Wissenschaftliche Untersuchungen
zum Neuen Testament · 2. Reihe

Herausgeber / Editor
Jörg Frey (München)

Mitherausgeber / Associate Editors
Friedrich Avemarie (Marburg)
Judith Gundry-Volf (New Haven, CT)
Hans-Josef Klauck (Chicago, IL)

254

Wenhua Shi

Paul's Message of the Cross as Body Language

Mohr Siebeck

WENHUA SHI, born 1968; Bachelor of Theology at Nanjing Union Theological Seminary, China; 2001 Master of Theology at Trinity Theological College, Singapore; 2008 PhD in New Testament at Durham University, England.

ISBN 978-3-16-149706-3
ISSN 0340-9570 (Wissenschaftliche Untersuchungen zum Neuen Testament, 2. Reihe)

The Deutsche Nationalbibliothek lists this publication in the Deutsche Nationalbibliographie; detailed bibliographic data is available in the Internet at *http://dnb.d-nb.de*.

The book was printed by Laupp & Göbel in Nehren on non-aging paper and bound by Buchbinderei Nädele in Nehren.

Printed in Germany.

Acknowledgements

This monograph is a revised version of my doctoral thesis submitted to the Department of Theology and Religion, Durham University. It represents not only years of hard work, but also the support and friendship of many. Although numerous people could be acknowledged, I would like to highlight those who have played the most significant roles in helping me bring this work to completion.

I am very grateful to my doctoral supervisor, Professor John Barclay, for his invaluable guidance. He has been a constant source of support and inspiration. I would certainly not have arrived at this point in my academic career without his expertise. Professor Barclay is not only the consummate English gentleman, but also a scholarly example, a man of graciousness and patience. Coming from China, I feel particularly privileged to have been a postgraduate student at Durham University, which is so well-known for its outstanding New Testament scholarship.

The ideas for the present study first began to take shape during my M.A. research under the supervision of Professor James Dunn. My interest in Pauline Studies truly started under his direction and I will always be indebted to him for this. Originally, the area of my M.A. dissertation was supposed to be the present study; however, Professor Dunn thought it would more appropriately be a subject for a doctoral thesis. At the same time, I also received the encouragement and support of Dr. Carol Harrison, Dr. Stephen Barton, Dr. Steven Croft and Dr. Chloe Starr. Without them my studies in Durham would not have been as pleasant as they were. The friendly environment at the Department of Theology and Religion made my years of study there very enjoyable.

Without the generous scholarship provided by the United Bible Societies, neither my studies at Trinity Theological College, Singapore nor Durham University would have been possible. I cannot express the depth of my gratitude to those who have made my studies financially possible. In this regard, the efforts of Mr. Kua Weeseng, Coordinator of the China Partnership of UBS, also merit particular mention. His fellowship and constant support have been a great blessing to me. The China Christian Council has also graciously endorsed my endeavours, for which I am most grateful.

Several friends cannot go without recognition. Steven, Chloe and Val Strickland warmly welcomed me at Cranmer Hall, St. John's College and helped me settle into their lovely Christian community. The friendship of Carolyn and Derek Rochester can only be described with the words "selfless love and caring." They received me into their home and treated me as

VI *Acknowledgements*

a member of their own family. Their devotion and passion for the Chinese community in Durham has been an inspiration to me. Other friends who merit mention are Jo West and Rita Chan, whose dear friendship has meant so much to me along with many other members of the Bible Study at the home of Dr. Zong Yongqiang and Jenny. Finally, the many friendships developed with fellow postgraduate students in Durham have been very meaningful and it is with much affection that I remember them here. As may be seen from the dedication, deepest love and thankfulness must be expressed to my family. Even from as far away as China, they have been a constant source of support to me.

A special thanks is owed to Professor Dr. Jörg Frey for accepting my manuscript into the prestigious *WUNT II* series. Dr. Henning Ziebritzki and Mr. Matthias Spitzner were generous with their time and also deserve credit in seeing this work to completion.

An important note is required in regard to the final version of this work. Although I am grateful to several friends who aided me in preparing my thesis for submission to Durham University, considerable credit needs to be given to Dr. Benjamin Wold for this final published version. His attention to editing the manuscript deserves recognition and many thanks.

Above all else, I would like to give glory to God for His amazing grace. May this research contribute something to a better understanding of God's message to us.

Tübingen, Summer 2008   Wenhua Shi

Table of Contents

Abbreviations

AB	Anchor Bible
ABD	*Anchor Bible Dictionary*. Edited by D. N. Freedman. 6 vols. New York, 1992
ABR	*Australian Biblical Review*
ANRW	*Aufstieg und Niedergang der römischen Welt: Geschichte und Kultur Roms im Spiegel der neueren Forschung*. Edited by Hildegard Temporini and Wolfgang Haase. Berlin, 1972-1982
ANTC	Abingdon New Testament Commentaries
BCE	Before the Common Era
BDAG	Bauer, W., F. W. Danker, W. F. Arndt, and F. W. Gingrich. *Greek-English Lexicon of the New Testament and Other Early Christian Literature*. 3d ed., Chicago, 2000
BDB	Brown, Francis, S. R. Driver and C. A. Briggs. *A Hebrew and English Lexicon of the Old Testament*. Oxford, 1907
BECNT	Baker Exegetical Commentary on the New Testament
BICS	*Bulletin of the Institute of Classical Studies*
BJRL	*Bulletin of the John Rylands University Library of Manchester*
BNTC	Black's New Testament Commentaries
CAAS	*Connecticut Academy of Arts and Sciences*
CBQ	*Catholic Biblical Quarterly*
CDP	Cambridge Dictionary of Philosophy
CUP	Cambridge University Press
DPL	*Dictionary of Paul and His Letters*. Edited by G. F. Hawthorne and R. P. Martin. Downers Grove, 1993
EC	Epworth Commentaries
EKKNT	Evangelish-katholischer Kommentar zum Neuen Testment
Herm	*Hermeneia*
HTR	*Harvard Theological Review*
IBC	Interpretation: A Bible Commentary for Teaching and Preaching
ICC	International Critical Commentary
IEJ	*Israel Exploration Journal*
Int	*Interpretation*
JBL	*Journal of Biblical Literature*
JCE	*Journal of Christian Education*
JECS	*Journal of Early Christian Studies*
JETS	*Journal of the Evangelical Theological Society*
JR	*Journal of Religion*
JRH	*Journal of Religious History*
JRS	*Journal of Roman Studies*
JSNT	*Journal for the Study of the New Testament*
JSNTSup	Journal for the Study of the New Testament Supplement Series
JSOT	*Journal for the Study of the Old Testament*
JSP	*Journal for the Study of the Pseudepigrapha*
KEK	Kritisch-exegetischer Kommentar über das Neue Testament (Meyer-Kommentar)

LCL	Loeb Classical Library
LSJ	Liddell, Henry George, Robert Scott, and H. Stuart Jones. *A Greek-English Lexicon*. 9th ed. with revised supplement. Oxford, 1996
LXX	Septuagint
2 Macc.	*2 Maccabees*
4 Macc.	*4 Maccabees*
m.	Mishnah
MNTC	Moffatt New Testament Commentary
NICNT	New International Commentary on the New Testament
NIGTC	New International Greek Testament Commentary
NIV	New International Version
NovT	*Novum Testamentum*
NRSV	New Revised Standard Version
NT	New Testament
NTS	*New Testament Studies*
NTT	New Testament Theology
OEED	*Oxford Encyclopedic English Dictionary*
OT	Old Testament
OTP	*Old Testament Pseudepigrapha*. Edited by J. H. Charlesworth. 2 vols. New York. 1983, 1985
OUP	Oxford University Press
OWC	Oxford World's Classics
PBSR	*Papers of the British School at Rome*
QJS	*Quarterly Journal of Speech*
RSV	Revised Standard Version
SacPag	Sacra Pagina Series
SBL	Society of Biblical Literature
SBLDS	Society of Biblical Literature Dissertation Series
SBLSP	*Society of Biblical Literature Seminar Papers*
SBLSS	Society of Biblical Literature Semeia Studies
SE	*Studia Evangelica*
TAPA	*Transactions of the American Philological Association*
TDNT	*Theological Dictionary of the New Testament*. Edited by Gerhard Kittel and Gerhard Friedrich. Translated by G.W. Bromiley. 10 vols. Grand Rapids, 1964-76)
TynBul	*Tyndale Bulletin*
UBS	United Bible Societies
WBC	Word Biblical Commentary
ZNW	*Zeitschrift für die neutestamentliche Wissenschaft und die Kunde der älteren Kirche*

Classical & Non-biblical Texts

Aristophanes
Cl.   *Clouds*

Aristotle
Eth. nic.   *Ethica nicomachea*
Rhet.   *Rhetorica*

Pol.   *Politica*

Artemidorus
Oneir.   *Oneirocritica*

Augustine
Civ.   *De civitate Dei*

Callistratus
Dig.   *Digesta*

Cassius Dio
Cocceianus
Hist. rom.   *Historia romana*

Cicero
Br.   *Brutus*
Cl.   *Pro Cluentio*
Deiot.   *Pro Rege Deiottaro*
Fin.   *De Finibus*
Inv.   *De inventione rhetorica*
Leg.   *De legibus*
Off.   *De Officiis*
Opt.   *De Optimo Genere Oratorum*
Or.   *De Oratore*
Orat.   *Orator*
Part.   *De Partitione Oratoria*
Pis.   *In Pisonem*
Rab. Perd.   *Pro Rabirio Perduellionis*
Rep.   *De republica*
Tusc.   *Tusculanae disputationes*
Verr.   *In Verrem*

Clement of
Alexandria
Paed.   *Paedagogus*

Curtius Rufus,
Quintus
Hist. Alex.   *Historia Alexandri Magni*

Demetrius
Elo.   *De Elocutione*

Dio Chrysostom
Or.   *Orationes*

Diodorus, Siculus
Bibl. Hist.   *Bibliotheca Historica*

Diogenes Laertius
Vit. Phil.   *Vitae Philosophorum*

Dionysius of Halicarnassus	
Ant. rom.	*Antiquitates romanae*
Ennius, Quintus	
Ann.	*Annales*
Epictetus	
Diss.	*Dissertationes*
Eusebius	
Hist. Eccl.	*Historia ecclesiastica*
Gaius	
Inst.	*Institutiones*
Gellius, Aulus	
Noct. Att.	*Noctes Atticae*
Gorgias	
Hel.	*Helen*
Homer	
Il.	*Iliad*
Odyss.	*Odyssey*
Horace	
Sat.	*Satirae*
Ignatius, Bishop of Antioch	
Ep.	*Epistolae*
Isocrates	
Antid.	*Antidosis*
Panegyr.	*Panegyricus*
John Chrysostom	
Hom.	*Homiliae*
Josephus	
Ant.	*Antiquitates judaicae*
B.J.	*Bellum judaicum*
Justin Epitomator	
Dig.	*Digest*
Justin Martyr	
Apol.	*Apologia*
Dial. Tryph.	*Dialogus cum Tryphone*

Juvenal
Sat.   *Satirae*

Lucian
Cat.   *Cataplus*
Dem.   *Demonax*
Dial. d.   *Dialogi deorum*
Dial. Mer.   *Dialogi Meretricii*
Fug.   *Fugitivi*
Gall.   *Gallus*
Iudic. voc.   *Iudicium vocalium*
Jup. Trag.   *Juppiter Tragoedus*
Peregr.   *De morte Peregrini*
Phil.   *Philopseudes*
Prom.   *Prometheus*
Sat.   *Saturnalia*
Somn.   *Somnium*

Marcus Aurelius
Med.   *Meditationes*

Minucius Felix
Oct.   *Octavius*

Origen
Cels.   *Contra Celsum*

Petronius
Satyr.   *Satyricon*

Philo
Cher.   *De Cherubim*
Flacc.   *In Flaccum*
Leg. All.   *Legum allegoriae*
Post.   *De posteritate Caini*
Quod Omn.   *Quod Omnis Probus*
Somn.   *De somniis*
Spec.   *De specialibus legibus*
Virt.   *De virtutibus*

Philodemus
De Rhet.   *De Rhetorica*

Philostratus
Vit. Apoll.   *Vita Apollonii Tyanae*

Plato
Apol.   *Apologia*
Cr.   *Crito*
Euthyd.   *Euthydemus*
Euthyph.   *Euthyphro*
Gorg.   *Gorgias*

Leg.	*De Legibus*
Men.	*Meno*
Phaed.	*Phaedo*
Phaedr.	*Phaedrus*
Protag.	*Protagogas*
Rep.	*De Republica*
Resp.	*Respublica*
Soph.	*De Sophista*

Plautus
As.	*Asinaria*
Aul.	*Aulularia*
Bacch.	*Bacchides*
Cap.	*Capitivi*
Cas.	*Casina*
Cur.	*Curculio*
Ep.	*Epidicus*
Mil.	*Miles gloriosus*
Most.	*Mostellaria*
Per.	*Persa*
St.	*Stichus*

Pliny the Elder
Nat.	*Naturalis hisroria*

Pliny the Younger
Ep.	*Epistulae*

Plutarch
Caes.	*Caesar*
Cat. Min.	*Cato Minor*
Cons. ad Apoll.	*Consolatio ad Apollonium*
Mor.	*Moralia*
Per.	*Pericles*
Vit.	*Vitae illustrium virorum*

Ps. – Quintilian
Decl.	*Declamationes*

Quintilian
Inst. orat.	*De Institutio Oratoria*

Rhet. ad Her.	*Rhetorica ad Herennium*

Seneca
Apoc.	*Apocolocyntosis*
Beat.	*De vita beata*
Ben.	*De Beneficiis*
Clem.	*De Clementia*
Cons.	*De consolatione ad Marciam*
Ep.	*Epistulae Morales*
Ir.	*De Ira*

| *Prov.* | *De Providentia* |

Suetonius
Aug.	*Augustus*
Cal.	*Caligula*
Claud.	*Claudius*
Gal.	*Galba*
Jul.	*Julius*
Ner.	*Nero*

Tacitus
| *Ann.* | *Annals* |
| *Hist.* | *Historiae* |

Terence
| *Eun.* | *Eunuch* |

Tertullian
| *Apol.* | *Apologeticus* |
| *Pat.* | *De Patientia* |

Virgil
| *Aen.* | *Aeneid* |

Xenophon
Ages.	*Agesilaus*
Cyr.	*Cyropaedia*
Eph.	*Ephesiaca*
Mem.	*Memorabilia*

Introduction

The study to follow is concerned with body language: the message of the cross as body language in Paul's Corinthian polemics as an inversion of the Greco-Roman social ethos. Within the English language, 'body language' may broadly be defined as 'the process of communicating through conscious or unconscious gestures and poses.'[1] However, the focus on 'body language' here is how it may be understood in the ancient Greco-Roman world.[2] Body language in crucifixion, for instance, was conveyed not only through gestures and poses, but also in powerful and effective symbols. The body of the crucified victim was symbolic of the worst of human suffering and pain, humiliation and degradation. Similarly, the physical pain that Paul endured through floggings, lashes and beatings (2 Cor. 11.23–25) also conveys vivid and poignant body language. The same is also true in regard to Paul's bodily presence, which was considered to be weak by his critics (10.10). It almost goes without saying that one of the clearest forms of body language was communicated through the various gestures and poses of the Greco-Roman orator. A powerful and impressive self-presentation on their part, as of any agent, also carried with it signs and traits of masculinity which were vital to a man's status in Greco-Roman society.

The message of the cross refers not only to the content of Paul's gospel, but also to the manner of his proclamation and delivery as well as his apostolic life. This is because, as far as Paul is concerned, the message he carried could hardly be separated from his manner of presentation and his *modus operandi* as Christ's apostle. Indeed, Paul decided to know nothing among the Corinthians except Jesus Christ crucified (1 Cor. 2.2), a decision which governed the content of his gospel. Moreover, his proclamation was 'not with plausible words of wisdom' (2.4), as his whole life, including his personal tribulations, was characterised by 'weakness' (2 Cor. 11.30). These three aspects of body language – the message of the cross, its presentation and Paul's own personal life – become particularly apparent in Paul's Corinthian polemics and may be seen to invert the current social ethos.[3]

---

[1] JUDITH PEARSALL, *The Oxford Encyclopedic English Dictionary* (New York: OUP, 1995), 158.

[2] See D. L. CAIRNS (ed.), *Body Language in the Greek and Roman World* (Swansea: Classical Press of Wales, 2005)

[3] The word 'body' or 'body language' also appears in other contexts in the Corinthian correspondence, for example, with reference to the Christian's body as 'a temple of the Holy Spirit' (1 Cor. 6.19); the Corinthian congregation as 'one body' (10.17), which was

Three specific areas concerning body language in Paul's Corinthian polemics may be identified with special reference to their socio-historical contexts and relevant passages in the Corinthian correspondence. The three areas which constitute the three divisions of this study are: (1) Crucifixion and noble death in antiquity; (2) Greco-Roman rhetoric with special emphasis on its delivery; and (3) *Peristasis* catalogues, or tribulation lists, which may be perceived both positively and negatively. Body language is the vital link between these three. On the basis of socio-historical studies of these three areas it may be argued not only that Paul was conscious of his intentions, but also that there is consistency in his inversion of the current social ethos in each area. Consequently, the following key questions shall be dealt with as well as minor questions related to them: (1) Why did Paul decide to know nothing among the Corinthians except Jesus Christ crucified' (1 Cor. 2.2)? (2) Why did Paul decide not to proclaim 'the mystery of God' in 'lofty words or wisdom' when he came to Corinth (2.1)? Why did he come to Corinth 'in weakness and in fear and in much trembling' (2.3)? (3) After providing the whole list of personal tribulations (*peristaseis*) in 2 Cor. 11.23–29, why should Paul conclude by saying that 'if I must boast, I will boast of the things that show my weakness' (11.30), instead of strength, like his Greco-Roman counterparts did?

1. Corinthian Studies: The General Situation and Approach

The study of Paul's Corinthian letters is among the most fascinating and yet at the same time the most complex in New Testament studies. As early as the 1830s Ferdinand Christian Baur already held that the early church was largely divided into two camps led by Paul and Cephas. For many decades, this position was dominant in the study of early Christianity.[4] Although Baur's view has often been criticized and abandoned by many, its influence and support remain considerable to this day.[5] In the early 20th

Christ's body (12.12, 27) in the contexts of the Lord's Supper as well as in Paul's teaching on spiritual gifts (12.12–31). But in all these and similar cases 'body' or 'body language' are used symbolically or as signs or metaphors in the contexts of Paul's teaching, and not as inversion of current social ethos.

[4] F. C. BAUR, *Paul, The Apostle of Jesus Christ, His Life and Work, His Epistles and His Doctrine* (Edinburgh/London: Williams & Norgate, 1875), 1.267–320.

[5] M. Y. MACDONALD, 'The Shifting Centre: Ideology and the Interpretation of 1 Corinthians', in E. ADAMS and D. G. HORRELL (eds.), *Christianity at Corinth: The Quest for the Pauline church* (Westminster John Knox Press: Louisville, 2004), 273–94, at 277. J. D. G. DUNN, 'Reconstructions of Corinthian Christianity and the Interpretation of 1 Corinthians', in *Christianity at Corinth,* 295–310. M. GOULDER, 'Sophia in 1 Corinthians', *NTS* 37 (1991), 516–34.

century, the *Religionsgeschichtlicheschule* was initiated by scholars who put the study of both Jewish and Christian religions in a much broader context and in close connection, even on *par,* with other religious traditions, thereby challenging the unique status which the Judeo-Christian tradition enjoyed for centuries. In addition, the category of 'Gnosticism' was also characteristically used to interpret Corinthian Christianity or theology by scholars such as Walther Schmithals[6] and Ulrich Wilckens.[7]

Critical of Gnosticism as the appropriate background of Corinthian studies, Richard Horsley advocates the perspective of 'Hellenistic Judaism' to interpret Corinthian theology.[8] Under Baur's influence, in the 1950s and 60s Corinthian studies tended to be Paul-centred, focusing merely or predominantly on Paul's thought rather than on 'a full understanding of the Corinthian community as a whole.'[9] Pauline scholarship between the 1960s and 70s may be regarded as Christianity-centred since 'the *ekklesia* of 1st century Corinth' was quite commonly perceived as being representative of Christianity.[10] This was followed by the historico-sociological movement, which has gradually shifted to become society-centred, using the Greco-Roman social context to interpret the Corinthian correspondence.[11] This shift has serious implications for the following ap-

---

[6] W. SCHMITHALS, *Gnosticism in Corinth* (Nashville: Abingdon, 1971).

[7] U. WILCKENS, *'Sophia'*, *TDNT* 7.519–22. Cf. R. A. HORSLEY, 'Wisdom of Word and Words of Wisdom in Corinth', *CBQ* 39 (1977), 224–39; B. A. PEARSON, *The Pneumatikos-Psychikos Terminology in 1 Corinthians: A Study in the Theology of the Corinthian Opponents of Paul and its Relation to Gnosticism* (SBLDS 12; Missoula, MT: Society of Biblical Literature, 1973), 27–43.

[8] HORSLEY, 'Gnosis in Corinth: I Corinthians 8.1–6', *NTS* 27 (1981), 32–52. J. A. DAVIS, Wisdom and Spirit: An Investigation of 1 Corinthians 1.18–3.20 against the Background of Jewish Sapiential Traditions in the Greco-Roman Period (Lanham, MD: University Press of America, 1984). HORSLEY, 'Pneumatikos vs. Psychikos: Distinctions of Spiritual Status among the Corinthians', *HTR* 69 (1976), 269–88; DUNN, 1 Corinthians, 37–38. R. MCL. WILSON, 'How Gnostic Were the Corinthians?' *NTS* 19 (1972-73), 65–74.

[9] MACDONALD, 'The Shifting Centre', 280. Cf. C. K. BARRETT, 'Christianity at Corinth', *BJRL* 46 (1964), 269–97. K. STENDAHL, *Paul among Jews and Gentiles* (Philadelphia: Fortress Press, 1976). N. A. DAHL, 'Paul and the Church at Corinth', in *Christianity at Corinth*, 85–95.

[10] MACDONALD, 'The Shifting Centre', 285. SCHMITHALS, *Gnosticism in Corinth*. HORSLEY, 'Gnosis in Corinth: I Corinthians 8.1–6', 32–52.

[11] E. A. JUDGE, *The Social Pattern of Christian Groups in the First Century* (London: The Tyndale Press, 1960). JUDGE, *Rank and Status in the World of the Caesars and St Paul* (Christchurch, N. Z.: University of Canterbury Publications, 1982). G. THEISSEN, *The Social Setting of Pauline Christianity* (Philadelphia: T. & T. Clark, 1982). S. C. BARTON, 'Paul and the Cross: A Sociological Approach', *Theology* 85 (1982), 13–19. W. A. MEEKS, *The First Urban Christians: The Social World of the Apostle Paul* (New Haven: Yale University, 1983). B. HOLMBERG, *Sociology and the New Testament* (Minneapolis: Fortress, 1990). J. K. CHOW, *Patronage and Power: A Study of Social Networks in*

proach, with its focus on the message of the cross in relation to the prevailing social ethos.

Feminist approaches have also developed and play an important role in Corinthian studies. Elisabeth Schüssler Fiorenza's book, *In Memory of Her: A Feminist Theological Reconstruction of Christian Origins,* published in 1983, is representative of this concern. Her work has aroused considerable interest in interpreting the role or status of women in the Corinthian church.[12]

More recently, new interest in Greco-Roman rhetoric has emerged with special reference to the Corinthian context.[13] The approach taken here recognizes the importance and value of both the socio-historical approach and more recent rhetorical studies.

Andrew Clarke contends that the Pauline corpus alone does not provide sufficient evidence to reconstruct the situation as it existed in Corinth. Multi-disciplinary approaches and perspectives are thus necessary.[14] Current Corinthian studies have been well summarised by Edward Adams and David Horrell:

Corinth (JSNTS 75; Sheffield: JSOT, 1992). D. B. MARTIN, *The Corinthian Body* (New Haven: Yale University Press, 1995). MARTIN, *The Social World of the Apostle Paul* (New Haven: Yale University Press, 1983). D. G. HORRELL, *The Social Ethos of the Corinthian Correspondence* (Edinburgh: T. & T. Clark, 1996). HORRELL (ed.), *Social-Scientific Approaches to New Testament Interpretation* (Edinburgh, T. & T. Clark, 1999). D. F. WATSON, 'Paul's Boasting in 2 Corinthians 10–13 as Defense of His Honour: A Socio-rhetorical Analysis', in A. ERICKSSON, *et al.* (eds.), *Rhetorical Argumentation in Biblical Texts: Essays from the Lund 2000 Conference* (Harrisburg, PA: Trinity Press International, 2002), 260–75.

[12] E. S. FIORENZA, *In Memory of Her: A Feminist Theological Reconstruction of Christian Origins* (New York: Crossroad, 1983). A. C. WIRE, *Corinthian Women Prophets: A Reconstruction through Paul's Rhetoric* (Minneapolis: Fortress, 1990). FIORENZA (ed.), *Searching the Scriptures. Vol 2: A Feminist Commentary* (London: SCM, 1995). A.–J. LEVINE, *A Feminist Companion to Paul* (London and New York: T & T Clark, 2004). J. ØKLAND, *Women in Their Place: Paul and the Corinthian Discourse of Gender and Sanctuary Space* (London: T & T Clark, 2004).

[13] G. A. KENNEDY, *Classical Rhetoric and Its Christian and Secular Tradition from Ancient to Modern Times* (London: Croom Helm, 1980); L. L. WELBORN, 'On the Discord in Corinth: 1 Corinthians 1–4 and Ancient Politics', *JBL* 106 (1987), 85–111; WATSON, 'The New Testament and Greco-Roman Rhetoric: a Bibliography', *JETS* 31/4 (1988), 465–72; S. M. POGOLOFF, *Logos and Sophia: The Rhetorical Situation of 1 Corinthians* (Atlanta: Scholars Press, 1992); D. LITFIN, *St Paul's Theology of Proclamation: 1 Cor 1–4 and Greco-Roman Rhetoric* (Cambridge: Cambridge University Press, 1994); M. MITCHELL, *Paul and the Rhetoric of Reconciliation: An exegetical Investigation of the Language and Composition of 1 Corinthians* (Tübingen: Mohr Siebeck, 1991).

[14] A. D. CLARKE, *Secular and Christian Leadership in Corinth: A Socio-Historical and Exegetical Study of 1 Corinthians 1–6* (Leiden: Brill, 1993), 6.

Thus the task of reconstructing earliest Christianity at Corinth will continue in diverse ways. While some branches of New Testament scholarship may eschew historical reconstruction ... others will continue to make use of the wide range of ancient evidence in order to reconstruct a setting in ancient Corinth with which to better understand Paul and the Corinthians.... One general area in which there does seem to be a convergence of opinion, unsurprising, perhaps, given the general collapse of the illusion that scholarship can ever be simply objective and disinterested, is in recognizing the need for critical and theoretical reflection, on the ways to use and interpret ancient evidence (Meggitt), on the ways to employ social-scientific resources (Holmberg), and on the interests and ideologies that shape scholarship (MacDonald).[15]

In the early 20th century, the German New Testament scholar Adolf Deissmann came up with a view which later came to be known as the 'Old Consensus'. In this view New Testament writers belonged to the lower classes of society on the basis of their use of the vulgar *koinē,* except for Paul whose social status was rather ambiguous.[16] This was also thought to be the case of the Pauline congregations, including the Corinthian church. A very different view is put forward by Edwin Judge, who believes that 'Christianity was a movement sponsored by local patrons to their social dependents.'[17]

Gerd Theissen and Wayne Meeks, who agree with many of Judge's finding (a position now dubbed as the 'New Consensus'), have also asserted that the Pauline communities comprised a cross-section of society, including some from the higher strata. Based on 1 Cor. 1.26, they argue for the existence of affluent groups within the Corinthian communities.[18] John Chow also suggests that patronage played a vital role in the Corinthian church, so that the few powerful patrons who possessed outstanding social status and wealth not only associated themselves with other powerful people in the colony, but also were dominant figures who 'through lawsuits, marriage or social fellowship with the powerful leaders in the colony, constantly sought to gain more, including possessions, power and honour.'[19]

---

[15] ADAMS, *Christianity,* 42–43.

[16] A. DEISSMANN, *Paul: A Study in Social and Religious History* (London: Hodder & Stoughton, 1926), 29–51. See J. J. MEGGITT, *Paul, Poverty and Survival* (Edinburgh: T&T Clark, 1998).

[17] JUDGE, 'The Early Christians as a Scholastic Community', *JRH* 1 (1960–61), 4–15, 125–37, at 8.

[18] THEISSEN, *The Social Setting,* 72–92; MEEKS, *The First Urban Christians,* 54–73.

[19] CHOW, *Patronage,* 166. See also R. P. SALLER, *Personal Patronage under the Early Empire* (Cambridge: Cambridge University Press, 1982). A. WALLACE-HADRILL (ed.), *Patronage in Ancient Society* (Routledge: London, 1990). A. C. MITCHELL, 'Rich and Poor in the Courts of Corinth', *NTS* 39 (1993), 562–86. L. SCHOTTROFF, '"Not Many Powerful": Approaches to a Sociology of Early Christianity', in D. G. Horrell (ed.), *Social-Scientific Approaches to New Testament Interpretation* (Einburgh, T & T Clark, 1999), 275–87.

Theissen's work provides valuable insights into the social situation of
the Corinthian church, especially its class membership and the nature of its
conflicts. John Schütz, the editor and translator of Theissen's essays,
writes that Theissen's work is not only marked by 'bold hypothesis', but is
also 'balanced with exegetical insight and patience for detail.'[20] Clarke
criticizes the imbalance in Pauline studies between theological perspective
and social approach: 'either they are too narrowly constructed on the theological ideals of the Pauline material; or they are too strongly dictated by
modern social theory without taking sufficient cognizance of the socio-
historical context.'[21]

The approach taken here seeks to keep a necessary balance between social study and exegetical insight. On this particular point, Judge's critique
of Bengt Holmberg's work is worth noting:[22]

It couples with New Testament studies a strong admixture of modern sociology, as
though social theories can be safely transposed across the centuries without verification.
The basic question remains unasked: What are the social facts of life characteristic of the
world to which the New Testament belongs? Until the painstaking field work is better
done, the importation of social models that have been defined in terms of other cultures is
methodologically no improvement on the 'idealistic fallacy' [of the theologians]. We
may fairly call it the 'sociological fallacy.'[23]

The Corinthian church situation in Paul's day was in a state of serious crisis, both in matters of faith and conduct. One of the most serious crises
was that of church 'quarrels' (1 Cor. 1.11) or 'jealousy and strife' (3.3).
Otherwise, Paul would not have singled it out at the very beginning of 1
Corinthians. The matter became more serious and complex when Paul himself was personally caught in the controversy. There was evidently a highly
organized and formidable force in Corinth that was working against Paul
so that a great deal of the content in the two letters was interspersed with
heated polemics between the apostle and his critics. The following en-
deavour seeks to show that Paul's polemics were conducted intentionally
and consistently from the perspective of the cross, which turned out to be a
drastic inversion of the current Greco-Roman social ethos.

---

[20] J. H. SCHÜTZ (trans.), *The Social Setting*, Introduction.

[21] CLARKE, *Leadership*, 129.

[22] See B. HOLMBERG, *Paul and Power: The Structure of Authority in the Primitive
Church as Reflected in the Pauline Epistles* (Lund: Liberlaromede/Gleerup, 1978).

[23] JUDGE, 'The Social Identity of the First Christians, A Question of Method in Religious History', *JRH* 11 (1980), 201–17, at 210. Moreover, J. M. G. BARCLAY has also
pointed out: 'Sociological study of Paul's churches should investigate not just social
status but also social interaction and should cease generalizing about "Pauline Christians."' Abstract of 'Thessalonica and Corinth: Social Contrast in Pauline Christianity',
JSNT 47 (1992), 49–74. The crucial question seems obvious: How to make good use of
the studies and findings of the various disciplines critically.

Clifford Geertz defines a people's ethos in terms of the tone, character, and quality of their lives as well as the style and mood of morals, aesthetics and their worldview. He helpfully describes the religious belief and practice of a group's ethos as 'rendered intellectually reasonable by being shown to present a way of life ideally adapted to the actual state of affairs the world-view describes, while the world-view is rendered emotionally convincing by being presented as an image of an actual state of affairs peculiarly well arranged to accommodate such a way of life.'[24]

Bruce Malina, following on from Geertz's views, suggests that social ethos is 'a system of symbols which acts to establish powerful, pervasive, and long-lasting moods and motivations in people, formulating conceptions of value-objects, and clothing these conceptions with such an aura of factuality that the moods and motivations are perceived to be uniquely realistic.'[25] Malina's concept of social ethos helps in understanding the Corinthian context and some of the basic problems of the Corinthian church.

The Corinthian correspondence will be read within its social context to determine if the Corinthian crises were actually linked to the Greco-Roman social ethos with which the Corinthians were accustomed, especially in regard to the society's perception of honour, status, prestige and power. In regard to power, one needs to note the emphasis on human wisdom and eloquence which find concrete expression in Greco-Roman rhetoric. Why was the message of the cross such foolishness to Gentiles and a stumbling block to Jews (1.23)? Was the Corinthians' preoccupation with wisdom and eloquence largely responsible for their apparent failure to understand the message of the cross and its implications for their life and witness?

Horrell argues that the Corinthian correspondence 'not only offers rich material for a study of the social ethos of early Christian teaching, but also … enables a focus on a specific community and on change over time.'[26]

Stephen Chester writes that, at least in terms of social setting, the study of the Corinthian correspondence may be more precise than other Pauline documents. He contends that Paul sends the Corinthian correspondence during the sixth decade of the 1st century. As such, one may situate the 'Corinthian understanding of conversion more precisely within the wider context of the Graeco-Roman culture than would otherwise be possible'.

---

[24] C. GEERTZ, 'Religion as a Culture System', in M. BANTON (ed.), *Anthropological Approaches to the Study of Religion* (London: Tavistock Publications, 1966), 1–46, at 3.

[25] B. J. MALINA, *The New Testament World: Insights from Cultural Anthropology* (Louisville: Westminster/ John Knox Press, 1993), 23. See also GEERTZ, *The Interpretation of Cultures: Selected Essays* (London: Fontana, 1993).

[26] HORRELL, *The Social Ethos*, 4.

Given the vast archaeological record on hand for studying 1st century Corinth, there is considerable evidence for such a study.[27]

It is with this recognition of the importance of the social setting of Corinth that more than half of this work is devoted to socio-historical studies on context, which may demonstrate a consistent pattern in all three distinct parts. Each part begins with socio-historical background studies before the exegesis of the relevant Corinthian passages is undertaken.

2. Crucifixion and the Message of the Cross in Socio-historical Perspective

The social perspective here is indebted to the findings and insights of several modern scholars in Corinthian studies, particularly Kathy Coleman, Raymond Pickett, Michael Gorman, David Horrell, Timothy Savage and several others.[28] However, a balance is sought between socio-historical studies and exegesis of the relevant Corinthian passages. The findings and insights of socio-historical studies provide the context for reading Paul's theology.

When it comes to the socio-historical study on crucifixion in antiquity, special acknowledgement is owed to Martin Hengel's research, which serves as a helpful introduction to much of the relevant primary literature. The common practice of crucifixion as a form of capital punishment in the ancient world leads Hengel to conclude that 'it is crucifixion that distin-

---

[27] S. J. CHESTER, *Conversion at Corinth: Perspectives on Conversion in Paul's Theology and the Corinthian Church* (London: T & T Clark, 2003), 32.

[28] K. M. COLEMAN, 'Fatal Charades: Roman Executions Staged as Mythological Enactments', *JRS* 80 (1990), 44–73. R. PICKETT, *The Cross in Corinth: The Social Significance of the Death of Jesus* (Sheffield: Sheffield Academic Press, 1997). M. GORMAN, *Cruciformity: Paul's Narrative Spirituality of the Cross* (Grand Rapids: William B. Eerdmans, 2001). HORRELL, *The Social Ethos.* T. B. SAVAGE, *Power Through Weakness: A Historical and Exegetical Examination of Paul's Understanding of the Christian Ministry in 2 Corinthians* (Cambridge: CUP, 1996). A. R. BROWN, *The Cross and Human Transformation: Paul's Apocalyptic Word in 1 Corinthians* (Minneapolis: Fortress Press, 1995). A. J. DEWEY, 'A Matter of Honour: A Social-Historical Analysis of 2 Corinthians 10', *HTR* 78 (1985), 209–17. D. L. BALCH, 'Paul's portrait of Christ Crucified (Gal. 3.1) in Light of Paintings and Sculptures of Suffering and Death in Pompeiian and Roman Houses', in D. L. BALCH and C. OSIEK (eds.), *Early Christian Families in Context: An Interdisciplinary Dialogue* (Grand Rapids: William B. Eerdmans, 2003), 84–108. C. EDWARDS, 'The Suffering Body: Philosophy and Pain', in J. I. PORTER (ed.), *Constructions of the Classical Body* (Ann Arbor: University of Michigan Press, 1999), 252–68. J. PERKINS, *The Suffering Self: Pain and Narrative Representation in the Early Christian Era* (London: Routledge, 1995). T. G. WEINANDY, *Does God Suffer?* (Edinburgh: T & T Clark, 2000).

guishes the new message from mythologies of all other peoples' and that 'the death of Jesus by crucifixion was one of the main objections against his being the son of God.'[29] Indeed, Hengel perceptively summarises: 'the reason why in his letters he [Paul] talks about the cross above all in a polemical context is that he deliberately wants to provoke his opponents, who are attempting to water down the offence caused by the cross. Thus in a way the "word of the cross" is the spearhead of his message.'[30] In some ancient writings 'madness' (μανία) was also used – such as by Justin Martyr[31] and some pagan authors – to describe the Christian message about the cross alongside the description 'folly' (μωρία).[32] While indebted to Hengel's initial work, this research depends on a fresh reading of primary sources related to crucifixion and focuses on its main features, especially as it relates to body language.

Coleman's research seeks to link ancient writings on crucifixion with some modern scholars' views on execution and punishment in the Roman world. Coleman agrees with Harding and Ireland that 'the history of punishment is not seen as a chronological development from "primitive" to "civilized" but rather as a constantly adjusting balance of techniques of social control determined by the physical resources, moral basis, and belief system of any given society.'[33] Agreement is found with Coleman's point that 'penalties of degradation', which sometimes entailed a public spectacle of punishment, were a 'pervasive penal practice' in the ancient world.[34] Moreover, the execution of crucifixion as a 'public spectacle of punishment' also made its body language particularly powerful and effective.

Consequently, demonstrating that a human being could not have suffered any greater pain, agony and humiliation than being publicly put on a cross, and quite often completely naked, merits further investigation. The public nature of Roman execution seems to have been designed to alienate the victim from his social context, so that the spectators, regardless of class, were united in a feeling of moral superiority as they ridiculed him, as was the case of Jesus. To achieve such a desired goal in Roman society, 'the mockery of a condemned person was sometimes performed spontaneously by parties other than the legal adjudicators. The best-known example from our period is the soldiers' mockery of Jesus ... the humiliation of the offender seems to be an integral part of the punishment, and it is obvious

---

[29] M. HENGEL, *Crucifixion in the Ancient World and the Folly of the Message of the Cross* (Philadelphia PA: Fortress Press, 1977), 1.

[30] HENGEL, *Crucifixion*, 89.

[31] Justin, *Apol.* 1.13.4.

[32] Pliny, *Ep.* 10.96.4–8; Horace, *Sat.* 2.3.79; Tacitus, *Ann.* 15.44.3.

[33] COLEMAN, 'Fatal Charades', 45. See C. HARDING and R. W. IRELAND, *Punishment: Rhetoric, Rule, and Practice* (London: Rouledge, 1989).

[34] COLEMAN, 'Fatal Charades', 45.

that this feature is going to bulk large in the context of executions performed in the course of spectacular enactments in the arena.'[35]

Paul's message of the cross and its foolishness is viewed from this perspective of crucifixion. The inquiry on the subject also seeks to learn if,
and to what extent, the execution of crucifixion was inseparable from the
very rigid social class distinction in Roman society. Coleman endorses Peter Garnsey's suggestions and holds that 'a crucial factor in the Roman penal system was the evolution of differentiated penalties for offenders of
different status: *humiliores and honestiores*. This is a phenomenon that is
characteristic of societies with a strongly differentiated class – or caste-
system, and it follows that, when the upper classes are equated with true
humanity, the lower classes are sub-human and therefore legitimately liable to cruel treatment.'[36] It is also for this reason that Roman citizens
were particularly horrified by any attempt to have any of their members
crucified.

As the primary emphasis is on body language, effort is made to show
that what happened at the scene of crucifixion was not just events and actions, but also a demonstration of the power and impact of body language
which was vividly and graphically conveyed through the suffering victim
and had serious social implications.

Pickett's sociological analysis of the Corinthian situation in a Greco-
Roman context has much to commend it, and he has largely succeeded in
putting the Greco-Roman and Christian socio-ethical values in clear and
pointed contrast.[37] This helps to explain the mystery of the cross of Christ
in paradoxical and dialectical terms. Pickett's use of the cross as 'symbol'
is highly relevant. The cross is indeed a very powerful symbol; however, it
should be borne in mind that for Paul it was the historical event and reality
of the cross of Christ that gave true meaning to the symbol.

Gorman, who coined the term 'cruciformity', describes that 'conformity
to the crucified Christ' is 'central to Paul's theology and ethics.'[38] Gorman's primary concern is the experience of the Christian: 'the purpose of
Paul's letters generally … is not to teach theology but to mould behaviour,
to affirm or – more often – to alter patterns of living, patterns of experience. The purpose of his letters, in other words, is pastoral or spiritual before it is theological.… It is appropriate, therefore, to consider Paul first
and foremost as a pastoral or spiritual writer, rather than as a theologian

---

[35] COLEMAN, 'Fatal Charades', 47.

[36] COLEMAN, 'Fatal Charades', 55. See P. GARNSEY, *Social Status and Legal Privilege in the Roman Empire* (Oxford: OUP, 1970).

[37] PICKETT, *The Cross*.

[38] GORMAN, *Cruciformity*, 4. See GORMAN, *Apostle of the Crucified Lord: A Theological Introduction to Paul and His Letters* (Grand Rapids: William B. Eerdmans,
2004), 115–30.

(or ethicist).'[39] It may be ventured that Paul himself would likely object to such one-sided thinking, since Christian life and practice could hardly be artificially separated from sound teaching or theology. The New Testament shows serious interest in wrong Christian behaviour or practice, which is often expressed as the direct or indirect result of wrong teaching or theology.

Savage notes that at the very core of Paul's position in 2 Corinthians lies an important paradox 'which finds expression in a number of different antitheses and which drives to the very heart of what it means to Paul to be a minister of Christ.'[40] He convincingly concludes that 'the Corinthian church was embroiled in a conflict between two opposing viewpoints: the worldly outlook of the Corinthians and Paul's own Christ-centred perspective, the so-called "wisdom of this age" and the "wisdom of God" ... it was precisely this conflict which seems to have evoked Paul's paradoxical teaching of power through weakness.'[41]

3. The 'Rediscovery' of Greco-Roman Rhetoric, Self-presentation and Masculinity

Although wisdom is an important issue in both Greco-Roman and Jewish traditions, it is beyond the present scope of this research to investigate it as fully deserved. While the issue of wisdom occupies a prominent place in Corinthian polemics, as was the case in the first two chapters of 1 Corinthians, discussion on the issue is confined to the context of Paul's message of the cross.[42] This is because, in the final analysis, Paul's interest is not in the usual wisdom speculation as such, but rather in the demonstration of divine wisdom in and through the cross of Christ. Moreover, it is also argued that in much of Paul's inversion strategy, human wisdom and divine wisdom are placed in the sharpest possible contrast in his Corinthian polemics.

The following statements in the Corinthian correspondence convey a simple but crucial point in regard to the relevance and importance of rhetoric for polemics: 'Christ did not send me to baptize but to preach the gospel, and not with eloquent wisdom, lest the cross of Christ be emptied of its power' (1 Cor. 1.17). 'Where is the debater of this age' (1.20)? 'Not ... in lofty words or wisdom ... and my speech and my message were not in

---

[39] GORMAN, *Cruciformity*, 4.

[40] SAVAGE, *Power,* Introduction.

[41] SAVAGE, *Power Through Weakness,* 188.

[42] See P. LAMPE, 'Theological Wisdom and the "Word about the Cross": The Rhetorical Scheme in 1 Corinthians 1–4', *Interpretation* 44/2 (1990), 117–31.

plausible words of wisdom' (2.1–4). 'They say, "His letters are weighty and strong, but his bodily presence is weak, and his speech of no account"' (2 Cor. 10.10).

For about two or three decades now Greco-Roman rhetoric has been generally recognized as an essential key to understanding a number of intriguing issues in the Corinthian letters, especially in 1 Cor. 1–4. This is demonstrated in the works of modern scholars such as Laurence Welborn, Stephen Pogoloff and Duane Litfin among many others.[43]

Pogoloff attempts a fresh reading of 1 Cor. 1–4 and stresses the importance of the 'rediscovery of and renewed appreciation for ancient rhetoric.'[44] This rediscovery now shows that rhetoric affected virtually all Greco-Roman culture and a whole host of different aspects of society.

Litfin contrasts the Corinthian orators' style and goal with Paul's *modus operandi*: 'The Apostle Paul's view of a preacher contrasted sharply with that of the Greco-Roman orator.'[45] While the Greco-Roman orators exploited rhetorical skill to achieve their self-seeking and self-promoting goal, Paul as a faithful preacher of Christ crucified refuses to follow that kind of style and goal. Bruce Winter points out that Paul's letters to Corinth contain evidence of the 1st century sophistic movement. He suggests that the apostle's language is essentially 'anti-sophistic'.[46] In Litfin's view, the reason why the Corinthians were not impressed by Paul's public speaking is because 'he came far short of the polish and sophistication in word choice, in diction, in voice, physical charm and self-possession that was indispensable to impress and move a Greco-Roman crowd.'[47]

Studies on Greco-Roman rhetoric in the discussion to follow seek to demonstrate that the art of rhetorical training and practice was an essential part of ancient Greco-Roman education for males. Detailed instructions about rhetoric, especially its delivery[48] which involved the whole human body (literally from 'head to toe'), were repeatedly given in the writings of: Aristotle (*De arte Rhetorica*), Cicero (*De Oratore*), Quintilian (*Instititio Oratoria*) and the work of an unknown author believed to be a contemporary of Cicero (*Rhetorica ad Herennium*).

---

[43] See above n. 13.

[44] POGOLOFF, *Logos*, 3.

[45] LITFIN, *Proclamation*, 247. See also M. JONES, *St Paul as Orator: A Critical, Historical and Explanatory Commentary on the Speeches of St Paul* (London: Hodder and Stoughton, 1910).

[46] B. W. WINTER, *Philo and Paul among the Sophists* (Cambridge: Cambridge University Press, 1997), 148.

[47] LITFIN, *Proclamation*, 162.

[48] T. H. OLBRICHT, 'Delivery and Memory', in S. E. PORTER (ed.), *Handbook of Classical Rhetoric in the Hellenistic Period* (330 B.C.–A. D. 400) (Leiden: Brill, 1997), 159–67.

Closely connected with the subject of rhetoric is the concern for masculinity in Greco-Roman society. Here the contributions of scholars such as Maud Gleason, Jennifer Larson and Jennifer Glancy are duly acknowledged.[49] Of importance is to question whether Paul's physical unattractiveness, including the possibility of a physical disability or handicap, was the main reason for the Corinthians' low esteem of him and prejudices against him. Did the Greco-Roman concept of masculinity have any direct bearing on a man's authority in society, including the apostolic authority of Paul? How crucial was this in the Corinthian controversy?

Gleason's work aims 'to refocus our attention on the social dynamics of rhetoric as an instrument of self-presentation, and in the process refine our appreciation of the functional aesthetics of a profoundly traditional performance genre.'[50] Gleason's conclusions are particularly helpful for a clear understanding of the ethos of rhetoric, especially the crucial issue of masculinity in Greco-Roman society.

Rhetorical training in the Greco-Roman society was a necessary process through which upper-class men were 'made'. In the end, education (παιδεία) for both Greek and Roman gentlemen became a valuable form of capital investment. Greco-Roman rhetoric was an ongoing, life-long process and discipline in a society which was seriously preoccupied with male socialization and also in which gender identity, social status and the self-esteem of men were all interconnected.

In an article on the masculinity of Paul, Larson suggests that despite all the attention given to the historical setting of the Corinthian controversy, one crucial aspect of the invective of the apostle Paul's opponents has been neglected, namely: 'How the criticisms of Paul engaged cultural expectations about manliness and its relationship to authority (cf. 2 Cor. 10–13).'[51] Larson's view that Paul and his opponents were functioning within a context of Greco-Roman social values and expectations is indeed convincing. The ultimate clash between two diametrically opposed sets of values and expectations was, in the end, inevitable.

---

[49] M. W. GLEASON, *Making Men: Sophists and Self-Presentation in Ancient Rome* (Princeton: Princeton University Press, 1995). J. LARSON, 'Paul's Masculinity', *JBL* 123/1 (2004), 85–97. J. A. GLANCY, 'Boasting of Beatings (2 Cor. 11:23–25)', *JBL* 123/1 (2004), 99–135. See also D. J. A. CLINES, 'Paul, the Invisible Man', in S. D. MOORE and J. C. ANDERSON (eds.), *New Testament Masculinities* (Society of Biblical Literature Semeia Studies 45; Atlanta: Society of Biblical Literature, 2003), 181–92. R. WARD, 'Pauline Voice and Presence as Strategic Communication', *SBLSP* (1990), 283–92. C. A. WILLIAMS, *Roman Homosexuality: Ideologies of Masculinity in Classical Antiquity* (New York: Oxford University Press, 1999).

[50] GLEASON, *Making Men*, xx.

[51] LARSON, 'Masculinity', 85–86.

With regard to the perceptions of gender in the Greco-Roman society, Larson elaborates:

Personal dignity, bodily integrity, and specific details of one's appearance were all factors in individual self-assessment and in men's evaluation of one another's masculinity. Elite men of the day were constantly concerned with the maintenance of their masculinity, because it both displayed and justified their positions of power. Unlike noble birth, which was immutable, masculinity was a matter of perception. While elites always represented their masculinity to outsiders as innate, among insiders it was implicitly recognized that masculinity was a performance requiring constant practice and vigilance.[52]

One need hardly make the case that body language was conveyed by such a constant performance.

Given the socio-historical context of Paul's time, especially in relation to ancient rhetoric, it is not at all surprising that he should be judged by his critics according to current convention. In 2 Cor. 10.10, Paul's opponents openly challenge his skills as a public speaker. 'Proper tone of voice, posture, gestures, dress, personal adornment, and other less concrete qualities', says Larson, were 'routinely cited by professionals as requirements for success. We have good reason to believe that Corinthians of the first century, even those with a lesser education, would have been experienced with regard to the evaluation of speakers.'[53] If that were truly the case, criticisms against Paul and deep dissatisfaction with him might not be confined to a few leaders, but rather shared among a much larger group.[54]

Larson's study reveals a great deal about a speaker's self-presentation. Since the performance of a speaker was also gender performance, a man's deficiency in self-presentation could easily create an opening for his rivals to ridicule him as 'effeminate' (*mollior*). Paul's bodily presence was described as weak. It remains to be seen if, and to what extent, the Greco-Roman perception of self-presentation has to do with the opponents' criticism against Paul. John Harrill suggests that 'attacks against one's outward appearance and speaking ability, as in 2 Cor. 10.10, must be interpreted in light of these cultural beliefs about deportment as a system of signs that reveal both one's self-control and one's fitness to rule others.'[55] The serious-

---

[52] LARSON, 'Masculinity', 86.

[53] LARSON, 'Masculinity', 87.

[54] Plutarch has a list of important figures, including an orator, a poet, a general, a rich man and a king who were regarded as 'handsome, gracious, liberal, eminent, rich, eloquent, learned, philanthropic', in strong contrast to those who were 'ugly, graceless, illiberal, dishonoured, needy ... unlearned, misanthropic' (*Mor.* 472A, 485A).

[55] J. A. HARRILL, 'Invective against Paul (2 Cor. 10.10), the Physiognomics of the Ancient Slave Body, and the Greco-Roman Rhetoric of Manhood', in A. Y. COLLINS and M. M. MITCHELL (eds.), *Antiquity and Humanity: Essays on Ancient Religion and Philosophy Presented to Hans Dieter Betz on His 70th Birthday* (Tübingen: Mohr-Siebeck, 2001), 189–213, at 204.

ness of 2 Cor. 10.10 together with its profound implications should be perceived in this particular context. In this connection, an important question deserves further investigation: Was Paul deficient in masculine virtues or did he willingly allow them to be abrogated? According to the Greco- Roman concept of masculinity, a real man did not cede power or control to another, as slaves and women did. As masculinity was closely tied to concepts of personal freedom and power over others, only the fool would abrogate them. Was Paul a 'fool' and if so in what sense?

4. *Peristasis* (περίστασις) Studies

Paul, in his *apologia,* refers to his tribulations for the sake of Christ, most notably in 1 Cor. 4. 8–13 and 2 Cor. 11.23–33. These references become all the more meaningful in the context of the use of *peristasis* catalogues among the Greco-Roman sages and philosophers. Therefore, the study of *peristasis* catalogues in Greco-Roman tradition, with special reference to Stoicism, is necessary.

Generally speaking, περίστασις, especially in the Stoic tradition, was perceived positively as an occasion for sages or philosophers to demonstrate their human virtues (e.g. courage, endurance, manliness). This positive attitude towards περίστασις in the Greco-Roman tradition has also been supported by modern scholars such as John Fitzgerald. He is convinced that his study of classical literature demonstrates that the Greco-Roman sage generally welcomed περίστασις. Fitzgerald infers that it is mainly for this reason that Paul in 2 Corinthians so often refers to the theme of his suffering and hardship.[56]

Fitzgerald's view, however, represents only one side of the coin. The other side, that is the mirror opposite view, was also current in Greco-Roman society, as the research of Glancy shows. It is reasonable to assume that it was this negative or derogative use of the *peristasis* catalogues which was the main concern of Paul who was trying to witness, paradoxically, to the divine power made manifest in and through his own weakness.

Glancy, in an article about 2 Cor. 11.22–25, contends that according to the social ethos of Paul's time the apostle's testimony concerning his own weakness and the abusing of his body was undoubtedly perceived by his opponents as a mark of servile submission and insignia of humiliation.[57] As such they were unworthy of a man of any social standing, dignity and

---

[56] J. T. FITZGERALD, *Cracks in an Earthen Vessel: An Examination of the Catalogues of Hardships in the Corinthian Correspondence* (Atlanta: Scholars Press, 1988), 44.

[57] GLANCY, 'Boasting', 99–135

honour. Glancy makes an important point that 'it is the Christians ... that revolutionize these values wholly by their total inversion.'[58]

The conflict between Paul and his critics in matters of social ethos and values deserves attention with regard to the physical body of a man in Roman society. Glancy agrees with Harrill that 'social status was somatically expressed', and since Paul's bodily appearance was weak (1 Cor. 2.3; 2 Cor. 10.10; 11.30) his critics naturally questioned his manhood and right to authority.[59]

Welborn describes that 'Paul was governed by a social constraint in his discourse of the cross and in his account of the sufferings of the apostles of Christ.' Like his contemporaries Horace and Seneca, 'Paul employs the language and imagery of the mime, when he speaks about these socially shameful subjects.'[60] Welborn also writes that 'Paul's exposition of the folly of the message of the cross is best understood in the context of an intellectual tradition which, for want of a better term, we have designated the "comic-philosophic tradition."'[61] The term suggests that 'a common cultural perspective connects Socrates, satire, and the mime.'[62] The wise fool, according to this tradition, was the hero Aesop of the folk-tale. For the intellectuals, however, Socrates was the model of the wise man whose wisdom was hidden in apparent foolishness. Welborn believes that 'Paul participates fully in this tradition in his discourse about the folly of the word of the cross.' The major points of Paul's argument in 1 Cor. 1–4, such as the divine reversal of wisdom and foolishness, 'find their closest analogies in the tradition that valorizes Socrates, Aesop, and the mimic fool.'[63]

Welborn's contributions and insight are noteworthy; nonetheless, the parallels drawn may at times be over-stretched. On the one hand, there seems to be a significant difference between the fool in the Greco-Roman comic-philosophic tradition and the apostle Paul. For instance, while the fool of the mime is an enacted figure on a stage, although he could be reflective of people in real life, he remains fictitious. On the other hand, Paul as a fool of Christ is completely personal and existential in real life, and is absolutely inseparable from his whole *modus operandi* as an apostle of Christ.

Paul's tribulations may not be confined only to the wounds and scars inflicted by others on his body, but also may be partly due to his manual labour as a tentmaker. As Ronald Hock observes, Paul's tentmaking profes-

---

[58] GLANCY, 'Boasting', 126.

[59] GLANCY, 'Boasting', 127–28.

[60] WELBORN, *Paul, the Fool of Christ: A Study of 1 Corinthians 1–4 in the Comic-Philosophic Tradition* (London: T & T International, 2005), 3

[61] WELBORN, *Fool*, 12.

[62] WELBORN, *Fool*, 12.

[63] WELBORN, *Fool*, 12–13.

sion (1 Cor. 4.12; cf. Acts 18.3) is often taken quite innocently and even positively as his ability (and pride) to support himself, thus making the gospel free to others. Hock's discussion helps demonstrate that Paul's manual labour was very much the trade of a slave or person of very low social status.[64] As such, Paul's choice of manual labour and decision to remain in this lowly esteemed trade, even as an apostle of Christ, could also be regarded as an inversion of the current social ethos.

Paul's hunger and thirst, mentioned in the Corinthian correspondence, may be indications that this trade did not always provide sufficiently for him. Paul's tentmaking labour was also a serious social σκάνδαλον in this status-conscious society. The social prejudice and stigma that his manual labour brought would have added further suffering to Paul besides the daily chores and physical pains that the manual labour itself brought. Yet, the apostle was not ashamed to stay in such a dishonourable profession for the sake of Christ and the Gospel. On the whole, the study on περίστασις indicates that Paul's physical suffering caused another σκάνδαλον in terms of the Greco-Roman social ethos in which human virtues, masculinity and social status were greatly cherished.

5. Aim, Limits and Structure

It should not be underestimated what an important feature the body is in ancient understandings of crucifixion and noble death. This is the case in Greco-Roman rhetoric, especially its preoccupation with delivery and masculinity, as well as in the Greco-Roman concept of *peristasis* (i.e. a catalogue of suffering). The socio-historical studies of the three areas provide the necessary contexts for the exegesis of the relevant passages in Paul's Corinthian polemics. There is a deliberate attempt on the part of Paul to invert the current social ethos in his dealings with these areas. The choice of these three areas sets a limit to the scope of this study, not only in its socio-historical studies, but also in its reference to the Corinthian passages. Consequently the exegesis is mainly confined to 1 Cor. 1.18–31; 2.1–5, 4.8–13 and 2 Cor. 10.10; 11.23–33. While the choice of these passages may initially seem arbitrary, it will be demonstrated that they are directly related to the three socio-historical areas under consideration.

A balance between the socio-historical and the exegetical-theological is carefully sought in the ensuing discussion. Each of the three parts begins with socio-historical studies. *Part I*: Crucifixion in Antiquity and Noble Death in Greco-Roman and Jewish Traditions. *Part II*: Rhetoric, Delivery,

---

[64] R. F. HOCK, *The Social Context of Paul's Ministry: Tentmaking and Apostleship* (Philadelphia: Fortress, 1980), 31–35.

Body Language and Masculinity in Greco-Roman Social Ethos. *Part III*:
Hardship (*Peristasis*) in Greco-Roman Social Ethos and Pauline Understanding. These socio-historical studies are respectively followed by exegesis on the relevant Corinthian texts.

Part I begins with socio-historical studies on crucifixion in antiquity
based on primary texts from Plato, Plutarch, Cicero, Seneca, Josephus and
Philo. These seek to elaborate why Paul's 'message of the cross' (ὁ λόγος
ὁ τοῦ σταυροῦ) was such an obvious 'folly' (μωρία) and great offence
(σκάνδαλον) to the Greco-Roman world. This is followed by studies on the
idea of 'noble death' in both Greco-Roman and Maccabean traditions.
These contextual studies help provide the necessary background for an
exegesis of 1 Cor. 1.18–31.

Part II focuses primarily on rhetoric, delivery, body language and masculinity in the Greco-Roman tradition. This exercise is necessary because
much of the Corinthian polemics has to do with human eloquence and self-
presentation in society. With this background as its socio-historical context,
the interpretation of 1 Cor. 2.1–5 and 2 Cor. 10.10 explains why Paul deliberately chooses not to use lofty words or wisdom in Corinth and why his
bodily presence was so adversely perceived by his Corinthian critics.

Part III is devoted to the study of περίστασις with special reference to
Stoicism in its positive use. This is followed by a close look at an opposing
view of the catalogues which highlights humiliation and human degradation in close relation to Paul's personal tribulations mentioned in the Corinthian correspondence. These background studies help shed light on the
exegesis of 1 Cor. 4.8–13 and 2 Cor. 11.23–33.

All three areas are connected in their concern with the body and together help demonstrate that Paul's polemics were nothing less than a drastic inversion of key elements in the current social ethos. The word 'inversion' in the title as well as its frequent use is admittedly bold. It is used to
indicate not only Paul's intention, but also the intensity of the Corinthian
polemics. The case made is built on this important assumption and each of
the three parts attempts to justify the appropriateness of its use.

Part I

Crucifixion in Antiquity and Noble Death
in Greco-Roman and Jewish Traditions

Chapter 1

Crucifixion in Antiquity

1.1 Introduction

In order to understand the apostle Paul's 'message of the cross' as well as his approach to the Corinthian crisis an analysis of the practice of crucifixion in antiquity and prevalent perceptions associated with it is necessary. Paul's main theological position is openly stated in 1 Cor. 1.18–31, almost immediately after his opening remarks in 1 Corinthians. It is reasonable to assume that Paul was knowledgeable about the practice of crucifixion in antiquity and current public perception about it when he acknowledges that 'the message of the cross' (ὁ λόγος ὁ τοῦ σταυροῦ) was 'foolishness' (μωρία) to those who rejected it (1.18).

Division in the Corinthian church evidently created a very serious crisis which threatened unity and fellowship. Judging from Paul's description of the situation (1.10–17) as well as his immediate response (1.18–31), it is sufficiently clear that the Corinthian division, in the final analysis, was largely due to a vital failure to understand the message of the cross, which was essential to both the faith and conduct of the Corinthians. Why was the message of the cross such foolishness to those who rejected it? And why was its theology so difficult even for the Corinthian Christians to grasp, although several years had passed since Paul first brought the message to them (i.e. assuming Paul arrived in Corinth c. 49/50 AD and 1 Corinthians was written c. 54/55)? The main problem apparently lay with people's perception about the cross in the Greco-Roman world. This chapter addresses these as well as other related issues *vis-à-vis* the social ethos of Greco-Roman society. Crucifixion as a form of capital punishment is not the only concern, but also the very powerful and graphic 'body language' conveyed by it as well as its serious social implications.

At a number of points this study is indebted to Hengel's research on crucifixion which refers to several crucial primary sources relevant to an analysis on the subject in ancient Greco-Roman writings. If Hengel modestly regards his work as 'no more than "historical preliminaries" for a presentation of the *theologia crucis* in Paul,'[1] than this inquiry is mainly an

---

[1] HENGEL, *Crucifixion*, xii.

attempt to provide a necessary socio-historical background to help explain why Paul's message of the cross was such foolishness to those who rejected it.

The beginning point here will be a general survey of crucifixion in antiquity, based primarily on ancient sources. This then is followed by an investigation of: (1) crucifixion and Roman law enforcement; (2) the victims of crucifixion; (3) the social symbolism of crucifixion; and (4) the emphasis on 'body language' conveyed by this form of capital punishment.

1.2 Crucifixion in Antiquity: A General Survey

The work of Hengel on the origins and parallels of Roman crucifixion in ancient writings is widely acknowledged as the most significant research on the subject.[2] His survey indicates that from the time of Plautus (c. 3rd cent. BC onwards), *crux* is already used as a 'vulgar taunt' among people of the lower classes, including slaves and prostitutes. Indeed, he argues that *crux* is a vile word that would not have sounded any better in the ears of slaves or foreigners (*peregrinus*) than to a member of the Roman nobility.[3]

Among scholars, the *opinio communis* seems to be that the practice of crucifixion was begun by the Persians. This is largely due to the witness of the Greek historian Herodotus (c. 484–425 BC): for instance, Herodotus records that after conquering Babylon for the second time, the Persian king Darius 'crucified (ἀνεσκολόπισε) about three thousand men [Babylonians] who were chief among them.'[4] Similarly, Darius wanted to impale (ἀναὸ κολοπιεῖσθαι) Egyptians 'for being less skilful than a Greek.'[5] Herodotus also mentions that Oroetes killed Polyerates of Samos and then crucified him (ἀνεσταύρωσε).[6]

Hengel's analysis of ancient sources demonstrates that quite a variety of 'barbarian peoples' such as Assyrians, Indians, Scythians, Taurians and Celts used crucifixion as a mode of execution. Even more significant was

---

[2] Another significant work on the subject is that of H.–W. KUHN, 'Die Kreuzesstrafe während der frühen Kaiserzeit. Ihre Wirklichkeit und Wertung in der Umwelt des Urchristentums', in H. TEMPORINI and W. Haase (eds.), *Aufstieg und Niedergang der römischen Welt: Geschichte und Kultur Roms im Spiegel der neueren Forschung* (Berlin: Walter De Gruyter, 1982), vol. 25.648–793. The works of Kuhn and Hengel discuss, for the most part, the same ancient source literature.

[3] HENGEL, *Crucifixion*, 9–10, esp. ref. Plautus, *Aul.* 522; *Bacch.* 584; Terence, *Eun.* 383.

[4] Herodotus 3.159.

[5] Herodotus 3.132.

[6] Herodotus 3.125.

the practice of this dreadful form of execution by the Carthaginians, especially for high treason, from whom the Romans might have learnt and perfected this form of capital punishment.[7]

In Roman practice, crucifixion was used almost exclusively for non-Romans. However, Greek and Roman historians generally tend to stress the barbaric nature of crucifixion and play down their own practice of this mode of execution. The crucifixions by Mithridates, Rome's arch-enemy, and of the two kings of Thrace, are given as 'deterrent examples' in the Hellenistic period.[8] The Greek philosopher Plato is already familiar with the practice of crucifixion, and from his *Gorgias* it is clear that crucifixion was often preceded by various kinds of torture.[9] As far as the Greeks are concerned, the many crucifixions Alexander the Great conducted are well known. A horrific example is the siege of Tyre in which Alexander crucified two thousand able-bodied survivors.[10]

Following the death of Alexander, Perdiccas came to power and 'tortured and impaled/crucified' (ἀνεσταύρωσε) the king [Ariarathes] and all his relatives in 322 BC.[11] The same practice was continued in the Hellenistic monarchies, although reports about it are few. Josephus writes about crucifixions in Judaea in 167 BC when Antiochus IV persecuted Jews.[12]

Hengel argues that there would have been no less awareness, fear and dread of crucifixion in the east of the Empire than the west. This would have been especially true among lower classes. One may reasonably assume that by the time of Paul, crucifixion would have been the *summum supplicium* throughout the entire Empire. This historical reality is of utmost importance because when Paul proclaimed the 'message of the cross' or 'Christ crucified' (e.g. 1 Cor. 1.23; 2.2; Gal. 3.1) in various parts of the Empire, many hearers would have known that this 'Christ', whom his followers regarded as the Son of God or even the very God himself, had been put on trial before Pontius Pilate like a criminal, found guilty (or at least presumed to be so) and was eventually crucified. That this crucified Jesus of Nazareth could truly be the Messiah sent to earth, the Son of God, Lord of all, as well as coming Judge at the world's end, would most certainly have been thought lunacy and foolishness to any educated person.[13]

---

[7] Among the cases cited are the crucifixion of the Median king Pharnus by the Assyrian king Ninus; the crucifixion of Cyrus by the Scythians. HENGEL, *Crucifixion*, 22–23.

[8] HENGEL, *Crucifixion*, 23–24.

[9] Plato, *Gorg.* 473BC.

[10] Curtius Rufus, *Hist. Alex.* 4.4.17.

[11] Diodorus, Siculus 18.16.3.

[12] Josephus, *Ant.* 12.256. Hengel suggests that Josephus' record could have come from a Hellenistic source (*Crucifixion*, 74–75).

[13] Cf. HENGEL, *Crucifixion*, 83.

In keeping with Hengel's view, it seems best to keep the Gentile 'μωρία' of the cross (1 Cor. 1.23) in the foreground and to deal separately with the subject within Jewish traditions.[14] In the following discussion, the former will be attended to more than the latter. However, due to Paul's reference to 'Christ crucified' being 'a stumbling block to the Jews' (1.23), a short discussion on crucifixion and 'curse' related to 'noble death' in Jewish literature will be offered in a later section (§2.4).

Many of the seats of Roman power, such as Syrian Antioch, Pisidian Antioch, Lystra, Iconium, Thessalonica, Philippi, Troas, Corinth and Ephesus were also centres of Paul's missionary activity. It would be reasonable to assume that the Roman governors and officials in those places would have followed the Roman practice and used crucifixion as a major capital punishment. Not only would a Roman citizen like Paul be familiar with it, crucifixion as a horrible execution would also be a matter of common knowledge, although attitudes to it might vary. The Romans and the law-abiding subjects would quite understandably welcome it as a necessary and effective instrument for the maintenance of social order and security. For the violent and rebellious as well as for the general public the response to crucifixion would naturally be one of fear and hatred. Despite its extreme cruelty and inhumanity, the ancient world as a whole did not seem to have the will or desire to abolish this form of execution.

Even if crucifixion were regarded as something evil by the more 'enlightened' or 'civilized', like the Greco-Roman philosophers Cicero and Seneca, it remained a 'necessary evil'.[15] Cicero simply describes crucifixion as *summum supplicium* ('the most cruel penalty') and *istam pestem* ('that plague'), without any suggestion for its abolishment.[16] Philo describes it as 'punishment at the uttermost' (τὰς ἀνωτάτω τιμωρίας)[17] while Josephus portrays it as 'the most pitiable of deaths' (θανάτων τὸν οἴκτιστον).[18] Seneca calls the cross 'the accursed tree' (*infelix lignum*)[19]

---

[14] HENGEL, *Crucifixion*, 84.

[15] The relevance of crucifixion for today may be illustrated by Mel Gibson's 2004 film, *The Passion of the Christ*. While critics of the film have been concerned with who is portrayed as responsible for putting Jesus to death, another issue has been with how the actual crucifixion is depicted. Many have seen it as simply too violent, however even though Gibson exaggerates the passion for his own purposes, one should take note that crucifixion was in fact terribly gruesome. Had viewers been aware of the ancient practice, critiques of Gibson would likely have been phrased much differently.

[16] Cicero, *Verr.* 5.168, 162.

[17] Philo, *Flacc.* 126.

[18] Josephus, *B.J.* 7.202.

[19] Cf. Philo in *Post.* 24–26 who quotes from Deut. 21.23 'Hanging on a tree is cursed of God' (κεκατηραμένον ὑπὸ θεοῦ τὸν κρεμάμενον ἐπὶ ξύλου) but does not identify it explicitly with crucifixion.

and regards the pain of crucifixion as a 'climax' (*et novissime acutam crucem*).[20]

The extent of suffering in crucifixion prompts Seneca to ask some disturbing questions in *Epistulae Morales* (101.14ff):

> But what sort of life is a lingering death? Can anyone be found who would prefer wasting away in pain, dying limb by limb, or letting out his life drop by drop, rather than expiring once for all? Can any man be found willing to be fastened to the accursed tree [*infelix lignum* (or *arbor*) is the cross], long sickly, already deformed, swelling with ugly tumours on chest and shoulders, and draw the breath of life amid long-drawn-out agony? I think he would have many excuses for dying even before mounting the cross!

Seneca suggests that Maecenas should perhaps consider suicide as the last way to freedom from the suffering of crucifixion.[21]

Despite the diversity of their backgrounds and contexts, most ancient writers seem to have dealt with or at least mention some of the following significant points regarding crucifixion in antiquity.

(1) *The variety of people crucified*: criminals, rebels, slaves, Jews (including Jesus), Christians and sometimes even nobles and Roman citizens. This last category was understandably most shocking and unacceptable to the Roman public.

(2) *The utmost cruelty and maximum pain* (physical and mental) *that crucifixion inflicted on the victims*. There were various forms of execution, from the usual cross-shape to a tree or simply a piece of wood or beam. A variety of tortures, such as burning and flogging, were quite commonly applied to the crucified victims.

(3) *The public display of crucifixion*: sometimes even turning it into a dramatic spectacle for entertainment and amusement to the full satisfaction of the most sadistic of the spectators. It was also in this context that the total alienation of the victims from the rest of human society would understandably be most deeply felt.

(4) Perhaps in no other way was the total helplessness and powerlessness of a *human* (if the victim was still worthy of such description!) more graphically shown than the very sight of crucifixion itself.

---

[20] Seneca, *Ep.* 101.14. As such, Hengel has every reason to regard crucifixion as 'a "barbaric" form of execution of the utmost cruelty', which is the title of chapter 4 of his book (*Crucifixion*, 22).

[21] Seneca, *Ep.* 101.14f: 'Thence came that most debased of prayers, in which Maecenas does not refuse to suffer weakness, deformity, and as *a climax the pain of crucifixion* (*et novissime acutam crucem*) – provided only that he may prolong the breath of life amid these sufferings.' Yet, as Hengel observes 'while the Stoic Seneca ascribes the abomination of crucifixion and other tortures to the worst of all passions, anger, he takes it for granted that criminals have to be executed in this way' (*Crucifixion*, 37. See also *Ir.* 3.6).

(5) *The public dishonouring of the human body* (often in total nakedness and full exposure); the depriving of a decent burial and even the possibility of the corpse or body remains being turned into food for beasts and birds were norms rather than exceptions in crucifixion.[22]

These points will be explored further.

1.3 Crucifixion and Roman Law Enforcement

Before investigating crucifixion as a capital punishment for people of different classes in Roman society, it is necessary to have a general view about the vital link between punishment and social status, as well as Roman law enforcement and *Pax Romana*.

Roman theories of punishment are characterized by a respect for status based on conventional socio-political relationships in society. This is more clearly reflected in the actions and attitudes of judicial officials than in legal theory.[23] Garnsey elaborates that when 'investigating the treatment given to defendants of different status in the various courts, it was found that low-status defendants were brought before the Senate or Emperor more often for punishment than for trial, and that if they were subjected to a relatively full examination and found guilty, they received harsher penalties than high-status defendants on the same charges.'[24]

Summum supplicium was the most serious penalty for offenders of low status. This covered several aggravated forms of the death penalty, including exposure to wild beasts (*bestiis dari*), crucifixion (*crux*) and being burned alive (*vivus uri, or crematio*).[25] As noted previously, crucifixion was already notorious as the cruelest and most humiliating penalty at the time of Paul, especially for slaves and people of the lower strata of Roman society. Roman citizens, on the other hand, were rarely punished by crucifixion according to the social convention of the time, although there were some exceptional cases. Such class consciousness and social distinction were very significant, especially with reference to the crucifixion of Jesus and Paul's 'message of the cross' as well as the apostle's approach to the Corinthian crisis.

The Roman's concern for social peace and order had almost become pathological.[26] As such, even enlightened philosophers agreed that it was necessary to punish criminals severely to maintain Roman law and the *Pax*

---

[22] Some primary textual evidences for these points will be cited in section (§1.3–1.4).

[23] GARNSEY, *Social Status*, 1–2.

[24] GARNSEY, *Social Status*, 99–100.

[25] GARNSEY, *Social Status*, 104.

[26] C. A. BARTON, *The Sorrows of the Ancient Romans* (Princeton, N. J.: Princeton University Press, 1993), 180.

Romana. It was also generally agreed that for the law against criminals to be effectively carried out, physical punishment to the utmost was necessary, although the idealistic philosopher Plato also believed in the *corrective* purpose of punishment.[27] The execution was usually preceded by various kinds of torture, such as burning the criminal's eyes and flogging. There is evidence too that torture was at times inflicted even on members of the criminal's family.[28]

The Stoic philosopher Seneca cites three main concerns in Roman criminal law: (1) correction, (2) deterrence and (3) the restoration of security. He believes that the best corrective was *severitas* (severity), but that it must not be over-used.[29] This is also largely the position of Gellius.[30]

There was also the element of retribution which met the primitive demand of: 'an eye for an eye and a tooth for a tooth.' Indeed, it was the duty of the Roman authorities to ensure that retribution was carried out.[31] Seneca holds that retribution and revenge are the chief factors motivating emperors in their punishment of crimes.[32] Retribution reasserted the status of the person who had been wronged and ensured that due respect was paid to him (Gellius, *Noct. Att.* 7.14.3).[33]

Philo's work also shows clearly how crucifixion was thought to be fitting for the worst criminals.[34] Plutarch simply refers to crucifixion as a form of execution for the criminal with the important qualification that the

---

[27] Plato, *Gorg.* 525B: 'And it is fitting that every one under punishment rightly inflicted on him by another should either be made better and profit thereby, or serve as an example to the rest, that others seeing the sufferings he endures may in fear amend themselves.' See Coleman, 'Fatal Charades', 47.

[28] Plato, *Gorg.* 473C: 'If a man be caught criminally plotting to make himself a despot, and he be straightway put to the rack and castrated and have his eyes burnt out, and after suffering himself, and seeing inflicted on his wife and children, a number of grievous torments of every kind, he be finally *crucified* (ἔσχατον ἀνασταυρωθῇ) or burned in a coat of pitch, will he be happier than if he escaped and make himself despot, and pass his life as a ruler in his city, doing whatever he likes, and envied and congratulated by the citizens and the foreigners besides?'

[29] Seneca, *Clem.* 1.22.2.

[30] Gellius (*Noct. Att.* 7.14.2) mentions three aspects of punishments: correction (κόλασις or νουθεσία), deterrence (τιμωρία), and the upholding of the crime victim's status (παράδειγμα).

[31] COLEMAN, 'Fatal Charades', 45.

[32] Seneca, *Clem.* 1.20.1.

[33] COLEMAN, 'Fatal Charades', 46.

[34] Philo, *Leg.* 3.151–152: '... he [the lawgiver] ordained another penalty as an addition, and ordered the manslayers to be *crucified* (ἀνασκολοπίζεσθαι). Yet after giving this injunction he hastened to revert to his natural humanity and showed mercy to those whose deeds were merciless when he says "Let not the sun go down upon the *crucified* (ἀνεσκολοπισμένοις) but let them be buried in the earth before sundown."'

victim 'must carry his own cross'.[35] The crucifixion of robbers by the young Caesar in Pergamum in c. 75 BC was recorded by Plutarch.[36]

Suetonius reports that Caesar had a particular group of pirates' throats cut before crucifying them, but actually places emphasis on the emperor's 'merciful' nature rather than on the cruel nature of the execution itself.[37] The cutting of the pirates' throats before execution on the cross, which one assumes causes death, was apparently meant to remove or reduce the victims' lingering suffering. Hence, the emperor's 'merciful' nature is better understood in this passage. Generally speaking, Coleman is convincing when he states that 'the humanitarian notion that execution should be carried out with dignity, speed, and discretion is a modern idea.'[38]

Deterrence was given jurisprudential recognition by Callistratus in *Dig.* 48.19.28.15: 'the practice approved by most authorities has been to hang notorious brigands on a gallows in the place which they used to haunt, so that by the spectacle others may be deterred from the same crimes.'[39] But as Coleman points out 'to be an effective deterrent, a penalty should arouse horror and aversion; no doubt audiences in the amphitheatre experienced these sensations, but so effective was the gulf created between spectacle and spectators that the dominant reaction among the audience was pleasure rather than revulsion' (see §1.5.2 for more on crucifixion as an occasion for public entertainment).[40]

Despite its extreme cruelty and inhumanity, crucifixion was quite generally thought to have contributed significantly to the maintenance of peace and order in Roman society against the threat of the worst criminals. Its employment was thus largely thought to be justified in the vast Empire where the *Pax Romana* needed to be maintained at all cost. The governor of Syria, Quadratus, for example, crucified some during a troublesome disturbance in the procuratorship of Cumanus.[41] Felix did the same with many brigands in order to restore order. Josephus also records a considerable number of people who were regarded as 'robbers/brigands' being crucified by Felix in Judaea.[42]

---

[35] Plutarch, *Mor.* 554 AB: 'Every criminal who goes to execution must carry his own cross on his back (ἕκαστος κακούργων ἐκφέρει τὸν αὑτοῦ σταυρόν)' (Cf. Jn. 19.17).

[36] Plutarch, *Caes.* 2.2–4: 'Caesar went to Pergamum, took the robbers out of prison, and *crucified* them all (ἅπαντας ἀνεσταύρωσεν), just as he had often warned them on the island that he would do, when they thought he was joking.'

[37] Suetonius, *Jul.* 74.1.

[38] COLEMAN, 'Fatal Charades', 46.

[39] COLEMAN, 'Fatal Charades', 50.

[40] COLEMAN, 'Fatal Charades', 50.

[41] Josephus, *Ant.* 20.129.

[42] Josephus, *B.J.* 2.253: 'Felix took prisoner Eleazar, the brigand chief, who for twenty years had ravaged the country, with many of his associates, and sent them for trial to Rome. Of the brigands whom he crucified (ἀνεσταυρωθέντων), and of the common

Broadly speaking, throughout the 1ˢᵗ century people in the Empire generally enjoyed the *Pax Romana* in which the law was largely effective and
the administration basically functioned well.[43] As such, a hard line was
usually taken against those criminals and robbers who threatened both social peace and political security, so much so that the use of crucifixion
against them often gained general approval. As such, contempt for those
who suffered it was something to be accepted. Not only was this gruesome
form of execution able to produce its desired deterrent effect, but also the
victim(s) who had suffered at the hands of the criminal could also draw
some satisfaction from viewing it.

As Justin Epitomator quite clearly states: *ut et conspectu deterreantur
alii ab isdem facinoribus et solacio sit cognatis et adfinibus interemptorum
eodem loco poena reddita, in quo latrones homicidia fecissent* (that the
sight may deter others from such crimes and be a comfort to the relatives
and neighbours of those whom they have killed, the penalty is to be ex-
acted in the same place where the robbers did their murders).[44]

It is in this particular context that Quintilian hails the crucifixion of
criminals as good work: *quotiens noxios crucifigimus celeberrimae eligun-
tur viae, ubi plurimi intueri, plurimi commoveri hoc metu possint. omnis
enim poena non tam ad (vin)dictam pertinet, quam ad exemplum* (whenever we crucify criminals, the most heavily used routes are chosen where
the greatest number of people can watch and be influenced by this threat;
for every penalty is aimed not so much at the offence as at its exemplary
value).[45]

1.4 Victims of Crucifixion

1.4.1 Crucifixion of Slaves

Although slavery was practised in most ancient cultures, ancient Greece
and Rome are two societies in world history which seem to have been
based on slavery. Independently, the Greeks and Romans apparently transformed slavery into an institutionalized system of large-scale employment

---

people Ps.–who were convicted of complicity with them and punished by him, the number was incalculable' (Cf. *B.J.* 7.202).

[43] According to the Roman historian Suetonius (*Aug.* 98.2), the sailors of Alexandria
actually paid tribute to Caesar Augustus for the *Pax* they enjoyed: *per illum se vivere, per
illum navigare, libertate atque fortunis per illum frui* (by him they lived, by him they
sailed and by him they enjoyed liberty and good fortune).

[44] Justin Epitomator, *Dig.* 48.19.28.15.

[45] Ps. – Quintilian, *Decl.* 274. 13.

of slave labour in both the countryside and the cities.[46] The system of slavery was fully developed and stabilized as a socio-legal institution by the 2nd century BC.

In Roman society the law common to all people (*ius gentium*) was perceived to be different from the law of nature (*ius naturale*). Slavery was regarded as an institution of the *ius gentium,* something essentially contrary to the law of nature and the basic principle of human equality. The institution resulted from human activities, especially wars. Also, under the laws of property, the slave was treated as a *res mancipi,* a classification that placed the slave in the same category as land and cattle. Slaves were also held to be *pro nullo* at law and were thus legally without rights or duties.[47] In other words, under Roman law, slaves could own nothing and were subject to their master's absolute control.[48] They had no right to marry and no rights in relation to their children, who belonged to their master.[49]

Garnsey notes that the punishments deem appropriate for *humiliores* are derived from those applied to slaves. Crucifixion was the standing form of execution for slaves.[50]

In their writings, Cicero, Valerius Maximus, Tacitus, Livy and Plautus clearly mention crucifixion as 'slaves' punishment' (*servile supplicium*).[51] Moreover, Callistratus records that slaves were traditionally punished more severely than free men.[52]

In real life situations slaves generally received little or no protection from Roman society. Thus their fate depended very much on the whim and fancy of their masters and other members of the Roman household. As such, they lived constantly under the threat of the *servile supplicium* which, in the system of slavery during the period, often meant crucifixion. The term became practically synonymous with crucifixion itself. The following dialogue between a Roman matron and her husband is revealing:

'Crucify that slave!' says the wife. 'But what crime worthy of death has he committed?' asked the husband; 'where are the witnesses? Who informed against him? Give him a hearing at least; no delay can be too long when a man's life is at stake!' 'What, you num-

---

[46] M. I. FINLEY, *Ancient Slavery and Modern Ideology* (London: Chatto & Windus, 1980), 67.

[47] W. W. BUCKLAND, *The Roman Law of Slavery* (London: Cambridge University Press, 1970), 1, 10.

[48] Gaius, *Inst.* 2.96. For a concise discussion of the legal aspects of *peculium,* see A. WATSON, *Roman Slave Law* (Baltimore: John Hopkins University Press, 1987), 95–96.

[49] Aristotle, *Pol.* 1.4–5. FINLEY, *Ancient Slavery,* 69–77, 95–97.

[50] GARNSEY, *Social Status,* 127.

[51] Cicero, *Verr.* 5.169; Valerius Maximus 2.7.12; Tacitus, *Hist.* 4.11; Livy 29.18.14; Plautus, *Mil.* 539–40; *Most.* 1133, 359–64; *Per.* 855–56.

[52] Callistratus, *Dig.* 48.19.28.16.

skull? You call a slave a man, do you? He has done no wrong, you say? Be it so; but this is my will and my command: let my will be the voucher for the deed.' (*'Pone crucem servo.' 'meruit quo crimine servus supplicium? quis testis adest? quis detulit? audi; nulla umquam de morte hominis cunctatio longa est.' 'o demens, ita servus homo est? nil fecerit, esto: hoc volo, sic iubeo, sit pro ratione voluntas.'*)[53]

The Roman matron's command – 'crucify that slave' (*pone crucem servo!*) reminds one of the cry of the chief priests and guards during the trial of Jesus before Pontius Pilate: 'Crucify him! Crucify him!' (σταύρωσον σταύρωσον, Jn. 19.6). Such shouting may very well have been familiar with the crucifixion of slaves in the ancient world. Whatever the case may be, as a well informed citizen of Rome and a seasoned traveller, Paul should have no difficulty identifying the crucified Christ with a crucified slave, as he had apparently done in the 'Philippian hymn' (Phil. 2.5–11) – assuming that the hymn could be of Pauline origin.

A negative attitude towards slaves was reflected even in the mind of enlightened philosophers. Cicero defends King Deiotarus who was accused by his runaway slave of misconduct. In Cicero's opinion: 'according to the practice of our ancestors, it is illegal to seek evidence from a slave against his master.' Cicero was so angry with what he believed to be a false accusation of the runaway slave that he thinks even the cruel penalty of crucifixion was not adequate as a torture for him. 'Can the cross inflict adequate torture upon this runaway?' asked Cicero.[54]

In very vivid terms, Cicero also describes the crucifixion of slaves who were suspected of conspiracy:

Those men, after being convicted of the crime of conspiracy, handed over to execution, and bound to the stake ... how effectively he frightened them into keeping quiet! He has ordered arrests to be made – that must have terrified them all; he has summoned their masters to their trial – what can alarm slaves more than that? ... What is the next step? The lash, the fire, and that final stage in the punishment of the guilty and the intimidation of the rest, the torments of crucifixion (... *Quid deinde sequitur? Verbera atque ignes et illa extrema ad supplicium damnatorum, metum ceterorum, cruciatus et crux*).[55]

According to Welborn, 'the most vivid references to crucifixion in ancient literature are found in the comedies of Plautus, in which the lives of slaves are portrayed with unparalleled sympathy. It is here that one encounters a phenomenon that is essential to an understanding of Paul's dictum on the "folly" of "the word of the cross": references to crucifixion in Plautus' comedies almost always take the form of jokes!'[56] Gallows humour is a mark of Plautus' writings.[57] Even more frequent are places where slaves

---

[53] Juvenal, *Sat.* 6.219.
[54] Cicero, *Deiot.* 26.
[55] Cicero, *Verr.* 5.11–12, 14.
[56] WELBORN, *Fool*, 134.
[57] Plautus, *Mil.* 372–73, 539–40, 610–14; *Per.* 855–56; *St.* 625–26; *Ep.* 359–64.

use the word *crux* in vulgar taunts, calling one another 'cross-meat', 'cross-bird'[58] and bidding one another to 'go be hanged!'[59]

Welborn has also found that the report of the crucifixion of a slave was sometimes 'sandwiched between a mimic dance and a gymnastic spectacle.'[60] Welborn has the story: 'Trimalchio gets drunk and invites his wife to perform a lascivious mimic dance, while he proceeds to imitate the gestures of the actor Syrus, to the choral accompaniment of the whole household. In the midst of these theatrical follies, the notice of the slave's death is suddenly read out: "the slave Mithridates was crucified for having damned the soul of our Gaius"'[61]

The theme of crucifixion with comic features is also found in novels and romances.[62] Gallows humour also appears in satirists' books.[63] The connection between crucifixion and comedy even occurs in political writing.[64]

For a Roman in the ancient world, speech was a most crucial element in the assertion of a man's power and authority as well as status in society. It was a tangible way of demonstrating his masculinity. For a slave who had already been deprived of all civil and human rights for life, one would perhaps expect him to have at least the opportunity to voice his grievances during the time of his crucifixion. Yet even that basic 'human right' was sometimes denied him when the tongue of a crucified slave was cut out so that he could no longer utter words or give evidence. Cicero actually cites such a case. While not objecting to the crucifixion itself, Cicero nonetheless objects strongly to the cutting of a slave's tongue.[65]

The crucifixion of slaves was particularly significant to Paul's message of the cross because Jesus Christ himself 'took on the form of a slave' (μορφὴν δούλου λαβών, Phil. 2.7) when he was crucified, and Paul proudly uses 'slave of Christ' (δοῦλος Ἰησοῦ Χριστοῦ, Rom. 1.1) as his own self-designation.

1.4.2 Crucifixion of Jews

In the Roman tradition those who were guilty of betraying their own people to foreign enemies were to be subjected to utmost dishonour and

---

[58] Plautus, *Aul.* 522; *Bacch.* 584; *Cas.* 416; *Most.* 359–64; Terence, *Eun.* 383; Petronius, *Satyr.* 126.9; 58.2.

[59] Plautus, *As.* 940; *Bacch.* 902; *Most.* 1133; *Cas.* 93, 641, 977; *Cur* 611.

[60] Petronius, *Satyr.* 53.3. WELBORN, *Fool*, 138.

[61] WELBORN, *Fool*, 137–38. Cf. Petronius, *Satyricon* 53.3.

[62] Petronius, *Satyr.* 111–13. Xenophon, *Eph.* 4.2; cf. B. P. REARDON, *Collected Ancient Greek Novels* (Berkeley: University of California Press, 1989), 155–57.

[63] E.g. Horace, *Sat.* 1.3.76–77, 82–83; Petronius, *Satyr.* 52; Juvenal, *Sat.* 6.219–23.

[64] Philo, *Flacc.* 72–85.

[65] Cicero, *Cl.* 187.

shame. In light of this, the crucifixion of eight hundred Pharisees by Alexander Jannaeus, recorded by Josephus, may be explained.[66] King Herod seemed to have refrained from using crucifixion as a form of execution and Josephus has no record of any crucifixion from Herod's time. The excessive use of crucifixion by the Romans in Judea had so put the Jews off that from the time of direct Roman rule it became almost taboo to use it as a mode of capital punishment among Jews. Such a change of attitude is also reflected in a rabbinic interpretation of Deuteronomy 21.23. Hengel explains:

> Varus had already had two thousand prisoners crucified around Jerusalem, and AD 70, the year of terror, brought a sorry climax in this respect too. Nevertheless, the cross never became the symbol of Jewish suffering; the influence of Deuteronomy 21.23 made this impossible. So a crucified messiah could not be accepted either. It was here that the preaching of the earliest Christians caused particular offence in the mother country itself. It also explains why the theme of the crucified faithful plays no part in Jewish legends about martyrs. The cross had become too much a sign of the passion of Jesus and his followers – though in the Talmudic literature we have a whole series of references to the crucifixion of Jews during the later empire.[67]

Josephus remains our key witness as far as the crucifixion of Jews is concerned. Josephus, who is well-known as having served as advisor to Titus when Jerusalem was under siege, witnessed many scenes of crucifixion. To him this form of capital punishment was 'the most wretched of deaths' (θανάτων τὸν οἴκτιστον).[68]

The terms 'cross' and 'crucifixion' occur in Josephus' writings *Jewish Antiquities* and *The Jewish War* quite frequently and in various contexts. They are used by Josephus in some very remarkable ways, for instance in his interpretation of Ezra in relation to those who disobeyed or transgressed commands.[69] In the Roman Empire, some Jews caused offence when following their customs and adhering to a worship of their own God, which at times resulted in crucifixion. Similarly, those rebelling against Romans or acting as robbers or brigands were also treated in such a manner. Indeed, the numbers crucified were considerable.[70]

According to Josephus the Jews were so horrified by crucifixion that when their Roman besiegers threatened to crucify a Jewish prisoner, the garrison eventually surrendered in exchange for safe conduct.[71] Josephus also refers to the flogging and crucifixion of Jews who were 'Roman knights' (ἄνδρας ἱππικοῦ τάγματος) in Jerusalem by the Roman procura-

---

[66] Josephus, *B.J.* 1.97ff; *Ant.* 13.380–83.

[67] HENGEL, *Crucifixion*, 85.

[68] Josephus, *B.J.* 7.203.

[69] Josephus, *Ant.* 11.17; 11.103; 11.208; 6.374.

[70] Josephus, *B.J.* 2.306. *Ant.* 12.256; 17.295; 20.102, 129.

[71] Josephus, *B.J.* 7.202ff.

tor Gessius Florus just before the outbreak of the Jewish War (66 AD).[72] The crucifixion of these Roman knights would have been very disturbing and shocking to the status-conscious Roman audience of Josephus. Josephus' account of a later stage of events is of the tragic end of Jewish fugitives during the siege of Jerusalem. This is among the most moving of his accounts:

> When caught, they were driven to resist, and after a conflict it seemed too late to sue for mercy. They were accordingly scourged and subjected to torture of every description, before being killed, and then crucified opposite the walls (μαστιγούμενοι δὴ καὶ πρὸ βασανιζόμενοι τοῦ θανάτου πᾶσαν αἰκίαν ἀνεσταυροῦντο τοῦ τείχους ἀντικρύ). Titus indeed commiserated their fate, five hundred or sometimes more being captured daily; on the other hand, he recognized the risk of dismissing prisoners of war, and that the custody of such numbers would amount to the imprisonment of their custodians; but his main reason for not stopping the crucifixions was the hope that the spectacle might perhaps induce the Jews to surrender, for fear that continued resistance would involve them in a similar fate. The soldiers out of rage and hatred amused themselves by nailing their prisoners in different postures (προσήλουν ... ἄλλον ἄλλῳ σχήματι πρὸς χλεύην); and so great was their number, that space could not be found for the crosses and nor crosses for the bodies (χώρα τ᾽ ἐνέλειπε τοῖς σταυροῖς καὶ σταυροὶ τοῖς σώμασιν).[73]

1.4.3 Crucifixion of Roman Citizens

Garnsey has contributed significantly to understanding Roman citizenship and the privileges attached to it. The emphasis is on the inequalities associated with legal procedures in both civil and criminal spheres. The period with which Garnsey is primarily concerned stretches from the middle of the 1st century BC to the early 3rd century AD. Garnsey believes that despite drastic socio-political changes which marked this period, the structure and ethos of Roman society remains basically unaltered. In actual practice favouritism was quite widespread throughout the period. Pliny clearly rejects juridical equality just as he rejects political equality.[74]

Garnsey's finding is largely shared by Coleman who holds that 'a crucial factor in the Roman penal system was the evolution of differentiated penalties for offenders of different status: *humiliores and honestiores.* This is a phenomenon that is characteristic of societies with a strongly differentiated class – or caste-system, and it follows that, when the upper classes are equated with true humanity, the lower classes are sub-human and therefore legitimately liable to cruel treatment.'[75]

Despite all the privileges and legal protection that they generally enjoyed, there are still cases of Romans who were executed on the cross.

---

[72] Josephus, *B.J.* 2.308.
[73] Josephus, *B.J.* 5.449–51.
[74] GARNSEY, *Social Status*, 2.
[75] COLEMAN, 'Fatal Charades', 55.

This was understandably shocking to members of the privileged class. A good example would be Cicero's accusation of Verres, former governor of Sicily, for inflicting the cruel penalty of crucifixion on a Roman citizen, Gavius, without adequate investigation and proof to show that he was indeed a spy. This unjust action of Verres was clearly unbearable and scandalous to Cicero, since crucifixion was already notorious as the most cruel and humiliating form of execution, which, with some rare exceptions, should never be inflicted upon Roman citizens. Cicero found Verres' crucifixion of Gavius particularly unacceptable as he was being dragged off to be crucified in spite of his repeated claim that he was a Roman citizen. Cicero challenges Verres thusly:

> Out of your own mouth I accuse you: the man claimed to be a Roman citizen. If you, Verres, had been made prisoner in Persia or the remotest part of India, and were being dragged off to execution, what cry would you be uttering, save that you were a Roman citizen? This is exactly what you, Verres, say, this is what you admit, that he kept proclaiming himself a Roman citizen, that this mention of his citizenship had not even so much effect upon you as to produce a little hesitation, or to delay, even for a little, the infliction of that cruel and disgusting penalty (*crudelissimum taeterrimumque supplicium*).[76]

Cicero's description of Gavius' suffering in the hands of Verres is certainly vivid. It was the greatest misfortune for a Roman citizen to be flung down, stripped naked and tied up in the open market-place and finally crucified.[77] Cicero expresses his horror and anger that: '... he [Gavius] hung there, suffering the worst extreme of the tortures inflicted upon slaves (*servitutis extreme summoque supplicio affixum*). To bind a Roman citizen is a crime, to flog him is an abomination, to slay him is almost an act of murder: to crucify him is – What? There is no fitting word that can possibly describe so horrible a deed.'[78] In his defence for the victim Gavius against Verres, Cicero clearly shows that while he objects to inflicting the extreme penalty of crucifixion on Roman citizens, like nearly all Romans, he readily accepts its practice in the case of slaves.

Another case about the crucifixion of Romans is found in Cicero's defence of Rabirius, a Roman noble and a senator who was threatened with the death penalty of crucifixion. Hengel suggests that this is 'one classic case in which the death penalty was even asked for over a member of the Roman nobility and a senator, with a reference to the old custom of hanging those guilty of high treason on the *arbor infelix*.'[79] The trial of Rabirius was instituted by Caesar in 63 BC. The prosecution was made by the trib-

---

[76] Cicero, *Verr.* 5.165–68. Cicero's reference to Persia and India is interesting, as crucifixion is also known to be used in these places.

[77] Cicero, *Verr.* 5.158, 161; cf. 4.24, 26; 1.9, 13.

[78] Cicero, *Verr.* 5.169–70.

[79] HENGEL, *Crucifixion*, 41.

une T. Labienus, a committed supporter of Caesar, and the defence was led in a masterly way by Cicero himself. The accused was charged with the murder of a tribune of the people which had taken place some thirty-seven years earlier.[80] Note how powerful Cicero's rhetoric against Labienus is:

'Veil his head, hang him to the tree of shame.' Such phrases, I say, have long since disappeared from our state, overwhelmed not only by the shadows of antiquity but by the light of Liberty.... Even if we are threatened with death, we may die free men. But the executioner, the veiling of the head, and the very word 'cross' should be far removed not only from the person of a Roman citizen but from his thoughts, his eyes and his ears (*Mors denique si proponitur, in libertate moriamur, carnifex vero et obductio capitis et nomen ipsum crucis absit non modo a corpore civium Romanorum sed etiam a cogitatione, oculis, auribus*).[81]

Cicero's indignant expression clearly shows how abhorrent crucifixion was for him and his fellow Romans. Again, the great 'foolishness' (μωρία) and 'madness' (μανία) of Paul's message of the cross must be viewed from this perspective.

If the crucifixion of a Roman, however noble but still human, was so unacceptable, it is certainly not be too difficult to imagine what the reaction would be when it came to the crucifixion of the one who was proclaimed as the very 'Son of God' and 'Saviour of the world'. Similarly, it should not be too hard to perceive how the unbelieving Roman society would regard Paul when he publicly declared that he had decided to know nothing 'except Jesus Christ, and him crucified' (1 Cor. 2.2). With this in mind, it is easier to see how this turns the conventional social ethos on its head; it is an inversion to the highest degree as far as Greco-Roman society was concerned.

Like Cicero, Josephus, Suetonius and Livy also find the crucifixion of Romans deplorable.[82] Suetonius also accuses the cruel governor Galba of crucifying a Roman citizen without sympathy: 'when the man invoked the law and declared that he was a Roman citizen, Galba, pretending to lighten his punishment by some consolation and honour, ordered that a cross much

---

[80] HENGEL, *Crucifixion*, 41–45.
[81] Cicero, *Rab. Perd.* 4.13–16.
[82] Josephus, *B.J.* 2.308: 'For Florus ventured that day to do what none had ever done before, namely, to scourge before his tribunal and nail to the cross (σταυρῷ προσηλῶσαι) men of *equestrian rank*, men who, if Jews by birth, were at least invested with that Roman dignity.' Suetonius, *Cal.* 27.3–4: 'Many men of honourable rank were first disfigured with the marks of branding-irons and then condemned to the mines, to wild beasts; or else he shut them up in cages on all fours, like animals, or had them sawn asunder.' *Cal.* 12.2 '... or even strangled the old man with his own hand, immediately ordering the *crucifixion* (*crucem*) of a freedman [Roman citizen] who cried out at the awful deed.' *Gal.* 9.1. Livy, 30.43.13; 29.9.10; 29.18.14.

higher than the rest and painted white be set up, and the man transferred to it.'[83]

1.4.4 Crucifixion of Christians

Records of the crucifixion of Christians, apart from a couple of those found in the writings of Roman historians like Tacitus and Suetonius, were not a matter of general public interest, although controversies, ridicule and Christian apologetics continued to centre around the crucifixion of Christ: How could a crucified Jew be the 'Messiah', the 'Son of God' and even 'God' himself?

From the viewpoint of New Testament studies, Josephus' reference to the crucifixion of Jesus under Pontius Pilate is particularly significant, although scholars have doubts and, rightfully, raise serious reservations about the authenticity of Josephus' designation of Jesus as 'the Messiah'.[84] Garnsey comments: 'a political charge was at least aired in the trial of Christ (see e.g. Jn. 18.33; 19.12, 19); later, the cross was frequently used for the punishment of Christians, at least from the time of Nero.'[85]

Not only was a political charge aired in the trial of Christ as Garnsey has convincingly argued, but the very title that was put on the cross of Jesus – 'Jesus of Nazareth, the King of the Jews' (Ἰησοῦς ὁ Ναζωραῖος ὁ βασιλεὺς τῶν Ἰουδαίων, Jn. 19.19) – would quite certainly be read by the ignorant and uncritical as a kind of formal verdict against the crucified Jesus, especially when it was written in three languages: Hebrew (or Aramaic), Greek and Latin. The political implication of Jesus' title or verdict was in fact consistent with the origin and historical development of the practice of crucifixion, beginning from the Persians and Carthaginians down to the time of the Romans, when crucifixion had been a major political punishment. Those who were not politically minded would at least tend to assume that the crucifixion of Jesus, just like other criminals or rebels, was a necessary and just punishment for his 'crime', whatever it might be in precise terms.

In Roman society as well as others in ancient times, the guilt of the crucified was quite readily assumed. The stigma that was attached to Jesus' crucifixion must therefore be understood in this socio-historical context, especially at the time of Jesus when people in the empire generally enjoyed the *Pax Romana* and when Roman law was by and large quite effectively

---

[83] Suetonius, *Gal.* 9.2. Cf. *Claud.* 25.3.

[84] Josephus, *Ant.* 18.64: 'Jesus who was a wise man who won over many Jews and Greeks. He was the Messiah. Pilate had condemned him to be crucified (σταυρῷ).'

[85] GARNSEY, *Social Status*, 127.

administered. In order to maintain the *Pax Romana*, the crucifixion of Jesus and his followers was regarded as legitimate punishment.[86]

Such an environment naturally made the defaming, both publicly and privately, of the crucified victim like Jesus much easier and more credible, not only socio-ethically, but also religiously, since the claims of Jesus had all these implications. And in the Jewish context, the burden of the stigma that was attached to the crucifixion of Jesus would be heavier if the 'curse' in Deuteronomy 21.23 was believed to be related to crucifixion (see §2.4).

The description of how some Christians were treated by Romans in the first century is similar to that of Jews. Indeed, condemned Christians are sometimes burnt with fire, thrown to the beasts or crucified.[87] However, in the history of the early church, what draws attention is not the crucifixion of Christ's earliest followers, but rather the 'crucified Christ' himself and the Christian 'message of the cross' (ὁ λόγος ὁ τοῦ σταυροῦ) which openly claims that the crucified Jesus was in fact the Messiah, the Son of God, even the very God Himself.

Justin Martyr writes that Christian belief in Christ crucified was so offensive to the opponents that they regarded it not just as 'folly' but also as 'madness' (μανία).[88] Commenting on the word μωρία, which is used by Paul in 1 Cor. 1.18, Hengel writes that 'the Greek word μωρία which he uses here does not denote either a purely intellectual defect nor a lack of transcendental wisdom. Something more is involved.'[89] Hengel suggests that Justin Martyr actually 'puts us on the right track' when he uses the word μανία to describe the strong reaction of the ancient world to the Christian message about the crucified Christ, the Son of God.[90]

Tacitus bluntly calls the Christian belief *exitiabilis superstitio* ('pernicious superstition') and describes crucifixion as an extreme penalty. Tacitus' basic historical data is right: *Auctor nominis eius Christus Tiberio imperitante per procuratorem Pontium Pilatum supplicio adfectus erat.* (Christus, the founder of the name, had undergone the death penalty in the reign of Tiberius, by sentence of the procurator Pontius Pilate).[91]

---

[86] Suetonius, *Ner.* 16.2; Tacitus, *Ann.* 15.44.

[87] Tacitus, *Ann.* 15.44.4; Suetonius, *Ner.* 16.2; Seneca, *Beat.* 59. 3; Cassius 63.13.2; Justin, *Dial. Tryph.* 110. 4; Tertullian, *Apol.* 12.3.

[88] Justin, *Apol.* 1.13.4: 'They say that our madness consists in the fact that we put a crucified man in second place after the unchangeable and eternal God, the Creator of the world.'

[89] HENGEL, *Crucifixion*, 1.

[90] HENGEL, *Crucifixion*, 1.

[91] Tacitus, *Ann.* 15.44.3.

Tacitus also accuses Jesus of having instigated the 'evil' or 'disease' (*malum*) which soon found its way even to the imperial capital Rome.[92] Hengel understands that Tacitus' precise account of Christ and his followers may well have come from the trials of Christians which he himself conducted while serving as the governor of Asia.[93]

Lucian ridicules Christians as 'poor wretched devils' (κακοδαίμονες), who deny 'the Greek gods and worship that crucified sophist himself' (ἃ νεσκολοπισμένον ἐκεῖνον σοφιστὴν) and live under his laws.[94] Lucian interprets the letter 'T' as an 'evil instrument' as it is shaped in the form of a *tau* on which tyrants crucify men.[95]

According to Origen, Celsus contemptuously links the crucifixion of Jesus to his humble upbringing as a carpenter and ridicules the Christian ideas of 'the tree of life' and the 'resurrection of the flesh through the wood [of the cross]': 'What drunken old woman, telling a story to lull a small child to sleep, would not be ashamed of muttering such preposterous things?'[96]

The deep-seeded prejudice of Pliny, Caecilius, Suetonius, Tacitus and others allows them to use such phrases as 'new sect of a form of *amentia*',[97] 'senseless and crazy superstition (*vana et demens superstitio*)', 'sick delusions (*figmenta male sanae opinionis*)',[98] and 'new and pernicious superstition (*superstiti nova et malefica*)'[99] to describe the Christian belief. Yet despite all these, Hengel justifiably holds that it 'is the crucifixion that distinguishes the new message from mythologies of all other peoples' and

---

[92] Tacitus, *Ann.* 15.44.3. Hengel thinks that Tacitus' precise account of Christ and his followers could have probably come from the trials of Christians which he himself conducted while serving as the governor of Asia (3).

[93] HENGEL, *Crucifixion*, 3.

[94] Lucian, *Peregr.* 13: 'The *poor wretched devils* have convinced themselves, first and foremost, that they are going to be immortal and live for all time, in consequence of which they despise death and even willingly give themselves into custody, most of them. Furthermore, their first lawgiver persuaded them that they are all brothers of one another after they have transgressed once for all by denying the Greek gods and by worshipping that crucified sophist himself and living under his laws.'

[95] Lucian, *Iudic. Voc.* 12: 'Men weeping and bewail their lot and curse Cadmus over and over for putting Tau into the alphabet, for they say that their tyrants, following his figure and imitating his build, have fashioned timbers in the same shape and crucified (ἀνασκολοπίζειν) men upon them; and that it is from him that the sorry device gets its sorry name (σταυρός). For all this do you not think that Tau deserves to die many times over? As for me, I hold that in all justice we can only punish Tau by making a T of him.'

[96] Origen, *Cels.* 6.34.

[97] Pliny the Younger, *Ep.* 10.96.4–8.

[98] Minucius Felix, *Oct.* 11.9; 9.2.

[99] Suetonius, *Ner.* 16.3: 'Punishment was inflicted on the Christians, a class of men given to a *new and mischievous superstition (superstitio nova et malefica).*' Cf. Tacitus, *Ann.* 15.44.3.

that 'the death of Jesus by crucifixion was one of the main objections against his being the son of God.'[100] The theme of 'crucified' god is very rare in ancient writings, so much so that Hengel comments: 'the extraordinary paucity of the theme of crucifixion in the mythical tradition, even in the Hellenistic and Roman period, shows the deep aversion from this cruellest of all penalties in the literary world.'[101]

The prejudices and charges against the crucifixion of Christians were so persistent and overwhelming that even the Christian Octavius found his apologetics quite ineffective. Hengel's explanation is very clear: 'Octavius cannot deny the shamefulness of the cross and therefore he is deliberately silent about the death of Jesus.... He avoids the real problem, namely, that the Son of God died a criminal's death on the tree of shame. This was not appropriate for a form of argument which was concerned to prove that the one God of the Christians was identical with the God of the philosophers.' Hengel perceives something even more serious in Octavius' evasion, because the Christian dilemma 'all too easily led educated Christians into docetism.'[102]

1.5 The Social Symbolism of Crucifixion

This concern here is primarily with certain social features which are found in the practice of crucifixion. They must be examined in vital relation to the social ethos of the Greco-Roman world. When Paul publicly acknowledges in 1 Cor. 1.18 that 'the message of the cross is foolishness' to those who rejected it, he appears to have the current Greco-Roman social ethos in mind. The crucifixion of Jesus, like most other crucifixions, was a public event as well as a social occasion, and what people perceived in their mind in the context of their conventional social setting was just as significant as what they actually saw with their eyes. This was where the social symbolism of crucifixion, including that of Jesus, became relevant. The following are some of the main features of the social symbolism of crucifixion.

1.5.1 The Presumed Guiltiness of the Crucified Victim

The presumed guilt of the crucified victim was not only the opinion of the condemning party and executioners, that is those who held power, but perhaps more significantly also that of the (often ignorant and innocent) pub-

---

[100] HENGEL, *Crucifixion*, 1.

[101] HENGEL, *Crucifixion*, 14.

[102] HENGEL, *Crucifixion*, 4. Hengel elaborates on this important point much further in his section on 'Docetism as a way of removing the "folly" of the cross' (15–21).

lic. As such, the presumed guiltiness of the crucified victim could be said
to be largely responsible for the public prejudice against the crucified victim.

As noted earlier, the use of this severe and cruel capital punishment was
considered a highly effective as well as just way of eradicating a presumed
social menace, for the sake of the *Pax Romana*, and in the name of which
no sacrifice was too great. For the undiscerning general public, the crucifixion of Jesus would most probably be perceived in such a context. Jesus
clearly died as a kind of 'rebel' in the eyes of those who did not have the
whole and true picture, although according to the witness of the gospels Pilate found no guilt or crime in Jesus. Tacitus, Suetonius, Celsus and Pliny
seem to have no real knowledge of the gospels.

Whatever the case might be, the title that was given to Jesus on the
cross – 'Jesus of Nazareth, the King of the Jews' – would most probably
have been taken by the ignorant and innocent as the crime of the crucified
Christ as well as a kind of official verdict on him, although the title was
quite clearly written by Pilate as a mockery. And those who were in the
know as well as the perceptive spectators would probably be able to read
Jesus' title on the cross as a possible mockery and insult to him personally
as well as to the Jews nationally. The response of the Jewish chief priests
to the title indicated that they would have nothing to do with a *crucified*
'King of the Jews'. Instead, they suggested that the appropriate title or
verdict should be: 'this man said, I am King of the Jews' (Jn. 19.21). Pilate's response was: 'what I have written I have written' (ὃ
γέγραφα, γέγραφα, 19.22).

The title given by Pilate is perhaps one of the greater ironies in human
history, because what was intended as a derisive insult turned out to be a
statement of truth, at least from the Christian point of view! For Jesus of
Nazareth was 'the King of the Jews', indeed more than just King of the
Jews. The Christian confession went on to describe the crucified Jesus of
Nazareth as 'the King of kings'. Yet, on that day when Jesus of Nazareth
was hanging on the cross, the title of the crucified victim or the verdict on
him would most probably have implied some kind of treason or crime in
the Roman context, at least as far as the general public was concerned. As
Paul himself states: 'none of the rulers of this age understood this; for if
they had, they would not have crucified the Lord of glory' (1 Cor. 2.8).

Augustine mentions an oracle of Apollo which was intended as a reply
to a question from a husband who is seeking to prevent his wife from becoming a Christian. The negative answer of the oracle is indicative of the
Roman prejudice against the crucifixion of Christ:

Let her continue as she pleases, persisting in her vain delusions, and lamenting in song as
a god one who died for delusions, who was condemned by judges whose verdict was just,
and executed publicly by the worst iron-bound death (*Pergat quo modo uult inanibus fal-*

laciis perseuerans et lamentari fallaciis mortuum Deum cantans, quem iudicibus recta sentientibus perditum pessima in speciosis ferro vincta mors interfecit).[103]

The oracle is consistent with the view of Pliny, Tacitus and Caecilius about the crucified 'God': A 'dead God' was the greatest contradiction in itself.[104] Walter Bauer sees the Christian dilemma here after his survey of the Christians opponents' response to the whole passion of Jesus: '*Wie hätten sie sich auch sein Leiden und Sterben und was damit zusammenhing entgehen lassen sollen. Wenn irgendwo, so konnte hier die vernichtendste Kritik einsetzen. Jesus ist verfolgt und getötet worden, doch nicht als ein Gerechter, ein neuer Sokrates. Vielmehr ward er als Verbrecher belangt, überführt, strafwürdig befunden und dem Tode überantwortet.*'[105]

1.5.2 The Public Nature of Crucifixion

The whole drama of crucifixion in the Greco-Roman world was often not confined to the very act of nailing or binding of the victim to the cross or wooden beam. What went before, such as insult, mockery and all sorts of verbal and physical abuses was just as entertaining and exciting as the final act itself. And as crucifixion was often deliberately executed in prominent public places, its desired goal, whether it was for deterrent purposes or public entertainment – or both – could quite easily be achieved. Not only was Christ publicly 'displayed' on the cross, the messengers of 'the message of the cross' were similarly put on stage for full public viewing as Paul himself says in 1 Cor. 4.9: 'For I think that God has exhibited us apostles as last of all, as though sentenced to death, because we have become a spectacle (θέατρον) to the world, to angels and to mortals.'

Garnsey's study indicates that 'in non-legal literary sources *supplicium* has three basic meanings: torture, death and punishment generally. The suggestion has been made that it is the first meaning (torture), that is preserved in the legal term *summum supplicium*.'[106] For the general public who were at the scene of crucifixion, the torture that was inflicted upon the victim could either arouse natural human sympathy or provide an occasion for entertainment. As the crucified victim was usually presumed to be guilty, the latter was often more apparent.

---

[103] Augustine, *Civ.* 19.23.

[104] HENGEL, *Crucifixion*, 19.

[105] W. BAUER, *Das Leben Jesu im Zeitalter der neutestamentlichen Apokryphen* (Tübingen: Mohr Siebeck, 1909; reprinted, 1967), 476, 'How could they [early Christians] avoid suffering, dying and what is connected with it? At any time damning criticism could be leveled. Jesus was persecuted and killed, but not as a righteous man, a new Socrates. But rather he was prosecuted as a criminal, convicted and found worthy of punishment, even to be turned over to be put to death' (Translation by B. G. WOLD).

[106] GARNSEY, *Social Status*, 122.

Crucifixion as an extreme form of execution was regarded as abhorrent by ancient people, precisely because of the various kinds of torture that were employed, usually prior to the final act of crucifixion (stripping, flogging, hanging, etc.), and the considerable length of time that elapsed before death.[107]

Martyn offers a helpful description of the practice, explaining that on most occasions the convicted man was nailed to a beam of wood, which would likely have a cross section, while he remained alive. This act would be followed by a slow and obscene death before a public audience. The primary reason for crucifixion, regardless of whether there was a sadistic origin to the practice, was based on the assumption that a hideous manner of punishment would inspire fear and respect for the law among the onlookers.[108]

Hengel's survey shows that not only in the ancient world generally, but even in the Roman Empire where some norms were to be expected, the form of execution varied considerably.[109] As such, crucifixion became a punishment in which 'the caprice and sadism of the executioners were given full rein ... there were too many different possibilities for the execu- tioner.'[110] Philo, Plutarch, Seneca and Lucian all make reference to the various forms of execution in their writings.[111] Beating and torturing the convicted before crucifixion was customary Roman practice.[112]

Inhumanity and cruelty were blatantly shown not only in the suffering of the victim, but also disgustingly demonstrated in the 'satisfaction' that spectators derived from it. Coleman elaborates:

A lingering death that lasts hours if not days, did not offer the same spectacular appeal as the other 'aggravated' death penalties that were commonly imposed: burning and beasts. But the actual moment of death may be relatively insignificant in relation to the satisfac- tion spectators derived from witnessing preliminaries that culminated in the hoisting of the body onto the cross. It is also possible that a combined penalty was envisaged such as

---

[107] Plutarch even described a crucified person who suffered for ten days. *Per.* 28.3 re- fers to crucifixion carried out by Pericles: '... Pericles had the Samian trierarchs and ma- rines brought into the market-place of Miletus and crucified (σανίσι προσδήσας "bound to planks") there, and that then, when they had already suffered grievously for ten days, he gave orders to break their heads in with clubs and make an end of them, and then cast their bodies forth without burial rites.'

[108] J. L. MARTYN, *Galatians: A New Translation with Introduction and Commentary* (New York: Doubleday, 1997), 277.

[109] Examples cited by Hengel are: 'a flogging beforehand, and the victim often carried the beam to the place of execution, where he was nailed to it with outstretched arms, raised up and seated on a small wooden peg' (25).

[110] HENGEL, *Crucifixion*, 25.

[111] Philo, *Post.* 61; *Somn.* 2.213; Plutarch, *Mor.* 449D; Seneca, *Cons.* 20.3; cf. *Ir.* 2.2; *Beat.* 19.3; Lucian, *Prom.* 1.2; *Dial. d.* 5 (1).1.

[112] *Dig.* 48. 19.8.3; Cassius, 2.11.6.

that suffered by the martyr Blandina, who was hung on a post as bait for the animals in a posture that is explicitly likened to crucifixion (Musurillo 5.1.41). Similarly the martyrdom of Pionius, who was nailed ... and burnt, combined crucifixion and *crematio* (Musurillo 10).[113]

Sometimes it was animals and not human beings for whom the spectators showed sympathy. As far as the audience was concerned, the very sight of violence in action was quite enough to bring great fascination. Plato, who had some knowledge of the extent of the cruelty that was associated with crucifixion, describes an innocent man who suffered the extreme form of execution: 'the man will have to endure the lash, the rack, chains, the branding-iron in his eyes, and finally, after every extremity of suffering, he will be crucified/impaled (τελευτῶν πάντα κακὰ παθὼν ἀνασχιν δυλευθήσεται).'[114]

The public nature of Roman execution was also designed to alienate the offender from his entire social context so that the spectators, regardless of class, were united in a feeling of moral superiority as they ridiculed him. To achieve the desired goal in Roman society, 'the mockery of a condemned person was sometimes performed spontaneously by parties other than the legal adjudicators. The best-known example from our period is the soldiers' mockery of Jesus ... the humiliation of the offender seems to be an integral part of the punishment, and it is obvious that this feature is going to bulk large in the context of executions performed in the course of spectacular enactments in the arena.'[115]

Joel Marcus suggests that 'irony was exactly their intention: this strangely "exalting" mode of execution [i.e. the raising of the crucified victim] was designed to mimic, parody, and puncture the pretensions of insubordinate transgressors by displaying a deliberately horrible mirror of their self-elevation.... Crucifixion was intended to unmask, in a deliberately grotesque manner, the pretension and arrogance of those who had exalted themselves beyond their station; the authorities were bent on demonstrating through the graphic tableau of the cross what such self-promotion meant and whither it led. Crucifixion, then, is a prime illustration of Michel Foucault's thesis that the process of execution is a "penal liturgy" designed to reveal the essence of the crime.'[116] The motive of deterrence behind the public display of crucifixion was obvious when the cross was erected in a prominent place for the full view of the public.[117]

---

[113] COLEMAN, 'Fatal Charades', 56.
[114] Plato, *Rep.* 361E–362A.
[115] COLEMAN, 'Fatal Charades', 47.
[116] J. MARCUS, 'Crucifixion as Parodic Exaltation', *JBL* 125 (2006), 73–87, at 78–79.
[117] Ps. – Quintilian, *Decl.* 274.

The writings of Philo,[118] Cicero,[119] Seneca,[120] Plutarch,[121] Suetonius[122] and Artemidorus[123] all emphasize the public nature of crucifixion. The public place of execution, including the Roman amphitheatre, naturally provided a conducive environment for public entertainment and amusement. Considerable numbers of early Christian martyrs at the time of Nero were thrown into an arena of beasts for Roman entertainment.[124] Crucifixion was another such entertainment except that its cruelty, inhumanity, horror and impact were harder to match. Hengel puts it quite bluntly, that 'crucifixion satisfied the primitive lust for revenge and the sadistic cruelty of individual rulers and of the masses.'[125]

Josephus provides a vivid picture of Titus having a number of Jewish prisoners crucified, even describing the Roman soldiers as taking great pleasure and amusement in nailing them to the cross (§1.3.2).[126] Gleason describes Titus as seeking to use the crucifixion of some captives to instil terror in the besieged Jews of Jerusalem so that they would surrender. These displays would also be part of a power strategy as the audience unwillingly and by force had to witness what they would really rather not, thus creating a view that the circumstances were not under their control but the directive of their adversary.[127]

Josephus also notes that Gaius watched with satisfaction when a play was presented by the dancer Cinyras in which the hero and his daughter were crucified (σταυροῦται).[128] Philo provides an abhorrent account of the Roman prefect Flaccus' crucifixion of Jews in Alexandria, which was part and parcel with a theatrical presentation for the populace:

But Flaccus gave no orders to take down those who had died on the cross. Instead he ordered the crucifixion of the living (ζῶντας δ' ἀνασκολοπίζεσθαι προσέτατεν).... And he did this after maltreating them with the lash in the middle of the theatre and torturing

---

[118] Philo, *Spec.* 3.160.

[119] Cicero, *Verr.* 5.158.

[120] Seneca, *Ep.* 14.5: 'Picture to yourself under this head the prison, the cross, the rack, the hook, and the stake which they drive straight through a man until it protrudes from his throat.'

[121] Plutarch, *Per.* 28.3.

[122] Suetonius, *Gal.* 9.2. *Claud.* 25.3.

[123] Artemidorus, *Oneir.* 2.53.

[124] Tacitus, *Ann.* 15.44.4: 'And additional derision accompanied their end: they were covered with wild beasts' skins and torn to death by dogs; or they were fastened on crosses and, when daylight faded, were burned to serve as lamps by night.'

[125] HENGEL, *Crucifixion*, 87.

[126] Josephus, *B.J.* 5.451.

[127] GLEASON, 'Mutilated messengers: Body language in Josephus', in S. GOLDHILL (ed.), *Being Greek under Rome: Cultural Identity, the Second Sophistic and the Development of Empire* (Cambridge: Cambridge University Press, 2001), 50–85, at 82.

[128] Josephus, *Ant.* 19.94. Cf. Suetonius, *Cal.* 57.4.

them with fire and the sword. The show had been arranged in parts. The first spectacle lasting from dawn till the third or fourth hour consisted of Jews being scourged, hung up, bound to the wheel, brutally mauled and haled for their death march through the middle of the orchestra. After this splendid exhibition came dancers and mimes and flute players and all the other amusements of theatrical competitions.[129]

Indeed, the entertaining and amusing effect of crucifixion as described here needs no further elaboration. Crucifixion, it would seem, tuned in to a sadistic side of human nature, a primal lust for vengeance and satisfied the cruelty of individuals, rulers and the masses.

Besides physical pain, the mental and 'spiritual' anguish that crucifixion brought to the victim was equally great, perhaps even greater than the physical aspect. The total loss of human dignity; the great shame and utter humiliation associated with execution; the public exposure of the human body and the denial of burial (especially for Jews) left behind virtually nothing that could be regarded as 'manhood' or masculinity.

No human situation or gesture could perhaps demonstrate the hopelessness and powerlessness of a human being more than the scene of crucifixion. Some victims were even forced to witness the execution of their own wives and children but were unable to do anything except to watch helplessly. Thus the agony they had to endure was both physical and mental. Crucifixion, which included a victim's family, is evidenced as far back as Plato's time.[130]

Philo witnessed in detail the tortures that were inflicted upon family members and relatives of runaway debtors. He describes the executioner who: 'filled a large basket with sand and having hung this enormous weight by ropes round their necks set them in the middle of the market-place in the open air, in order that while they themselves sank under the cruel stress of the accumulated punishments, the wind, the sun, the shame of being seen by the passers-by and the weights suspended on them, the spectators of their punishments might suffer by anticipation. Some of these, whose souls saw facts more vividly than did their eyes, feeling themselves maltreated in the bodies of others, hastened to take leave of their lives with the aid of sword or poison or halter, thinking that in their evil plight it was a great piece of luck to die without suffering torture.'[131]

1.5.3 Crucifixion as 'Body Language'

Gleason finds Josephus' references to the human body and 'body language' particularly instructive in terms of semiotics, especially in the context of crucifixion publicly executed. He elaborates:

---

[129] Philo, *Flacc.* 84ff.
[130] Plato, *Gorg.* 473C. Josephus, *B.J.* 1.96.
[131] Philo, *Spec.* 3.160.

What I am fishing for in these murky waters is some understanding of the semiotic context – of the ways the human body functions as a signifier in that time and place.... But I speak of gestures, including acts of violence, as language.... Even if 'body language' is only a metaphor, the metaphor helps our investigation because languages are systems of communication that admit of degrees of familiarity.... The relish with which Josephus narrates both ways of using the body as *tours de force* of self-presentation makes it clear that he did not consider body language a 'natural' concomitant of strong emotion, but a system of conventional signs whose deployment was subject to conscious control.[132]

Gleason goes on to consider how bodies could be manipulated. A particularly helpful example is found in the Hasmonean king Alexander Jannaeus (88 BC) and his spectacular use of bodies in pain. When his authority was challenged during a rebellion, Jannaeus crucified eight hundred Pharisees in the middle of Jerusalem.[133] Before crucifying them, Jannaeus forced them to 'watch the execution of their wives and children, while he reclined publicly amongst his concubines to watch the spectacle-within-a-spectacle.'[134] Subsequently, the very sight of the king became an effective spectacle itself and produced an intense emotional reaction in the audience: the next night some eight thousand more rebels who got the message were absolutely horrified and fled the country. Gleason draws attention to the visual aspect of this event, which was significant because it emphasizes both 'the spectatorship of the crucified and the visibility of the chief spectator.'[135]

Gleason attaches great significance to the control of the bodies of the enemies and the body language it sought to convey in a battle such as the siege of Jerusalem. In this siege, where so much was at stake, of paramount concern for the battle was not simply to win control of the movements of people, but to control the very meaning of a body's movement. The combatants sought to use human bodies as symbols within a type of primitive sign language. Gleason concludes that 'mutilated messengers' in Josephus' narrative are sufficiently explained by this analysis.[136]

The body of the crucified victim was fully exposed. The shame of nudity accompanied the other tortures heaped upon the victim. This served as vivid and powerful 'body language'. It robbed one of human dignity. It brought dishonour. Degradation was visited upon them. The crucified became weak and helpless beyond what chains or even death could bring. Powerlessness was, one could argue, given the fullest possible expression in nakedness.

---

[132] GLEASON, 'Mutilated Messengers', 50–51.
[133] Josephus, *B.J.* 1.97–98.
[134] GLEASON, 'Mutilated Messengers', 78. See Josephus, *Ant.* 13.14.2.
[135] GLEASON, 'Mutilated Messengers', 78.
[136] GLEASON, 'Mutilated messengers', 83–84.

A crucified person was usually deprived of the honour of a decent burial. Instead, the human corpse or bodily remains were meant for the consumption of beasts and vultures. All these must be put in the context of the social ethos of the time concerning human dignity, especially masculinity, power and honour. The crucified victim became the very embodiment or epitome of shame, indignity, 'foolishness' (μωρία) and 'madness' (μανία), the latter according to the tradition from Justin Martyr.

Since body language was meaningless in the Roman world apart from the real physical human body, understanding the Roman view of body in relation to manhood, especially masculinity, power and authority, social honour and status, becomes essential. Substantial works have already been done by several modern scholars in this important area.

Barton observes that 'honour was, for the Romans, synonymous with "being". It was not, as it is for us, some minor and dispensable aspect of life.' It would, therefore, be a most unbearable thing should that honour be lost.[137] David deSilva argues that 'honour' has several synonymous meanings. It is, then, necessary for one to begin with a basic inventory of places in which the vocabulary of honour and dishonour are used when one investigates the honour discourse within a text. This would include words such as: reputation, honour, dishonour, reproach, outrage, noble, praise and scorn. This list could be expanded by considering synonyms and by looking for other forms (e.g. verbs, adjectives, etc.) built on the same roots as the words above.[138]

Malina describes that from a symbolic point of view, in the Mediterranean world, honour relates to one's rightful location in society and social standing. The 'honour position' is distinguished by boundary markers which include degrees of power, gender and location on a social scale.[139] From a functionalist point of view, honour could be described from the perspective of how one sees themselves or how others within the society view them (i.e. internal/external honour views). This could also be stated as a personal claim to worth and an acknowledgement from society about value.[140] When there is a physical affront to one's honour – and these are symbolic affronts – they require a response, and failure to adequately counter the affront leads to dishonour and disgrace.[141]

According to Malina's understanding, the crucified Christ obviously failed to mark off social boundaries. This was simply because as a crucified victim there was, humanly speaking, absolutely no way for Jesus to

---

[137] BARTON, *The Sorrows*, 186.

[138] D. A. DESILVA, *The Hope of Glory: Honor Discourse and New Testament Interpretation* (Collegeville: The Liturgical Press, 1999), 9.

[139] MALINA, *The New Testament World*, 54.

[140] MALINA, *The New Testament World*, 54, 32.

[141] MALINA, *The New Testament World*, 55.

display his 'power' and exhibit his manly 'gender status'. Nor was Jesus able to choose his 'location' when he was helplessly nailed to the cross. Therefore, Paul's 'message of the cross' (λόγος τοῦ σταυροῦ) was offensive not only to the Roman authorities but also to the whole populace, according to the general social ethos.[142] One can only imagine the sort of response Paul would receive when telling the Corinthians he had decided to know nothing among them 'except Jesus Christ and him crucified' (1 Cor. 2.2). Within this culture it would be difficult to find a statement that would more radically invert the values of the audience.

For a crucified victim hanging helpless and shamefully exposed in public view, it would be a blatant mockery to speak about honour, worth and a host of other social values, morals and virtues. Because his '*body* language' clearly testified that he no longer possessed or was capable of any of them! Moreover, if, as Malina has suggested, 'physical affronts are always symbolic affronts that require a response' and 'failure to respond means dishonour, and disgrace', a crucified victim in his absolute helplessness and powerlessness on the cross could only accept the dishonour and disgrace as a predestined fate. There was simply and matter-of-factly no way to respond in this condemned and humiliated state.

One could perhaps relate this again to the scene of Christ's crucifixion. It was quite clearly in recognition of Jesus' utter powerlessness that some of the passers-by reviled him, shaking their heads and saying, 'Aha, you who were going to destroy the temple and build it in three days! Save yourself! Come down from the cross! Similarly the chief priests.... He saved others; Himself He cannot save ...' (Mk. 15.29–31). Christ's own seemingly desperate cry–'*Eloi, Eloi, lama sabachthani?*' (15.34) – no doubt could only further confirm his absolute helplessness as far as the spectators were concerned. And yet, here lies the real 'foolishness' and 'madness' of it all, because Paul told the Corinthians in no uncertain terms that 'the message of the cross' (ὁ λόγος ὁ τοῦ σταυροῦ) is (ἐστίν) 'the power of God' (δύναμις θεοῦ, 1 Cor. 1.18) and that the apostle himself had decided to know nothing among them 'except Christ and him crucified' (εἰ μὴ Ἰησοῦν Χριστὸν καὶ τοῦτον ἐσταυρωμένον, 2.2).

For ancient people in general, and for the Greeks and Romans in particular, there was perhaps nothing more shameful and humiliating than the public display of the crucified person, including the public exposure of the body. deSilva argues that the physical body must be taken into serious consideration in the matter of honour:

A more complex system of symbolizing the honour of a person is to be located in the treatment of the physical body, for there existed an intimate relation between honour and the physical person.... Corporal punishment, such as flagellation or crucifixion, is an act

---

[142] HENGEL, *Crucifixion*, 5.

of degradation imposed upon a body, a token of the lack of esteem in which criminals who are so punished, are held. Such observations should lead us, then, to pay careful attention to details touching the physical person and the treatment of that person by others as indications of honour exchanges.[143]

deSilva's observation is important for understanding the scandalous nature of crucifixion as well as the physical abuse which the victim suffered. As has already been observed by both ancient writers and modern scholars, public display of the victim's corpse on the cross was exposed to general abuse and mockery.

Michael Satlow's research demonstrates that Jewish sources from the period portray the nudity of men in a fairly consistent way. For males in antiquity, to be fully exposed is to offend the sacred. Likewise, when considering the divine and the relation of earthly representatives to the divine (e.g. kings, priests or rabbis), one does not reveal himself to social subordinates.[144]

Gleason suggests that although one cannot be certain that Romans generally understood Jews to be especially sensitive about nudity in the presence of social inferiors, 'the verb αἰκίζεσθαι, commonly used for scourging, well conveys the injury to status that such punishment involved.'[145] John's Gospel describes not only the dividing of Jesus' clothes by the soldiers at the time of crucifixion, but also the robbing of his tunic (19.23, 24). This may have communicated further exposure of Jesus' body and the dishonouring of it.

Burial was equally important for a normal person in ancient culture. The burial of the dead person was indicative of his social rank, honour and public identity. In his *De Legibus*, Plato discusses funerary legislation: (1) funeral rites are required for the dead to be performed in respect of the gods; (2) burial should be carried out on the third day; (3) burial should be held outside of the city and with moderate mourning and (4) mourning and lamentation should be appropriate and controllable.[146]

According to Donna Kurtz's study, the burial of the Greeks was concerned with tomb architecture and memorials as well as rites. Some possessions of the dead were destroyed or buried with them. Greeks regarded death as a slow transition to another form of life.[147] Kurtz notes that 'by the Classical period Greek burials seem to have developed as far as they possibly could to satisfying the living, within a sequence of rites which

---

[143] DeSilva, *The Hope of Glory*, 14.

[144] M. L. Satlow, 'Jewish Constructions of Nakedness in Late Antiquity', *JBL* 116/3 (1997), 429–54, at 453.

[145] Gleason, 'Mutilated messengers', 81.

[146] Plato, *Leg.* 958D–960B.

[147] D. C. Kurtz and J. Boardman, *Greek Burial Customs* (London and Southampton: Thames and Hudson, 1971), 329–32.

preserved traditional practice, yet which gave scope to expression of human grief, admiration, even hope.'[148]

In his *De Legibus*, Cicero describes funerary regulation at great length.[149] Cicero for the most part preserves Plato's view on burial custom: (1) rites for the dead are in honour of the gods; (2) the corpse should be buried before daybreak; (3) burial or cremation should be held outside of the city apart from famous persons and emperors;[150] (4) limitations of funeral expenses like monuments and mourning are set; (5) offerings are in honour of the dead and (6) laws for the protection of graves given (2.10–26). In the Roman period, burial tended to be luxurious and extravagant monuments, columns and tombs often constructed.

Romans believed strongly in the afterlife and the survival of the soul after death.[151] Plautus' story refers to the spirits of the dead which were believed to be able to haunt the dwellings of the living.[152] Cicero thought that the dead could be harmful if they were neglected.[153] The living honoured the dead by remembering their virtues and achievements.[154]

Jocelyn Toynbee's observation is also significant: 'all Roman funerary practice was influenced by two basic notions – first, that death brought pollution and demanded from the survivors acts of purification and expiation; secondly, that to leave a corpse unburied had unpleasant repercussions on the fate of the departed soul.'[155]

According to Jewish customs, burial of the dead took place immediately after death and by sunset on the day of death. The corpse was washed and wrapped tightly with linen cloths around the body (*m. Semahot* 12.10) and placed in a coffin/tomb. Byron McCane's dissertation has shown that 'early Christians and Jews in Roman Palestine shared common rituals, theologies, and cultural values of death and burial.'[156]

---

[148] KURTZ, *Greek*, 332–33.

[149] Cicero, *Leg.* 2.22.56; cf. Xenophon, *Cyr.* 8.7.25.

[150] According to Cicero, both cremation and inhumation were practised in the fifth century BC (*Leg.* 2.23.58).

[151] Cicero, *Pis.* 7.16; Livy 3.58; Virgil, *Aen.* 6.743.

[152] Plautus, *Most.* 499–500; *Cap.* 598.

[153] Cicero, *Leg.* 2.9.22.

[154] Propertius 4.2.99–102: *causa perorata est. flentes me surgite, testes, dum pretium vitae grata rependit humus. moribus et caelum patuit : sim digna merendo, cuius honoratis ossa vehantur avis.* (The case for my defene is done. Rise up, my witnesses, who weep for me, while kindly Earth requites my life's deserts. Even heaven has unbarred its gates to virtue. May I be found worthy that my bones be borne to join my honoured ancestors.)

[155] J. M. C. TOYNBEE, *Death and Burial in the Roman World* (London and Southampton: Thames and Hudson, 1971), 43.

[156] B. R. MCCANE, *Jews, Christians, and Burial in Roman Palestine* (Ann Arbor: UMI Dissertation Services, 2005), 236.

A crucified victim was usually deprived of the above burial customs and rituals. As such he was virtually cut off from his society and became an outcast in his death, because of the crucifixion. Instead, as has been noted, the human corpse or the bodily remains were often meant for the consumption of beasts and vultures.

Josephus, with his bi-cultural background, thus considers the throwing out of the bodies in nakedness and without burial a violent and humiliating act, especially for aristocratic Jews: 'Bodies that had lately worn the sacred garment, that had presided over cosmic ceremonies and received prostrations from every corner of the globe, were seen naked, thrown out as carrion for dogs and wild beasts (ἐρριμμένοι γυμνοὶ βορὰ κυνῶν καὶ θηρίων ἐβλέποντο).'[157]

As Gleason observes, in a culture where autonomy and social control were articulated in body language, 'the Greco-Roman aristocrats were expected to display a body free from the scars of mutilating punishment or manual work, and for aristocratic Jews, the stakes were even higher. Since aristocratic physical perfection encoded not only the social history of the body, but also its fitness for divine service, physically imperfect men could not assume priestly duties.'[158]

1.6 Conclusion

This overview of crucifixion in antiquity and its main features help demonstrate, in its socio-historical context, how the practice would have been understood and perceived. Some of the most abhorrent aspects of human degradation and humiliation were present in crucifixion. The considerable examples cited from primary sources and further fleshed out by recent scholarship provide the background against which to further understand body language and the cross. Special weight has been given to the crucifixion of people from the lower strata of society, including slaves and Jews, because such a detestable form of capital punishment was commonly applied to them, among whom one could include Jesus. The kinds of degradation and humiliation that the crucified victims endured were self-evident in many of the accounts provided here.

The public nature of crucifixion, the kind of 'body language' conveyed by the crucified victims and the entire scene of execution – including the inhuman treatments victims often received both before and during the final

---

[157] Josephus, *B.J.* 4.324–25. The Roman general ordered the captive [Eleazar] stripped naked, placed 'in the spot most visible to those watching from the wall', and savagely scourged (*B.J.* 7.200).

[158] GLEASON, 'Mutilated messengers', 84.

act itself – made this form of capital punishment the most horrific and cruellest manner of capital punishment known from Roman antiquity. Thus the cross became not only a powerful visual symbol, but also a very impressive description of body language. Those cases of crucifixion and the commentaries on them are not made in a vacuum, but in the concrete and harsh reality of the social ethos before as well as during Paul's time.

Hengel warns against attempts, both ancient and modern, 'to blur the sharp contours of Paul's remarks about the cross of Christ ... in symbolic-allegorical or cosmic terms.'[159] This is because, for Paul and his fellow Christians of the time, the cross of Christ 'was not a didactic, symbolic or speculative element but a very specific and highly offensive matter', which brought a great burden to the life and witness of the earliest Christians. It was for this very reason that the relatively young Christian church in Corinth sought, according to Hengel, 'to escape from the crucified Christ into the enthusiastic life of the spirit, the enjoyment of heavenly revelations and an assurance of salvation connected with mysteries and sacraments.'[160] But for the Christians themselves as well as for their opponents and critics, there was actually no way for the 'spiritual' Corinthians to escape and still remain true to the historical reality of the crucifixion of Christ at the same time.

Paul's open acknowledgement in 1 Cor. 1.18 that 'the message of the cross is foolishness to the perishing', as well as the entire passage of 1.18–31, should be understood and perceived in the overall context of crucifixion in antiquity as well as in close connection with the conventional social ethos of the apostle's time.

---

[159] HENGEL, *Crucifixion*, 17–18.
[160] HENGEL, *Crucifixion*, 18.

Chapter 2

Noble Death in Greco-Roman and Jewish Traditions

2.1 Introduction

The study of crucifixion in antiquity helps demonstrate one of the primary reasons why Paul's 'message of the cross' was perceived as 'foolishness' (μωρία). There might, however, be other important factors that contributed to prejudice against the teaching of Paul. Recent studies indicate that by the time of Paul a concept was prevalent among Greeks, Romans and Jews referred to as 'noble death'. In the Greco-Roman world, the most classic example of noble death is generally assumed to be the famous death of Socrates – the philosopher *par excellence*. For Jews, the deaths of the Maccabean martyrs likely served as models. There remains much to be said about noble death in both Greco-Roman and Jewish traditions. How this theme relates to the death of Jesus, especially within Paul's message of the cross, is the focus here. The aim is to throw into relief the message of the cross as a teaching denuded of any face-saving elements of 'nobility'.

The death of Socrates will serve as a point of departure in this study of noble death in the Greco-Roman tradition, followed by a survey of noble death in Jewish tradition with special reference to the Maccabean martyrs as well as to the Jewish σκάνδαλον (1 Cor. 1.23). A brief review of recent studies on noble death will also assist in understanding how this subject may help elucidate Paul's message.

2.2 Noble Death in the Greco-Roman Tradition

2.2.1 Socrates, the Philosopher Par Excellence

Like Jesus and a few other great religious teachers and philosophers, Socrates (470–399 BC) wrote nothing. Memory of him has been passed on, as is well-known, largely from the writings of Plato. There is a general view of Socrates as 'a man of great intellectual brilliance, moral integrity, personal magnetism, and physical self-command.'[1] It is also now generally

---

[1] R. KRAUT, 'Socrates', in R. AUDI (ed.), *The Cambridge Dictionary of Philosophy* (Cambridge: Cambruge Uiversity Press, 1995), 749–50, at 749.

agreed that all the dialogues of Plato were written after Socrates' death. Aristophanes' *Clouds*, which first appeared in 423 BC, may be the only evidence from Socrates' own lifetime.[2] Plato's portrayal of Socrates in his *dialogues* remains largely consistent. But they should not be read as a technical 'biography' of the great philosopher. Plato wrote as an apologist in order to present Socrates as 'the ideal embodiment of philosophy, unjustly traduced by confusion with bogus practitioners (Sophists) and unjustly condemned for his dedication to the philosophic life.'[3]

Much of Socrates' time and energy was preoccupied with wisdom, truth and right conduct, although he only regarded himself as a fellow seeker of truth and a lover of wisdom (φιλόσοφος), but not a wise man (σοφός). Socrates' critical and inquisitive mind made him a role model for the serious and thoughtful seekers of truth, but at the same time, it also rendered him exceedingly unpopular with the complacent, powerful and self-conceited, including the σοφοί of Athens. In the spring of 399 BC Socrates was formally prosecuted by the court and condemned to death. Meletus was the main accuser of Socrates in Plato's *Apology*. Two main charges were brought against him. (1) Impiety (ἀσέβεια) towards the gods of the city. Instead of recognising the gods of the state, he was alleged to have introduced new deities to the city. (2) Corrupting the mind of young Athenians, thereby threatening the stability of society and challenging basic traditional assumptions. In the words of *Apology* 24B: 'Socrates is guilty of corrupting the minds of the young, and of believing in deities of his own invention instead of the gods recognized by the State.' Socrates subsequent death after drinking a cup of poison hemlock is well-known. His 'noble death' turned him into a kind of martyr so that his influence became even more lasting and widespread than when he was alive.

Socrates is also the hero of Xenophon. Although his *Memorabilia* is 'as much a work of art as any Platonic dialogue', his view on Socrates is quite different from that of Plato. In Plato's idealism, Socrates was a great martyr, and for Xenophon, the great sage is pre-eminently a moral teacher.[4] But for both Xenophon and Plato, the death of Socrates is undoubtedly "noble".

On the noble death of Socrates, Xenophon praises his glory and dignity, writing: 'how could any one have died more nobly than [Socrates]?' Fur-

---

[2] C. C. W. TAYLOR, 'Socrates', in H. TED (ed.), *The Oxford Companion to Philosophy* (Oxford: Oxford Univesity Press, 1995), 836–37, at 836.

[3] TAYLOR, 'Socrates', 836.

[4] A. D. LINDSAY, *Socrates Discourses by Plato and Xenophon* (London: J. M. Dent & Sons, Ltd., 1918), ix–xi.

thermore, Xenophon finds Socrates' method of death honourable, happy and most acceptable to the gods.[5]

The accounts of Socrates' trial and its aftermath are recorded in three of Plato's works. The *Apology* is primarily concerned with Socrates' defence at his trial. *Crito* provides Socrates' reasons for not taking the opportunity to escape from prison and head into exile. The day before Socrates' trial was the first day of the annual Mission to Delos which had taken so long that Socrates was kept in prison for a month. There was an opportunity for Socrates to escape and leave the country. Though Socrates' friends tried hard to persuade him to escape, he refused and expressed his strong conviction in response to Crito when he begged him to do so: 'The really important thing is not to live, but to live well.... And that to live well means the same thing as to live honourably or rightly.'[6] *Phaedo* is a fascinating and moving story of the great philosopher's final hours. It contains Socrates' basic philosophy of life, attitude towards death and belief in the immortality of the soul.

2.2.1.1 Socrates' Apology and Sense of Mission

In response to a charge of impiety towards the gods of the city, Socrates claims that he had consistently been a faithful servant to his god as well as a dedicated and caring citizen of Athens. In an inspirational speech, he says that he has done nothing but seek to persuade all citizens to make their primary concern not their body but their soul.[7] In conclusion Socrates

---

[5] Xenophon, *Mem.* 4.8.3: 'How could any one have died more nobly than thus? Or what death could be more honourable than that which any man might most honourably undergo? Or what death could be happier than the most honourable? Or what death more acceptable to the gods than the most happy?' Cf. 4.8.11: 'To me, being such as I have described him, so pious that he did nothing without sanction of the gods; so just, that he wronged no man even in the most trifling affair, but was of service, in the most important matters, to those who enjoyed his society; so temperate, that he never preferred pleasure to virtue; so wise, that he never erred in distinguishing better from worse, needing no counsel from others, but being sufficient in himself to discriminate between them ... he seemed to be such as the best and happiest of men would be.' 4.8.2: 'It is indeed acknowledged that no man, of all that are remembered, ever endured death with greater glory ... let it be considered, throughout all the former part of his life he had been admired beyond all men for the cheerfulness and tranquility with which he lived.' 1.2.18: 'I know that Socrates made himself an example to those who associated with him as a man of honourable and excellent character, and that he discoursed admirably concerning virtue and other things that concern mankind.' 1.2.62: 'To me, therefore, Socrates, being a man of such a character, appeared to be worthy of honour rather than of death; and any one, considering his case according to the laws ... Socrates was the most innocent of all men.'

[6] Plato, *Cr.* 48AB.

[7] Plato, *Phaed.* 30A: 'This, I do assure you, is what my God commands; and it is my belief that no greater good has ever befallen you in this city than my service to my God;

states he is ready 'to die a hundred deaths,' which gained him great admiration from the Stoic philosopher Seneca, who strongly believed in a true philosopher's consistency of word and deed (*Ep.* 24.15). Indeed, for Epictetus, death is the best opportunity for a true philosopher to set an example leading others to this way of life (3.20.13).

These words of Socrates in *Phaedo* express the philosopher's strong sense of mission: 'If you doubt whether I ... have been sent to this city as a gift from god.... Does it seem natural that I should have neglected my own affairs and endured the humiliation of allowing my family to be neglected for all these years ... going like a father or an elder brother to see each one of you privately, and urging you to set your thoughts on goodness? ... The witness ... is ... my poverty.... If you put me to death, you will not easily find anyone to take my place ... all day long I never cease to settle here, there, and everywhere, rousing, persuading, reproving every one of you.'[8] Socrates was convinced that his trial was absolutely unfair: 'I am willing to die ten times over if this account is true ... Other heroes of the old days [also] met their death through an unfair trial.'[9]

2.2.1.2 Noble Death

In the Greco-Roman tradition, the condemned Socrates in Plato's *Phaedo* is clearly perceived as one who welcomed a 'noble death' (64A). Socrates' alleged 'death wish' was undoubtedly governed by his overall view on the human body as a prison of the soul and his belief in the immortality of the soul in relation to the quest for truth (66B; cf. 64E). Paul Gooch describes Socrates' attitude towards the physical body as 'somatic indifference': 'Now if we had to employ but one category for Socrates' relation to his body, it would be self-control ... the ruling element in Socrates' psyche, we are led to believe, is reason.... So I now suggest that we use a phrase like *somatic indifference*, not just somatic self-control, to characterize Socrates' attitudes to body.'[10] Socrates was thought to be such a master over his own body through self-control, reason and somatic indifference that the hemlock poison was not able to have its normal torturous effect on him.[11] Socrates' legendary composure has not only contributed much to the alleg-

---

for I spend all my time going about trying to persuade you, young and old, to make your first and chief concern not for your bodies nor for your possessions, but for the highest welfare of your souls ... you know that I am not going to alter my conduct, not even if I have to die a hundred deaths.'

[8] Plato, *Phaed.* 30B–31A.

[9] Plato, *Phaed.* 42A.

[10] P. W. GOOCH, *Reflections on Jesus and Socrates: Word and Silence* (New Haven and London: Yale University Press, 1996), 194–95.

[11] GOOCH, *Reflections*, 196–97.

edly 'noble' character of his death, but is also sometimes used to compare his death favourably with that of Jesus.

One should not forget that Plato's *Phaedo* was designed as a type of eyewitness account. Gooch draws attention to how Plato constructs the account right from the beginning to evoke admiration for him.[12] In the role of eyewitness is Phaedo, who reports his own emotional response, or lack thereof, feeling no grief when Socrates dies nobly and fearlessly (58E). As the dialogues come to an end, there are the famous lines about the end of our friend, described as the best, wisest and most just man of his time. One also sees that it is not only the friends of Socrates who are moved by his final moments, but also the jailer. As this character looks on he can scarce contain his tears as he praises him as the best and gentlest of all men.

Phaedo's account does not seem to have been seriously questioned in the Greco-Roman world. Epictetus greatly admires Socrates' resolute decision to prefer a noble death to living on dishonourably: 'he saves himself by dying, not by flight' (4.1.165). Epictetus' admiration of Socrates as a paradigm is sufficiently well stated in Epictetus 4.1.159–69 where Socrates' honour, obedience, reverence and courage are particularly highlighted.[13]

Gooch also points out that 'Plato makes certain that we know at the beginning of the dialogue that for Socrates philosophy itself is a kind of dying. His entire way of life has been preparation for this final day.... If philosophy seeks the wisdom and truth that is to be found in soul, not body, then the final separation of soul from body may be welcomed as the fitting culmination of the philosophical quest.'[14]

In the discussion about Socrates' 'death wish' and 'noble death' one simple but relatively significant factor is often overlooked, that is, his ad-

---

[12] GOOCH, *Reflections*, 246.

[13] Epictetus 4.1.159–69: '... take Socrates and observe a man who had a wife and little children, but regarded them as not his own, who had a country, as far as it was his duty, and in the way in which it was his duty, and friends, and kinsmen, one and all subject to the law and to *obedience* to the law. That is why, when it was his duty to serve as a soldier, he was the first to leave home, and ran the risks of battle most ungrudgingly; and when he was sent by the Tyrants to fetch Leon, because he regarded it as disgraceful, he never deliberated about the matter at all, although he knew that he would have to die, if it so chanced. And what difference did it make to him? For there was something else that he wished to preserve; not his paltry flesh, but the man of *honour*, the man of reverence.... If we were useful to men by living, should we not have done much more good to men by dying when we ought, and as we ought? And now that Socrates is dead the memory of him is no less useful to men, nay, is perhaps even more useful, than what he did or said while he still lived.'

[14] GOOCH, *Reflections*, 247.

vanced age when confronted with the prospect of death.[15] In Plato's account (*Phaedo*), the age of Socrates is not mentioned; however, Socrates
himself in *Apology* (38C) refers to his being elderly and not far from a
natural death. Indeed, knowing that Socrates has experienced a long and
rich life has a subtle role in one's estimation of his death. As *Phaedo* goes
on, it is learned that his is a painless end and the hemlock poisoning does
not interfere with his lucidity or even distance him from his own death.[16]
Thus, one may ask the question: Had Socrates been much younger, say
near to the age of Jesus, would he have responded much differently in
those final moments of his life journey? And if so, would his death be regarded as less 'noble'?

2.2.1.3 Divine Sign

Both Plato's *Euthyphro* and Xenophon's *Memorabilia* mention Socrates'
belief in some kind of divine 'sign' or 'voice' for guidance thereby arousing his critics' suspicion of the soundness of his mind and teaching. Socrates also speaks about a dream in *Phaedo* (61B): 'In the course of my life I
have often had the same dream, appearing in different forms at different
times, but always saying the same thing: "Socrates, practise and cultivate
the arts".... I meant that the dream ... was urging me on to do what I was
doing already, that is, practising the arts; because philosophy is the greatest of the arts, and I was practising it....'

Plato qualifies Socrates' 'death wish' with reference to the divine necessity: 'then perhaps from this point of view it is not unreasonable to say
that a man must not kill himself until god sends some necessity upon him
(πρὶν ἂν ἀνάγκην τινὰ θεὸς ἐπιπέμψῃ), such as has now come upon
me' (*Phaed.* 62C). The works of Cicero, Seneca, Plutarch and Epictetus
also mention Socrates' 'divine sign'.

Cicero clearly believes that when a divine sign is given, one should welcome death obediently and joyfully as Socrates and Cato had done:

Cato departed from life with a feeling of joy in having found a reason for death; for the
God who is master within us forbids our departure without permission. When, however,
God himself has given a valid reason, as he did in the past to Socrates and in our day to
Cato and to many others, then with certainty your true wise man will joyfully go forth
from the darkness here into the light beyond ... he will go forth at the summons and re-

---

[15] See Xenophon, *Mem.* 4.8.1: 'Let him consider, in the first place, that he was already
so advanced in years that he must have ended his life, if not then, at least not long after;
and, in the next, that he relinquished only the most burdensome part of life, in which all
feel their powers of intellect diminished, while, instead of enduring this, he acquired
great glory by proving the firmness of his mind, pleading his cause, above all men, with
the greatest regard to truth, ingenuousness, and justice, and bearing his sentence at once
with the utmost resignation and the utmost fortitude.'
[16] GOOCH, *Reflections*, 247.

lease of God. For the whole life of the philosopher, as the same wise man says, is a preparation for death.[17]

Cato was believed to have committed suicide after reading *Phaedo.*[18] Lucilius was similarly set free from the fear of death.[19] Seneca links Cato's courage in the face of death to his desire for true freedom.[20] Plutarch thinks that the death of Cato was inspired by the example of Socrates.[21] Epictetus firmly believes that one should accept death willingly when a 'signal to retreat' was given by god, as Socrates had done.[22]

2.2.1.4 The Body as Bondage of the Soul & Death as its Liberation

Socrates consistently holds that the body is the soul's prison: 'is not what we call death a freeing and separation of soul from body? Certainly, said Socrates. Such was the desire of a true philosopher: And the desire to free the soul is found chiefly, or rather only, in the true philosopher; in fact the philosopher's occupation consists precisely in the freeing and separation of soul from body. Isn't that so?'[23]

---

[17] Cicero, *Tusc.* 1.74; 1.118: 'For our part, if it so fall out that it seems a sentence delivered by God, that we depart from life, let us obey joyfully and thankfully and consider that we are being set free from prison and loosed from our chains, in order that we may pass on our way to the eternal home which is clearly ours, or else be free of all sensation and trouble.' Similar to *Phaedo*, Cicero believes that an individual should not depart from life until God gave him the signal: 'For unless that God, whose temple is everything you see, has freed you from the prison of the body, you cannot gain entrance there' (*Rep.* 6.15–16). Cicero praises Cato for his resolve in the face of death: 'Indeed, such diversity of character carries with it so great significance that suicide may be for one man a duty, for another [under the same circumstances] a crime.... But Cato had been endowed by nature with an austerity beyond belief, and he himself had strengthened it by unswerving consistency and had remained ever true to his purpose and fixed resolve; and it was for him to die rather than to look upon the face of a tyrant' (*Off.* 1.112).

[18] Seneca, *Ep.* 24.6–7.

[19] Seneca, *Ep.* 24.12–21.

[20] Seneca, *Prov.* 2.9–10: '"I do not know what *nobler sight* Jupiter could find on earth ... than the spectacle of Cato, after his cause had already been shattered more than once, nevertheless standing erect amid the ruins of the republic." "Although," said he, "all the world has fallen under one man's sway, although Caesar's legions guard the land, his fleets the sea, and Caesar's troops beset the city gates, yet Cato has a way of escape; with one single hand he will open *a wide path to freedom*. This sword, unstained and blameless even in civil war, shall at last do good and noble service: the freedom that it could not give to his country it shall give to Cato!"'

[21] Plutarch, *Cat. Min.* 67–68.

[22] Epictetus 1.29.29: 'only let me not give up my life faintheartedly, or from some casual pretext. For again, God does not so desire; for he has need of such a universe, and of such men who go to and fro upon earth. But if he gives the signal to retreat, as he did to Socrates, I must obey him who gives the signal, as I would a general.'

[23] Plato, *Phaed.* 67CD; cf. 66E.

Socrates advocates that there is one way in which 'a man can be free from all anxiety about the fate of his soul; if in life he has abandoned bodily pleasures and adornments ... with self-control, and goodness, and courage, and liberality, and truth – has fitted himself to await his journey to the next world.'[24]

Whether of philosophy or religion, the Socratic attitude towards death was evidently based on the Greek belief in the immortality of the soul as well as its ability to find true wisdom 'in the other world.'[25]

Seneca describes that one could accept death with determination, presumably even through suicide, as long as 'the way to freedom' from slavery was opened. His thinking was thus very much in line with that of Socrates, in regarding death as the path to true freedom, although Socrates was apparently not so ready to commit suicide as Seneca (*Prov.* 6.7; *Ir.* 1.112).

For Epictetus death is a sort of 'harbour' or 'refuge': 'And this is the harbour of all men, even death, and this their refuge. That is why none of the things that befall us in our life is difficult. Whenever you wish, you walk out of the house and are no longer bothered by the smoke' (4.10.27; 3.24.96–102).

2.2.1.5 Fearless and Noble before Death

In classical Greco-Roman tradition perhaps no true courage could have been better typified than the serenity with which Socrates faced death. Socrates is consistently and emphatically portrayed as being fearless before death. In Plato's *Phaedo* (58E), Phaedo says that, 'since he seemed to me to be happy, both in his bearing [manner] and in his words, he was meeting death so fearlessly and nobly (ἀδεῶς καὶ γενναίως).'

In *Phaedo* 64A, Socrates teaches that a true philosopher should welcome death: 'a man who has really devoted his life to philosophy should be cheerful in the face of death, and confident of finding the greatest blessing in the next world when his life is finished.' Socrates also likens himself to a soldier who took the order absolutely.[26]

In an attempt to comfort his followers, Socrates says, 'but you also, judges, must regard death hopefully and must bear in mind this one truth, that no evil can come to a good man either in life or after death, and God does not neglect him. So, too, this which has come to me has not come by chance (αὐτομάτου), but I see plainly that it was better for me to die now

---

[24] Plato, *Phaed.* 115A.

[25] Plato, *Phaed.* 67E–68B. Cf. 82C.

[26] Plato, *Apol.* 28D–29A: 'For thus it is, men of Athens, in truth; wherever a man stations himself, thinking it is best to be there, or is stationed by this commander, there he must, as it seems to me, remain and run his risks, considering neither death nor any other thing more than disgrace.'

and be freed from troubles. That is the reason why the sign (σημεῖον) never interfered with me, and I am not at all angry with those who condemned me or with my accusers' (*Apol.* 41D).

Once the philosopher was convinced of the divine will he 'cheerfully and quietly' accepted his fate, offered a final prayer: 'he took it [the cup], and very gently (μάλα ἵλεως) ... without trembling or changing colour or expressions (οὐδὲν τρέσας οὐδε διαφθείρας οὔτε τοῦ χρώματος οὔτε τοῦ προσώπου) but looking up at the man with wide open eyes, as was his custom, said: "what do you say about pouring a libation to some deity from this cup? May I, or not?" "Socrates," said he, "we prepare only as much as we think is enough." "I understand," said Socrates; "but I may and must pray to the gods that my departure hence be a fortunate one; so I offer this prayer, and may it be granted". With these words, he raised the cup to his lips and very cheerfully and quietly drained it (μάλα εὐχερῶς καὶ εὖ 'κόλως ἐξέπιεν), quite calmly and with no sign of distaste, he drained the cup in one breath.'[27]

2.2.1.6 Final Verdict

This is how Phaedo concludes his story about the death of Socrates, with emphasis on his courage, wisdom and uprightness: 'Such was the end, Echecrates, of our friend, who was, as we may say, of all those of his time whom we have known, the best (ἀρίστου, "noblest or bravest") and wisest (ἄλλως φρονιμωτάτου) and most righteous man (δικαιοτάτου)' (*Phaed.* 118).

2.2.1.7 More on 'Noble Death' in the Socratic Tradition

Other ancient sources beside the writings of Plato clearly show the abiding and widespread influence of Socrates' alleged 'noble death'. Aristotle, following this Socratic tradition, also highly regards the sacrifice of philosophers for friends or for other worthy causes as noble death:

But it is also true that the virtuous man's conduct is often guided by the interests of his friends and of his country, and that he will if necessary lay down his life in their behalf. For he will surrender wealth and power and all the goods that men struggle to win, if he can secure nobility for himself; since he would prefer an hour of rapture to a long period of mild enjoyment, a year of noble life to many years of ordinary existence, one great and glorious exploit to many small successes.[28]

This view is also shared by Diogenes Laertius: 'tell us that the wise man will for reasonable course make his own exit from life, on his country's behalf or for the sake of his friends, or if he suffers intolerable pain, muti-

---

[27] Plato, *Phaed.* 117BC.
[28] Aristotle, *Eth. nic.* 1169a.

lation, or incurable disease' (7.130; Philostratus, *Vit. Apoll.*). Epictetus had
very high regard for Diogenes.[29] Seneca lists a number of models who died
for others. Evil fortune made them great exemplars.[30] The metaphor of
'sacrifice' was sometimes used to describe the death of noble persons, such
as that of Socrates and Demonax, the latter being an enactment of the former.[31]

Historically, Socrates' noble death also became an inspiration and consolation for several illustrious Romans who ended their own lives after
they had fallen into disgrace. Such was the opinion of the Roman historian
Tacitus with reference to the suicides of Seneca and Thrasea Paetus.[32] Barton's comments on honour as it relates to death are particularly insightful.
She writes that Roman *virtus*, which is related to the aggressive and self-
aggrandizing nature of a warrior, was controlled and balanced by a self-
sacrificial aspect. More to the point, there was honour in death not as a
wasting of life, but rather an act of shaping life, or as Barton expresses it:
'to will death was not to deny life but to carve its contour.'[33]

Jan van Henten and Friedrich Avemarie make a significant comparison
between Greeks' and Romans' respective attitude toward death. While the
'death wish' of the Greeks was often governed by their negative view on
the human body as a kind of 'prison' and their belief in the immortality of
the soul, the Romans had their own views about noble death. They regarded it as a kind of self-sacrifice such as by those who were on military
duty or as a dedication to the deities, with the hope that the act would ultimately bring about victory. A certain idea of 'atonement' or 'substitution'
seems to be associated with this kind of self-sacrifice.[34]

---

[29] Epictetus 4.1.152–55: 'But I can show you a free man, so that you will never again
have to look for an example. Diogenes was free.... He knew the source from which he
had received them, and from whom, and upon what conditions. His true ancestors, indeed,
the gods, and his real Country he would never have abandoned, nor would he have suffered another to yield them more obedience and submission, nor could any other man
have died more cheerfully for his Country. For it was never his wont to seek to *appear* to
do anything in behalf of the Universe, but he bore in mind that everything which has
come into being has its source there, and is done on behalf of that country, and is entrusted to us by Him who governs it.'

[30] Seneca, *Prov.* 3.4: 'The same is true of Forture. She seeks out the bravest men to
match with her; some she passes by in disdain. Those that are most stubborn and unbend-
ing she assails, men against whom she may exert all her strength. Mucius she tries by fire,
Fabricius by poverty, Rutilius by exile, Regulus by torture, Socrates by poison, Cato by
death. It is only evil fortune that discovers a great exemplar (*magnum exemplum*).'

[31] Tacitus, *Ann.* 15.62–64. Lucian, *Dem.* 1.11.

[32] J. W. VAN HENTEN and F. AVEMARIE, *Martyrdom and Noble death: Selected texts
from Graeco-Roman, Jewish and Christian Antiquity* (London: Routledge, 2002), 3–14.

[33] BARTON, *Roman Honour*, 41–43.

[34] Cf. Epictetus 1.9.16, 22–26; 2.1.17; 4.10.27; Cassius 59.8.3; 63.13.10–15. VAN
HENTEN, *Martyrdom*, 19–21.

Latin sources refer to a special form of self-sacrifice as duty, called *devotio* such as the 'dedication' by military persons of themselves, the enemy's army, or both, to the gods of the underworld or other deities. This ceremonial death was apparently regarded as the ultimate means to bring about victory.[35] van Henten has found that ancient Greeks placed several kinds of 'glorious death' in one category of *biaiothanasia* ('violent death') which included death on the battlefield, execution as well as different forms of self-sacrifice and suicide. Descriptions of these deaths were found in different genres and literary forms, including elegies, tragedies, apologies, funeral orations, histories, biographical narratives *(teleute, exitus illustrium virorum),* diatribes, letters and so-called 'acts' of pagan martyrs.[36] Readiness to acccpt violent death rather than to compromise one's conviction and the profound desire to sacrifice for others are all stressed in pagan as well as in Jewish [37] and Christian writings.[38] However, van Henten's study also reveals that unlike Christian and Jewish martyrs, willingness to sacrifice their life for religious motives was rare among pagans.

In view of the abiding and widespread influence of the Socratic tradition on 'noble death' in the Greco-Roman society, it is significant that the 4th century church father John Chrysostom contends that the Christian martyrs were far superior to Socrates. Firstly, Chrysostom claims to be able to list 'ten thousand' Christian martyrs for every Socrates. Secondly, Chrysostom argues that Socrates had no choice but to accept death, whereas the Christian martyrs went to their deaths willingly.[39] Thirdly, unlike Jesus and many of his followers, Socrates was of old age when he was confronted with death: 'For not against their will did the martyrs endure, but of their will, and being free not to suffer.... This you see is no great wonder: that he [Socrates] whom I was mentioning drank hemlock; it being no longer in his power not to drink, and also when he had arrived at a very great age.... But show me someone enduring torments for godliness' sake, as I show you ten thousand everywhere in the world. Who, while his nails were being torn out, nobly endured? Who, while his joints were being wrenched asunder? Who, while his body was being cut in pieces, member by member? Who, while his bones were being forced out by levers? Who, while being placed on frying-pans without relief? ... Show me these instances. For [Socrates] to die by hemlock is like falling asleep, even more pleasant than

---

[35] Cf. Livy 8.9.4–9; 8.10.11–14; 8.6.13. VAN HENTEN, *Martyrdom*, 19.

[36] VAN HENTEN, *Martyrdom*, 5.

[37] *2 Macc.* 6–7; Josephus, *B.J.* 7.323–88; *Ant.* 12.256, 21–22.

[38] *1 Clement* 5–6; Ignatius, *Romans* 1–7.

[39] A. J. DROGE and J. D. TABOR, *A Noble Death: Suicide and Martyrdom Among Christians and Jews in Antiquity* (San Francisco: HarperSanFrancisco, 1992), 139.

sleep.'[40] If the death of Socrates was regarded as 'noble', in the opinion of Chrysostom the martyrdom of many Christians would certainly be more so.

2.2.1.8 A Summary

Any study faces the challenge of fair and objective comparison and contrast between two great historical figures who come from such different traditions. However, the association between Socrates and Jesus, no matter from what perspective it is perceived, is clearly a historical reality which one should not easily pass by. In the opinion of Gooch, at least in the history of the Christian church, Socrates' association with Jesus has in fact elevated the reputation of the Greek philosopher to a kind of 'sainthood,' especially because of his attitude towards death. Indeed, when one considers Socrates in relation to martyrdom, his death is seen to bring him closer to Jesus.[41]

Whatever the case may be, with this relatively detailed account about Socrates' noble death and the Socratic tradition, it is possible to see whether there is any significant point of contact between Socrates and Jesus with special reference to Paul's message of the cross.

In general, it may be fair to suggest that while Paul could be familiar with noble death in the Greco-Roman tradition; such an idea was evidently alien to the apostle's understanding of the death of Jesus on the cross. If there were any nobility in the death of Jesus, it could only be perceived from the divine perspective and not from any human point of view.

The previous historical survey on crucifixion in antiquity seeks to demonstrate that the crucifixion of Jesus belonged to the most ignoble death of the time. It was ignoble in the eyes of the Romans because they did not think that he was dying for the gods, for the nation or for any other noble cause. What was even worse was the fact he was crucified with the sanction of the highest Roman official in Palestine. And his death was not without struggle; recall the prayer in the garden for the possible removal of the 'cup' of suffering before his arrest and the outcry on the cross for being alienated from God (cf. the legendary 'calmness' of Socrates in the face of death). According to the gospels, for the Jews the death of Jesus was well-deserved based on the charge of 'blasphemy'.

In light of these observations, it is not terribly surprising that in 1 Corinthians 1–2 Paul not only shows no interest in the Greco-Roman notion of 'noble death', but actually puts forward ideas which were diametrically opposed to the commonly accepted social ethos of the time. After raising the thorny issue of church divisions in 1.10–12, Paul goes straight into the message of the cross: 'Was Paul crucified for you?' (1.13). The force of

---

[40] John Chrysostom, *Homilies on 1 Corinthians* 4.7.
[41] GOOCH, *Reflections*, 276–77.

Paul's rhetoric is clear and simple: Only the one who was crucified for you, namely Jesus Christ, deserves the total allegiance of the Corinthians. As such, Paul first rebukes those (one should perhaps say *especially* those) who gave him their loyalty, because having received Paul's message of the cross and being his supporters they should have known better.

For Paul, the crucifixion of Jesus was no mere historical reality, important as it was, but the very substance of his proclamation and the only purpose of his mission (1.17) and existence. The 'eloquent wisdom' of man was incompatible with the 'power' of God, which was demonstrated on the cross of Christ (1.17). Paul was fully aware that the message of the cross was foolishness to those who rejected it, but salvation to those believing (1.18). The wisdom of God in and through the proclamation of the cross had thus turned the social perceptions of their world upside down (1.18–21). Paul knew that Jews demanded signs and Greeks desired wisdom (1.22). And yet he had committed himself to the proclamation of 'Christ crucified', which was a stumbling block to Jews and foolishness to Gentiles (1.23).

Paul's commitment was thus a direct and deliberate challenge to both Jews and Greeks of his time, because for them the absolute horror of crucifixion as a form of execution and all the sufferings (both physical and mental), shame, inhumanity and indignity that were associated with it were notorious. There was thus nothing noble about Jesus' death, as Socrates' death was commonly regarded to be. As such, only a 'fool', according to the social ethos of the time, would have committed himself to the proclamation about the crucified Jesus, having been prosecuted and condemned by the government. Yet, Paul was no fool, his commitment was based on the conviction that the crucified Christ had demonstrated clearly that 'God's foolishness is wiser than human wisdom, and God's weakness is stronger than human strength' (1.25).

If one were looking for some significant points of contact between Socrates and Jesus with special reference to Paul's message of the cross in the opening chapters of 1 Corinthians, the result could be rather disappointing. But paradoxically, the absence of any significant point of contact between the two cases is itself revealing because it serves to demonstrate rather clearly that Socrates and what he symbolizes and embodies do not quite fit the picture of Paul's crucified Christ in the final analysis. This is so despite the fact that Socrates has been a commonly respected and admired figure throughout the history of the church, especially for his commitment to the search for truth and for his courage in the face of great adversity, including death itself. But the mission and death of Jesus Christ have to be understood, perceived and interpreted in an entirely different way, especially in light of the way Paul communicates in the opening chapters of 1 Corinthians. The uniqueness of the cross of Jesus lies precisely in its incomprehensible nature, humanly speaking. And it is this that allows Paul to describe his message as 'a stumbling block to Jews and foolishness to Gentiles.'

2.3 Noble Death in *2* and *4 Maccabees*: A Jewish Tradition

The origin and title of *2 Maccabees* are quite clearly explained by Jonathan Goldstein. Clement of Alexandria and Origen are believed to be the earliest of the Church Fathers to mention the books by name. They were called *Ta Makkabaïka*, ('Maccabaean Histories'). The earliest use of the term 'Maccabees' for the heroes was found in Tertullian's *Adversus Judaeos* 4 (c. 195 AD). After that, the title 'Books of Maccabees' came into frequent usage in the writings of the Church Fathers.[42]

The structure of *2 Maccabees* at first glance appears rather odd. It begins with two letters. The first (1.1–10a) may be called Epistle 1, and Epistle 2 consists of 1.10b–2.18. 2.19 begins with a history in which (2.19–32) the writer refers to an 'abridgment' of the work of Jason of Cyrene who wrote about 'Judas Maccabaeus and his brothers, the purification of the "greatest" of temples and the dedication of the altar, the wars against Antiochus IV Epiphanes and Antiochus V Eupator, and the miraculous divine interventions and glorious victories which then occurred.'[43] Goldstein accepts the claims of the abridger (2.19–23). The abridger evidently paid much greater attention to the sufferings of the martyrs (6.10–7.42) than other matters.[44] The themes of his history are also fairly apparent: the covenantal relationship between God and His chosen people, the sanctity of the Jerusalem temple, the Hasmonaean dynasty and their pious opponents, the martyrdom of the Jews and the belief in resurrection.[45]

Although Jason and the abridger appear to have followed the most popular stylistic and narrative patterns of Greek historians, Goldstein suggests that 'despite all these Greek elements, the abridged history is profoundly Jewish.'[46] A careful reading of the Maccabean narratives and their theology leads one to agree with Goldstein's view.

Based on the first letter (*2 Macc.* 1.9) van Henten argues that the date of *2 Maccabees* is c. 124 BC and the author was likely a member of the Hasideans.[47] Moreover, *4 Maccabees*, especially in its historical contexts of

---

[42] J. A. GOLDSTEIN, *II Maccabees* (Garden: Doubleday & Company, 1983), 3–4.

[43] GOLDSTEIN, *II Maccabees*, 4.

[44] GOLDSTEIN, *II Maccabees*, 5–6.

[45] GOLDSTEIN, *II Maccabees*, 12.

[46] GOLDSTEIN, *II Maccabees*, 20–21.

[47] VAN HENTEN, *The Maccabean Martyrs as Saviours of the Jewish People: A Study of 2 and 4 Maccabees* (Leid: Brill, 1997), 296.

martyrdom, is believed to have been largely derived from *2 Maccabees* and came into being in c. 100 BC.[48]

In Goldstein's view, *2 Maccabees* 7 constitutes 'the earliest surviving examples of elaborate stories of monotheists suffering martyrdom and are the direct source for the patterns that thereafter prevailed in Jewish and Christian literature.' So much so that he even makes a convincing case that Hebrews 11.35–36 alludes to *2 Maccabees* 6.18–7.42 and that from this time forward, and especially in Christian traditions, the idea of redemptive power and martyrdom are present.[49]

2 Maccabees has three stories of 'noble death': (1) the ninety-year old scribe Eleazar, (2) the anonymous mother and (3) her seven sons (6.18–31; 7). The nobility of such death was set in the context of covenant.[50] David Seeley makes a convincing case that the martyrdom of the elderly Eleazar was a particularly important source of encouragement and strength for his fellow Jews (6.31).[51] He singles out three aspects of Eleazar's death: obedience, the military context and the overcoming of physical vulnerability. In addition, there is also another aspect of Eleazer's death which is particularly noble: its vicariousness.[52]

In the Maccabean writings the martyrs were regarded as Jewish philosophers whose thoughts and virtues provided a guideline for the Jewish way of life. van Henten elaborates that the Jewish philosophy is understood to measure up to Greek philosophy in every regard. In fact, because the Jewish has divine origins it is not just equal, but superior to Greek. When one understands this view, the scene which takes place before the king – where there is a refusal to renounce εὐσέβεια ('piety') and the philosophical way of life stemming from it – is better understood.[53]

The idea of bodily resurrection of Jewish martyrs is one of the most significant elements in the Maccabean belief in divine vindication. Resurrection displays God's power over life and death to bring justice about. Divine sovereignty is also communicated through the conversion of Antiochus IV to Judaism just before his death.[54] In chapter 9 one learns of Antiochus falling to the ground and being shown the power of God, whereupon he remarks that it is 'right to submit to God' and that he will proclaim Jerusalem a free city. Antiochus also promises to adorn the temple and bring votive offerings to it. At the end of this speech, these words are

---

[48] VAN HENTEN, *Martyrs*, 82.

[49] GOLDSTEIN, *II Maccabees*, 282–83.

[50] VAN HENTEN, *Martyrdom*, 46.

[51] DAVID SEELEY, *The Noble Death: Graeco-Roman Martyrology and Paul's Concept of Salvation* (Sheffield: JSOT Press, 1990), 89.

[52] SEELEY, *The Noble Death*, 91.

[53] VAN HENTEN, *Martyrs*, 294.

[54] *2 Macc.* 9.8–17. van Henten, *Martyrs*, 303.

placed on his lips by the author of 2 *Maccabees*: 'I shall become a Jew and shall make a tour of the entire inhabited world, telling of the might of God' (2 *Macc.* 9.8–17).

In Hugh Anderson's view, the writer of 4 *Maccabees*, while familiar with Greek thought and especially Stoic ideas, was not really concerned to promote them among his Jewish readers as such, but rather to use them in the service of his own people and make the great virtues of Greek self-control, courage, justice and temperance subordinate to Jewish Law.[55] deSilva shares this same basic view.[56] An excellent example of this is found in 4 *Maccabees* 1.16–19: 'Reason, I suggest, is knowledge of things divine and human, and of their causes. And this wisdom, I assume, is the culture we acquire from the Law, through which we learn the things of God reverently and the things of men to our worldly advantage. The forms of wisdom consist of prudence, justice, courage, and temperance.'[57]

John Barclay in *Jews in the Mediterranean Diaspora* seeks to interpret the thesis of 4 *Maccabees* in relation to Jewish identity and tradition. In his view, the author places the Maccabean martyrdoms 'within the framework of the thesis that "religious reason is master over the passions"' right from the start (1.1–3.18).[58]

The author of 4 *Maccabees* was familiar with the relation between reason and passions, which was a main issue in contemporary philosophy, especially in Stoicism. But to the author, it was Jewish philosophy which was superior (5.22, 35; 7.7, 9, 21) and all philosophies must serve Jewish interests. Barclay suggests that the author's use of the first person plural 'we' in relation to wisdom (σοφία), education (παιδεία) and Jewish law (νόμος) is indicative of the author's strong sense of solidarity with his Jewish community. This also implies that ultimately the author was only interested in the Jewish form of wisdom and philosophy.[59]

While 4 *Maccabees* appears to share the Stoic belief that religion is an ingredient of reason, the repeated occurrences of the words 'godly reason' (εὐσεβὴς λογισμός; 1.1; 5.38; 7.16, etc.) and 'godliness' (εὐσέβεια) suggest that reason was to be understood in a Jewish religious context, especially in relation to the examples of great Jewish figures in history. They all conquered passions with their godliness (7.21–22).[60]

---

[55] H. ANDERSON (trans.), '4 Maccabees', in J. H. CHARLESWORTH (ed.), *OTP* (New York: Doubleday & Company, 1985), vol. 2.531–64, at 537–38.

[56] DeSILVA, *4 Maccabees* (Sheffield: Sheffield Academic Press, 1998), 51.

[57] cf. *4 Macc.* 1.6; 5.7–13, 17–25; 13.19; 14.2.

[58] BARCLAY, *Jews in the Mediterranean Diaspora* (Edinburgh: T & T Clark, 1996), 369.

[59] BARCLAY, *Jews*, 371.

[60] BARCLAY, *Jews*, 372–73.

Returning to Socrates, one could ask how he responded when confronted by death. Although it almost sounds like colloquial English, the Greek philosopher may have responded: 'he took it like a man'. This response, in fact, is the basic title of a significant paper written by Stephen Moore and Janice Anderson based on their study of *4 Maccabees*.[61]

Moore and Anderson focus on the issue of masculinity in their Maccabean studies. They note that while the definitive masculine trait usually includes both control of others and self-control in most of the Greek and Latin writings, *4 Maccabees* regards self-control as the supreme index of masculinity compared with the control of others.[62] The 'masculinity' of old Eleazer, the widowed mother and her seven young sons is powerfully demonstrated in their self-control when confronted with death (14.11; cf. 15.23, 28–30; 16.14, 2).

Moore and Anderson single out four cardinal virtues – φρόνησις ('prudence'), σωφροσύνη ('temperance'), δικαιοσύνη ('justice'), ἀνδρεία ('courage' = 'manliness') – in the Greco-Roman society which were thought to have been articulated by Plato, especially in *Phaedo* 69C. These four virtues were subsequently cherished by Aristotle, the Stoics as well as Philo. The author of *4 Maccabees* is believed to have taken over these virtues and applied them to the Mosaic Law. The Maccabean author demonstrates that Eleazar, the mother and her seven sons all died with great courage (ἀνδρεία) which was considered essentially a masculine virtue.[63]

True maturity was thought to be mental and not physical. When the sixth son is faced with death, he proudly says to Antiochus, 'I am younger in age than my brothers, but just as mature mentally' (11.14; cf. 5.31). Similarly in 5.23, Eleazar challenges Antiochus: 'you mock at our philosophy as though our living under it were contrary to reason. On the one hand, it teaches us temperance so that we are in control of all our pleasures and desires; and it gives us a thorough training in courage [ἀνδρεία] so that we willingly endure all hardship.' The Jewish Maccabean martyrs were models of masculine virtue not only for the Jews but also for the Gentiles (*2 Macc.* 7.12; *4 Macc.* 17.16–24).

Ironically, Antiochus, the powerful ruler who appeared to have absolute control over his captives became a slave of his own passions (8.2). He was defeated for not being able to force his captives to eat defiling food. In a violent rage he loses control of himself (10.17). For the author of *4 Maccabees*, true masculinity is clearly something internal. Therefore, for him the real battle is between the martyrs and themselves. In popular Hellenistic moral philosophy a clear distinction was made between the man who

---

[61] MOORE and J. C. ANDERSON, 'Taking It like a man', *JBL* 117 (1998), 249–73.
[62] MOORE 'Taking It', 250.
[63] MOORE, 'Taking It', 252–53.

was 'stronger than himself' (κρείττων ἑαυτοῦ; i.e. one who was able to control his passions and appetites) and the man who was 'weaker than himself' (ἥττων ἑαυτου; i.e. the person who became a slave to his own passions and appetites). [64] Plato thus says in his *De Republica* that for he who is master of himself would also be subject to himself, and he who is subject to himself would be master. [65] In his *De Legibus*, Plato clearly states that being defeated by oneself is not only the most shameful but also worst of all defeats. [66] Moore and Anderson argue the reason for this is that it is equivalent to defeat at the hands of women or slaves. [67]

Ironically, in *4 Maccabees* King Antiochus, who possessed absolute power over others, turned out to be powerless and unmanly when confronted with an elderly man, a widowed mother and her seven boys. To appear powerless was a public shame for the king, since manhood was essentially a matter of public perception in the ancient Mediterranean world. By marked contrast, the tortured old Eleazar's manly behaviour was greatly admired and he is described as a person 'adorned with the beauty of his piety ... the great soul and the noble man' (6.2, 5). Seeley's understanding and definition of 'noble death' is largely based on the death of Eleazar, in which he finds four important elements: (1) obedience to the divine Law; (2) a military context, which involved a war against Antiochus and the Hellenisers; (3) the overcoming of physical vulnerability and (4) sacrificial metaphors since the deaths of the martyrs in *4 Maccabees* are considered 'vicarious'. Moreover, judged by the way that stories are told in *4 Maccabees* there is hardly any doubt that its author regarded the martyrs as examples mimetically to be followed (cf. 7.8–9; 14.9; 9.30; 11.24–25). [68]

Moore and Anderson note that 'in the ancient Mediterranean world, μαλακός ('soft'; Latin *mollis*) was the adjective supremely used to differentiate women, girls, boys, youths, effeminate males, catamites, and eunuchs from "true men"'. [69] In the highly dramatized encounter between Antiochus and his Jewish captors, the latter clearly emerged as the winners. Even the widowed mother became a true man – that is she took it like a man. The Maccabean author has particularly great admiration for the suffering mother (17.1; 14.12; 15.15) and concludes with this remark: 'how numerous, then, and how great were the torments that the mother suffered while her sons were tortured on the wheel and with the searing irons' (15.22). [70] The Maccabean author's great admiration became the more re-

[64] MOORE, 'Taking It', 257–58; 261.
[65] Plato, *Rep.* 430E–431A.
[66] Plato, *Leg.* 1.626DE.
[67] MOORE, 'Taking It', 262.
[68] SEELEY, *The Noble Death*, 147.
[69] MOORE, 'Taking It', 263.
[70] MOORE, 'Taking It', 265.

markable since he himself shared the popular view that the female was 'the weak-spirited, weak-souled, and weaker sex'. But as Moore and Anderson observe, 'it is precisely this "innate" disability that the mother is depicted as heroically overcoming, thereby proving herself worthy of one of the more curious compliments that a Hellenistic male author could bestow upon a female character.'[71] In this particular context, Kerstin Aspegren's comment is also insightful: 'if a woman achieved something good or distinguished herself in ethical, religious or intellectual matters, she was not praised as being a woman of good qualities but as a woman who had become manly. Unable to measure up to men in the arena of virtue, the best woman could hope for was to be declared an honorary man.'[72]

Although much of what Moore and Anderson present about Greco-Roman masculinity in the Maccabean stories is not particularly new, they nonetheless make a few points which are insightful and instructive. These may be summarized as follows:

(1) On a number of occasions as well as in conclusion they mention that 'mastery' is synonymous with 'masculinity' in most of Greek and Latin texts surviving from antiquity. They place emphasis on the inner self-control of a person as being far superior to the outward domination of others. This point has been made well with special reference to *4 Maccabees* in which the inner self-control of the Jewish captors – Eleazer, the mother and her seven boys – enabled them to emerge as 'manly' winners in their confrontation with the pagan ruler. Antiochus becomes a loser in the end and thus sufferes from great shame and humiliation according to the social ethos of the Greco-Roman society. Honour belongs to his Jewish sufferers. To use their expression, Antiochus is 'feminised'.

(2) The paradoxical way of presenting the overall case is attractive. For example, in the Maccabean story, it is the 'weak' that defeat the 'strong'; 'the conquered' that shame 'the conqueror' and self-mastery displaces political mastery of others. Such significant paradoxes are also present in Paul's 'message of the cross' (1 Cor. 1.18–31). However, it is important to point out that while the author of *4 Maccabees* constructs a Jewish version of masculinity, it is still largely based on the Hellenistic social ethos and values of the world of Antiochus, a pagan tyrant. Moore and Anderson thus note a very significant problem in the Maccabean author's continuity with the Hellenistic tradition with regards to masculinity: 'victory is achieved in 4 Maccabees only by accepting and reaffirming the dominant hierarchical continuum along which ruler and ruled, master and slave, male and female were positioned.'[73]

---

[71] Moore, 'Taking It', 266.
[72] K. Aspegren, *The Male Woman: A Feminine Ideal in the Early Church* (Stockholm: Almqvist & Wilksell, 1990), 11.
[73] Moore, 'Taking It', 272.

While Moore and Anderson are pleased to see 'the elite, hegemonic concept of masculinity' being modified by *4 Maccabees* by elevating self-mastery or self-control over mastery of social inferiors, the old Greco-Roman ethos remained basically unchallenged. Even in *4 Maccabees* it is still taken for granted that women are predestined to be subservient to men. In the end it is still masculinity or manliness that is being glorified. The Jewish martyrs' victory over their pagan oppressor is only one side of the story. The other side of the story is the simple fact that these martyrs are 'implicated in a contest of manhood that is itself inherently oppressive.'[74]

In *4 Maccabees* the author makes a remarkable contrast between honour and shame. deSilva comments that the tortures and bodily malestations to the martyrs are not considered by the author as effecting their honour negatively.[75] Whereas similar treatment could be perceived in some contexts as harmful to honour and one's place in society, in the case of martyrs it is just the opposite: 'dishonour' becomes honour. On this significant point *4 Maccabees* differs markedly from Greco-Roman perception and apparently comes closer to the crucifixion of Jesus in which he suffered great bodily 'dishonour' and 'shame'. Paul, in his imitation of Christ, was evidently not ashamed of the 'dishonouring' of his body and spoke very openly about it (cf. 1 Cor. 4.9–13; 2 Cor. 11.22–32). Paul knew full well that while those sufferings he refers to in 1 and 2 Corinthians would be causes for shame within Greco-Roman society (ch. 1); it was an honour for the sake of the 'message of the cross'. Paul undoubtedly derived his inspiration and strength from the crucifixion of Jesus. As such, he is able to say, 'For I decided to know nothing among you except Jesus Christ, and him crucified' (1 Cor. 2.2).

Unlike the Maccabean author who readily accepts the Greco-Roman ethos about masculinity, honour/shame, strength and weakness, Paul deliberately disassociates himself from such ethos in his message of the cross, including the manner of his appearance and speech. Paul evidently opts for a clear-cut discontinuity with the social ethos of the time as far as his life and witness are concerned. Ultimately, it is not man's glory that Paul seeks but God's, and his commitment is to true godliness and not manliness. The significance of this latter point within this study must not be overlooked.

Noble death in the Maccabean tradition, very much like the Greco-Roman tradition, is also largely a human perception. Therefore, in comparison to the death of, say, the Maccabean martyr Eleazar, the death of Jesus is also far from being 'noble'.

---

[74] MOORE, 'Taking It', 273.

[75] DESILVA, 'The Noble Contest: Honour, Shame, and the Rhetorical Strategy of 4 Maccabees', *JSP* 13 (1995), 31–57, at 54.

However, there is one common element in Paul's theology of the cross and the Maccabean martyrdom that makes a comparison between the two cases meaningful: *there is a shared element of profound paradox present in both cases.* Quite similar to the Pauline case in which the power of God is believed to have been revealed in the 'weakness' of Jesus' crucifixion, the paradoxical nature of the Maccabean martyrdom is also evident when the old and weak (Eleazar), the female (the widowed mother) and her seven young boys ultimately triumph over the seemingly strong and powerful.

Finally, there is the crucial identity issue which is a main concern not only in the Maccabean martyrdom, but also in the death of Jesus as well as in Paul's response to the Corinthian crisis. It is here that Barclay's effort to place the theology and spirit of *4 Maccabees* at the centre of Judaism, especially in relation to the vital issue of Jewish identity, becomes particularly relevant and helpful. In Barclay's opinion, the greatest contributor to the maintenance of the fundamental bond of the ethnicity and identity of the Jews in Diaspora has been *ta patria*, the customs passed down from one generation to the next. But unfortunately, it is this very strength which often caused the resentment of other ethnic communities who considered the Jews to be 'unassimilable'. However, what has been perceived as offensive by non-Jews is the very distinctive feature, namely the Jewish tradition, which provides the impetus for their survival in the Diaspora for two more millennia under the most extreme and devastating circumstances. The problems and challenges they face today are even greater.[76]

The Maccabean martyrs are clearly regarded as heroes and role models for the Jews, especially in the context of Jewish identity. van Henten has thus suggested that both 2 and *4 Maccabees* attempt to 'deal with issues of self-definition and Jewish identity in both the religious-cultural and the political spheres.'[77] The martyrs' refusal to submit to the pagan ruler and their subsequent noble deaths are taken as powerful signs of their Jewish identity.[78]

The identity issue is important because the Corinthian problem is also essentially an identity crisis and Paul clearly takes the matter of Christian identity very seriously right from the start of his Corinthian letter when he solemnly reminds the Corinthian Christians that they are 'sanctified in Christ Jesus, called to be saints (ἡγιασμένοις ἐν Χριστῷ Ἰησοῦ, κλητοῖς ἁγίοις, 1 Cor. 1.2), and that they have already been 'called into the fellowship of his [God's] Son, Jesus Christ our Lord' (1.9). That, for Paul, is the Corinthian Christians' true identity. As such, it was sheer fool-

---

[76] BARCLAY, *Jews*, 444.
[77] VAN HENTEN, *Martyrs*, 6.
[78] VAN HENTEN, *Martyrs*, 7, 11.

ishness for them to think that they belong to Paul, Apollos or Cephas
(1.12). And such a mentality which had clearly led to the very serious conflicts and divisions in the Corinthian Church was a very clear indication
that the trouble-making Corinthians were still very much enslaved by the
social ethos of the time. It was clearly an identity issue. Had they taken
their Christian identity seriously and understood all its profound implications from the perspective of the cross, they would not behave in the way
they were. And they most certainly would not challenge Paul's *modus operandi.*

2.4 Crucifixion and the 'Curse'

It is almost impossible to discuss the matter of noble death, especially the
Jewish σκάνδαλον (1.23), without considering the important idea of
'curse' in close connection with the cross – at times referred to as 'tree'.

Paul's reference to the Old Testament Scriptures twice in 1 Cor. 15.3, 4
– 'according to the scriptures' (κατὰ τὰς γραφὰς) – is very significant. It
may serve apologetically as a direct response to the Jewish σκάνδαλον
(particularly in view of Deut. 21.23) as well as the Greco-Romans' charac-
terization of the 'message of the cross' as 'foolishness'. Unfortunately,
Paul does not point to any particular passage or passages of Scriptures he
may have had in mind when he wrote 15.3–4. However, one is naturally
tempted to recall Isaiah 53, where the death (vv.7–8), burial (v.9) and vindication (resurrection?) (vv.10–12) of the 'suffering servant' were all mentioned or at least implied.

What Paul fails to do in 1 Cor. 15.3–4 (i.e. pinpointing particular verses
of Scripture), he does in Galatians 3.13, with special reference to the Deut.
21.23 concerning 'the curse of the law.' Just like 1 Cor. 15.3–4, Gal. 3.13
also belongs to the very core of Paul's gospel or 'the message of the cross',
although its expression is different from the Corinthian passage. In terms
of the present research, especially on the crucial issues of crucifixion and
noble death, Gal. 3.13 is very important because the verse is about the
manner of Jesus' death in relation to Deut. 21.23. As mentioned previously,
the Greeks and Romans' characterisation of the message of the cross as
foolishness was basically due to the manner of Jesus' death. And as far as
the unbelieving Jews were concerned, besides the problem of crucifixion,
there was also the religious problem surrounding the death of Jesus. This
problem basically had to do with Jewish messianic expectations (a topic
that is already the subject of so many volumes) and a Jewish understanding
of the 'curse' in Deut. 21.23.

In Galatians 3.13 Paul refers to Christ's sacrificial death in close connection with 'the curse of the law' of Deut. 21.23. In this regard, a parallel

Yigael Yadin draws attention to in *Pesher Nahum* (4Q169) 3–4 i lines 7–8 and *11QTemple* 64 lines 6–13 is of great value.[79] John Allegro first published this fragmentary *pesher* in 1956[80] and then in 1971 Yadin published his own revision. This portion of the *pesher* interprets Nah. 2.12–14, where the fall and plundering of Nineveh (612 BC) are the main concern. The author(s) of the Qumran *pesher*, according to Fitzmyer, reapplies Nahum's words to the situation in Judea in the early 1st century in order 'to present its own interpretation of what God has done to certain elements in that people.'[81]

It is generally agreed that *Pesher Nahum* refers to a historical event according to which Demetrius III the Seleucid ruler (95–78 BC) was invited by the enemies (the Pharisees) of Alexander Jannaeus (the Sadducee high priest, 103–76 BC) to assist them in Jerusalem. When the expansionist and war-like Alexander Jannaeus eventually regained Jerusalem, he punished the Pharisees by public crucifixion, as discussed in chapter one, in Jerusalem.[82]

There are different identifications of the *pesher's* sobriquet 'Lion of wrath', although he is most often thought to be Alexander. Yadin begins his argument for this association with two observations: (1) Here, the 'Lion of wrath' is God's instrument (cf. Hos. 5.13–15) and (2) 'Wrath' in the Bible is most often associated with God's anger.[83] Therefore, the 'Lion of wrath' within the *pesher* was regarded as God's judgment against the דורשי החלקות ('seekers of smooth things'). Fitzmyer has identified the phrase 'seekers of smooth things' as the Pharisees, the opponents of the 'Lion of Wrath' (=Alexander Jannaeus).[84]

Yadin suggests that *11QTemple* 64 lines 6–13 are closely related to *Pesher Nahum*. The *Temple Scroll* makes clearer the ambiguous crimes of Deut. 21.22–23, these are: (1) political treason such as conspiring to hand-over one's own people and (2) attempting to escape the death penalty by fleeing. Yadin argues that these specific crimes are likely references to the historical events concerning Demetrius III and Alexander.[85] The

[79] Y. YADIN, 'Pesher Nahum (4Q pNahum) Reconsidered', *IEJ* 21 (1971), 1–12. Cf. J. A. FITZMYER, 'Crucifixion in Palestine, Qumran, and the New Testament', in *To Advance the Gospel: New Testament Studies* (Grand Rapids: William B. Eerdmans, 1981), 125–46. J. M. BAUMGARTEN, 'Does TLH in the Temple Scroll Refer to Crucifixion"? *JBL* 91 (1972), 472–81. M. WILCOX, '"Upon the Tree" – Deut 21:22–23 in the New Testament', *JBL* 96 (1977), 85–99.
[80] J. M. ALLEGRO, 'Further Light on the History of the Qumran Sect', *JBL* 75 (1956), 89–95.
[81] FITZMYER, 'Crucifixion', 130.
[82] FITZMYER, 'Crucifixion', 131. See Josephus, *Ant.* 13.379–80; cf. *B.J.* 1.93–98.
[83] YADIN, 'Pesher Nahum', 3.
[84] FITZMYER, 'Crucifixion', 131–32. Cf. YADIN, 'Pesher Nahum', 12.
[85] YADIN, 'Pesher Nahum', 8–9.

דורשי החלקות would have passed on information to Demetrius III, which led to this disaster in Jerusalem.[86] The awful events are described by Josephus: in the wake of the crucifixions, the 800 rebels learn that Alexander forced the families of the crucified to watch the execution, all the while looking on as he consorted with his concubines – this story led the opponents to flee in horror.[87]

The Seleucid backed Pharisees who passed information on to the enemy, considered treasons, were crucified.[88] As previously discussed, the purpose of hanging was not merely to inflict the greatest pain and suffering on the victim, but also to serve as a public deterrence. However, *11QTemple* 64 line 12, which rewrites Deut. 21.22–23, instructs that execution must be followed by burying the hung corpse before sundown.[89] The instruction is seen to be in line with the Torah in such cases.

Yadin seeks to restore lines 7–8 of *Pesher Nahum* as follows: '*its interpretation concerns the Lion of wrath* [who ... sentence of] *death* דורשי החלקות (and) *who hangs men alive* [*on the tree as this is the law*] *in Israel as of old since* the hanged one is called alive on the tree.'[90] Yadin explains that the group behind the *pesher*, strict observers of the law, could have based their interpretation on the customs of ancient Israel with reference to Deut. 21. Yadin points to Josh. 8.23–29 where the king of Ai is seen to be hanged alive, but his corpse is treated according to the regulations of Deut. 21.23.[91] Fitzmyer, who accepts the plausibility of Yadin's restoration, suggests that there is one common idea among various restorations: that the group behind the *pesher* expresses horror at such crucifixion.[92]

If Yadin is right in seeing a connection between *Pesher Nahum* and *11QTemple*, and that 'to hang' in both cases refers to crucifixion, the implication is that Romans would not be the only ones in Palestine to use this mode of execution.[93] One should add that Jews in this period would likely not have accepted crucifixion as an acceptable way to deal with their enemies – whether from a 'legal' or 'religious' perspective. The argument of Yadin points to an understanding of causes for crucifixion in Deut. 21 and a Mosaic injunction for dealing with a corpse after crucifixion. One would suspect that the 'Lion of Wrath', that is Alexander, would only have been endorsed by the Qumranites in so far as he was an instrument of judgment

---

[86] Josephus, *Ant.* 13.376–83.

[87] Josephus, *B.J.* 1.97–98.

[88] YADIN, 'Pesher Nahum', 9.

[89] FITZMYER, 'Crucifixion', 134.

[90] YADIN, 'Pesher Nahum', 12.

[91] YADIN, 'Pesher Nahum', 10–11.

[92] FITZMYER, 'Crucifixion', 132.

[93] FITZMYER, 'Crucifixion', 135.

against the wicked treasons. However, with this said, the author(s) of the *pesher* would have believed Alexander also to be an enemy of Israel.

The evidence from Qumran, for this study, is especially significant because it makes a clear contribution to language associated with crucifixion. Within early Jewish literature there is a paucity of references using such language as 'to hang alive on the tree' (לתלוי חי על העץ), especially in connection to Deuteronomy (21.22): 'and you shall hang him on a tree' (ותלית אתו על עץ).

The study of the Qumran texts in relation to Deut. 21.22–23 has significant implications for the crucifixion of Jesus, especially in connection with Gal. 3.13, a passage highly relevant for the discussion about noble death, or, in the case of Jesus, ignoble death. The case is well put by Fitzmyer, who begins his explanation with a statement that the *opinio communis* is that *Pesher Nahum* refers to Alexander crucifying his enemies.

These lines of the *pesher* could be described as a 'missing link' in pre-Christian Palestinian writings that there were Jews who considered "hanging" (תלוי), in reference to Deut. 21.22–23, as a way to describe crucifixion. Before this evidence, 'hanging on a tree' was often explained in relationship to the crime of *perduellio* ('high-treason'), which was punished within the Roman Empire by a statutory penalty of crucifixion.[94] However, even before the *pesher*, it was never doubted that crucifixion was practised in Roman Palestine, whether by the Romans or Alexander in Hasmonean times. However, the application of Deut. 21.22–23 to crucifixion has been puzzling, and nearly universally taken for granted in commentaries. The significance of *Nahum Pesher* is that it provides the extra-biblical documentation to demonstrate how Deut. 21.23 was likely interpreted by Jews at this time: to be hung on a tree is understood as crucifixion.[95]

In Gal. 3 and 4 Paul uses the story of Abraham in Genesis to argue for his doctrine of justification by faith. Gal. 3.13 is part of the first of four midrashic developments of the Abraham story in Genesis. The first midrashic development is found in Gal. 3.6–15. Starting from Gen. 15.6, Paul in Gal. 3.6–15 concludes that the true children of Abraham are those, like the Christians, who put their faith in God. By contrast, however, 'all who rely on the works of the law are under a curse; for it is written, 'cursed is everyone who does not observe and obey all the things written in the book of the law' (3.10), which is clearly a reference to Deut. 27.26.

---

[94] Cicero, *Rab. Perd.* 4.13: *CAPVT OBNVBITO, ARBORI INFELICI SVSPENDIT* ('Veil his head, hang him to the tree of shame'). Cicero implied the punishment of crucifixion derives from pre-Republican times. Livy also showed the same opinion (1.26.6–7, 11).

[95] FITZMYER, 'Crucifixion', 136–37.

Although Paul in Gal. 3.6–15 does not refer to the crucifixion of Jesus explicitly, crucifixion or the cross is quite clearly implied in 3.13 when Paul boldly declares that 'Christ redeemed us from the curse of the law by becoming a curse for us' with a specific reference to Deut. 21.23: כי קללת אלהים תלוי ('for anyone hung on a tree is under God's curse', NRSV).[96] Important to note is that Paul in his reference to Deut. 21 in Gal. 3.13 omits 'by God' and adds 'on a tree'. This is not found in the MT, but in the LXX, because without the 'tree' it would be difficult to link Deut. 21.23 to the hanging of Jesus on the 'cross.' Exegetically, it has been diffi-cult to take the 'tree' in Deut. 21.23 and apply it to the 'cross' of Jesus. The Qumran texts seem to have quite clearly indicated that there was in fact a pre-Christian understanding of crucifixion as 'hanging on a tree' and this is especially true of *4QpNah*. Paul, in an analogous way, also relates Deut. 27.26 to Deut. 21.22–23 to expound his vicarious and soteriological theology. To apply the 'hanging' in Deut. 21.23 to Jesus is evidently a Christian *theologoumenon*, which does not have a precursor in the Qumran text.[97]

In the studies of Fitzmyer, Yadin and others the Qumran texts in rela-tion to Gen. 22, Deut. 21 and Gal. 3 also have other implications. For the present study on noble death, especially with reference to the crucifixion of Jesus, it is sufficient to note that a vital link between the 'tree' in Deut. 21.23 (LXX) and the 'cross' in Gal. 3.13 is established in writings pre-dating Paul.

Understanding this intellectual background further helps the present discussion, as the 'curse' is turned into God's means of salvation for all, whether or not such a death of Jesus was regarded as 'noble' or not. Even if it should be regarded as 'ignoble' within the society, be it Jewish or Greeks and Romans, Paul would argue, as he does in 1 Corinthians 1.18–31, that God in his true σοφία has in fact used the 'ignoble' to shame the 'noble'. In view of Paul's consistent use of paradox in the Corinthian cor-respondence, one may safely infer that the crucifixion of Jesus was for Paul an 'ignoble' death according to the conventional social ethos.

2.5 Conclusion

On the matter of noble death, it may be helpful to cross-reference Romans 5.6–8 in which Paul makes a significant but rare remark about the death of Christ: 'For while we were still weak, at the right time Christ died for the ungodly. Indeed, rarely will anyone die for a righteous person – though

---

[96] LXX: ὅτι κεκατηραμένος ὑπὸ θεοῦ πᾶς κρεμάμενος ἐπὶ ξύλου·

[97] FITZMYER, 'Crucifixion', 138.

perhaps for a good person someone might actually dare to die. But God proves his love for us in that *while we still were sinners Christ died for us.*'[98] The deaths of Socrates and the Maccabean martyrs were indeed noble because they died not only for themselves, but also for others (presumably including the 'righteous' and the 'good' also). They died for nation as well as for God. The same was seen in regard to Paul's view of Christ, except as he significantly highlights, and a point which seems to be absent in the 'noble death' of both Greco-Roman and Jewish traditions, the death of Jesus was for 'sinners' – people who were not worth dying for. Such an act of Christ is naturally subject to various value judgments, even diametrically opposed ones. For the cynical and the unbelieving, to die for sinners was surely a foolish act. On the contrary, for the believing (people who are conscious of their own sinfulness) it was a most selfless and noble act – for one even to die for the unworthy and ignoble sinners.

The study of crucifixion in antiquity demonstrates that the crucifixion of Jesus was a most ignoble death as far as the unbelieving world was concerned. This would form a sharp contrast with the concept of 'noble death' according to the current social ethos. The classic example of noble death in contemporary Roman culture was surely the death of Socrates. According to this tradition, the condemned Socrates welcomed a noble death. The Stoic philosopher Epictetus greatly admires Socrates' resolute decision to choose a noble death rather than living with dishonour (4.1.16). For Jews, the classic example would most likely be the martyrdoms described in Maccabees.

Could any meaningful comparison be drawn between Socrates and Jesus or between Jesus and the Maccabean martyrs on the issue of death? One may answer both 'yes' and 'no'. Yes, because like Socrates who died for his 'mission' (which included the quest for truth, true wisdom and philosophy as well as for the people of Athens) and the Maccabean Martyrs (who died for faith and conviction, as well as for nation and God), Jesus also died for his 'mission' (for humanity and for God). A definite 'no' may be given in regard to a specific comparison to the manner of Jesus' death, because the manner of Jesus' death was most ignoble. The crucifixion of Jesus has been seen as the most ignoble death from the perspective of the wider perception of society, and additionally a 'curse' according to the reading of scripture (Deut. 21.23) at the time.

Paradoxically, it is this 'no' side of the comparison, especially between Socrates and Christ, that is most significant, revealing and challenging from the Christian perspective, because it brings out sharply the uniqueness of Christ crucified, making the message of the cross such utter μωρία and σκάνδαλον to the world, turning its ethos upside down. Contextualis-

---

[98] Italics mine.

ing these statements and viewing Paul's words as they may have sounded – an overturning of the current social ethos – creates new resonances for modern readers and challenges one to re-think the message.

According to the main categories of the crucified victims, namely the crucifixion of rebels, the lower class, slaves, Jews, Christians and even Romans, Jesus could be said to have died the death of each of these categories, except the Romans who were distinguished from all the rest. This point is profoundly significant in relation to the foolishness of the message of the cross. Christ clearly died as a kind of 'rebel' in the eyes of those who did not have the true picture about it, although according to the witness of gospel writings Pilate found no crime in Jesus. The title that was put on the cross – '*Jesus of Nazareth, the King of the Jews*' – would most probably have been taken by the uninitiated as Jesus' true crime or as a kind of official verdict on him. The title on the cross could also imply treason in the Roman context of the time. Treason was evidently a paramount concern of the Roman authorities as it was a direct challenge to the *Pax Romana.*

A significant point has also been made in relation to the manner of Christ's death in Paul's reasoning, which was markedly different from the Roman and Jewish examples provided. In the end one may only conclude that it was the manner of Jesus' death that was ignoble and consequently made the message of the cross a stumbling block to Jews and foolishness to Gentiles. Had Christ died in a way other than crucifixion, one could speculate that a significant difference would have been made in the attitude of ancient audiences to Paul's message. At the very least, in the Corinthian context it was clearly the 'cross' (σταυρός) which made the message foolish. The cross was really the issue in Paul's response to the Corinthian crisis as well as to the world's characterisation of the message.

No disagreement is found with the views of Seeley, Droge and van Henten that noble death, voluntary death and martyrdom enjoyed a general acceptance in a wide array of traditions from the time. However, none of the cases cited by these scholars on the subject include a means of death by crucifixion. It is precisely at this crux that the study of noble death needs to stop and ponder the details of the paradigm. If any of these deaths had occurred by this particular method, would one still be able to argue that it was 'noble' in the ancient world? On account of deep-seeded prejudices against crucifixion as a capital punishment for the worst criminals, including slaves, the answer seems to be 'no'. When understanding this cultural response, one begins to see the challenge Paul faced in teaching the Corinthians: he was to turn what was considered an ignoble death of his Lord into what he believed to be the most noble.

Chapter 3

Exegesis of 1 Corinthians 1.18–31

3.1 Introduction

The study of crucifixion in antiquity in chapter one provides the necessary background to explain why Paul's 'message of the cross' (ὁ λόγος ὁ τοῦ σταυροῦ) was perceived contemptuously and subsequently rejected. Indeed, it has been argued that this was a radical inversion of the social ethos of Greco-Roman society. According to the study on 'noble death' in chapter two, in both Greco-Roman and Jewish traditions the death of Jesus was seen to be blatantly ignoble. Not only was the death of Christ on the cross no ordinary death, but also it was no simple death when placed in the social context of Paul's world. The body language and social symbolism that crucifixion conveyed were just as significant as its physical or literal aspect, especially in the case of Christ's crucifixion. This is because of the alleged or perceived crime Jesus committed, as well as the extraordinary claims of his immediate followers about him. Crucifixion as the most abhorrent form of capital punishment was symbolic of practically everything negative: shame, humiliation, human degradation and indignity. And for the crucified victim himself, this most detestable form of execution was vividly and powerfully symbolic of human helplessness and powerlessness. In terms of body language, both witnesses to and hearers of the event would understand the powerful imagery and have been deeply effected by it.

When placed in a Jewish religious context of the time, there was also the additional and crucial element of divine 'curse' in crucifixion. As Paul was brought up and moved extensively in a multi-cultural environment, how ever one may nuance Judaism and Hellenism, it may be reasonably assume that few of the observations made here would have been lost to him. This point is crucial in the exegesis of Corinthian passages which touch on the important subject of Christ's crucifixion and Paul's message of the cross. 1 Cor. 1.18–31 is a natural place to begin after chapters one and two, for it is in this crucial passage that Paul not only openly acknowledges the 'foolishness' of his message, but also he places the rejection of his message in a broader context, especially as it relates to perceptions of wisdom and power. The exegesis is sequenced as follows: (1) The de-

thronement of human wisdom by foolishness and foolishness as divine
power (1.18–25) and (2) Absolutely no grounds for boasting by both human and divine standards, and Christ the wisdom, righteousness, sanctification and redemption (1.26–31).

3.2 The Dethronement of Human 'Wisdom' by 'Foolishness', and 'Foolishness' as Divine Power (1.18–25)

The problem of divisions in the Corinthian church was not only a personal
challenge to Paul's leadership and authority, it also revealed, in the final
analysis, the Corinthians' failure to understand that it was Christ alone who
was crucified for them and thus rightly deserved their absolute allegiance.
This was ultimately a theological question concerning the cross. Closely
linked to the problem of church divisions was the issue of 'wisdom'. In
Paul's judgment, church divisions in Corinth were a clear indication that
those who were involved in them had actually adopted the *modus operandi*
of the world, especially in their understanding of wisdom and power. The
subject of wisdom had a long history in both Jewish and Hellenistic traditions and Paul may be assumed to be broadly knowledgeable about it.
However, he seems to have had no intention to deal with the speculative
aspects of those traditions in the Corinthian letters. In the Corinthian context, the word σοφία appears to be referring to two different and yet
closely related entities.[1] (1) It could refer to certain exalted (religio-
philosophical) knowledge that was often thought to be only in the possession of a privileged group of people and which brought them special status
both socially and spiritually in society. (2) It could more tangibly mean
special skills, usually rhetorically trained and acquired, which enabled a
person to publicly express himself with great eloquence, power and persuasion, and by means of which the possessor of such skills earned social
esteem and popularity.

   Paul attempts to deal with these two aspects of σοφία in his response to
the Corinthian crisis, including the troubling issue of church divisions
(σχίσματα). In response to the exalted wisdom, which was often socio-
philosophically conceived, Paul presents a marked contrast between the
perceived wisdom of the Corinthians and that of God. It is Paul's conviction that divine wisdom was revealed and powerfully demonstrated in the
crucified Christ (1 Cor. 1.17–2.9). The Corinthians' perceived that wisdom
was also very much in line with the second aspect of σοφία, which heavily
depends on human eloquence. This aspect of σοφία was acquired technically through rhetorical training, including the indispensable aspect of

---

[1] BARRETT, 'Cephas and Corinth', 28–39 (See §4.2).

one's physical appearance and delivery (hence, the importance of 'body language').[2] Wisdom, power, rhetoric, eloquence were all fundamental elements and basic values of the most cherished social ethos of the Corinthians.

A relatively careful reading of 1.10–17, which provides the immediate background for the exegesis of 1.18–31, indicates that church divisions (1.10) in Corinth were a major issue that greatly troubled Paul.[3] Some of the factors that might have caused the Corinthian σχίσματα could be explained socially, such as the Corinthians' preoccupation with σοφία, social status and power. However, the crux of the matter was also essentially theological, especially in relation to the crucifixion of Jesus. To be more exact, the disturbing issue of σχίσματα had to do primarily with the Corinthians' lack of understanding of the cross of Christ. This crucial point was evidently reflected in the most vital question which Paul poses to the divided church in 1.13 as soon as the matter of σχίσματα is raised ("Was Paul crucified for you?), as well as in the very strong statement made in 1.17 ('For Christ did not send me to baptize but to proclaim the gospel … the cross of Christ'). Paul's solution is, therefore, both a social and theological response to some of the fundamental values of the cultural milieu of the Corinthians from the perspective of the cross.

The social values of the Corinthians included wisdom, eloquence, power, honour, and other status symbols. They were passionately cherished and jealously guarded by members of society. Consequently, immediately after making his strong statement in 1 Cor. 1.18a, that "the message of the cross is foolishness" to those who rejected it, Paul launches straight into a direct confrontation with the crucial issues of human wisdom and power in 1.18b–25 in very polemical and paradoxical terms. In the end, the whole passage goes far beyond mere discussion on the subjects of wisdom and power as these subjects were ultimately perceived in terms of a direct encounter between two diametrically opposed world views.

Paul's deliberate attempt to challenge the basic social ethos of the Corinthians may also be regarded as simultaneously risky and courageous. Risky because when calling into question the fundamental social values of the Corinthians – especially with 'the message of the cross' which was already acknowledged even by Paul himself to be 'foolishness' – his strategy clearly could have backfired. Paul was fully prepared to take the risk and openly declare that he had already 'decided to know nothing … except Jesus Christ, and him crucified' (2.2). Paul may be described as courageous

---

[2] Certain key passages and verses in the Corinthian letters should be read in this important context: 1 Cor. 1.17–20; 2.1–5; 2 Cor. 10.10; 11.22–25. See below chapters 4–5.

[3] See BARTON, '1 Corinthians', in J. D.G. DUNN and J. W. ROGERSON (eds.), *Eerdmans Commentary on the Bible* (Grand Rapids, MI: W.B. Eerdmans, 2003), 1314–52.

because he directly confronted a firmly established social norm. One should bear in mind again that while Paul's main argument was ultimately theological, the cause of the Corinthian crisis had deep roots in the social. Since Paul's intention was to invert the social ethos of those who were involved in the divisions, his rhetorical approach was understandably and appropriately paradoxical.

1.18 Ὁ λόγος γὰρ ὁ τοῦ σταυροῦ τοῖς μὲν ἀπολλυμένοις μωρία ἐστίν, τοῖς δὲ σῳζομένοις ἡμῖν δύναμις θεοῦ ἐστιν. *('For the message of the cross is foolishness to those who are perishing, but to us who are being saved it is the power of God')*

The Greek γὰρ ('for') in 1.18 is intended to link 1.18–31 with preceding 1.17. In 1.17, Paul emphasizes that his mission was primarily the preaching of the gospel. He did it 'not with eloquent wisdom (οὐκ ἐν σοφίᾳ λόγου), so that the cross of Christ might not be emptied of its power (ἵνα μὴ κενωθῇ ὁ σταυρὸς τοῦ Χριστοῦ)' (1.17b). With this statement in 1.17b, Paul is already setting a sharp contrast between his manner of proclamation and the style of his Corinthian critics who cherished 'eloquent wisdom', in line with what would have naturally appealed to their audience. This point will be returned to in more detail in reference to rhetoric.

Ὁ λόγος ὁ τοῦ σταυροῦ ('the message of the cross') here clearly referred to Paul's gospel message and the emphasis was deliberately on 'the cross', which is the heart of the matter in Paul's response to the Corinthian crisis in 1.18–31. It was precisely this point that was regarded as μωρία by many in the audience.

In most of the Wisdom writings, for instance, in Proverbs and Psalms, the word ἄφρων is used almost exclusively for the fool.[4] In Philo's writings the concept of folly refers to all worldly wisdom.[5]

Welborn argues that the term μωρία implies 'stupidity' rather than 'absurdity' in Paul's time and its social stigma was not generally associated with the English word 'folly'. The term μωρία 'designated the attitude and behaviour of a particular social type: the lower class moron. The "foolishness" of this social type consisted in a weakness or deficiency of intellect, often coupled with a physical grotesqueness. Because the concept of the laughable in the Greek-Roman world was grounded in contemplation of the base and defective, those who possessed these characteristics were deemed to be "foolish."'[6] As such, what Paul actually meant to say was

---

[4] The fools are those who lack true knowledge of God, and thus fail to acknowledge God as God. BERTRAM, *TDNT* 4. 833.
[5] Philo, *Cher.* 116; *Leg. All.* 2.70.
[6] WELBORN, *Fool*, 1–2.

that the message of the cross was regarded by the cultural elite of his day as 'a coarse and vulgar joke'.[7]

Welborn's point leads on to a question concerning who first labelled his message with this word. Was μωρία used in the Corinthian correspondence as a defensive reaction, that is those who rejected the message of the cross had previously levelled this charge? Or was it somehow 'preemptive', employed by the messenger himself who understood from the start that both the content and manner of his proclamation would arouse such negative reaction? Welborn thinks that μωρία was probably applied to Paul by certain members of the Corinthian church to describe the impression they had about the apostle and his gospel. The term could also be a judgment of Paul's critics upon his preaching.[8] Because Paul's allegedly unimpressive physical appearance and manner of speech could have easily caused his critics to apply the term μωρία to him personally as well as to his message, Welborn's point may well be correct.

In 1.18, Paul is very specific that the message of the cross is μωρία to those who are 'perishing'. This naturally leads to a more likely possibility, namely, Paul would have been alert and culturally astute enough to perceive that his message of the cross would initially be viewed contemptuously as 'foolishness' by much of his audience. This possibility should be taken more seriously in the context of the current social ethos and how wide-spread views on crucifixion and noble death were in the period. One might consider, for instance, that if the death of Socrates was commonly regarded as noble, it would be sheer foolishness to claim that the one who died the most ignoble death on the cross could in any way be the saviour of the world and the Son of God.

The message of the cross is central to Pauline theology in the Corinthian correspondence and also, in varying degrees, in other Pauline writings. Crucifixion language is distinctively Pauline and unlike other references to the death of Jesus it is exclusively used by Paul in polemical situations.[9] Although Paul's description of the gospel as 'foolishness' is only found in one epistle (1 Cor 1.18–25, 27; 2.14; 3.18–19; 4.10), it has played a crucial role in the history of Christian thought.[10]

Historical research has shown that the term 'folly' is nowhere connected with the cross in pre-Christian literature, whether in Greek or Latin tradition. In the ancient world the cross was described with words such as: terrible, infamous, barren, criminal, and an evil instrument. Moreover, cruci-

---

[7] WELBORN, *Fool*, 2.

[8] WELBORN, *Fool*, 102–03.

[9] Rom. 6.6; 1 Cor. 1.17, 18; 2.2; 2 Cor. 13.4; Gal. 2.19; 3.1, 13; 5.11; 6.12, 14; Phil. 2.8; 3.16. C. B. COUSAR, *A Theology of the Cross: The Death of Jesus in the Pauline Letters* (Minneapolis: Fortress, 1990), 23.

[10] WELBORN, *Fool*, 15.

fixion was regarded as cruel and disgusting, shameful, the supreme penalty and the most wretched of deaths. But nowhere was the cross associated with 'foolishness'. Paul's expression about the message of the cross in 1 Corinthians was therefore unique, not only in Pauline writings, but also within the New Testament.[11] For that matter, μωρία is not found as such in the Old Testament.

It is worthwhile at this juncture to return to a point made by Welborn. He points out that as language of the cross emerges in Paul's message, writers such as Cicero and Varro attest that such vocabulary was cruel, disgusting and the cultural elite of the Roman world would not have wanted to hear it. Welborn describes the cross strikingly as 'an ominous lacuna at the centre of public discourse.'[12] As such, Paul, the 'fool' for Christ's sake, must have been thought to have turned the world upside down by describing his gospel most provocatively as 'the message of the cross' (1 Cor. 1.18). Paul chooses such a single phrase knowing full well that this expression would surely be regarded by those who were perishing as utter μωρία (1.18). When Paul preaches his message, one can begin to imagine how vulgar and utterly shocking the language of cross would have sounded to the educated Corinthians.[13]

Studies of other NT documents, including Paul's earlier wrings such as 1 Thessalonians, indicate that cross language does not occur in pre-Pauline kerygmatic formulac. But the case is very different when it comes to the Corinthian correspondence (e.g. 1.13, 17, 18, 23; 2.2, 8).[14]

For Paul, the decision to use the language of the cross was never casual or incidental. One should assume that it was only after careful consideration that Paul had finally decided (ἔκρινα) to know nothing among the Corinthians 'except Jesus and him crucified' (1 Cor. 2.2). In view of crucifixion and noble death in antiquity, there must be a certain rationale behind Paul's deliberate choice of the cross in his response to the Corinthian crisis. One may even be tempted to conjecture that Paul could have intended to use the cross as a kind of 'shock' tactic.[15] Some of the main problems in the Corinthian church, such as church divisions, the Corinthians' preoccupation with power and social status, as well as their low estimation of Paul, were clear indications that they were still very much entrenched in their traditional social ethos and incapable or unwilling to see past it.

For Paul the herald, 'the message of the cross' is never neutral. It demands a crucial response from the hearer. They could either reject it to

---

[11] WELBORN, *Fool*, 21–23.

[12] WELBORN, *Fool*, 251.

[13] WELBORN, *Fool*, 252.

[14] WELBORN, *Fool*, 252.

[15] HORRELL, *The Social Ethos*, 132.

their own ultimate destruction, or receive it for their own salvation. This is clearly the intent and force of Paul's statement in 1.18. One's response to the message of the cross would subsequently divide humanity into two entirely different categories: those who were 'perishing' and those who were 'being saved'. Moreover, the rejection and reception of the message also represented two diametrically opposed world views; one 'of the world' (1.20), and the other 'of God' (1.21). In Paul's view, a person's positive response to the message was actually not entirely an arbitrary human perception, because it was 'spiritually discerned' (πνευματικῶς ἀνακρίνεται, 2.14).

The Greek σταυροῦ in the phrase ὁ λόγος γὰρ ὁ τοῦ σταυροῦ is genitive. It is probably intended to denote the theme of Paul's gospel message, namely, the core of Paul's message is the cross itself. Hence Charles Kingsley Barrett comments: 'the gospel is simply a placarding (cf. Gal. 3.1) of Christ crucified; its effects are twofold: it is foolishness to those who are on the way to destruction, but to us who are on the way to salvation it is God's power (cf. 2 Cor. 2.15f.).'[16] The phrase – 'the message of the cross' – as a description of the gospel message is first found in Paul's writing. The term 'the word' or 'the message' (ὁ λόγος) seems to refer to the form or manner of Paul's preaching while 'the cross' in the genitive (τοῦ σταυροῦ) means the core content of the message proclaimed.

Anthony Thiselton has argued that one may define Paul's gospel with the cross.[17] Hans Conzelmann sets forth a near identical view that the word of the cross (2.1f.) describes the content of the gospel.[18] Litfin makes a further point that Paul wants to keep the message and the cross together, stating that: 'the repeated article in the construction serves to prevent the focus from shifting away from form to content and balances the stress between the two.'[19] This point should not be taken lightly because, as will be demonstrated further below, the critics of Paul focused on both the core content of his message and the manner of his proclamation. Paul was apparently very conscious of this in his response. Thus, for example in 1.17, the phrase 'not with eloquent wisdom' refers to the manner of Paul's proclamation, and 'the cross of Christ' essentially means the core content of the gospel. While some distinction between the two may be valid, it is, however, neither necessary nor helpful to press the issue too hard, since in the case of Paul, the content of the gospel and the manner of its proclamation

---

[16] BARRETT, *The First Epistle to the Corinthians* (London: Adam & Charles Black, 19-68), 19.

[17] A. C. THISELTON, *The First Epistle to the Corinthians: A Commentary on the Greek Text* (Carlisle: Paternoster Press, 2000), 154.

[18] H. CONZELMANN, *1 Corinthians: A Commentary* on the First Epistle to the Corinthians (Hermeneia; Philadelphia: Fortress Press, 1975), 41.

[19] LITFIN, *Proclamation*, 194.

could not be artificially separated. The paradoxical nature of the message is particularly clear and is also pointed out by Horrell who writes: 'the symbolic order of the gospel, as Paul sees it, centred upon the cross of Christ, inverts the values of the dominant social order. Anyone who wants to count themselves "in" must cease to regard themselves as strong and wise "in this age" and become weak and foolish in order to discover the power of God.'[20]

The words 'perishing' and 'being saved' also seem intended to cause those this-worldly Corinthians to think of the eschatological dimension of the message of the cross, a dimension that was in danger of being forgotten in the Corinthians' many preoccupations and problems. Conzelmann suggests that the two contrasting present participles – 'perishing' and 'being saved' – are eschatologically defined.[21] This is in fact understandable since the crucifixion of Christ itself is an eschatological event. For that matter, Paul's sense of the *eschaton* may be felt even in his salutation: '... as you wait for the revealing (ἀποκάλυψιν) of our Lord Jesus Christ.... He will also strengthen you to the end (τέλους) so that you may be blameless on the day of our Lord Jesus Christ' (1.7, 8).

Beside the strong contrast between 'who are perishing' and those 'who are being saved', the verbal form of the expression 'who are being saved' is also worth noting. The Greek verb σῳζομένοις is a present participle, and it might well be intended by Paul as a reminder to the Corinthians that Christian salvation was still a process and not yet a full reality, humanly speaking. While eschatologically it is correct to regard the Christians as having been saved already, it is equally true to think that it is still not yet, existentially speaking. Here lies the tension in the Christian's experience. This point may have special meaning in the Corinthian context because certain members of the church thought that they had already reached full maturity or had arrived at the final point (4.8–10). 'Already you have all you want! Already you have become rich! Quite apart from us you have become kings!' Paul laments in 4.8 with a touch of sarcasm.

Paul divides people into two categories according to their response to the message of cross: lost and saved. Richard Hays makes the observation that Paul's sharp division is made from the apocalyptic perspective.[22] For Paul, the cross not only makes this new division, it also inaugurates the new age, so that the foolishness of the cross now belongs to the old age mentality of those who were perishing.[23] Moreover, the expression 'who

---

[20] HORRELL, *The Social Ethos*, 137.

[21] CONZELMANN, *1 Corinthians*, 41.

[22] R. B. HAYS, *First Corinthians* (Louisville KY: Wesminster John Knox Press, 1997), 28.

[23] G. D. FEE, *The First Epistle to the Corinthians* (Grand Rapids MI: William B. Eerdmans, 1987), 69.

are being saved' also indicates the crucial issue of Christian identity. As noted previously, church divisions in Corinth which greatly troubled Paul (1.10–17) were also a serious identity crisis. Otherwise, they would not have pledged their allegiance to human personalities such as Paul, Apollos and Cephas. As Christians, and such should their true identity be, Christ alone deserves their total allegiance. On this point Pogoloff makes the comment that: 'the contrast in 1.18 between those who are perishing (ἀπολλυμένοι) and those who are being saved (σῳζομένοι) not only moves the discourse from cultural to community identity, it also locates that identity within the larger narrative of God's salvific activity.'[24]

Paul's use of antithesis and paradox in the Corinthian correspondence is striking, and the passage under consideration (1.18–31) is only the beginning of his use of it.[25] Such a use of paradox, one should consider, is a sign of the considerable rhetorical skills of Paul. At the very beginning of the passage Paul already sets up a profound antithesis between the 'foolishness' of the message of the cross and 'the power of God'.[26] Caution should be taken so that this antithesis is not misunderstood, he is not saying that the cross itself is foolishness. The real issue is perception about this form of capital punishment: the body language, social implications, prejudices and symbols that were associated with it. It is 'the message of the cross', which necessarily centred round the crucified Christ, that constituted foolishness as far as unbelievers were concerned.

Greco-Roman society attached great importance to word, speech and message (λόγος). In such a social context no *logos* was actually 'neutral' or value-free. In a society which was status-conscious, *logos* could often determine a person's worth in society. As such, the message (λόγος) of the cross could only belong to the lowest and most despised of the Greco-Roman society, such as slaves and criminals. It must therefore have been an astonishing and, indeed, horrendous act when Paul openly claimed that such a *logos* as this was 'the power of God' (δύναμις θεοῦ)! But such was his paradoxical message an approach to presenting his case.

Once Paul's antithesis and paradox were skilfully presented, they are established and he continues to use terms and expressions in his own special way. Within his own structure, he does not contradict himself. Thus, human wisdom suddenly becomes foolishness, and divine foolishness becomes wisdom. In the end there is virtually no substantial difference between God's wisdom or power and God's weakness, as he seeks to demon-

---

[24] POGOLOFF, *Logos*, 158.

[25] See MITCHELL, *Reconciliation*, 211–12.

[26] See R. W. FUNK, *Language, Hermeneutic, and Word of God: the Problem of Language in the New Testament and Contemporary Theology* (New York: Harper & Row, 1966), 302–03.

strate in the verses that follow. Pickett describes the paradox – weakness of
God (1.25) and power of God (1.18) – as synonymous: they are both defined in terms of the cross. The social values denoted by the antithesis of
folly-wisdom and weakness-strength are superseded by a different set of
values centred on the cross.[27] Thiselton also remarks on this antithesis, arguing that it constitutes the key to Paul's argument. Especially helpful is
his observation that the wisdom-folly contrast played a crucial role in the
cultural content and would undoubtedly have 'represented theological slo-
gans or catchwords.'

Paul's antithetical and paradoxical way of writing is aimed at turning
the social ethos of the time on its head. This drastic manoeuvre was apparently necessary because the troublesome Corinthians were still very much
fixed within the current social ethos. On Paul's deliberate inversion of the
Corinthians' social ethos, James Louis Martyn comments that: 'the gospel
is God's advent! And for that reason, those who are being redeemed discover that in the event of the gospel God invades their wills, rearranging
the very *fundamenta* of their existence. As event, the gospel is inseparable
from God because God himself comes on the scene in that proclamation in
the fullness of his power.'[28] Once the social ethos of the Corinthians was
turned upside down, the message of the cross is no longer within the purview of human evaluation or judgment, but is now part of the divine.

1.19 γέγραπται γάρ· ἀπολῶ τὴν σοφίαν τῶν σοφῶν καὶ τὴν σύνεσιν
τῶν συνετῶν ἀθετήσω. *('For it is written, "I will destroy the wisdom of
the wise, and the discernment of the discerning I will thwart."')*

Paul continues to dethrone worldly wisdom in its totality with a quotation
from Isa. 29.14 in 1.19. With this quotation his horizon shifts far beyond
the boundary of Corinth and on to universal views about divine judgment
on the wisdom of this world. But Paul obviously does not want to get himself entangled in the endless discussion and debate about the whole 'wisdom' issue at this stage. Despite his rejection of worldly wisdom, Paul
qualifies his point a little later, writing that 'among the mature, we do
speak wisdom, though it is not a wisdom of this age.... But ... God's wisdom' (2.6, 7). Wolfgang Schrage highlights the significance of the critical
destruction of worldly wisdom, which is not indicative of irrationality
(*credo quia absurdum* 'I believe it because it is absurd'). He explains that
it means instead that the cross is actually the sign to define all wisdom and
the scope of all 'faith-implied understanding and all theology.'[29] Unfortu-

---

[27] PICKETT, *The Cross*, 71.

[28] MARTYN, *Theological Issues in the Letters of Paul* (Edinburgh: T. & T. Clark,
1997), 219.

[29] *'Die kritische Destruktion der Weltweisheit bedeutet also keine Irrationalität, kein
credo quia absurdum. Wohl aber bedeutet es, dass das Kreuz tatsächlich Vorzeichen al-*

nately, very few, if any, of the Corinthians in Paul's judgment were in fact mature (τελείοις, 2.6). Paul makes it clear in 1.17 that his proclamation of the gospel was 'not with eloquent wisdom' (οὐκ ἐν σοφίᾳ λόγου), so that the cross of Christ might not be emptied of its power. As such, Paul desires the faith of the Corinthians to rest 'not on human wisdom but on the power of God' (μὴ ἦ ἐν σοφίᾳ ἀνθρώπων ἀλλ' ἐν δυνάμει θεοῦ, 2.5).[30]

In view of the crucial connection between 1.18 and 1.19, it is important to take the Greek γάρ ('for') in 1.19 seriously. Paul already states in 1.18 that the preaching of the message of the cross has resulted in the vital division of people into two distinct categories (i.e. saved and perishing). At first glance, this division in 1.18 merely appears like a statement of fact, resulting from two diametrically opposed responses to the message. Charles Cousar reads this in light of Isa. 29.14 in 1.19–20.[31] Thus, the word γάρ in 1.19 suggests that the division mentioned in the previous verse does not just occur as an empirical fact, but must ultimately be traced back to the sovereign God. In the words of Cousar: 'it is a part of the divine strategy to expose the wisdom of this age (1.19).'[32]

1.19 has a direct quotation from Isa. 29.14 (LXX: ἀπολῶ τὴν σοφίαν τῶν σοφῶν καὶ τὴν σύνεσιν τῶν συνετῶν κρύψω, 'I will destroy the wisdom of the wise, and will hide the understanding of the prudent'), except the verb κρύψω ('I will hide', 'conceal', 'keep secret') is replaced by ἀθετήσω ('I will set aside', 'bring to nought', 'nullify', 'confound'). In Barrett's view, Paul's variation may be due to Ps. 32.10 (LXX: κύριος δι̑ ασκεδάζει βουλὰς ἐθνῶν ἀθετεῖ δὲ λογισμοὺς λαῶν καὶ ἀθετεῖ βουλὰς ἀρχόντων, 'The Lord frustrates the counsels of the nations; he brings to nought also the reasonings of the peoples, and brings to nought the counsels of princes.'), in order to make the quotation more suitable to his argument.[33] This is because ἀθετέω is a much stronger verb than κρύπτω and has the same force as ἀπόλλυμι ('I destroy').

---

ler Weisheit und Horizont allen im Glauben implizierten Verstehens und aller Theologie ist.' W. SCHRAGE, *Der Erste Brief an die Korinther* (Zürich: Benziger Verlag, 1991), 192.

[30] Paul even warns the arrogant Corinthians that he would soon visit them, God willing, and if he did, he would find out 'not the talk of these arrogant people but their power' (οὐ τὸν λόγον τῶν πεφυσιωμένων ἀλλὰ τὴν δύναμιν, 4.19). This was because 'the kingdom of God depends not on talk but on power' (οὐ γὰρ ἐν λόγῳ ἡ βασιλεία τοῦ θεοῦ ἀλλ' ἐν δυνάμει, 4.20). If not for the fact that the Corinthians were so preoccupied with 'wisdom', so that Paul had to deal with it, he may well have chosen to talk about something else, or simply bypass it. The apostle's main concern is the cross of Christ and the divine power that it demonstrates.

[31] COUSAR, *Theology*, 29.

[32] COUSAR, *Theology*, 29.

[33] BARRETT, *The First Epistle*, 52.

1.19 not only enforces Paul's point in v.18, but also serves as a stern
warning to those who considered themselves 'wise' and who regarded the
message of the cross as μωρία.[34] Thiselton acknowledges the suitability of
the parallel which Paul draws between the context of Isaiah and his own:
'against the background of Isaiah 29 the contrast suggests a parallel between the vulnerability and fragility of time spent devising strategies for
self-presentation or self-enhancement as against seeking alignment of the
self with the divine purpose.'[35] In the Isaianic context, Isa. 29.14 from
which Paul quotes, belongs to Yahweh's judgment oracle against Judah
whose national leaders had put their trust in their own human wisdom and
devices by entering into a crucial treaty with Egypt rather than believing in
Yahweh through the words of His prophet. What is involved here is a 'wisdom' issue, that is human wisdom against that of Yahweh's as the original
text states: 'so I will do amazing things with this people, shocking and
amazing. The wisdom of their wise shall perish, and the discernment of the
discerning shall be hidden' (Isa. 29.14).

The emphasis of Yahweh's stern pronouncement is clearly on the destruction of the wisdom of the wise. Similarly, in the Corinthian case, the
crucial matter was also that of wisdom so that as long as human wisdom
prevailed, the message of the cross would be regarded as foolishness and
consequently rejected by the wise. Such wisdom, as was the case in Isa.
29.14, must be destroyed since 'the world did not know God through [its
own] wisdom'. The reason Isa. 29.14 is so attractive to Paul becomes,
upon closer scrutiny, quite apparent.

It is also noteworthy that Judah's reliance on her own human wisdom
was inseparably linked to the nation's lack of true worship and credible
spirituality. Human wisdom could be said to be the very root cause. Isa.
29.13 declares: 'The Lord said: Because these people drew near with their
mouths and honour me with their lips, while their hearts are far from me,
and their worship of me is a human commandment learned by rote.' The
historical contexts of Isaiah and Corinth were admittedly much different.
However, similar to the Isaianic case, the wisdom problem in Corinth was
also closely related to the important matters of worship and spiritual matters. Church divisions, the disorderliness in the administration of the
Lord's supper (ch. 11) and the abuse and misuse of spiritual gifts
(χαρίσματα in chs. 12–14) were clear examples. The words 'mouths' and
'lips' in Isa. 29.13 could remind one of human speech and eloquence,
through which human wisdom found expression. It was precisely in the
area of speech or eloquence that the Corinthians had serious trouble,
among other problems. Ironically, it was also particularly in 'speech and

---

[34] FEE, *The First Epistle*, 69–70.
[35] THISELTON, *The First Epistle*, 162.

knowledge of every kind' (ἐν παντὶ λόγῳ καὶ πάσῃ γνώσει) that the Corinthians had been most enriched as Paul himself readily acknowledges at the beginning of his letter (1.5). It is therefore natural and understandable that Paul should deal most firmly with 'wisdom' and 'speech' problems.

Finally, in both the Isaianic and Corinthian cases, the judgment was clear: the overthrowing of human wisdom and the vindication of God's wisdom; and in the Corinthian case, in and through Christ crucified. Paul in 1.19 quotes the second half of Isa. 29.14. But the first half of the verse was also meaningful when applied to the Corinthian situation, especially in relation to 'the message of the cross.' This was what the Lord said in Isa. 29.14a: לכן הנני יוסף להפליא את-העם-הזה הפלא ופלא ('so I will again do amazing things with this people, shocking and amazing.')[36] As the study on crucifixion in antiquity has shown, it was a most 'shocking' form of execution. But the utterly amazing thing was that God in His wisdom had now used this most shocking form of execution as His means of human salvation. While undoubtedly shocking to those perishing, who regarded it as μωρία, it was amazing to those being saved.

1.20 ποῦ σοφός; ποῦ γραμματεύς; ποῦ συζητητὴς τοῦ αἰῶνος τούτου; οὐχὶ ἐμώρανεν ὁ θεὸς τὴν σοφίαν τοῦ κόσμου; *('Where is the one who is wise? Where is the scribe? Where is the debater of this age? Has not God made foolish the wisdom of the world?')*

The purview of Paul's concern becomes even clearer in the next few verses (1.20–25) where he refers, in general terms, to the 'wise' and 'the scribe' as well as 'the debater of this age' and 'the wisdom of the world' (τὴν σοφίαν τοῦ κόσμου, 1.20). Similarly, the terms 'Greeks' and 'Jews' (1.22–24) must also be put in broader contexts. Here the insight of Martyn is helpful when recognizing that 'there are two opposing worlds in Paul's apocalyptic, that is the Old Age and the new creation,' and that 'Paul sees that the coming of Christ is the invasion of Christ. And as invasion, that event has unleashed a cosmic conflict, indeed *the* cosmic conflict.'[37]

Of significance is that Paul's emphasis is on God's wisdom which was revealed and powerfully demonstrated in and through Christ crucified as well as on the salvation of those who believed. There is no suggestion in Paul's argument that the Christian believers or those who are being saved have now been made wise or appear wise in human terms by virtue of

---

[36] LXX Isaiah 29.14: διὰ τοῦτο ἰδοὺ ἐγὼ προσθήσω τοῦ μεταθεῖναι τὸν λαὸν τοῦτον καὶ μεταθήσω αὐτοὺς καὶ ἀπολῶ τὴν σοφίαν τῶν σοφῶν καὶ τὴν σύνεσιν τῶν συνετῶν κρύψω ('Therefore behold, I will once again deal marvelously with this people, wondrously marvelous. And the wisdom of their wise men shall perish, and the discernment of their discerning men shall be concealed.').

[37] MARTYN, *Theological Issues*, 281–82.

their salvation. In fact, the believers would continue to be looked upon as foolish (1.27) by the unbelieving world as long as the message of the cross continued to be regarded as such by it (1.18).

The rhetorical questions in 1.20 suggest that Paul was going to elaborate on his argument against human wisdom from the perspective of the cross. Paul's questions – 'where is the one who is wise? Where is the scribe?' – may have OT Scriptures in the background, e.g. Isa. 19.12 (LXX: ποῦ εἰσιν νῦν οἱ σοφοί σου; 'where are now your wise men?') and 33.18 (ποῦ εἰσιν οἱ γραμματικοί; 'where are the scribes?'). The use of the interrogative was a form of argument which could be found also in early Jewish literature.[38]

Paul's reference to 'the wise' (σοφός), 'the debater' (συζητητὴς) and 'the scribe' (γραμματεύς) in 1.20 is polemical.[39] Based on 1.22–24 where Jews and Greeks are both mentioned, it is reasonable to suggest that 'the wise' and 'the debater' probably refer more to Greeks and their philosophers or rhetoricians, with 'the scribe' being more representative of the Jews. These three terms were also general enough to include Paul's critics in Corinth. It should be noted that the word συζητητὴς ('debater') occurs only here in the NT and in Ignatius (Eph. 18.1).[40] The word συζητητὴς, which may be translated 'skilful debater', seems to suggest that Paul is conscious that he was dealing with those who were well educated in rhetoric and were probably among his critics who had caused serious divisions in Corinth.

The phrases τοῦ αἰῶνος τούτου ('of this age') and τοῦ κόσμου τούτου ('of the world') occur in Paul's writings rather often: 'age' (αἰών) (31x), 'world' (κόσμος) (47x). Sometimes these terms are used by Paul synonymously. Similarly, Paul also uses expressions like 'wisdom of the world', 'wisdom of this age' and 'wisdom of this world' quite freely (1 Cor. 1.20; 2.6; 3.19).[41]

Barclay argues that '"this world" and "the present age" are spoken of in consistently derogatory terms throughout the letter, for they, together with their rulers, are doomed to imminent destruction (1.18–2.8; 3.18–20;

---

[38] CONZELMANN, *1 Corinthians*, 43. Cf. Baruch 3.15f, 29f; Plutarch, *Cons. ad Apoll.* 110d: *Ubi sunt, qui ante nos …*? 'Where are those before us …?'

[39] See A. ROBERTSON and A. PLUMMER, *A Critical and Exegetical Commentary: First Epistle of St Paul to the Corinthians* (Edinburgh: T. & T. Clark, 1967), 19–20. CONZELMANN, *1 Corinthians*, 43. THISELTON, *The First Epistle*, 164.

[40] CONZELMANN, *1 Corinthians*, 43. According to Greeven, the term συζητητὴς is used technically in secular literature to denote philosophical investigation, this meaning might be implied in Paul's reference to the search of the Greeks after wisdom in 1 Cor. 1.22 (*TDNT* 2.893).

[41] H. SASSE, *TDNT* 1.203.

7.31).'[42] Adams suggests that Paul adeptly changes the predictable ideological associations of κόσμος to his own advantage. When Paul joins κόσμος with ὁ αἰὼν οὗτος, the previous order which has been overthrown with the apocalyptic judgment of the cross, he sets the dominant social system normally associated with, and legitimised by, κόσμος in contrast with God's new order.[43] For Paul, the new 'age' or 'world' had already arrived with the crucifixion of Christ and his subsequent resurrection, although the end was still not yet. This point is already made in 1.8 where Paul refers to 'the day of our Lord Jesus Christ' (ἐν τῇ ἡμέρᾳ τοῦ κυρίου ἡμῶν Ἰησοῦ [Χριστοῦ]) and later in chapter 15 with regard to the believers' future resurrection.

Hermann Sasse discusses that while the OT and Jewish ideas are taken over by the NT, there are significant new developments because of the Christ event (cf. Heb. 1.10ff; 13.8; Rev. 1.17). That is, through the crucifixion and resurrection of Christ, eternity was already a present reality.[44] In this regard, Thiselton makes a point about the preferred translation of 'this world order' (τοῦ αἰῶνος τούτου) and writes: 'Apocalyptic contrasts express in temporal terms realities which in effect amount to a difference between two world orders.... Hence what appears as "folly" or "weakness" as it is judged within the values and frame of the old world order ... at once appears as "wisdom" and divine "power". The three status-related terms sage, expert, and debater receive a different evaluation within a different world order.'[45]

From what has been considered so far, it is not difficult to understand why Paul makes a sharp contrast between this age and the age to come in relation to wisdom and power issues, because two entirely different world views are involved.

Paul's follow-up question in 1.20b – 'Has not God made foolish the wisdom of the world?' (οὐχὶ ἐμώρανεν ὁ θεὸς τὴν σοφίαν τοῦ κόσμου τούτου;) – might actually be regarded as a kind of rhetorical answer to the first three in 1.20a. More precisely, God had indeed 'made foolish' (ἐμώρανεν) the wisdom of the world, including the wisdom of the σοφός, γραμματεύς and συζητητής through Christ crucified (1.23). The point of divine initiative (or pre-emptive act) must be clearly noted here. That is, God already had, in and through Christ crucified, taken the initiative to make foolish the wisdom of the world. In other words, such a crucial act was not an afterthought of God, as if God had made foolish the wisdom of

[42] BARCLAY, 'Thessalonica and Corinth', 59.

[43] ADAMS, *Constructing the World: A Study in Paul's Cosmological Language* (Edinburgh: T & T Clark, 2000), 113.

[44] SASSE, *TDNT* 1.202.

[45] THISELTON, *The First Epistle*, 165.

the world because the world in its wisdom had first regarded the message of the cross as 'foolish'. This is not the case, well before Paul's message of the cross was proclaimed, and at the very crucifixion of Christ, God had already 'made foolish the wisdom of the world'. This point may help to determine if the idea of 'foolishness' was first ascribed to the message of the cross by those who had rejected it (Welborn's position) or something which had already been anticipated by Paul who was keenly aware of the world's attitude towards the cross and crucifixion. The latter was quite obviously the case.

Given Paul's Jewish as well as Greco-Roman backgrounds, it is reasonable to assume that Paul (or Saul then) would most probably have shared the prejudice of both Jews and Romans concerning the cross in general and the crucified Christ in particular. The suggestion that Paul had already anticipated the rejection of 'the message of the cross' is thoroughly consistent with the study of crucifixion in antiquity and the concept of 'noble death' in the Greco-Roman tradition as well as the social ethos of Paul's time.

With regards to ἐμώρανεν, Conzelmann points out that Paul does not argue that God shows the world to be foolish, but rather that God makes the world's wisdom foolish.[46] The entire known world of Paul's audience has now been turned around. Hays, appreciating this point too, calls the cross the beginning point for an 'epistemological revolution'.[47] Paul's revolution provides the categories for a new and critical evaluation of divisions in the church. On a foundational level, one's understanding of wisdom, wealth and power are changed. When one comprehends the paradoxical logic of the argument, how the world is fundamentally perceived is altered.

Rhetorical eloquence was highly sought after and a respected skill in Paul's time. Eloquent orators in the period were to be compared with stars and even superstars in the contemporary world of entertainment or sports. It must, therefore, have been shocking to hear Paul say that God in Christ had now made this foolishness. 'Where are they now?' Paul asked rhetorically and most solemnly (cf. Isa. 19.12) about the eloquent orators.

---

[46] CONZELMANN, *1 Corinthians*, 43. 'Make foolish' (μωραίνω), is intransitive in classical Greek. The sense is illumined by v.18; for the content, see Isa. 44.25.

[47] HAYS, *First Corinthians*, 27.

1.21 ἐπειδὴ γὰρ ἐν τῇ σοφίᾳ τοῦ θεοῦ οὐκ ἔγνω ὁ κόσμος διὰ τῆς σοφίας τὸν θεόν, εὐδόκησεν ὁ θεὸς διὰ τῆς μωρίας τοῦ κηρύγματος σῶσαι τοὺς πιστεύοντας· *('For since, in the wisdom of God, the world did not know God through wisdom, God decided, through the foolishness of our proclamation, to save those who believe.')*

The opening statement in 1.21a implies that true knowledge about God did not belong to the will or autonomy of the world. Even if the world had the desire or will to know God through its own wisdom, such knowledge would still be denied them. Cousar comments on 1.21 that it 'is unequivocal about the incapacity of human wisdom'.[48] True knowledge of God, or about God, was a matter of divine initiative and it could only be given to the world as His gift. Paul's statement makes it clear that it was 'in the wisdom of God' (ἐν τῇ σοφίᾳ τοῦ θεοῦ) that such should be the case. The world's failure to know God 'through [its own] wisdom' happened within God's sovereign master plan.

David Garland finds six citations of Scripture in 1.18–3.23 (1.19, 31; 2.9, 16; 3.19, 20). Each of these citations make the same point that the world simply could not comprehend God's way through its own wisdom.[49] What has been said so far about the inadequacy or failure of human wisdom is also consistent with what Paul writes about divine revelation and the Spirit in 2.6–16. But the end of a person's road is the beginning of God's way. The last statement of 1.21 brought truly good news through divine wisdom, because 'God decided, through the foolishness of our proclamation, to save those who believe'. There is something paradoxical and ironical here: 'the wisdom of God' was revealed 'through the foolishness' (διὰ τῆς μωρίας) of the Christian proclamation.

The overall context of the Corinthian correspondence indicates that foolishness refers to both the content (message) and its proclamation ('not with eloquent wisdom', 1.17). Litfin contends that the term κήρυγμα, which occurs in 1.21, is crucial and indicative of Paul's two-fold emphasis on form and content.[50] Indeed, κήρυγμα is synonymous with the word of the cross found in 1.18. Similar to the first instance of μωρία, a few verses later it is not simply the cross which is foolishness, but also the proclamation of the cross. According to current rhetorical theory and practice, the very manner or form of Paul's presentation was also unimpressive and unacceptable. Paul was evidently conscious of this and needed to respond to it, which is why he repeatedly emphasises that he was sent 'to proclaim the gospel … not with eloquent wisdom' (εὐαγγελίζεσθαι, οὐκ ἐν σοφίᾳ λόγου, 1.17) and that his 'speech and … proclamation were not with plau-

---

[48] COUSAR. *Theology*, 29.
[49] D. E. GARLAND, *1 Corinthians* (Grand Rapids: Baker Academic, 2003), 59.
[50] LITFIN, *Proclamation*, 198.

sible words of wisdom' (ὁ λόγος ... καὶ τὸ κήρυγμά μου οὐκ ἐν πειθοῖ[ς] σοφίας [λόγοις], 2.4).

In summary, Paul's concern is far more than just a comparison or contrast between human and divine wisdom, but more significantly the encounter of two world orders. This point is pivotal if one is to understand the nuances of how Paul's message of the cross functions to invert the current social ethos.

1.22 ἐπειδὴ καὶ Ἰουδαῖοι σημεῖα αἰτοῦσιν καὶ Ἕλληνες σοφίαν ζητοῦσιν, ('For Jews demand signs and Greeks desire wisdom,') 23 ἡμεῖς δὲ κηρύσσομεν Χριστὸν ἐσταυρωμένον, Ἰουδαίοις μὲν σκάνδαλον, ἔθνεσιν δὲ μωρίαν, ('*but we proclaim Christ crucified, a stumbling block to Jews and foolishness to Gentiles,*')

1.22 further explains why the message of the cross is regarded as foolishness by the world, in relation to Jew or Greek: 'For Jews demand signs and Greeks desire wisdom.' The Jews' request for signs (σημεῖα) is known from elsewhere in the New Testament, for instance Mark 8.11 (and parallels). In the present context, the perception of Jewish demands for signs is negative, and is taken as an indication of scepticism and unbelief with reference to the message of the cross. Similarly, the Greek desire for wisdom is also set forth in a negative way, with the implication that the message of the cross was foolishness to them.

The first δέ in 1.23 should be translated as a strong 'but', in order to make the contrast between the world's way of thinking and that of God's: '*but* we proclaim Christ crucified' (ἡμεῖς δὲ κηρύσσομεν Χριστὸν ἐσταυρωμένον). However, it is more than just a striking contrast. The force of the statement – 'but *we* proclaim Christ crucified' – suggests that it was Paul's (as well as his fellow messengers') most uncompromising determination to want to continue with the proclamation of the message about Christ crucified – despite its rejection by the world. The present tense of κηρύσσομεν also has this strong sense.

Conzelmann suggests that categorising humanity from a salvation history point of view as Jews and Greeks may be viewed as a 'Jewish equivalent for the Greek classification "Greeks and barbarians."'[51] Although Conzelmann's suggestion is helpful, it should be borne in mind that in the context of the present passage Paul's division of humankind into those 'who are perishing' and those 'who are being saved' (v.18) is infinitely more important. Paul's overall concern for the salvation and calling of 'both Jews and Greeks' (v.24) also far outweighs their respective interests: the Jews in signs and the Greeks in wisdom. Krister Stendahl also comments on Paul's division of humanity. Whereas the pre-Christian Paul once

---

[51] CONZELMANN, *1 Corinthians*, 47.

divided humankind into two parts (Jews and Gentiles), the Christian Paul
begins to use the word 'all' in his writings to include both parts. The mission of Paul should be seen in this context.[52]

The qualifying statement in 1.23 – 'a stumbling block to Jews and foolishness to Gentiles' – serves to reinforce the idea that the world's rejection
of the Christian message is no surprise to Paul from the very beginning and
such rejection would continue to be a matter of fact as long as the world
judged it through its own wisdom.

The word σκάνδαλον is only found in the LXX, NT and Christian writings, while σκανδάληθρον ('trap') has the Hebrew equivalent מכשול at
Qumran.[53] In Pauline writings the words σκάνδαλον and σκανδαλίζω appear not only in 1 Corinthians (1.23; 8.13), but also in Romans (9.33; 11.9;
14.13; cf. Gal. 5.11). Gustav Stählin detects a NT reconstruction of
σκάνδαλον: 'in the sphere of this possibility of opposing effects inherent
in Christ and His Gospel the word σκάνδαλον becomes a term ... in which
the main OT meanings – "occasion of guilt" and "cause of destruction" –
are fused into a total unity in the NT reconstruction – for in the NT unbelief is the basic sin.'[54] Stählin's point serves to highlight the gravity of
Paul's use of the term σκάνδαλον in the present Corinthian context, because the proclamation of 'Christ crucified' not only causes the unbelieving Jews to stumble, but the rejection of the message of the cross actually
leads to eternal damnation. This is clearly the force of the word 'perishing'
in 1.18.

As previously discussed (§2.4) in relation to crucifixion and the curse, a
vital link between the 'tree' in Deut. 21.23 (LXX) and the 'cross' in Gal.
3.13 may be established in pre-Christian times on the strength of one of the
Qumran texts. This also helps to explain why the cross of Christ was such
a σκάνδαλον for the unbelieving Jews.

1.24 αὐτοῖς δὲ τοῖς κλητοῖς, Ἰουδαίοις τε καὶ Ἕλλησιν, Χριστὸν
θεοῦ δύναμιν καὶ θεοῦ σοφίαν *('but to those who are the called, both
Jews and Greeks, Christ the power of God and the wisdom of God.')*

That Paul's contemporaries would find his message of the cross utterly offensive and foolish is made sense of in light of crucifixion and noble death
in antiquity. In this context, the δὲ in the opening statement of 1.24 should

---

[52] STENDAHL, *Paul*, 1–6.

[53] מכשול most often occurs in relation to iniquity, see 1QS ii 12, 17; 1QH iv 15; viii
35 (chains of stumbling); ix 21, 27; x 17; xvi 15; and 4Q415 (*4QInstruction*) 11 7 where
one's wife appears to be a stumbling block to her husband. CONZELMANN, *1 Corinthians*,
47, n. 79. See B. G. WOLD, *Women, Men and Angels: The Qumran Wisdom Document
Musar leMevin and its Allusions to Genesis Creation Traditions* (WUNT II/201; Tübingen: Mohr Siebeck, 2005), 226–30.

[54] G. STÄHLIN, *TDNT* 7.352–53.

be understood as a forceful 'but', just as the case in 1.23, and thus serves effectively to provide the strongest contrast between two diametrically opposed perceptions. In the context of the Corinthian polemics, 'called' (κλητοῖς) here could well serve as a reminder to the self-conceited Corinthians that not only was their present Christian identity a divine gift (cf. 1.2), but also the vital knowledge that 'Christ [was] the power of God and the wisdom of God' was also of divine origin, which was revealed in and through Christ crucified. 'Called' in 1.24 as well as in 1.2 is inclusive language and reminds the divided Corinthian congregation of the divinely given oneness and fellowship in Christ crucified. Moreover, as a called community in Christ, the Corinthian church should truly be liberated from the enslavement of the conventional social ethos, including the rigid classification of social stratification.

It is remarkable that Paul is not simply saying that the cross of Christ reveals the wisdom of God, but that Christ is 'the wisdom of God' (θεοῦ σοφίαν, 1.24b). Similarly, Christ crucified demonstrates not only the power of God, but is himself 'the power of God' (θεοῦ δύναμιν, 1.24b).

1.25 ὅτι τὸ μωρὸν τοῦ θεοῦ σοφώτερον τῶν ἀνθρώπων ἐστὶν καὶ τὸ ἀσθενὲς τοῦ θεοῦ ἰσχυρότερον τῶν ἀνθρώπων. *('For God's foolishness is wiser than human wisdom, and God's weakness is stronger than human strength.')*

The opening word ὅτι, which could simply be rendered 'for', initiates Paul's concluding statement for the whole of 1.18–25. This section (1.18–25) is not an isolated paragraph, because it has 1.13–17 as its background and 1.26–31 as its immediate follow-up.

'Wisdom' and 'foolishness' are strongly contrasted throughout much of 1.18–24. In Paul's reasoning and subtle argument throughout the passage, the focus on the cross remains sharp. Paul's concluding statement in 1.25 basically reasserts the points which he so profoundly made earlier. As such, what is new in 1.25 is not so much its content as Paul's slightly different way of expression. Instead of bringing human and divine wisdom yet again in sharp contrast, Paul now makes a comparison between the two: 'God's foolishness is *wiser* than human wisdom, and God's weakness is *stronger* than human strength.' But the force of the earlier contrast between (human) foolishness and (divine) wisdom, and between (human) weakness and (divine) strength is still being retained.

At first glance, Paul's teaching about 'God's foolishness' and 'God's weakness' appears as a kind of concession. If this is indeed the case, it could only serve rhetorically within Paul's argument. It was not that Paul himself really thought that there was any 'foolishness' or 'weakness' on the part of God, for that would be absolutely impossible for Paul. Paul's subtle argument was really this: *even granted* that 'foolishness' could be ascribed to God or His act, 'God's [so-called] foolishness was [still] *wiser than* [so-called] human wisdom'. The same is true about 'God's weakness'. If that is the case, both 'human wisdom' and 'human strength' appear even more worthless. Here lies the force of Paul's rhetorical argument.

Johannes Weiss convincingly argues that the definite article τὸ before μωρὸν ('foolishness') and ἀσθενές ('weakness') respectively serves to highlight the singularity of God's act, that is the death of Christ on the cross, which is understood by the audience as a sign of foolishness and weakness.[55]

With reference to the manifestation of divine power in weakness, Savage sees Paul as having very little choice but to respond to his worldly critics with: 'when I am weak, then I am strong'.[56] Savage describes the Corinthian church as being engulfed in a conflict between two diametrically opposed viewpoints: (1) the worldly outlook of the Corinthians and (2) Paul's own Christ-centred perspective. These are summarised as the 'wisdom of this age' and the 'wisdom of God'. Savage significantly concludes that it is 'precisely this conflict which seems to have evoked Paul's paradoxical teaching of power through weakness.'[57]

Having set the worldly wisdom in sharp contrast with the divine, Paul now returns to a direct address to the Corinthian Christians. He draws their attention specifically to their own humble background and God's gracious calling (κλῆσις) of them (1.26–31).

3.3 Absolutely No Grounds for Boasting by both Human and Divine Standards – Christ the Wisdom, Righteousness, Sanctification and Redemption (1.26–31)

1.26 Βλέπετε γὰρ τὴν κλῆσιν ὑμῶν, ἀδελφοί, ὅτι οὐ πολλοὶ σοφοὶ κατὰ σάρκα, οὐ πολλοὶ δυνατοί, οὐ πολλοὶ εὐγενεῖς· *('Consider your own call, brothers and sisters: not many of you were wise by human standards, not many were powerful, not many were of noble birth.')*

1.26 already serves as a key reference for NT scholars when commenting on the social background of early Christianity. In the words of Wilhelm

---

[55] 'Natürlich ist τὸ μωρὸν und τὸ ἀσθενές vom Standpoint der Juden und Heiden aus gesagt. Die neutr. Adjektiva brauchen nicht, wie etwa II Kor 4₁₇; 8₈; Phl 4₅ ... für das abstrakte Substantiv zu stehen (Torheit, Ohnmacht) – vielmehr wird die ganz bestimmte (daher der Artikel) Einzelbetätigung Gottes, nämlich der Kreuztod Christi, hervorgehoben, welche den Menschen als Zeichen der Torheit und Schwäche gilt.' J. WEISS, *Der Erste Korintherbrief* (Göttingen: Vandenhoeck & Ruprecht, 1910), 34.

[56] SAVAGE, *Power*, 189–90.

[57] SAVAGE, *Power*, 188.

Wuellner: 'No other single verse of the entire New Testament was more influential in shaping popular opinion and exegetical judgement alike on the social origins of early Christianity than 1 Corinthians 1.26.'[58] For Justin Meggitt, who is critical of the New Consensus, it is striking that both the Old and New Consensus have found here 'a keystone for their respective reconstructions of Christian origins.'[59]

In the 2nd century, Celsus alleged that Christianity was a movement of the lower classes, including Jesus himself who was only able to win his disciples among members of the lower strata such as 'tax-collectors and sailors' and those 'who had not even been to a primary school.'[60] In the early 20th century Deissmann came to a similar view that early Christianity, including the Pauline congregation, came from the lower strata of society.[61] In contrast to Deissmann's view, Judge argues that 'Christianity was a movement sponsored by local patrons to their social dependents.'[62] He then proceeds to suggest that Paul could have been identified as a 'sophist' as he also had some intimate patronal relations.[63]

Following on Judge's view, Chow puts forward the suggestion that 'patronage was one of the important ways through which relationships in first-century Corinth were structured.'[64] Chow's assertion that Paul sided with the socially weak in the Corinthian church is not only consistent with the general impression that the correspondence gives, it is also in line with Paul's strategy to dethrone the powerful and wise in the city.[65] For Judge, the social pretensions of the Corinthians are not surprising: 'They were riddled with snobbery and divisions (cf. *supra.* 4.7): "debates, envyings, wraths, strifes, backbitings, whisperings, swellings, tumults" (2 Cor. xii. 20). But this was natural in a group that had enjoyed the attentions not only of the mercurial Paul, but also of the impressive Alexandrian theologian,

---

[58] W. H. WUELLNER, 'The Sociological Implications of 1 Corinthians 1:26–28 Reconsidered', in E. A. LIVINGSTONE (ed.), *Studia Evangelica IV* (Berlin: Akademie, 1973), 666–72, at 666.

[59] MEGGITT, *Poverty*, 102. See THEISSEN, 'Review Essay: Justin J. Meggitt, *Paul, Poverty and Survival*', *JSNT* 84 (2001), 51–64; 'The Social Structure of Pauline Communities: Soime Critical Remarks on J. J. Meggitt, Paul, Poverty and survival', *JSNT* 84 (2001), 65–84. MEGGITT, 'Response to Martin and Theissen', *JSNT* 84 (2001), 85–94. THEISSEN, 'Social conflicts in the Corinthian community: Further Remarks on J. J. Meggitt, Paul, Poverty and survival', *JSNT* 25/3 (2003), 371–91.

[60] Origen, *Cels.* 1.62.

[61] DEISSMANN, *Paul*, 29–51.

[62] JUDGE, 'The Early Christians as a Scholastic Community', 8.

[63] JUDGE, 'Cultural Conformity and Innovation in Paul: Some Clues from Contemporary Documents', *TynBul* 35 (1984), 3–24, at 23.

[64] CHOW, *Patronage*, 188.

[65] CHOW, *Patronage*, 188.

Apollos (Acts xviii. 24–28), and others, and was entertained by a number of generous patrons (Rom. xvi. 1, 2, 23; and also cf. *supra*. 36, 58).'[66]

While it may be true that Paul tends to be on the side of the poor when dealing with certain Corinthian problems, such as the food issue in 1 Cor. 8–10 and the Lord's Table in 11, his pastoral concern is undoubtedly that of church unity.[67]

Some of the terms used by Paul in 1.26–29 are significant in regard to the issue of social strata, specifically in reference to: the wise, powerful and those of noble birth. Paul combines these three terms and seeks to remind the self-conceited Corinthians that actually 'not many' of them deserved such social stratification.[68] Theissen finds parallels to these Pauline social terms in the writings of Philo.[69] 'Are not private citizens continually becoming officials, and officials private citizens, rich men becoming poor men and poor men of ample means, nobodies becoming celebrated, obscure people becoming distinguished, weak men (ἀσθενεῖς) strong (ἰσ χυροί), insignificant men powerful (δυνατοί), foolish men wise men of understanding (συνετοί), witless men sound reasoners?'[70] questioned Philo.

---

[66] JUDGE, *The Social Pattern of Christian Groups in the First Century*, 59. See JUDGE, 'The Early Christians as a Scholastic Community', 4–15, 125–37. Judge's social-historical approach has a significant impact on Pauline studies. In his book, Theissen presents insightful, convincing views from sociological approaches to the analysis of social problems in the Pauline communities (THEISSEN, *The Social Setting*). The social tension is sharply divided between the rich (i.e. strong) and poor (i.e. weak) in terms of the food issue in 1 Cor. 8–10 and social status differences between the haves and have-nots which resulted in divisions at the Lord's table. Paul's aim is to win over both the rich and poor in the Corinthian church (CHOW, *Patronage*, 21–22). Theissen concludes that a few Christian groups in Paul's congregation came from the upper class, which was the dominant or influential Christians. As such, the conflicts in the church were basically derived from differing strata (MEEKS, *The First Urban Christians*, 52–53).

[67] MITCHELL, *Reconciliation*, 237–43. HORRELL, *Solidarity and Difference: A Contemporary Reading of Paul's Ethics* (London: T. & T. Clark International, 2005), 166–203; 99–132.

[68] Theissen suggests that social levels within the Corinthian church were made diverse and were dominated by those who came from a higher class. Based on 1 Cor. 1.26–29, Theissen argues that the Corinthian church was stratified. He distinguishes three distinct groups: σοφοί 'wise' (the educated people), δυνατοί 'powerful' (the influential people) and εὐγενεῖς 'noble birth' (high status). These terms are set in contrast to their opposites, linking wisdom/foolishness and power/weakness and a third category which is more dramatic: noble birth is not merely set against lower born, but rather against the 'despised' and 'things that are not'. According to these social relationships, Theissen contends that this passage has both a strong sociological emphasis and theological implications.

[69] THEISSEN, *The Social Setting*, 72.

[70] Philo, *Somn.* 1.155.

Socially, it is clear that church divisions in Corinth were essentially due to the struggle for power and social status, very much along the lines of the conventional social ethos. As such, it was only natural and necessary that Paul should deal with them thoroughly in the form of a drastic inversion of current social ethos.

The fact that Paul states that there were few people who belonged to the upper class means that there were at least a few, while the majority of the Corinthian community remained poor and lowly. Ironically, precisely because there were 'not many' in the church, the elite became more important and influential and could thus more fully exploit their social position. Indeed, Clarke comes to the conclusion that within the congregation there were some who came from the ruling class of society.[71] Similarly, Winter concludes that 1.26 refers to the ruling class of Corinth 'from which orators and sophists came.'[72] So too, Barclay puts forward the view that Paul refers to 'the minority of Christians with relatively high social status.'[73]

The debate between 'old' and 'new' positions is ongoing.[74] Deissmann and Meggitt argue that Pauline Christians should be located among the poor and non-elite of the Roman Empire. The 'New Consensus', spearheaded by Theissen and Meeks, asserts that the Pauline communities comprised a cross-section of society, including some from the higher strata.[75] Given the data available, a rigid description of the social composition of the Corinthian church seems unwise and at many points even impossible. Ultimately, one has little more to work with than Paul's description that 'not many' of the Corinthian Christians were of the elite class. In light of this 'not many' statement, the implication is that the remainder would have belonged to the ordinary and lower strata of society. Thus, although there are many shades within any one picture, the New Consensus seems more in keeping with the statement found in 1 Corinthians.

Whatever the case may be, the intention of Paul in 1.26 would seem clear, he desires to confront the Corinthians with the harsh social reality so that they might not be too self-conceited and boastful. Paul's strategy and rhetoric are impressive. He appears to be saying to them that 'since you Corinthians are so concerned with power and social status, let us examine it by your own worldly standard. In the end even you yourselves will have to acknowledge the naked fact [however reluctantly!] that in reality "*not many of you ... are of noble birth* (etc.)."' The Corinthians' craving for

---

[71] CLARKE, *Leadership*, 45. See MEEKS, *The First Urban Christians*, 63.

[72] WINTER, *Philo*, 191.

[73] BARCLAY, 'Thessalonica and Corinth', 57.

[74] See S. J. FRIESEN, 'Poverty in Pauline Studies: Beyond the So-Called New Consensus', *JSNT* 26/3 (2004), 323–61.

[75] See Introduction, n. 15–17.

power and social status are among the more obvious reasons for church divisions.

Those terms used by Paul – 'wise' (σοφοί), 'powerful' (δυνατοί), 'noble birth' (εὐγενεῖς) – were all attractive catchwords of the time. They are representative of what people deeply desired to possess and are basic to the traditional social ethos. When Isocrates was asked about a person's path to glory, he simply answered, 'What was his birth and education?'[76] Aristotle regards wealth, honour, strength and noble birth as some essential elements of happiness or fortune.[77] Jerome Neyrey has offered a study on the shared honour and shame values among Greeks, Romans and Judeans. Whether one speaks of the time from Homer to Herodotus or from Pindar to Paul, the quest for honour was pivotal and men lived and died seeking fame, approval and respect.[78]

The Romans divided society into two primary categories: *honestiores* and *humiliores* (higher and lower status).[79] Honour belonged only to the former: *honestiores*. Barton observes that for the Romans, honour was synonymous with 'being'. Whereas in contemporary western society honour is a negligible issue, at this time and place it would have been absolutely unbearable should one lose their honour.[80] Malina makes this even clearer, speaking of the symbolic value of honour in the ancient Mediterranean world where it was associated with one's rightful place in society. Each person's position of honour would be delineated by markers related to power, gender and social location.[81]

If, as Barton has observed, honour was synonymous with 'being',[82] Paul's questioning of the Corinthians presumed that honour (i.e. being

---

[76] Isocrates, *Antid.* 308.

[77] Aristotle, *Rhet.* 1360b 3–5; *Eth. nic.* 1102a.

[78] J. H. NEYREY, '"Despising the Shame of the Cross": Honor and Shame in the Johannine Passion Narrative', in D. G. HORRELL (ed.), *Social-Scientific Approaches to New Testament Interpretation* (Edinburgh, T. & T. Clark, 1999), 151–76, at 155.

[79] GARNSEY, *Social Status,* 221.

[80] BARTON, *The Sorrows,* 186.

[81] MALINA, *The New Testament World,* 54. deSilva stresses the crucial importance in understanding the role of social values regarding honour and disgrace in ancient Mediterranean societies, especially as it relates to the maintenance of group values and boundaries. deSiva states: 'A person born into the first-century Mediterranean world, whether Gentile or Jewish, was trained from childhood to desire honour and avoid disgrace. These two coordinates – honour and disgrace – are central social values for people living around the Mediterranean from the time of Homer, extending even into the present day in the less urbanized areas.' It is therefore not surprising that honour should have become "the umbrella that extends over the set of behaviours, commitments, and attitudes that preserve a given culture and society; individuals raised with a desire for honour will seek the good of the larger group, willingly embodying the group's values as the path to self-fulfilment' (*The Hope of Glory,* 2, 3).

[82] BARTON, *The Sorrows,* 186.

'wise', 'powerful' and 'of noble birth') was tantamount to challenging their very being. This is not an overstatement, since Paul was, as a matter of fact, dealing with the being of the Corinthians when he reminded them of their call (κλῆσις, 1.26) [83] and God's election of them (1.27, 'God chose'). It was clearly this divine call and election that ultimately gave the Corinthians new being, although they seemed to have been forgetful about this, due to being bound within the current social ethos. Moreover, it was their new Christian being that gave the unworthy Corinthians their true identity (1.28). In the end, Paul's initial questioning of their true social status was designed to paradoxically lead to the re-affirmation of their true being and identity.

1.27 ἀλλὰ τὰ μωρὰ τοῦ κόσμου ἐξελέξατο ὁ θεός, ἵνα καταισχύνῃ τοὺς σοφούς, καὶ τὰ ἀσθενῆ τοῦ κόσμου ἐξελέξατο ὁ θεός, ἵνα καταισχύνῃ τὰ ἰσχυρά, ('But God chose what is foolish in the world to shame the wise; God chose what is weak in the world to shame the strong;') 28 καὶ τὰ ἀγενῆ τοῦ κόσμου καὶ τὰ ἐξουθενημένα ἐξελέξατο ὁ θεός, τὰ μὴ ὄντα, ἵνα τὰ ὄντα καταργήσῃ, ('God chose what is low and despised in the world, things that are not, to reduce to nothing things that are,')

In a characteristic way, Paul writes about God's overturning of the current social order in paradoxical terms in 1.27 and 28. The opening ἀλλά ('but') in 1.27 already anticipates something of the reversal: '*But* God chose what is foolish in the world to shame the wise; God chose what is weak in the world to shame the strong; God chose what is low and despised in the world, things that are not, to reduce to nothing things that are.' Richard Horsley argues that Paul views God as upending the present order; this has a clear foundation in Jewish biblical traditions. More specifically, Horsley points to the great songs devoted to extol God for his victory over the powerful and wealthy rulers on behalf of lowly Israel (e.g. Exod. 15; Judg. 5; 1 Sam. 2.1–10; cf. Lk. 1.46–55). [84]

Horsley suggests that when Paul uses the terms wise, powerful and noble birth there is yet another level which extends beyond social aspects and implications. This is the 'spiritualized' level, which was rather common among Hellenistic and Roman philosophers. The Stoics, for example, thought that only the truly wise might be regarded as really rich, powerful and qualified to be a king. Horsley's study indicates that Hellenistic Jews had adopted this 'philosophical spiritualization' of the old Greco-Roman ideals and applied it to their own devotion either to Yahweh or to the personified *Sophia*. The same was also true for Philo. Horsley cites the *Wis-*

---

[83] CHESTER, *Conversion*, 77–112.

[84] R. A. HORSLEY, *1 Corinthians* (Abingdon New Testament Commentaries; Nashville: Abingdon Press, 1998), 51.

dom of Solomon in which the heavenly *Sophia* is said to be conferring a kingdom on pious souls (6.20, 21; 10.14) as well as riches (7.8, 11, 13-14; 8.5, 18; 10.11) and noble birth (8.3).[85]

Horsley's study on this issue is relevant to the Corinthian context because, besides the Corinthians' craving and fighting for social wisdom, power and wealth, there were also serious attempts to use (or misuse) their spiritual gifts (1 Cor. 1.4, 5; 12-14) in order to further consolidate their social status. As such, what Paul states with a drop of sarcasm in 4.8–10 actually had both social and spiritual meanings and implications because the Corinthians were apparently fascinated by the 'spiritual' level of their attainment: 'Already you have all you want! Already you have become rich! Quite apart from us you have become kings! Indeed, I wished that you had become kings, so that we might be kings with you! ... you are wise in Christ.... You are held in honour....' The Corinthians' claim to spiritual maturity or superiority was also reflected in certain aspects of their views and behaviour. For example, at least some members were indifferent to sexual immorality (ch. 5) while others seemed to have gone to the other extreme of despising legitimate sexual and married life (ch. 7). There was also the lack of care and concern on the part of the (spiritually) strong and mature for those who were weak in relation to how they viewed food and related to how it had been offered to idols (ch. 8). Paul's skilful rhetoric in the whole section of 1.18-31 thus thoroughly turns both the social and 'spiritual' worlds of the boastful Corinthians upside down.

1.29 ὅπως μὴ καυχήσηται πᾶσα σὰρξ ἐνώπιον τοῦ θεοῦ. *('so that no one might boast in the presence of God.')*

Boasting was another feature in Greco-Roman society which was closely associated with power, wealth and status. Aristotle discusses it in *Rhetoric* (1360b–1362a; 1366ab). Beside the first virtue of prudence, Cicero considers the following external attributes praiseworthy: 'public office, money, connexions by marriage, high birth, friends, country, power' (*Inv.* 2.59.177). Quintilian includes wealth, power and influence as key subjects for praise (3.7.14). Plutarch highlights 'love of contention, love of fame, the desire to be first and greatest.'[86] Philo takes note of 'silver, gold, honour, office, [and a] beautiful body' (*Virt.* 187–226).

Here in 1.29, Paul solemnly reminds the self-conceited of the divine inversion of social order 'so that no one might boast in the presence of God.' The Greek ἵνα in 1.27 and 28 and ὅπως in 1.29 suggests that what God has done is not only purposeful, it also leaves absolutely no ground for human boasting. 'Boasting' was clearly a major Corinthian problem in

---

[85] HORSLEY, *1 Corinthians*, 52.
[86] Plutarch, *Mor.* 788E; 816A.

church divisions. Such audacity seems to be based on two factors. (1) association with some particular charismatic leader or hero and, hence, right relationship – crucial to one's standing in Greco-Roman society. (2) their own personal gifts (χαρίσματα) and accomplishments, whether real or imagined.

For those who were spiritually perceptive and sensitive, to be ἐνώπιον τοῦ θεοῦ ('in the presence of God') was a most awesome (even awful) and humbling state. As such, only the badly misguided or self-conceited would dare to think about boasting 'in the presence of God'.

Horrell comments on the symbolic order of the Pauline gospel. As Paul expresses it here, a sharp contrast occurs with the prevalent symbolic order of Greco-Roman society. The poor are despised in this order and the value of an individual is determined by education, wealth and breeding. In contrast, the cross turns the world on its head and stands for God's rejection of the world's hierarchy. Indeed, a total transformation takes place in how one evaluates social order.[87]

1.30 ἐξ αὐτοῦ δὲ ὑμεῖς ἐστε ἐν Χριστῷ Ἰησοῦ, ὃς ἐγενήθη σοφία ἡμῖν ἀπὸ θεοῦ, δικαιοσύνη τε καὶ ἁγιασμὸς καὶ ἀπολύτρωσις, *('He is the source of your life in Christ Jesus, who became for us wisdom from God, and righteousness and sanctification and redemption,')* *31* ἵνα καθὼς γέγραπται· ὁ καυχώμενος ἐν κυρίῳ καυχάσθω. *('in order that, as it is written, "Let the one who boasts, boast in the Lord.")*

God not only shows Himself to be truly wise in His salvation through Christ crucified, especially in saving those who were humble and lowly; 'He is [also] the source of your life in Jesus Christ' (1.30). In the statement that immediately follows, Paul is no longer discussing wisdom in abstract terms, but rather is concrete in his communication. Christ Jesus is regarded here as personified wisdom when Paul says that Jesus Christ ἐγενήθη σοφία ἡμῖν ἀπὸ θεοῦ ('became for us wisdom from God'). Barrett too finds Christ crucified becoming the personified figure of Wisdom as well as God's agent in creation (cf. 8.6). As such, Christ is God's means of restoring men to himself.[88]

There is much more to Christ in this passage than just personified Wisdom. For Christians, Jesus Christ also became their δικαιοσύνη τε καὶ ἁγιασμὸς καὶ ἀπολύτρωσις ('righteousness and sanctification and redemption'). Since the main theme of 1.18–31 is the message of the cross, the key theological term δικαιοσύνη ('righteousness') must be perceived in the whole context of Christ's sacrificial act on the cross; the act which

---

[87] Cf. 1.27–29. HORRELL, *The Social Ethos*, 134.
[88] BARRETT, *The First Epistle*, 60.

makes it possible for the Corinthian believers to stand before God as for-given sinners. This point is important for both Paul and the trouble-making Corinthians, because whatever problems Paul may have with them, he does not seem to question their Christian calling and identity. Instead, Paul re-minds them right from the start that they are "called to be saints" (κλητοῖς ἁγίοις, 1.2) and are 'being saved' (1.18).

The word ἁγιασμός ('sanctification') was also in the mind of Paul at the very beginning. The Corinthians, despite the many blemishes in their Christian faith and practice, are still regarded by Paul in 1.2 as having been ἡγιασμένοις ἐν Χριστῷ Ἰησοῦ ('sanctified in Christ Jesus'). It is possi-ble that Paul's use of this important word in 1.30 is intended to remind the Corinthians of their privileged status in Christ as well as to encourage them to lead a life that is fitting for those who have been set apart by God and for God. The term ἀπολύτρωσις ('redemption'),[89] with its rich im-agery borrowed from the ancient slave trade, could quite easily cause one to remember the classic case of God's liberation of Israel from Egyptian bondage which had become the prototype of divine salvation in and through Christ crucified. The 'words of institution' of the Lord's Supper in 11.23–26 are also a solemn reminder of this.

Slightly earlier, in 1.29, Paul leaves absolutely no ground for any hu-man boasting. However, in 1.31, which is a concluding statement for the whole section of 1.18–31, he gives room for the possibility of boasting. But such boasting could only be done ἐν κυρίῳ ('in the Lord'). 1.31, which is an adaptation of Jeremiah 9.23–24, and fits into the whole context of 1.18–31 very well because Jeremiah 9.23 refers to the boasting of the wise, the mighty, and the wealthy: 'thus says the Lord: do not let the wise boast in their wisdom, do not let the mighty boast in their might, do not let the wealthy boast in their wealth.' This verse could thus be appropriately applied to the boastful Corinthians in both social and spiritual terms. But Jeremiah actually says more than that in 9.24: 'but let those who boast boast in this, that they understand and know me, that I am the LORD; I act with steadfast love, justice, and righteousness in the earth, for in these things I delight, says the LORD.'

Jeremiah 9.24 helps provide a clearer context not only for the original prophetic words, but also for Paul's statement in 1.31. In other words, for Jeremiah as well as for Paul, the only grounds for boasting could be God, His work and nothing else. Therefore, Hays considers 1.31 as emphatically precluding any possibility of revelling in human wisdom. God is the source

---

[89] See P. ELLINGWORTH and H. A. HATTON, *Paul's First Letter to the Corinthians* (United Bible Societies Handbook; New York: United Bible Societies, 1994).

of salvation and He deserves all the glory. Room cannot be found for human self-assertion.[90]

3.4 Conclusion

In 1.18–31, Paul responds to perceived foolishness as it relates to the message of the cross, which is not only crucial but also highly complex. The
issues involved include the most sought-after wisdom, power and status in
Greco-Roman society. Methodologically, Paul skillfully uses antithetical
and paradoxical ways of speaking. He first does this by dethroning the
'wisdom of the wise' by the perceived foolishness of the message of the
cross and puts in its place the power and wisdom of God, which is revealed
and demonstrated in and through Christ crucified. However, both the
power and wisdom of God are not conceived by Paul in abstraction because they were effectual for those who were being saved. Moreover, both
the overturning of worldly wisdom and the salvation of those who had
been called are understood in light of God's absolute sovereignty. It is God
who 'made foolish the wisdom of the world' (1.20) and it is also He who
decided to save those who believed (1.21). As such, the dissolution of human wisdom is not an end in itself, but just the beginning of God's saving
grace.

The primary problem with the self-conceited Corinthians is that of
boastfulness, which is likely the most important contributing factor to their
divisions. But Paul's antithetical and paradoxical approach leaves them absolutely no grounds for any human boasting because even by the worldly
standard, or by their much cherished social ethos, 'not many' of them were
actually wise, powerful and of noble birth (1.26). Here lies the great divine
paradox: God chose what was foolish to shame the wise, the weak to
shame the strong. God chose what 'were not' to reduce to nothing the
things that 'were' (1.27, 28). In the end, what is presented by Paul in 1.18–
31 is a revolution of immense proportions and perhaps no inversion of the
current social ethos could be more radical.

Having dethroned the wisdom of the world and reaffirmed God's wisdom and power in His calling of those who were being saved, Paul concludes his response by reminding the Corinthians that Christ alone became
the 'wisdom from God, and righteousness and sanctification and redemption' for them. The Corinthians were now to understand fully their calling
and identity on this basis alone. If anyone dared to boast, they were to
'boast in (or of) the Lord', but on nothing else.

---

[90] HAYS, *First Chritinans*, 33–34.

Part II

Rhetoric, Delivery, Body Language
and Masculinity in Greco-Roman Social Ethos

Chapter 4

Rhetoric, Delivery, Body Language and Masculinity

4.1 Introduction

In *Part I*, Paul's message of the cross (ὁ λόγος τοῦ σταυροῦ) was set within its Greco-Roman socio-historical context. Likewise, reference was made to crucifixion in Jewish thought of the period. The study of the origin and practice of crucifixion in antiquity and the concept of noble death in both Greco-Roman and Jewish traditions begins to demonstrate why Paul's message was foolishness (μωρία) to unbelieving Gentiles and a stumbling block (σκάνδαλον) to Jews. In the preceding investigation, it was argued that Paul's message upturns the social ethos of his time. The exegesis of 1 Cor. 1.18–31 took this viewpoint as a point of departure and, in doing so, further helped display the significance of this inversion for reading the passage.

In this chapter, the first of two in *Part II*, the place of rhetoric will be assessed. Special attention will be given to delivery, which was a well established form of body language in Greco-Roman society. In addressing rhetoric, a primary concern will be to understand better Paul's decision 'to know nothing among the Corinthians except Jesus Christ, and him crucified' (2.2). Moreover, this investigation will be concerned with why his 'speech and proclamation' were 'not with plausible words of wisdom' (2.3) when he came to Corinth. The study of Greco-Roman rhetoric may also assist in answering the question of why Paul's 'bodily presence' and 'speech' were perceived by his Corinthian critics to be 'weak' and 'contemptible' (2 Cor. 10.10).

This chapter will begin with the rediscovery of the importance of rhetoric in New Testament scholarship, especially in Corinthian studies. Reference will first be made to some modern scholars who have made significant contributions to the rediscovery. The bulk of this chapter, however, focuses on the primary literature: Greco-Roman writers who discuss both the theory and practice of rhetoric. These ancient authors are especially relevant for understanding delivery as body language. The remainder of this section (ch. 5) is devoted to an exegesis of 1 Cor. 2.1–5 and 2 Cor. 10.10, passages which make best sense when placed within the social context of Greco-Roman rhetoric.

4.2 Importance of Rhetoric Rediscovered: A Review of Some Scholarly Views

In the last two decades, Greco-Roman rhetoric has generally come to be recognised as an essential key to interpreting a number of Corinthian passages which were arguably obscure beforehand. In this regard, the works of Barrett and Litfin, as well as several others, deserve special mention.[1]

The church schism in 1 Corinthians 1–4 is one such passage. Baur holds that the early church was, for the most part, divided into two large camps: one led by Paul and the other Cephas.[2] Weiss and Barrett also take Peter's influence on the Corinthian church seriously. Barrett sees clear allusions to this in his re-examination of passages such as 1 Cor. 1.12; 3.22; 9.5; 15.5.[3] Since Paul was the founder of the Corinthian Church, it is naturally far easier to assume the existence of a 'Pauline party'. Based on the repeated occurrences of the name of Apollos, especially in relation to Paul (1.12; 3.4–6, 22; 4.6) together with the interesting description of Apollos in Acts (18.24–28), scholars have reasonably assumed that there was also a formidable 'Apollos party' which posed a serious challenge to Paul's leadership.

Scholars appear to have searched in vain for the 'Christ party'. In a critical response to Baur, Johannes Munck acknowledges nothing more than the presence of certain 'cliques' in the church.[4] In view of the seriousness of the schism in the Corinthian Church, Munck's view may be an understatement. James Dunn argues that Munck's reaction to Bauer likely goes too far. Dunn's view is much more convincing, he points to that fact that Paul is confronted by sharp criticism and likely outright opposition from within the Corinthian Church (cf. the sharp responses in 1.17; 3.1–3; 4.18–21; 8.1–3 and 11.16).[5]

Of particular notice are two passages in 1 Corinthians: 'with me it is a very small thing that I should be judged by you' (4.3) and 'This is my defence to those who would examine me' (9.3). These brief references are sufficient to show that a very serious schism existed in the Corinthian Church and that Paul evidently felt that it warranted an equally serious response. Church schism is in fact the first problem he mentions in 1 Corinthians (1.10–17) among a host of other doctrinal, social and ethical problems.

---

[1] BARRETT, 'Cephas and Corinth', in *Essays on Paul* (London: SPCK, 1982), 28–39. See Introduction, n. 13.

[2] BAUR, *Paul*, 1.269–81.

[3] BARRETT, 'Cephas', 28–39.

[4] J. MUNCK, 'The Church without Factions: Studies in 1 Corinthians 1–4', in *Paul and the Salvation of Mankind* (London: SCM Press, 1959), 135–67.

[5] DUNN, *1 Corinthians* (Sheffield: Sheffield Academic Press, 1995), 32.

When discussing the language and themes of wisdom, especially in 1
Corinthians 1–4, three major hypotheses have been offered in the course of
the last century to explain them. Dunn summarises these as: (1) Gnosticism, (2) Hellenistic Judaism or (3) rhetoric.[6] It is beyond the scope of the
present study to delve into each of these three areas and thoroughly adjudicate their significance for interpreting these chapters. However, the subject
of rhetoric, as it relates to wisdom, has a direct bearing on the Corinthian
controversy.

The word σοφία occurs sixteen times in 1 Cor. 1–3 alone, and two of
these are in 1 Cor. 12.8 and 2 Cor. 1.12. The adjective σοφός follows a
similar pattern and appears ten times in 1 Cor. 1–3, once in 6.5 without any
technical meaning, and nowhere else in the two Corinthian letters. There
are different views on the use of the word in Paul's correspondence with
the Corinthians, Wilckens and Barrett are representative of the controversy. *Contra* Wilckens, who denies the existence of disharmony in the
various uses of σοφία in 1 Cor. 1–3, Barrett comments that 'if there is no
disharmony there is at least a good deal of polyphony'.[7] Barrett also rejects
Wilckens' argument that Paul could not have been opposing a rhetorical
expression because he knew nothing of the rhetorical styles of the formal
philosophies. Noteworthy for this study, Barrett thinks that Wilckens' assumption simply ignores the historical fact that rhetoric was very much
part of the life and life-style in Paul's time.[8]

Barrett's view is backed up by the studies of scholars like Litfin, Welborn, Pogoloff and Mitchell. It is with good reason that one consider that
Paul is familiar with traditional Greco-Roman rhetoric. Indeed, as the exegesis of 1 Cor. 1.18–31 indicates, Paul was rather accomplished in his rhetorical skills, especially judging from his response to the controversial issues of 'wisdom' and 'power', which is an impressive display of presenting profound antithetical and paradoxical arguments.

Barrett divides the meaning of σοφία into good and bad categories;
however, he warns against drawing these lines too sharply. He holds that
there is a group of passages where σοφία denotes 'a kind of eloquence, a
technique for persuading the hearer' and is harmless in itself. It only becomes 'vicious' when it comes to rely on 'human device and artifice, and
not on the divine power resident in Christ crucified and transferred by the
Spirit to the preaching which has Christ crucified as its theme'.[9] This kind
of σοφία belongs to the 'bad' category and Paul refuses to adopt it when
he first preaches to the Corinthians (see esp 1 Cor. 1.17; 2.1). For Paul, to

---

[6] DUNN, *1 Corinthians*, 34.
[7] BARRETT, 'Christianity', 7.
[8] BARRETT, 'Christianity', 7.
[9] BARRETT, 'Christianity', 8.

do so would be tantamount to providing a substitute for Christ crucified, which was his real worry.[10] For the apostle, Christ crucified alone was the power and wisdom of God (1.23, 24). The so-called 'bad' use of σοφία will be expounded upon in the exegesis of 1 Cor. 2.1–5 and 2 Cor. 10.10.

Litfin devotes a section of his work *St Paul's Theology of Proclamation* to the rhetorical background of 1 Cor. 1–4. He is convinced of the pervasive and powerful place of rhetoric in 1st century Greco-Roman society and believes that for the majority of the population it was a kind of commodity. In keeping with this analogy, he describes only a small number of the population who were producers while the rest were consumers.[11] For Litfin, the impact of this pervasive Greco-Roman rhetorical tradition on Paul and the Corinthians was unquestionable. He elaborates that the 1st century Corinthians held *logos* and *sophia* in the highest esteem, and yet were not the least reluctant to stand in judgment over the orators who spoke in their presence.[12] Litfin applies his background research to the situation in 1 Cor. 1–4, especially in relation to Paul's *modus operandi*.

Litfin also makes a case that Paul as preacher contrasted sharply with contemporary orators.[13] While the Greco-Roman speakers fully exploited rhetorical skills to achieve their self-seeking goal, Paul as a faithful preacher of Christ crucified refused to follow that kind of style and goal. To resort to human wisdom, especially eloquence and human dynamic through rhetoric, would be unworthy of a faithful preacher of the cross: 'The *modus operandi* Paul adopted to avoid usurping the power of the cross is summed up in the term *proclamation* – the simple, straightforward "placarding" of the cross.'[14] Litfin also points out that the contrast is not between reason and irrationality, but rather two different styles of bringing listeners to understand the truth of the proclamation.[15] While the Greco-Roman orator's message may change in the process of adaptation, Paul's message remains fixed and firm, rather than varying to fit a rhetorical need, the proclamation remains constant.[16]

Litfin's view on rhetoric, whether in ancient Greco-Roman tradition or in special reference to the Corinthian context, is persuasive. However, one may take issue with aspects of his assessment on Paul's *modus operandi*.

---

[10] Paul uses expressions such as 'the wisdom of the world' (1.20), 'the wisdom of men' (2.5), 'wisdom of this age or of the rulers of this age' (2.6), 'human wisdom' (2.13) and 'the wisdom of this world' (3.19) to describe the human 'substitute' for 'Christ crucified'.

[11] LITFIN, *Proclamation*, 132.
[12] LITFIN, *Proclamation*, 146.
[13] LITFIN, *Proclamation*, 247.
[14] LITFIN, *Proclamation*, 247.
[15] LITFIN, *Proclamation*, 248.
[16] LITFIN, *Proclamation*, 248.

Within the Corinthian context Paul is committed to proclaiming the crucified Christ, which Litfin regards as a fixed, unchanging message: a constant. In contrast, according to Liftin, Greco-Roman rhetoric was often
used to achieve the orator's desired self-seeking goal through the process
of adaptation, thereby endangering integrity. However, Litfin also agrees
that the majority of ancient speakers did not have this self-seeking goal as
their sole consideration. He even agrees with Wayne Booth's words that 'a
genuine rhetorical stance also involves a faithfulness to one's subject matter – in so many words, honesty – and this was a familiar theme of ancient
rhetorical theory.'[17]

There appears, in light of these inconsistencies in Litfin's views, to be
no compelling reason to consider Paul, who Litfin also gladly acknowledges as familiar with Greco-Roman rhetoric, to have not used the art skilfully (but not craftily) when packaging his message in order to achieve the
goal.[18] Judging from his well-reasoned argument and its eloquence in his
response to the 'wisdom' issue in 1 Cor. 1–4, it is hard to believe that Paul
had not in fact made skilful use of the Greco-Roman rhetoric of his day.
Moreover, as will be made clear in the survey of the tradition of rhetoric in
Greco-Roman society, a great deal of written work was intended to be read
or delivered orally. Very often it was when the message was orally delivered that the desired effect and ultimate goal were achieved.

Litfin is right in drawing attention to Paul's dependence on the power of
the Spirit when preaching the gospel. However, such crucial dependence
need not be incompatible with the use of human skill. Rhetoric may be
used with integrity and to achieve a noble goal. In the case of Paul, using
rhetoric in this manner should not be seen as compromising his overall
modus operandi. The words of Günther Bornkamm on the matter of faith
and reason, which Litfin agrees with, merit repeating: 'the Apostle [Paul]
nowhere advocates the abandonment of human reason as such – the so-
called *sacrificium intellectus*.'[19]

With regard to the 'wisdom' issue in 1 Cor. 1–4, Welborn points out
that scholars before World War II tended to overlook or deliberately bypass the political aspect of Corinthian factions, instead interpreting them
largely in terms of either Hellenistic mystery religions or syncretistic *gno-*

---

[17] LITFIN, *Proclamation*, 246.

[18] 1 Corinthians gives the clear impression that some of the 'wise' and 'powerful' in
Corinth did practise rhetoric. But there has been no written record of their words or
speeches. Similarly, it is largely on the basis of a short description in Acts that Bible
readers learn that Apollos was 'an eloquent man' (18.24), and hence a very likely candi-
date to practise rhetoric. Again, there has been no record of his actual words or speeches.
However, the apostle Paul had left behind clearly written words.

[19] LITFIN, *Proclamation*, 248–49.

sis.[20] Welborn finds it impossible not to have the impression that Paul describes the situation in the Corinthian Church 'in terms like those used to characterize conflicts within city-states by Greco-Roman historians'.[21] For example, Paul first speaks of σχίσματα in 1 Cor. 1.10. Besides σχίσμα, Welborn also refers to other similarly important terms such as ἔρις (1.11), ζῆλος (3.3) and μερίς (1.13) and their usage in the ancient the Greco-Roman world. He cites numerous classical examples and draws parallels between the ancient Greco-Roman world and the Corinthian situation. He is convinced that politics and rhetoric are the key to unlocking the wisdom mystery in 1 Cor. 1–4 and makes his claim forthrightly:

> It is no longer necessary to argue against the position that the conflict which evoked 1 Corinthians 1–4 was essentially theological in character. The attempt to identify the parties with the views and practices condemned elsewhere in the epistle, as if the parties represented different positions in a dogmatic controversy, has collapsed under its own weight.[22]

It is unwise to treat the Corinthian conflict only or essentially in terms of dogmatic controversy. The issues in 1 Corinthians 1–4 are not just political and rhetorical. In the Corinthian context, what are political and rhetorical to Welborn could hardly be separated in their entirety from the theological. For instance, was not the most serious and disturbing issue of church divisions (σχίσματα) also the result of a very grave theological failure to recognise that the church was the one undivided body of Christ? Even granted that those politically minded Corinthians were not aware of the serious theological implications of their divisions and conflict, Paul himself certainly is keenly aware of them. This is reflected in the questions he poses to them: 'has Christ been divided? Was Paul crucified for you? Or were you baptized in the name of Paul?' (1 Cor. 1.13). It would be better to suggest that in the Corinthian situation politics, rhetoric and theology were closely related and intermixed.

Welborn is so eager to draw close, even exact parallels, between ancient city-states and the Corinthian situation on issues of the socio-political conflict as well as on socio-economic inequality and class divisions that he is prepared to make the unqualified statement that 'Paul's goal in 1 Corinthians 1–4 is not the refutation of heresy but what Plutarch describes as the object of the art of politics – the prevention of *stasis*.'[23] On the one hand, agreement may be found with Welborn that the prevention of *stasis* was Paul's goal. On the other hand, how Paul seeks to achieve that goal should be questioned. Was this done by simply resorting to lofty words of wisdom

---

[20] WELBORN, 'Corinth', 86.
[21] WELBORN, 'Corinth', 86.
[22] WELBORN, 'Corinth', 88.
[23] WELBORN, 'Corinth', 93–101, 89–90.

(2.1) as the sophists and others were doing? There is no denying that Paul probably uses some such rhetorical methods in his response to the wisdom issue. But as a responsible pastor and theologian it is hard to imagine that he would not be equally concerned with theological substance as a real answer to the Corinthian problem. Perhaps this is a matter of definition and perception. Although there are many perceptions, one of the more convincing views is that what the Corinthians did according to 1 Cor. 1–4 was completely unacceptable (i.e. unduly strong attachment to particular leaders as heroes; setting up one particular leader against others so as to tear the church apart, as if Christ himself could be divided; glorifying human wisdom out of proportion, etc.). Had Paul not considered the thinking and practice of the Corinthians somehow wrong and thus theological in the ultimate sense, he would likely not have responded to the issue with the 'wisdom of God' and 'Christ crucified' which are theological motifs.

Paul most likely used the rhetorical method (i.e. 'form') to convey his theology (i.e. real 'substance'). In his conclusion, Welborn provides some recognition of Paul's theological interpretation:

> It is Paul's intention in 1 Corinthians 1–4 not merely to put an end to dissension but to transform the Corinthians' understanding of the conflict. The strife of the factions is no petty quarrel, no *Cliquenstreit*, but a mirror of the cosmic conflict between the rulers of the age and the power of God. *The theological interpretation that the apostle gives to the struggle is obviously designed to turn the Corinthian Christians away from politics* (italics mine). The fate of the community does not rest upon precepts of statecraft, but upon the word of the cross. Thus, its members need not look to political leaders, but can await redemption from God.[24]

In light of these remarks, a balanced position on the Corinthian controversy is one that gives credence to both sociological (or, in Welborn's own words, in terms of politics and rhetoric) and theological aspect to the first chapters of Paul's first letter to them.

Pogoloff seeks to read 1 Cor. 1–4 afresh based on what he refers to as three currents in present New Testament scholarship.[25] These three currents are interrelated and represent a major shift in interpretative stance. The first and foremost current is a 'rediscovery of and renewed appreciation for ancient rhetoric' which no longer regards rhetoric narrowly (i.e. 'mere rhetoric') in terms of style. This rediscovery appreciates that rhetoric affected virtually all Greco-Roman culture and practically every level of society, including early Christianity. The second current is found in the 'renewed interest in social factors', such as social status which had to be constantly maintained through fierce competition and boasting. Pogoloff believes reading 1 Corinthians *vis-à-vis* this current will allow a fresh

---

[24] WELBORN, 'Corinth', 109.
[25] POGOLOFF, *Logos*, 1–3.

reading of the letter. The third current relates to a 'change in hermeneutical theory'. Unlike the old, the new rhetorical criticism enables the interpreter to use the texts both literarily and historically. The point of connection between the two is the rhetorical.

On the whole Pogoloff's understanding of rhetoric in the socio-political context of the ancient Greco-Roman world is quite similar to Welborn's. Pogoloff's emphasis is on the social and cultural factors which fill out Paul's language.[26] Like those who are keen to promote rhetoric in New Testament studies, Pogoloff also has the tendency to downplay the importance of doctrinal and theological concerns in 1 Cor. 1–4. He readily assumes that in 1 Corinthians 'Paul is addressing an exigence of the ethical dimensions of division, not doctrinal divergence.'[27] Pogoloff's rather artificial separation between the ethical and doctrinal is not entirely convincing. Pogoloff himself has also observed that Paul is not responding to division itself, but rather to the values behind them.[28]

What are the values which lie behind Paul's response? Whatever they are, they should be seen as somehow relevant to Christian doctrine. Moreover, as Pogoloff observes, it is through an appeal to the narrative of the community's origin that he seeks to change behaviour and values. The narrative to which he refers is Christ crucified.[29] The relation of community origins to crucified Christ clearly evokes the Christian calling in 1 Cor. 1.26–30 and the gospel message at its centre (1.23; 2.2). Lest this analysis be perceived as not appreciating the research of Pogoloff, in conclusion to a review of his contribution, one should not overlook how valuable his insights are to better understanding rhetoric.[30]

Another contributor to the present discussion is Mitchell. For her, 1 Corinthians is a cohesive, purposeful letter which urges unity throughout on the divided Corinthian church.[31] Through exegetical investigation of the language and composition of the text, Mitchell concludes that Paul's political terms and *topoi* in 1 Corinthians were commonplace in Greco-Roman political texts concerning concord and factionalism. Her focus is

---

[26] POGOLOFF, *Logos*, 3.

[27] POGOLOFF, *Logos*, 104.

[28] POGOLOFF, *Logos*, 119.

[29] POGOLOFF, *Logos*, 119.

[30] Pogoloff remarks: 'Paul insists that modeling the church on such attitudes and behaviours of the outside world betrays the heart of the gospel. Christians … should not divide themselves from one another, because Christ suffered and died and rose again equally for all. The persuasiveness of Paul's message is not to be attributed to the status of rhetorical skill (even if he has it), but to the authority he derives from his master. This authority he not only speaks but acts in suffering, a humble attitude he enjoins the Corinthians to imitate' (*Logos*, 14).

[31] MITCHELL, *Reconciliation*, 296.

thus on the 'political' nature of 1 Corinthians.[32] In Mitchell's view, however, Paul's rhetoric of reconciliation in 1 Corinthians is a failure on at
least two grounds. Firstly, one may surmise from 2 Corinthians that the
rhetorical strategy of Paul, in which he appeals to himself as the respected
example to be imitated, was not well received at Corinth. Rather this was
viewed negatively, being interpreted as Paul's 'self-recommendation'.
Secondly, as a purposeful argument for unity, Paul's first letter to the Corinthians was an inherently risky undertaking. Rather than uniting the factions at Corinth, it appears that Paul's letter resulted in angering the others.[33] Mitchell also points out that despite its 'inaugural failure', 1 Corinthians remained a very important and popular document for appeals to
church unity and reconciliation.[34]

Winter also offers a study on the sophistic movements, focusing on Alexandria and Corinth. He concludes that Paul's letters to Corinth have information which is not found in other sophistic movements from the 1st
century.[35] Winter thinks that those Corinthians who were united in their
support for Apollos hoped that the rhetorically skilful orator would help
establish their social prestige in this Roman city (1 Cor. 16.12). This
choice of Apollos over Paul is understood as reflecting a preference of
'speaking' over 'writing' which goes back to Isocrates.[36] The observation
of Winter that the Corinthian correspondence reflects the spirit of the age,
where the value of public orators was on the rise, is significant.[37]

The works of Barrett, Litfin, Welborn, Pogoloff, Mitchell and others
discussed here help demonstrate that while there is a consensus among recent scholars concerning the importance of the rediscovery of Greco-
Roman rhetoric for Corinthian studies, there is not always unanimity on
what direction this focus should take or what conclusions should be
reached. While there is little doubt that each scholar makes a contribution
to perceiving Greco-Roman rhetoric better, one issue that has not been
adequately addressed is that of delivery or body language. Indeed, this under appreciated aspect of rhetoric within Corinthian studies is not taken seriously enough. A case will be made that proper delivery according to the
rhetorical teaching of the time needed to be conveyed by a powerful presentation of self (i.e. body language). When one recognizes this value, it
serves as a crucial background for understanding the opponents of Paul
and their criticisms of him. Moreover, within the apostle's own *apologia* is
evidence of the significance of body language.

---

[32] MITCHELL, *Reconciliation*, 300.
[33] MITCHELL, *Reconciliation*, 303.
[34] MITCHELL, *Reconciliation*, 303–04.
[35] WINTER, *Philo*, 232.
[36] WINTER, *Philo*, 241.
[37] WINTER, *Philo*, 241.

4.3 Rhetoric in Greco-Roman Culture

4.3.1 Rhetoric as Oral Culture in Greco-Roman Society: An Overview

A consideration of terms is a necessary beginning point for the conversation to follow. There are those who use 'oratory' to refer to the actual speech act while 'rhetoric' indicates the theory or technique of speaking.[38] Such a strict distinction shall not be held to in the discussion to follow. Ancient authors expressed a wide variety of views on the subject of rhetoric and oration. In *Gorgias*, Plato defines rhetoric as 'the artificer of persuasion' (πειθοῦς δημιουργός).[39] Within Platonic discussions on rhetoric, rhetoricians 'are often confuted as conjurers.'[40]

Aristotle defines rhetoric as 'the faculty of discovering the possible means of persuasion.'[41] Isocrates describes Πειθώ as a goddess by whom an orator could share her power (δύναμις) through eloquence.[42] Quintilian regards rhetoric as 'the science of speaking well (*bene dicendi scientia*)'.[43] Rhetoric is broadly acknowledged as involving both theory and practice.

The main feature of Greek rhetoric was oral expression with particular concern for clarity, vigour and beauty by the standard of the classical Greek mind. Ancient Greek society relied heavily on oral expression. Although literacy was already extensive in Athens in the 5th and 4th centuries BC, reading and writing were still quite inaccessible to most. Not only was education and poverty an issue, but so too the availability of materials, whether stone, bronze, clay, wood, wax or papyrus. Oral expression thus remained the primary method of communication.[44]

In instances where reading was undertaken, Greeks were accustomed to reading aloud even when they were alone.[45] It is a well-known fact that Homeric poems and a great deal of ancient Greek drama first existed orally before being formally set in writing. Speech did not lose its special significance even when the original oral literature was written.

---

[38] KENNEDY, *The Art of Persuasion in Greece* (Princeton: Princeton University Press, 1963), 9.

[39] Plato, *Gorg.* 453A.

[40] T. S. BARTON, 'Physionomics: *Voir, Savoir, Pouvoir*', in *Power and Knowledge: Astrology, Physiognomics, and Medicine under the Roman Empire* (Ann Arbor: University of Michigan Press, 1994), 95–131, at 97. Gorgias, *Hel.* 10. Plato, *Euthyd.* 288BC; *Protag.* 315A. According to Tamsyn Barton, the magical power of rhetoric was appreciated as early as the 5th century BC.

[41] Aristotle, *Rhet.* 1355b 2.

[42] Isocrates, *Antid.* 323

[43] Quintilian 2.15.34.

[44] KENNEDY, *Persuasion*, 3–4. See also C. HEZSER, *Jewish Literacy in Roman Palestine* (TSAJ 81; Tübeingen: Mohr Siebeck, 2001).

[45] KENNEDY, *Persuasion*, 4.

Oration was used a great deal in ancient philosophy, in the teaching of logical method, for the exposition of ideas and doctrines as well as for engagement in dialogues.[46] Even letters often sound like they were composed as a speech, as has been noted about certain New Testament epistles. In Colossians 4.16, for example, special instruction is given for the letter to be read in the church of the Laodiceans, and likewise for the Laodicean letter to be read in Colossae.

Besides letters and other written works, Greek oratory took a number of forms including philosophical writings, sermons, political pamphlets, educational treatises, funeral encomiums, as well as other intellectual exercises. In Greek oratory the form, especially its oral delivery, was just as important as its substance and often more so.

Due to the very prominent role of oratory in ancient literary activities, it is not surprising that literary criticism was essentially rhetorical in practice. Oratory often became the centre of attention; even the structure, approach, standards and terminology of literary criticism were largely borrowed from the rhetorical schools.[47] All these and other relevant factors contributed to the development of Greco-Roman oration as well as its firmly established place in the whole intellectual life and civilization of the Greco-Roman world in antiquity.

As the eloquence and power of oration would be quite meaningless without the hearer or audience, it is self-evident that Greco-Roman rhetoric could be defined as audience-centred. From very ancient times the Greeks were intuitively drawn to human eloquence. They revelled in it and were delighted to be swept away by it. They held such great expectations from the eloquence of speakers that they could suddenly become hostile toward a speaker who failed to satisfy them.[48] Litfin expresses the depth of anticipation as wanting to be 'lifted up and carried out of themselves by the sheer power of eloquent words.'[49]

Plato believes that persuasion could be accomplished by the power of words (διὰ ῥώμην λόγου).[50] On one occasion, Plato uses the term δύναμις to describe the function of speech (λόγου δύναμις).[51] In Aris-

---

[46] KENNEDY, *Persuasion*, 4–6.

[47] KENNEDY, *Persuasion*, 7–8. See also Usher, Stephen, 'Oratory', in J. Higginbotham (ed.), *Greek and Latin Literature: A Comparative Study* (London: Methuen, 1969), 342–89.

[48] Cf. Plato, *Protag.* 319B–323A; Xenophon, *Mem.* 3.6.1.

[49] LITFIN, *Proclamation*, 35.

[50] Plato, *Phaedr.* 267A: 'Shall we leave Gorgias and Tisias undisturbed, who saw that probabilities are more to be esteemed than truths, who make small things seem great, and great things small by the power of their words (διά ῥώμην λόγου).'

[51] Plato, *Phaedr.* 271D: Socrates says, 'since it is the function of speech (λόγου δύναμις) to lead souls by persuasion, he who is to be a rhetorician must know the various forms of soul.'

totle's rhetoric, the term ῥώμη is replaced by δύναμις, which is often translated as 'faculty' or 'capacity' although the essential meaning 'power' was never lost.[52] Quintilian uses the Latin term *vis*, which is the equivalent of the Greek δύναμις, to describe rhetoric as the power of persuasion.[53]

According to conventional theory and practice Greek rhetoric consists of five major parts: invention, arrangement, style, memory and delivery. (1) *Invention* (εὕρεσις, *inventio*) is mainly concerned with the subject matter and its relevant questions in preparation for the appropriate arguments to be used in proof or refutation. (2) *Arrangement* (τάξις, *dispositio*) involves the careful and formal organisation of a speech into parts. (3) *Style* (λέξις, *elocutio*) is based on the so-called 'four virtues', i.e. correctness, clarity, ornamentation and propriety. (4) *Memory* (μνήμη, *memoria*) is concerned with 'mnemonic devices'. (5) *Delivery* (ὑπόκρισις, *actio*) deals with rules for the control of voice and other bodily gestures of the orator.[54]

Historically, rhetoric seems to have arisen largely to serve democracy. For example, in Sicily and especially at Athens its main concern was largely with civil questions. Of the three basic elements in speech which are identified by Aristotle (*Rhet.* 1358a 38) – speech, speaker and audience – the first is often compromised due to its preoccupation with the last two. This point is particularly significant (see ch. 5) because Paul's primary concern is clearly with the content of speech (i.e. 1 Cor. 2.1 and 'the message of the cross' not with 'lofty words or wisdom' or 2.4 with 'plausible words of wisdom').

As a speaker or orator, Paul confesses openly that he did not come to Corinth with the strength and self-confidence which are expected of his Greco-Roman counterpart, but 'in weakness and in fear and in much trembling' (2.3). The meaning and implications of Paul's self-confession, or perhaps strategy, can only be appreciated in the context of Greco-Roman rhetoric. This crucial point will become clearer in the exegesis of certain Corinthian passages (esp. 1 Cor. 2. 1–5; 2 Cor. 10.10).

Athens held a unique place in ancient rhetoric. It was this cultural centre of Greece that Cicero describes as the birthplace of eloquence and location where it grew to maturity.[55] It was in Athens that rhetoric gained its place

---

[52] Aristotle, *Rhet.* 1356a 2: 'Rhetoric then may be defined as the faculty (δύναμις) of discovering the possible means of persuasion (πιθανόν) in reference to any subject whatever.' 1362b 14: 'Eloquence and capacity (δύναμις) for action; for all such faculties are productive of many advantages.'

[53] Quintilian 2.15.3–4: 'So the commonest definition is that "rhetoric is the power of persuading [*rhetoricen esse vim persuadendi*]." (What I call "power" many call "capacity," some "faculty." To avoid ambiguity, let me say that by "power" I mean *dynamis*). This view originates with Isocrates (if the "Art" Passing under his name is really his).'

[54] KENNEDY, *Persuasion*, 10–12.

[55] Cicero, *Br.* 10.39; 13.49–50; *Or.* 1.13.

of prominence among the common people and flourished. Litfin describes rhetoricians from all over the classical world making their way to Athens. What Paris is to fashion today, anyone of significance in this art form eventually travelled there. The city became known as the unquestioned 'capital of eloquence' and retains this title even to the present.[56]

Greek rhetorical theory is usually thought to be evident by the 4th century BC in Aristotle's *Rhetoric* and in the work known as the *Rhetorica ad Alexandrum*. The latter handbook is only preserved in the work of Aristotle. Modern scholars usually attribute it to Anaximenes of Lampsacus (*fl.* c. 550 BC).

Rhetoric underwent its greatest development in the Hellenistic period. The first complete handbook is the *Rhetorica ad Herennium*, an anonymous 1st century BC treatise once attributed to Cicero, largely because Cicero's early *De inventione rhetorica* parallels part of it. Traditional theory is found in Cicero's later works *De Oratore* and *Orator,* as well as *Partitiones Oratoriae*. The same is also true in the writings of Dionysius of Halicarnassus and the elder Seneca. But the most complete expression is found in Quintilian's *Institutio Oratoria*.[57]

4.3.2 Rhetoric as Core Education (παιδεία)

After learning how to read and write, together with some arithmetic, musical and gymnastic training, a Greek boy at the age of about fourteen would be sent to the school of the rhetorician for formal theoretical instruction in public speaking. This was most likely to continue throughout the course of his life. The sophists also adopted instruction in public speaking as an important part of their education.[58]

There has been controversy over the role of sophists in the development of Greco-Roman rhetoric. Sophists are often portrayed as professional educators, but not philosophers, who educated young men for high fees. Plato thus despises the sophists who, as he writes, 'profess to be teachers of virtue and advertise themselves as the common teachers of the Greeks, and are ready to instruct anyone who chooses in return for fees charged on a fixed scale.'[59] Plato distinguishes himself from the sophists because for him the true philosophers only seek truth and knowledge. Plato's rival Isocrates is a well-known sophist who places great emphasis on the social value of persuasive rhetorical presentation.

The contribution of Isocrates to rhetoric has been appreciated in our own time. For instance, Kennedy describes sophistry as having had a bad

---

[56] LITFIN, *Proclamation*, 22.

[57] KENNEDY, *Persuasion*, 13.

[58] KENNEDY, *Persuasion*, 7.

[59] Plato, *Men.* 91B. Cf. *Euthyd.* 271C–72B; *Rep.* 495E–96A.

name among critics of the time, however similar to rhetoric, one cannot generalise and describe it as depraved, decadent or in poor taste. Whereas rhetoric broadly places emphasis on the role of speaker and the process of learning to speak or write by imitating models, sophistry is one part within the rhetorical system that allows room for genius and inspiration.[60]

Donald Clark outlines three 'characteristic and divergent views on rhetoric': (1) the *moral philosophical view* of Plato who understood it in contradistinction to truth and the good life because it is concerned with appearances and pleasure; (2) the *philosophical scientific view* of Aristotle who sought to devise a theory or rhetoric that excluded either blame or praise of it; and (3) the *practical educational view* of rhetoricians such as Isocrates, Cicero and Quintilian who taught, practiced and lauded the art as a key part of any free and civilised society.[61] Where Paul fits within these three views will be discussed further below.

Plato's Academy came under considerable influence of Greek rhetoric and was responsible for Aristotle's decision to teach it. During this period of time rhetoric was regarded as the most certain way to fame and success. For centuries the orator was a powerful and attractive icon. In a society of diverse ideas and competing philosophies, rhetoric was perhaps the only learned discipline which provided a common basis for education.[62]

In view of the crucial role that rhetoric occupied in both education and the intellectual life of Greco-Roman society, it was only natural that most of the philosophical schools had rhetorical training in their core curriculum (*Quintilian* 3.1.15 and 12.2.23 ff). Philosophical interest in the great art of rhetoric might have also been prompted by the practical needs to attract disciples.[63] The immediate successors of Aristotle, Theophrastus and to a lesser extent Demetrius, made several significant advances in rhetorical theory and practice.[64]

Pogoloff makes the point that through education and the application of skills learned there, the culture itself came to be rhetorical.[65] Similarly, Henri Marrou places rhetorical παιδεία at the very centre of any genuine picture of Hellenistic civilization.[66] Such views are consistent with what Isocrates (436–338 BC) states in the 4th century BC concerning the all-

---

[60] KENNEDY, *Classical Rhetoric*, 39–40.

[61] D. L. CLARK, *Rhetoric in Greco-Roman Education* (New York: Columbia University Press, 1957), 24–25.

[62] KENNEDY, *Persuasion*, 271.

[63] KENNEDY, *Persuasion*, 272.

[64] KENNEDY, *Persuasion*, 272–73.

[65] POGOLOFF, *Logos*, 48.

[66] H. I. MARROU, *A History of Education in Antiquity*, trans. G. LAMB (New York: Sheed & Ward, 1956), 49.

importance of rhetorical education in his time. His words are worth repeating:

> Beautiful and artistic speech ... is the work of an intelligent mind. [Athens] knew that whether men have been liberally educated from their earliest years ... is made manifest most of all by their speech, and that this has proved itself to be the surest sign of culture (παιδεύσις) in every one of us, and that those that are skilled in speech are not only men of power in their own cities but are also held in honour in other states. And so far has our city distanced the rest of mankind in thought and in speech that her pupils have become the teachers of the rest of the world; and she has brought it about that the name 'Hellenes' (Ἑλλήνων) suggests no longer a race but an intelligence, and that the title 'Hellenes' is applied rather to those who share our culture (παιδεύσεως) than to those who share a common blood. [67]

Clark draws attention to the fact that in the Greco-Roman schools education was devoted almost exclusively to teaching rhetoric, a skill that was almost exclusively considered preparation for the life of a free man.[68] Litfin notes that Isocrates' use of the term 'Hellenes' no longer signifies merely an ethnic group or a race but could, in a broader sense, denote a διάνοια, a way of thinking 'which venerated wisdom and eloquence as man's highest achievement, a way of thinking shared by men of intelligence wherever Greek culture had spread.'[69]

Marrou also weighs in on the centrality of rhetoric, seeing eloquence as the highest level of culture in the Hellenistic and Roman periods.[70] Just like the rest of Greco-Roman society, Corinthian preoccupation with rhetoric and social values closely associated with it needs to be viewed against the backdrop of its overarching importance in education and society.

4.3.3 The Preoccupation with Delivery ('Body Language') in Greco-Roman Rhetoric

Delivery in Greek was ὑπόκρισις, which originally meant 'the playing of a part'. The word derives from ὑποκρίνεσθαι, a verb used very early to describe an actor's response to the chorus in Greek tragedy. The word for 'responding' or 'acting' soon came to mean 'delivering a speech'. Similarly, the word for actor, ὑποκριτής, was mainly used to denote the task of the speaker.[71] According to Philodemus:

[67] Isocrates, *Panegyr.* 48–50.
[68] CLARK, *Rhet.* 65.
[69] LITFIN, *Proclamation*, 74.
[70] MARROU, 'Education and Rhetoric', in M. I. FINLEY (ed.), *The Legacy of Greece* (Oxford: Clarendon Press, 1981), 185–201, at 195.
[71] R. NADEAU, 'Delivery in Ancient Times: Homer to Quintilian', *QJS* 50 (1964), 53–60, at 53.

... much of delivery is the natural and unconscious bodily expression of the emotions. Delivery depends, too, on natural endowment, beauty of voice, grace of body, self-possession [self-confidence], qualities the lack of which caused Isocrates to refrain from public appearances. But Demosthenes said that delivery was the first thing in oratory, and the second and the third, and actors say that it is everything in their art.[72]

In his work, Plutarch mentions Demosthenes who is challenged by the tragic actor Andronicus because Andronicus thought that Demosthenes' words were excellent but his delivery deficient.[73] Philodemus notes that even though Demosthenes 'was in the first rank of rhetors' Aeschines still criticises him for his shrill voice and loudness. Demetrius of Phalerum also upbraids Demosthenes for being too theatrical and lacking simplicity and nobility in his delivery.[74] In Philodemus' opinion, most ancient sophists had poor delivery. In the Greco-Roman tradition all the theories and practices of rhetoric were finally put to the test in delivery, so much so that it became almost synonymous with rhetoric itself.

Rhetoric in Latin literature is largely based on its Greek predecessor. The Romans began to appreciate the importance of the great art of persuasion around the late 3rd century BC when their city became a powerful state in the Mediterranean.[75] Before that, the status of a Roman citizen in society was largely dependent upon family prestige and wealth as well as personal authority and power.

A brief account may be offered as to how rhetoric developed in the later Roman Republic. The basic word for speech in Latin was *oratio*, which Cicero (*Off.* 1.132) subdivided into *contentio* (debate) and *sermo* (conversation). The original function of a Roman orator was basically that of a performer in official religious or political functions, primarily as a senator or lawyer, but in the last two centuries of the republic the word acquired new meanings. Rhetoric in Latin was basically derived from the Greek term *rhetorice*, or the more Latinized *rhetorica* (Quintilian 2.14), and the word *eloquentia*[76] was sometimes used to refer to *ars dicendi* ('the art of speaking').[77]

---

[72] Philodemus, *De Rhetorica,* trans. H. M. HUBBELL, 'The Rhetorica of Philodemus', *CAAS* 23 (1920), 243–382, at 301.

[73] Plutarch, *Mor.* 845B. Cf. *Lives, Demosthenes* 7. This comment sounds very similar to Paul's opponents' opinion about the apostle (2 Cor. 10.10).

[74] HUBBELL, 'Philodemus', 301.

[75] KENNEDY, *Rhetoric,* 4.

[76] R. MacMullen puts Greco-Roman society's preoccupation with eloquence (*eloquentia*) in a much broader socio-historical context: 'The one art in which cultivated people commonly expressed their cultivation, from the fifth century B.C. to the fifth century A.D. is [one] we no longer practice nor value, and tend to ignore. That was *eloquentia*. For a thousand years it remained at the heart of classical civilization, placing its heroes upon embassies, rostrums, richly endowed chairs, and the platforms of special theatres; at last, as statues, upon pedestals in the Roman forum itself.' *Enemies of the Roman Order:*

Actio, agere and *actor* in Latin mean, 'acting', 'to act' and 'actor' respectively. All three also refer to the delivery of a speech, to speak and speaker. The Romans also frequently use *pronuntiatio* when writing about delivery, *pronuntiare* in the verb form and *pronuntiator* (less frequently) as a noun. These words also have a theatrical background, especially with reference to reciting and declaiming. Thus for most people in antiquity, public and social activities such as delivering a speech, presenting a declamation, reciting poetry or playing a part on stage all had a lot in common.[78]

Details about delivery, including how to use the whole of one's body (lit. 'head to toe'), are repeatedly given in the writings of: (1) Theophrastus; (2) *Rhetorica ad Herennium,* a work by an unknown author commonly believed to be a contemporary of Cicero; (3) Cicero, *De Oratore*; and (4) Quintilian, *Instititio Oratoria.* Although Aristotle does not provide the details that these writings do, he shall serve as the beginning point of an overview on the subject of delivery in the writings of these ancient authors as he lays a foundation for their views on rhetoric.

4.3.3.1 Aristotle (384–322 BC)

Aristotle is of paramount importance as a Greek pioneer who made delivery one of the basic elements of the art of rhetoric (*Rhet.* 1403b 1–5). He holds that proofs (πίστεις) are effected by three means which form the core of rhetoric: character (ἦθος), emotion (πάθος) and logical reasoning (λόγος). Each of these is discussed as a means of effective persuasion at great length.[79] In the words of Aristotle:

Now the proofs furnished by the speech are of three kinds. The first depends upon the moral character of the speaker (τῷ ἤθει τοῦ λέγοντος), the second upon putting the hearer into a certain frame of mind, the third upon the speech itself, in so far as it prove or seems to prove.[80]

It was most probably from these well established and honoured means of persuasion in rhetoric that Paul's Corinthian critics judged him.

In addition to the above three means of persuasion, there were also other qualities which are expected of the good orator in order to effectively convince his audience: good sense (φρόνησις, i.e. way of thinking, intelligence), virtue (ἀρετή) and goodwill (εὔνοια, i.e. enthusiasm).[81]

Treason, Unrest, and Alienation in the Empire (Cambridge: Harvard University Press, 1966), 15.

[77] KENNEDY, *Rhetoric*, 7.

[78] NADEAU, 'Delivery', 53.

[79] Aristotle, *Rhet.* 1356a 7; *Eth. nic.* 1094ab.

[80] Aristotle, *Rhet.* 1356a 3.

[81] Aristotle, *Rhet.* 1378a 5–7.

According to Aristotle, an audience changes their opinion in regard to their judgments because of their wide array of emotions.[82] In the first half of book two Aristotle discusses the role of such *pathos* in detail.[83] This is how Aristotle describes the object of rhetoric:

> But since the object of rhetoric is judgement — for judgements are pronounced in deliberative rhetoric and judicial proceedings are a judgement — it is not only necessary to consider how to make the speech itself demonstrative and convincing (ἀποδεικτικὸς καὶ πιστός), but also that the speaker should show himself to be of a certain character and should know how to put the judge into a certain frame of mind. For it makes a great difference with regard to producing conviction — especially in demonstrative, and, next to this, in forensic oratory — that the speaker should show himself to be possessed of certain qualities and that his hearers should think that he is disposed in a certain way towards them; and further, that they themselves should be disposed in a certain way towards him.[84]

In regard to historical development, the Hellenistic rhetoricians (i.e. after Aristotle) developed and refined more and more rules of delivery and tended to neglect the other two aspects of delivery: *ethos* ('character') and logical argument. Such change is significant because Aristotle, like Socrates before him, quite consistently accepts eloquence based upon knowledge. While recognising the special need for emotions, especially in the peroration (1419b 10ff), depth of knowledge is seen to be the more important in successful speaking (1354a14 ff and 1354b 21ff).

Aristotle consistently insists that the logical side of rhetorical theory and practice are crucial. He describes two types of logical proof: deductive (the enthymeme) and inductive (the example).[85] Rhetorical speech should also be concerned with purity, which is the foundation of style. Purity consists of five rules: (1) the usage of the correct Greek language; (2) impressiveness or loftiness of style; (3) propriety in the echo from audience, the character of the speaker, the nature of the subject; (4) avoiding of rhythmic prose; and (5) the use of graphic language to paint things before the eyes of the audience.[86]

As logical reasoning is ultimately a matter for the listener or audience to evaluate, Aristotle was well aware of the significant role of the audience as judge. In Aristotle's own words: 'the object of rhetoric is judgment'.[87] However, Aristotle disapproves of using rhetoric inappropriately just for the sake of securing good judgment from the audience. He explains that it

---

[82] Aristotle, *Rhet.* 1378a 8.

[83] Aristotle, *The "Art" of Rhetoric*, trans. J. H. FREESE (Loeb Classical Library; London: William Heinemann LTD, 1959), xxxvii.

[84] Aristotle, *Rhet.* 1378a 2–3.

[85] FREESE, xxxii.

[86] Aristotle, *Rhet.* 1404a 4.

[87] Aristotle, *Rhet.* 1378a 2.

is wrong to pervert feeling, or to arouse anger, jealousy or compassion; he even compares such a use to making the rule one intends to use crooked.[88]

Greco-Roman audiences understood their role as judge and took such a role seriously. They enjoyed not only the power of oratory, but also their own power as listeners, especially in their judgment or evaluation of the speaker. This point about the audience being judge is relevant to the Corinthian context, not only because Paul's Corinthian critics know their role well, but also apparently play the role in relation to Paul. This point will be dealt with in the exegesis of the relevant Corinthian passages.

4.3.3.2 Theophrastus (c. 370 – c. 285 BC)

Theophrastus, a pupil of Aristotle, once gave an address to a group as large as 2,000 people wherein he paid particular attention to the technique of speaking (Diogenes Laertius 5.37) and especially body gestures (Athenaeus 1.21AB).[89] Theophrastus' influence on rhetoric is greatest in the areas of style and delivery. According to him, there are four virtues in delivery:[90] purity (ἑλληνισμός, *purus et Latinus*),[91] clarity (τὸ σαφές, *dilucide planeque*), [92] propriety (τὸ πρέπον, *decorum*) [93] and ornamentation (κατασκευῆς , *ornatus*).[94]

Theophrastus' influence on rhetorical work, and especially the subject of delivery, is quite considerable. His work, which is devoted entirely to delivery, is entitled Περὶ ὑποκρίσεως (see Diogenes Laertius 5.48). According to Athanasius, Demosthenes once said delivery is the first, the second and the third most important thing in rhetoric. Athanasius also refers to Theophrastus' high regard for delivery: 'Theophrastus the philosopher says that delivery is the greatest factor an orator has for persuasion, referring delivery to first principle and the passions of the soul and the knowledge of these so that the movement of the body and the tone of the voice may be in accordance with the whole science of delivery.'[95] In his work, *Lives of Eminent Philosophers*, Diogenes Laertius makes special reference to Theophrastus' work on delivery. In Harry Caplan's view, it is

---

[88] Aristotle, *Rhet.* 1354a 5. Cf. 1355a 12.

[89] KENNEDY, *Persuasion*, 273.

[90] Theophrastus' four virtues in delivery had also been taken up in *De Oratore* (3.37ff) in which each of the virtues was discussed in good order with other topics subordinated to it. Quintilian (8.1–11.1) also had something very similar to say in his long deliberation on the same subject.

[91] Cicero, *Or.* 3.40.

[92] Cicero, *Or.* 49.

[93] Demetrius, *Elo.* 114; Aristotle, *Rhet.* 1048a 10ff; 1413b 3ff; Cicero, *Or.* 3.210–12.

[94] Diogenes Laertius 7.59; Dionysius of Halicarnassus, *Isocr.* 3; Quintilian 10.1.27; Demetrius, *Elo.* 41; Cicero, *Or.* 3.184 ff; *Orat.* 228.

[95] KENNEDY, *Persuasion*, 283.

Theophrastus and not Aristotle who is probably first to make delivery the fourth formal duty of the orator (*officium oratoris*). Aristotle does not fully develop this theme (see *Rhet.* 1403b 1).[96]

4.3.3.3 Rhetorica ad Herennium

In *Rhetorica ad Herennium*, the unknown author (commonly held to be a contemporary of Cicero) adds memory and delivery to the three parts of the traditional theory of rhetoric, making it five altogether: invention, arrangement, style, memory and delivery.[97] For the writer 'delivery is the graceful regulation of voice, countenance, and gesture' (*Rhet. ad Her.* 1.2.3). This unknown writer also looks at the human voice in close relation to the orator's physical movement and gestures (i.e. 'body language'; 3.11.19). Voice quality (3.11.20–14.25) is characterised by three aspects: volume, stability and flexibility (3.11.20). Vocal flexibility is further divided into three tones: (1) the conversational; (2) the debating and (3) the tone of amplification.[98]

In order to maintain manly dignity in speaking the author particularly warns against a sharp voice, which is regarded as feminine (3.12.22). The writer is also aware of the intimate connection between body movement and voice (3.15.26–27). While voice and other body movements and gestures are important in good delivery, the writer also acknowledges that 'good delivery comes from one's heart' (3.15.27).

Rhetorica ad Herennium also takes facial expression as a crucial aspect of the orator's body gestures. Bringing the face closer to the audience is believed to be a wise move in public delivery, certainly far more desirable and effective than most violent body gestures (Quintilian 11.3.123).

4.3.3.4 Cicero (106–43 BC)

Cicero is one of the best known figures in rhetoric during the Roman Republic. He manages to combine the theory and practice of Demosthenes with Aristotle. Cicero lists five parts of rhetoric – invention, arrangement, expression, memory, delivery – and makes special connection between voice and body movement: 'Delivery is the control of voice and body in a manner suitable to the dignity of the subject matter and the style.'[99] Cicero explains: 'Why should I go on to describe the speaker's delivery? That needs to be controlled by bodily carriage, gesture, play of features and

---

[96] [Cicero], *Rhetorica ad Herennium*, eds. G. P. GOOLD, *et al.*, trans. H. CAPLAN, 190–91.

[97] The writer further suggests that all five parts could be acquired by three means, namely, theory, imitation and practice (*Rhet. ad Her.* 1.2.3).

[98] *Rhet. ad Her.* 3.13.23–24.

[99] Cicero, *Inv.* 1.7.9.

changing intonation of voice; and how important that is wholly by it-self.'[100]

Cicero repeatedly asserts that 'delivery is the dominant factor in ora-tory; without delivery the best speaker could not be of any account at all, and a moderate speaker with a trained delivery can often outdo the best of them.'[101] Cicero describes the importance of delivery for the transforma-tion of the orator in the eyes of his audience, saying that there is nothing else that so shapes and moulds who the speaker is as his presentation.[102] Cicero holds that the audience's judgment very much depends on the effec-tive speaker himself.[103] For Cicero, the ultimate goal of the speaker is to persuade and to win his audience over. Cicero regards the speaker's ability to sway his hearer's emotions as 'the orator's chief source of power (*plurimum pollere*).'[104]

Cicero divides the persuasive art of speaking into three functions: (1) the proof of the truth, (2) the winning of hearers' favour and (3) the stir-ring of their emotions.[105] These three functions resemble Aristotle's logical reasoning and pathos. Moreover, these three *officia oratoris* later become Cicero's key concept in rhetorical theory.[106] The comparison as well as contrast which Robert Sonkowsky makes between Aristotle and Cicero[107] is helpful:

---

[100] Cicero, *Or.* 1.18.

[101] Cicero, *Or.* 3.56.213.

[102] Cicero, *Br.* 37.142. Plutarch similarly repeats the same story about Demosthenes: 'Therefore when someone asked him what was the first thing in oratory, he replied "Delivery" (ὑπόκρισις), and what the second, "Delviery," and the third, "Delivery"' (*Mor.* 845B).

[103] Cicero, *Or.* 1.123–25. *Br.* 184–88.

[104] Cicero, *Br.* 79.276: 'There are three things which the orator must effect, to teach, to please and to move, two of these he possessed in the highest degree, namely, perfect lucidity of exposition and the ability to hold his audience by the charm of his words. The third merit, which consists in moving the listener and in arousing his emotions, – the ora-tor's chief source of power, as I have said – he lacked, and he was in fact quite without force and intensity (*nec erat ulla vis atque contentio*).' 80.279: 'Every one must ac-knowledge that of all the resources of an orator far greatest is his ability to inflame the minds of hearers and to turn them in whatever direction the case demands. If the orator lacks that ability, he lacks the one thing most essential (*maximum*).'

[105] Cicero, *Or.* 2.115: 'Thus the purposes of persuasion the art of speaking relies wholly upon three things: the proof of our allegations, the winning of our hearers' favour, and the rousing of their feelings to whatever impulse our case may require *(Ita omnis ratio dicendi tribus ad persuadendum rebus est nixa: ut probemus vera esse, quae defendimus; ut conciliemus eos nobis, qui audiunt; ut animos eorum, ad quemcumque causa postu-labit motum, vocemus).*' Cf. *Opt.* 4: There are three functions of speaker: to instruct (*do-cere*), delight (*delectare*) and to move the minds of the audience (*movere*).

[106] KENNEDY, *Rhetoric*, 207.

[107] J. WISSE, *Ethos and Pathos from Aristotle to Cicero* (Amsterdam: Hakkert, 1989).

It remained for Cicero to go back to the *ratio Aristotelia* and to apply his own talents to rhetoric.... It is also important to notice how Cicero's approach to the subject of the emotions differs from Aristotle's. Aristotle defines and describes *ethê* and *pathê* in themselves so as to give the knowledge needed by the orator for finding his means of persuasion. Cicero does less of this; instead he includes information on the external techniques to be used. He stresses the *signa* of the *leniores affectus* and recommends the proper tone of voice, facial expression, language and a certain technique of delivery whereby the orator can give the impression of being under involuntary compulsion when his attack is too vehement (*De or.* 2.182). Cicero assumes that ... the orator must himself feel the emotions of his speech in order to impart them to his audience (2.189).[108]

Sonkowsky's remarks also highlight Cicero's emphasis on the external techniques and body language in the orator's delivery.

Like several other great philosophers and orators, Cicero also recognises the endowment of 'nature' in oratory as it relates to good theory and practice: 'Therefore let art follow the leadership of nature in pleasing the ear. Certainly the natural excellence of voice to be desired is not in our power, but the use and management of the voice is in our power.'[109] In the end, nature and human training complement each other: 'We must, of course, look to Nature for both gifts. But distinctness may be improved by practice; the musical qualities, by imitating those who speak with smooth and articulate enunciation.'[110] While Cicero's comments are true, in actual practice it is the humanly created 'art' in delivery that seems to have precedence over the endowment of 'nature'.

A full treatment of delivery is given in Cicero's *De Oratore* (3.56.213–58.217), in which he writes: 'Nature has assigned to every emotion its own particular facial expression, tone of voice and gesture (*Omnis enim motus animi suum quemdam a natura habet vultum et sonum et gestum*).'[111] Sonkowsky points out that by 'nature' Cicero does not mean *sine arte,* but *natura ab arte perfecta.* In order to establish a *genus vocis* for each emotion, one must combine nature with training in the art of delivery.[112]

For Cicero, the orator's thoughts, words, emotions and delivery itself are all intimately and vitally connected.[113] The essence of eloquence is thought and language,[114] it is inseparable from wisdom and in his words is: 'nothing else but wisdom delivering copious utterance.'[115] As such, a truly eloquent orator is also a sound thinker: 'For no one can be a good speaker

---

[108] R. P. SONKOWSKY, 'An Aspect of Delivery in Ancient Rhetoric Theory', *TAPA*, XC (1959), 257–74, at 269.

[109] Cicero, *Orat.* 17.58.

[110] Cicero, *Off.* 1.37.133.

[111] Cicero, *Or.* 3.57.216; cf. Philodemus 1.196.8.

[112] SONKOWSKY, 'Delivery', 270.

[113] Cicero, *Or.* 3.57.216–17; 3.59.220.

[114] Cicero, *Or.* 3.5.19.

[115] Cicero, *Part.* 79.

who is not a sound thinker. Thus whoever devotes himself to true eloquence devotes himself to sound thinking (*prudenter intellegit*), which
even in the conduct of great wars cannot reasonably be dispensed with.'[116]
Yet, in the end, it is still the art of delivery which is both crucial and decisive: 'There is no thought which can bring credit to an orator unless it is
fitly and perfectly expressed.'[117] One should not forget the vital element of
grace in good delivery: 'For it is not enough to discern what is to be said
unless you have the ability to say it fluently and with some charm; nor
even is this enough unless what is said is recommended by some grace of
voice, facial expression, and action (*nisi id quod dicitur fit voce voltu mo-
tuque conditius*).'[118]

Although gracious or powerful delivery is itself an art, among rhetorati-
cians in the Greco-Roman period, including the great thinker Cicero, one
would not conceive of 'art for art's sake'. This is because, as Cicero himself points out, eloquence offers the greatest rewards in Roman society, it
leads to glory, honour, reputation, status and applause: 'From eloquence
those who have acquired it obtain glory and honour and high esteem.'[119]
Eloquence 'brings with it a large measure of popularity, glory and power
(*gratiae, gloriae, praesidi plurimum*).'[120] And 'through this he won not
only the highest reputation for talent, but also great applause (*summam in-
geni non laudem modo sed etiam admirationem est consecutus*).'[121]

On the matter of the much sought-after glory[122] in Roman society,
Cicero singles out one of his contemporaries: 'Gnaeus Pompeius my contemporary ... destined by nature to pre-eminence, would have enjoyed
greater glory for eloquence had not ambition for still greater glory drawn
him off to the prizes of a military career. His language had some elevation
and he possessed good judgement in discerning the question at issue but
chiefly a fine voice and great dignity of bearing made his delivery impressive.'[123] Cicero also regards Marcus Cornelius Cethegus as the first eloquent Roman who is 'sweet-speaking' (*suaviloquens*).[124] Hortensius' elo-

---

[116] Cicero, *Br.* 6.23.

[117] Cicero, *Orat.* 67.227.

[118] Cicero, *Br.* 29.110.

[119] Cicero, *Inv.* 1.5. *Br.* 49.182: 'Eloquence has held out the greatest rewards, all men
have desired to be speakers, no great number have ventured to try, few have been successful.'

[120] Cicero, *Orat.* 41.141.

[121] Cicero, *Br.* 43.159. Cf. *Or.* 3.14.53.

[122] Cicero, *Or.* 1.4.14: 'Our people [Romans] were fired with a really incredible enthusiasm for eloquence.' *Off.* 2.14.48: 'The eloquent and judicious speaker is received
with high admiration, and his hearers think him understanding and wise beyond all others.'

[123] Cicero, *Br.* 68.239.

[124] Cicero, *Br.* 14.57–58; Ennius, *Ann.* 304–05; Quintilian 11.3.31.

quence is described as 'worthy of the ears of Roman or even of Greece (*Romanis Graecique auribus digna*)'.[125]

Cicero calls *actio* a 'sort of language'[126] and 'a kind of eloquence of the body' (Quintilian 11.3.1). This point is particularly important because oratory is essentially understood as body language. But for body language to be effective, body movement must be in full harmony with the orator's mind and words. For Cicero the body talks: 'For by action the body talks (*Est enim actio quasi sermo corporis*), so it is all the more necessary to make it agree with the thought; and nature has given us eyes ... to indicate the feelings of the mind, so that in the matter of delivery which we are now considering the face is next in importance to the voice; and the eyes are the dominant feature in the face' (*Or.* 3.59.223). On the expression of the orator's eyes, which is deemed to be very crucial in delivery, Cicero writes, 'For as the face is the image of the soul, so are the eyes its interpreters, in respect of which the subjects under discussion will provide the proper limits for the expression of joy or grief.'[127] When each of these important elements is harmoniously combined, the result is excellent oration which achieves the effects the speaker desires.

Earlier on, Cicero mentions that what makes a speaker's delivery impressive is an excellent voice combined with great dignity of bearing. In Roman society at the time of Cicero, it would have been understood by all that a fine voice and great dignity could only come from man. From this point on voice and bearing emerges the crucial matter of masculinity in Roman rhetoric, especially in the skill of delivery which is the prerogative of men. A good speaker takes great pains to manage his voice and all other body gestures well so that nothing effeminate appears, but only manly features: 'The superior orator will therefore vary and modulate his voice; now raising and now lowering it, he will run through the whole scale of tones. He will also use gestures in such a way as to avoid excess: he will maintain an erect and lofty carriage, with but little pacing to and fro, and never for a long distance. As for darting forward, he will keep it under control and employ it but seldom. There should be no effeminate bending of the neck, no twiddling of the fingers, no marking the rhythm with the finger-joint. He will control himself by the pose of his whole frame, and the vigorous and manly attitude of the body (*virili laterum flexione*), extending the arm in moments of passion, and dropping it in calmer moods. Furthermore, what dignity and charm is contributed by the countenance, which has a role second only to the voice.'[128] In view of such descriptions, the proper

---

[125] Cicero, *Br.* 2.6.
[126] Cicero, *Or.* 3.59.222. See *Orat.* 55.
[127] Cicero, *Orat.* 17.60.
[128] Cicero, *Orat.* 18.59–60.

use of body language is defined in part by masculinity over and against a
negatively conceived femininity.

4.3.3.5 Quintilian (c. 35–100 AD)

If the early Roman Empire is regarded as 'one of the most eloquent periods
in human history', Quintilian's writing would most probably be the best
resource about oratory of the time.[129] Quintilian's *Institutio Oratoria* consists of twelve books in which he skilfully adapts some of the features of
Aristotle's *Rhetorica* and of Cicero's *De Oratore* and *Orator*.[130] Like his
predecessors, Quintilian adopts the five parts of rhetoric: 'The art of oratory, as taught by most authorities, and those the best, consists of five
parts: invention, arrangement, expression, memory, and delivery or action
(the two latter terms being used synonymously)' (3.3.1).

For Quintilian, rhetoric is not only a matter of speaking well, it should
also include other virtues and character of the orator since no man can
speak well unless he is a good man (2.15.34) or *vir bonus* (11.3.10). Only
good and virtuous men may possess oratory.[131] Quintilian's emphasis on
the importance of the moral character of the orator distinguishes him from
some of his predecessors, including Aristotle and Cicero.

Quintilian has a grand view of the whole man in his philosophy of education. For him, the accomplished orator is 'the greatest human type'. With
this noble goal in mind, Quintilian readily assumes the role of a serious
educator, especially in the training of great orators. Such thinking may be
described as being in line with the ethos of his time, which had begun 'to
see human beings as individuals rather than as cogs in society.'[132]

Since oratory is essentially body language, it is natural that a kind of
rhetorical theory about the body develops in Greco-Roman tradition. There
is, for instance, a well-known Roman idiom that: 'The body of the orator
must be the body of the good man. This body is good to the extent that it
betrays itself to be a mere vessel, given its virtue and value by the soul of
the good man of which it is the bearer. Bodily excellence cites and per-
forms the authority of the good man.'[133] It is thus clear that Quintilian does
not just want to train a skilful actor, but an actual man who is morally
good. The body of the orator is only good when it reveals 'the goodness of
the orator himself.'[134] Moreover, the orator must also be a man who may

---

[129] KENNEDY, *Rhetoric*, 428.

[130] KENNEDY, *Rhetoric*, 496–97.

[131] Quintilian 2.17.43. Cf. 12.1.9

[132] KENNEDY, *Rhetoric*, 498.

[133] E. GUNDERSON, *Staging Masculinity: The Rhetoric of Performance in the Roman
World* (Ann Arbor: University of Michigan Press, 2000), 61.

[134] GUNDERSON, *Masculinity*, 61.

truly be called wise and not only perfect in moral character (Quintilian 1. pr. 18–19).[135]

Quintilian never seriously doubts the great power and charm of a good delivery and its tremendous impact: 'Delivery itself has a marvellously powerful effect in oratory' (11. 3. 2). He continues that he has 'no hesitation in saying that even mediocre speech, made attractive by the power of Delivery, will carry more weight than the best speech deprived of this help. After all, when Demosthenes was asked what was the most important thing in the whole business of oratory, he gave the prize to Delivery.'[136]

Lest one get the wrong impression that for an orator to be successful he must necessarily be overbearing or even aggressive, Quintilian makes a contrary suggestion. For him, an orator should also possess some of the most attractive qualities such as humanity, approachability, moderation and kindness (11.1.42). According to Quintilian, the perfection of oratory may only be achieved when the orator of noble personal character acquires the essential skills of the art and delivers them accordingly.[137] Quintilian is also concerned about the orator's personal character with special reference to decorum or propriety: 'An impudent, disorderly, or angry style of delivery is unseemly in any speaker.... Speech indeed is very commonly an index of character, and reveals the secrets of the heart. There is good ground for the Greek saying that a man speaks as he lives.'[138]

Although Quintilian agrees with Aristotle in theory that 'delivery is a matter of nature rather than of art,'[139] he qualifies it by saying that 'nothing comes to perfection unless nature is assisted by art.'[140] Quintilian thus elaborates on the importance of voice, other training and practice at considerable length (11.3.19, 22).

Like other educators of oratory, Quintilian also takes for granted that this art is the prerogative of man. Masculinity must, therefore, be maintained and displayed at all costs and at all times. The dull, coarse, hard and stiff voice of a man is just as bad as an effeminate voice which is thin, empty, grating, feeble and soft.[141] As such, when Quintilian speaks about body gesture he is referring to that of a man in rhetorical training. Such body gesture is literally from head to toe as 'gesture conveys meaning

---

[135] GUNDERSON, *Masculinity*, 87–88.

[136] Quintilian 11.3.5–8; cf. also Philodemus 1.196.3; Cicero, *Br.* 37.142, *Orat.* 17.56; Plutarch, *Mor.* 845B.

[137] Quintilian 11.1.10: 'Indeed, since words are very powerful by themselves, and the voice adds its own contribution to the content, and gestures and movements have a meaning, then, when they all come together, the result must be perfection.'

[138] Quintilian 11.1.29–30.

[139] Quintilian, *Instititio Oratoria*, vol. V, trans. D. A. RUSSELL, Introduction, 5.

[140] Quintilian 11.3.11. See Cicero, *Or.* 3.42; *Br.* 137.

[141] Quintilian 11.3.30–32.

without the help of words' (11.3.66–67). Due to the crucial role that gesture play in the body language of delivery, the respective roles that members of a man's body play, with special reference to Quintilian's instruction, merit individual attention.

The Head

Quintilian's instruction on body gesture begins with the head: 'It is the head which occupies the chief place in Delivery (as it does in the body itself).... (1) For seemliness, it must first be upright and natural.... (2) The head conveys meaning in many different ways. Apart from the movements of assent, denial, and agreement, there are others, well-known and universally used, which express modesty, doubt, surprise, and indignation' (11.3.69–71).

From the head Quintilian then focuses more specifically on the face as the head's dominant feature. From there he moves orderly downward to the neck, then the shoulders, the arms and the hands (11.3.72–84).[142]

The Face and the Eyes

'The face is sovereign', according to Quintilian, because 'it is this that makes us humble, threatening, flattering, sad, cheerful, proud, or submissive; men hang on this; men fix their gaze on this; this is watched even before we start to speak; this makes us love some people and hate others; this makes us understand many things; this often replaces words altogether' (11.3.72).

Of the face itself the most important and obvious feature is the eyes: 'The mind shines through especially in ... the eyelids and the cheeks. Much also is done by the eyebrows' (11.3.75–78).[143] Whatever one does with the various parts of the body, all feminine mannerisms must be avoided, warned Quintilian.[144]

Neck and Shoulders

Good posture is appreciated by Quintilian who not only describes it, but also provides moral commentary. Quintilian reveals the status-conscious side of Roman society when he equates a gesture of servitude with hypocrisy. 'The nape of the neck must be straight, not stiff or bent back ...

---

[142] GUNDERSON, *Masculinity*, 76.

[143] Quintilian 11.3.76 (eyes), 78–79 (eyebrows), 69 (head), 83 (shoulders), 126 (feet), 128-29 (swaying), 165. Compare Seneca, 'A sexually impure man is revealed by his gait, his gestures, sometimes by his answers, by his finger touching his head, and by the shifting of his eyes' (*Ep.* 52.12).

[144] A. CAESAR, *Taking it Like a Man: Suffering, Sexuality and the War Poets: Brooke, Sassoon, Owen, Graves* (Manchester; Manchester University Press, 1993), 63.

Rarely is it becoming to shrug or hunch the shoulders, because this short-ens the neck and produces a gesture of humiliation and servility (*gestum quendam humilem atque servilem*), suggesting hypocrisy, because people use it when they are pretending to flatter, admire, or fear' (11.3.83).

Hands

Quintilian links the use of the hands as an important body gesture to that of 'deauthorization and silencing' of one's rivals, including political oppo-nents.[145] In general, the hands are given an exceptionally important value for the speaker: 'As for the hands, without which the delivery would be crippled and enfeebled, it is almost impossible to say how many move-ments they possess, for these almost match the entire stock of words. Other parts of the body assist the speaker: the hands, I might almost say, speak for themselves' (11.3.85–87).

Feet

So long as one does so with great moderation, the use of feet and particu-larly foot-stomping is seen to be a helpful gesture. 'Stamping the foot can be opportune on occasion, as Cicero says, at the beginning or end of a pas-sage of aggressive argument, but if it is done often it shows the speaker to be a fool, and ceases to attract the judge's attention.'[146]

Gestures Mimicking Action

For Quintilian, gestures which mimic action must be avoided. Thus, imitat-ing parts of a scene which one describes detracts from the overall efforts of the speaker. 'An orator has to be very different from a dancer; he must adapt his gesture to his sense more than to his words – which indeed was the practice of the more serious actors too. I would readily let him move his hand towards himself when he speaks about himself, or towards a per-son whom he wishes to point out, and a few things like that; but I do not approve of his miming attitudes and making a visual display of whatever he says. This caution applies not only to the hands, but to the whole range of gesture and voice.'[147]

Inappropriate Gestures Taboo

Certain movements are singled out as being particularly important to avoid. It appears that these are either coarse or repetitive actions. 'Take care not to thrust the chest or stomach forward. This arches the back, and all bending backwards is unsightly. The side must be in tune with the ges-

---

[145] GUNDERSON, *Masculinity*, 83.
[146] Quintilian 11.3.128. See Cicero, *Or.* 3.220.
[147] Quintilian 11.3.88–90.

ture, for the movement of the whole body is important, so much so that Cicero says that more is done by this than by the hands themselves. This is what he says in the Orator: "No twiddling of the fingers, no marking the rhythm with the finger joint; he controls himself more by the pose of his whole body and the manly flexing of the side."' (11.3.122; See Cicero, *Orat.* 18.59).

Harmonious Coordination

In the mobilization of the various body parts in delivery great emphasis is placed on good co-ordination and harmony, similar to an orchestra: 'Not only is the body carefully articulated in its parts, it is also coordinated and organized such that its elements will be orchestrated into a harmonized whole' (11.3.122; 11.3.70).

Dress

Although no specific clothing is regarded as better than others, the theme of masculinity arises in relation to dress. 'As for dress, there is no special form for the orator, but his is noticed more. As with all men of standing, it should be distinguished and masculine' (11.3.137). Certain extreme actions related to dress are also mentioned: 'Of course, wrapping your left hand in your toga and tying it round you is almost insane, and throwing back the fold from its bottom onto the right shoulder is foppish and effeminate' (11.3.146).

Jane Gardner's comments on dress and masculinity emphasise that there was indeed a dress code. When discussing masculinity in this regard, she notes that it is not sufficient simply to be a man, but one must act according to an expected gender role. That is, beyond the biological gender boundary there is a psychological one. Moreover, Gardner draws attention to the severity of views on gender, that it was practically anathema to intentionally imitate a woman as this was to degrade oneself.[148]

According to Gardner, Roman lawyers actually defined what men's and women's clothing was based upon social assumptions about masculine behaviour.[149] Paulus also comments that clothing is indicative of what was or was not appropriate for a man to do because certain garments or manners of dress would have shamed him and damaged his masculine image.[150] Therefore, one may better gain insights into masculinity *vis-à-vis* the legacy of male (and female) clothing.

---

[148] J. F. GARDNER, 'Sexing a Roman: imperfect men in Roman law', in L. FOXHALL and J. SALMON (eds.), *When Men Were Men: Masculinity, Power, and Identity in Classical Antiquity* (London: Routledge, 1998), 136–52, at 147.

[149] GARDNER, 'Sexing a Roman", 136.

[150] Paulus, *Sent.* 3.6.80. Cf. *Dig.* 34.2.23.2.

The Orator and Actor

It is also noteworthy that Quintilian seeks to make a clear distinction between a comic actor and a true orator: 'I do not want my pupil to be a comic actor, but an orator' (*non enim comoedum esse, sed oratorem volo*).[151] Quintilian remarks that Cicero gives the best advice on this matter: 'Nowadays, however, a somewhat more agitated style of delivery is regarded as acceptable, and is indeed appropriate in some contexts; but it needs to be under control, lest, in our eagerness to pursue the elegance of the performer, we lose the authority of the good and grave man (*dum actoris captamus elegantiam, perdamus viri boni gravis auctoritatem*).'[152]

Quintilian also sets *actio* and *imitatio* against each other and insists that the orator's performance is not just an imitation of a 'thing', that is the orator's delivery must be seen as a performance of essence or of character. Only in this way is the orator a true actor of himself (11.3.5). Only this self, in Quintilian's view, is the *vir bonus et gravis* ('the good and serious man'). This point is important for Quintilian because a true orator may only be an actor or imitator for himself and not for others.

In his conclusion, Quintilian cites the good example of Cicero, and hails Marcus Antonius as an orator *par excellence* in the art of delivery in gesture, voice and words which agree with the course of his thoughts.[153]

Of all the great masters of Greco-Roman rhetoric cited, Quintilian may well be described as the most engaged on the subject of the moral character of the orator. Within a conversation about Corinthians, this point is significant. In Paul's polemics against his critics, some of whom were practitioners of Greco-Roman rhetoric, admirers of it or both, Paul's perception of the practice, especially its emphasis on delivery and eloquence, is quite understandably negative. As such, Quintilian's emphasis on the moral character of the orator may, to a certain extent, serve as the other side of the coin. One may perceive the moral character of the orator as a kind of counter-balance, although the considerable attention given to delivery would possibly not escape the apostle's criticism.

Sonkowsky comes to the conclusion that within this tradition, the techniques of delivery are a crucial component to the very act of writing a composition. Issues of oration are not considered in an *ad hoc* manner long after writing is completed, but is an integral part of the process.[154] And Quintilian is important not only for a brief span of time, but rather has an enduring influence. As Nadeau sums up so well: 'From Quintilian's time through the Middle Ages and well into the Renaissance and beyond it,

---

[151] Quintilian 11.3.182.
[152] Quintilian 11.3.184. Cf. Cicero, *Orat.* 41.141.
[153] Quintilian 11.3.184. See Cicero. *Br.* 37.141.
[154] SONKOWSKY, 'Delivery', 273.

rhetoric and commentaries provide a repetition of classical theory with whatever modifications are required to adapt it to the times.'[155]

Sonkowsky's point is important because of the intimate relationship between literary composition and public presentation, which are both part and parcel of the process of ancient rhetoric. In the case of Paul, the distinction between literary composition and public presentation is not always clear, nor is it the apostle's particular concern to make them distinct. For Paul, the two could hardly be separated. Thus, when he mentions the 'message (λόγος) of the cross' he most likely has in mind the content of his message (i.e. literary composition) and its proclamation (i.e. public presentation). However, 2 Cor. 10.10 seems to suggest that Paul's critics make a distinction between his literary composition (i.e. his letters which they consider 'weighty and strong') and his bodily presence and speech (regarded as 'weak' and 'contemptible'). The critics' distinction between literary composition and public presentation as well as their negative judgment on the latter are quite understandable in the case of Paul in the context of Greco-Roman rhetoric. In its later development, as the previous survey indicates, Greco-Roman rhetoric takes the public presentation (i.e. delivery) more seriously than literary composition because it is body language which proves to be far more powerful and attractive than mere written words or speech without gestures.

4.4 Recent Contributions on Masculinity

Rhetoric occupied an important place in Greco-Roman society and was exclusively a manly game. This is most evident when delivery is analysed: positive body language is to be properly masculine. When this point is brought into conversation with Paul and the Corinthian controversy, it may be observed that Paul's masculinity is called into question. Therefore, how the theme of masculinity is evaluated is of significance and may, especially, illuminate one's reading of 1 Cor. 2. 1–5 and 2 Cor. 10.10.

Within recent New Testament studies significant attention has been given to the place of masculinity in surrounding cultures. Indeed, any study on Greco-Roman rhetoric would be incomplete that did not take masculinity seriously.[156]

---

[155] NADEAU, 'Delivery', 59.

[156] For an up-to-date survey of works on this subject see MOORE, '"O Man, Who Art Thou ...?": Masculinity Studies and New Testament Studies', in S. MOORE and J. C. ANDERSON (eds.), *New Testament Masculinities* (SBLSS 45; Atlanta: Society of Biblical Literature, 2003), 1–22.

One work that merits special mention is that of Maud Gleason.[157] Her work seeks to shift attention to the social dynamics of rhetoric and how it was used to present oneself. In focusing on this angle, appreciation is found for the 'functional aesthetics' of what she calls a 'profoundly traditional performance genre.'[158] Gleason's findings are particularly helpful for understanding the ethos of rhetoric, especially the crucial issue of masculinity. Her focus is most relevant to the Corinthian problem because Paul's opponents were critical of his weak self-presentation and, by implication, the crucial absence of manliness expected of any good orator.

Gleason describes those who read ancient rhetoric in the 20th century, or 21st as is the case now, as 'entirely an armchair affair'. As such, they often fail to appreciate some of the basic aspects of the training and discipline which were essential to serious rhetorical education (παιδεία). These were the necessary processes through which men, especially upper-class men, were made. In addition to comments made in the preceding conversation, Gleason comments that for both Greek and Roman gentlemen παιδεία was a form of 'symbolic capital'. In her words: 'Its development required time, money, effort, and social position ... eloquence was the essential precondition of its display.'[159]

According to Gleason, it is through παιδεία in public speaking and constant competition with peers that a Roman displays his cultural capital, thereby distinguishing authentic members of the elite from the non-elite of society. When competing for status dominance, the very best performers attracted large audiences. The result of such dramatising, which included symbolic violence, was to further impress upon the audience the gap between educated and uneducated. So effective were these performances that the difference between the classes came to be seen not as a difference in education, but in the biology itself.[160]

Gleason demonstrates that in the 2nd century there was increased concentration on training in posturing, which was seen as the very embodiment of manhood. However, deportment exercise was not static, but an ongoing dynamic process of male socialisation in which gender identity and public identity were among the most essential parts of an interconnected whole. Self-presentation largely determined a man's standing in society.[161] Viewed from this perspective, Paul's apparent lack of good self-presentation and impressive public identity (1 Cor. 2.1–5; 2 Cor. 10.10) would only have made him an easy target of his critics' contempt.

---

[157] GLEASON, *Making Men*.

[158] GLEASON, *Making Men*, xx.

[159] GLEASON, *Making Men*, xx–xxi.

[160] GLEASON, *Making Men*, xxi.

[161] GLEASON, *Making Men*, xxvi.

The lives and careers of two popular 2nd century rhetoricians, Favorinus and Polemo, provide Gleason fascinating material and insights into the way ancient Romans perceived and constructed masculinity during a time when men, especially those of the upper class, were preoccupied with concerns about manly deportment. In Gleason's view, Favorinus and Polemo represent opposing paradigms of masculinity.

The relatively late material of Gleason (2nd cent.) may at first glance appear to be a weak point in her analysis. However, under closer scrutiny the date of the sources are a strength when applied to Corinthian studies because they may well serve to demonstrate historical continuity in the development of Greco-Roman rhetoric from the time of Aristotle to Quintilian. Moreover, since Greco-Roman rhetoric is well established within the broader social ethos of the Greco-Roman world in the course of at least three centuries, and most of its theories and practices remained relatively constant, the 2nd century materials used by Gleason may reasonably be assumed as relevant witnesses to Paul's time.

Gleason's findings are far more than just rhetorical studies of 2nd century Roman society. They also involve the Sophistic movement of the time and reveal a lot about the function and meaning of an elite culture. She is right in pointing out that it was the *Pax Romana* that provided the aristocrats the environment to challenge each other's masculinity while they remained absolutely sure of their 'collective dominance'.[162]

The Sophistic movement was primarily a Greek movement in the 5th century BC. Soon after the time of Christ a new movement appeared and was given the name 'Second Sophistic' by the sophist Philostratus, who wrote about its history up to around 200 AD.[163] This movement became very popular during the 2nd century and took the form of a kind of public entertainment, although it also had its place in some important cultural functions. Its popularity brought some sophists a great deal of wealth and turned them into fashionable preachers who inculcated belief in traditional religious and moral values in the most refined and elegant form.

Aelius Aristides and Herodes Atticus must be counted among the most famous sophists of the 2nd century.[164] However, due to the perceived pagan origin of sophistry the movement was often criticised by Christians, especially in its earlier stage. Christian criticism mainly targets the sophists' celebration of the beauties, derived from pagan mythology, as well as special attention given to oratory and other cherished aspects of the lifestyle of the time. This situation seems to have changed significantly when its influence on Christianity (c. 2nd cent.) became rather considerable.[165] Glen

---

[162] GLEASON, *Making Men*, 162.
[163] KENNEDY, *Classical Rhetoric*, 37.
[164] KENNEDY, *Classical Rhetoric*, 38.
[165] KENNEDY, *Classical Rhetoric*, 39.

Bowersock describes the sophists in the second movement as established 'public speakers who offered a predominantly rhetorical form of higher education, with distinct emphasis on its more ostentatious forms.'[166]

The history of classical antiquity is almost exclusively a history of men. Lin Foxhall describes women as being excluded from 'the structure of power perpetrated by dominant masculine ideologies.'[167] Foxhall identifies maleness as something that one is born with – male body and genitalia – and regardless of later social or even physical events a man (and his hierarchical position) could not easily be lost.[168] Dominic Montserrat elaborates that it was the male body in antiquity which provided a significant and symbolic measure within power discourses, social position and identity. The male form was not only physically superior to others, but may be understood as a blank canvas upon which power relations could be painted. The 'unmarked, unspecified and unqualified human body was male' and other forms were gauged in relation to it.[169] From Montserrat's observations about the physical body of a man, one also perceives a close connection with the social ethos and values of the time, especially in relation to power and status. As such, the symbolic nature of man's body in social terms was just as important, if not more so, as its physical aspects.

The legal implications of male identity were just as important as its social aspects. Gardner draws attention to the role of men within Roman law, they performed the role of *paterfamilias* and could exercise their *potestas* over the other members of the family. Men, in other words, were predetermined to have a superior legal standing because of their masculinity. Women, however, were restricted in regard to their legal capacities when engaging in transactions and acting as a head of the house.[170]

Barton makes a subtle but significant distinction between males and men: they are not synonymous. A male in Roman culture was not necessarily a man. The distinction is that 'to be male' is an ontological statement while 'to be a man' an existential one. One may be born human (*homo*) and male (*mas*), however one must transform themselves into a man (*vir*).[171] As such, becoming a man was not taken for granted. The making of a man and the maintenance of manhood/masculinity help to explain the fierce competition which was part and parcel of Greco-Roman society.

---

[166] G. W. BOWERSOCK, *The Second Sophistic: A Cultural Phenomenon in the Roman Empire* (London: Routledge, 1993), 1.

[167] FOXHALL, *When Men Were Men*, 1.

[168] FOXHALL, *When Men Were Men*, 5.

[169] D. MONTSERRAT, 'Experiencing the male body in Roman Egypt', in *When Men Were Men,* 153–64, at 153.

[170] GARDNER, 'Sexing a Roman', 136.

[171] BARTON, *Roman Honour*, 38.

When considering fierce competition, Gleason is particularly mindful of how terrifying defeat and public humiliation would have been.[172] There was a great deal at stake, indeed it was a matter of survival, and usually only the fittest survived. This may, in part, account for the existence of divisions and quarrels (1 Cor. 1.10, 11) and their seriousness in the Corinthian church. In this context, the Corinthian conflict was essentially the result of fierce competition between the men: Paul, Cephas and Apollos (even Christ). While these leaders themselves might not personally approve of such unwarranted competition, as Paul himself had clearly done (1 Cor. 1.13–17), their respective parties thought otherwise. As such, these enthusiastic party supporters were only behaving as the ordinary Corinthians did: according to the social ethos and practice of the time. It was this kind of social ethos and practice which Paul was in process of inverting. Given the social context, Paul's actions were very risky.

The establishment of masculinity and its maintenance were demanding tasks. David Gilmore finds a number of ways to describe these undertakings: it is hardy work; requires incredible self-discipline; manhood is practically a cult and it involves ideologies.[173] The ideologies of manhood require men to meet certain demands lest they lose their very identity, which would have been perceived as worse than death. A particular moral structure was in place to guarantee that men accepted a code of appropriate behaviour.[174] One may well imagine that there was an enormous stress involved in preserving and solidifying one's manhood.

Greco-Roman society was so committed to the forming as well as the maintaining of true masculinity that Gilmore describes men as being expected to tame nature. Real men were seen to create values where none were present and this was done through qualities of discipline, self-reliance and self-direction. As men, they were the ones who maintained kinship units within society and this was perceived as nothing less than heroic.

---

[172] 'The sheer sweat of exertion involved in projecting an unamplified voice before a large outdoor audience, the demands of managing the heavy folds of the cloak or toga, the exhilarating risk of stumbles and solecisms lying in wait for a moment's loss of nerve, the vibrant immediacy of a collaborative live audience, ready to explode with jeers or applause. We must imagine the intoxicating sense of power that surged through the performer as he mastered the crowd, overwhelming sceptics and hecklers with the hypnotic charm of a beautifully controlled voice in full spate. We must also try to remember the terror of defeat and public humiliation, the courage required to risk both.' (GLEASON, *Making Men*, xx). The fierce competition between or among men and the relentless struggle for power, dominance as well as survival in the Greco-Roman society must be understood in this context. It is also in such social ethos that church divisions in Corinth must be perceived.

[173] D. D. GILMORE, *Manhood in the Making: Cultural Concepts of Masculinity* (New Haven: Yale University Press, 1990), 220.

[174] GILMORE, *Manhood*, 221.

Moreover, to be a man was to be a procreator.[175] When such perceptions are understood to have penetrated the whole of ancient Roman society, then Paul's challenges to current perceptions on masculinity – whether in relation to his self-presentation, manner of speech or his own perception of 'weakness' – were quite drastic.

That rhetoric, with its strong emphasis on masculinity, was an exclusive game of men is also very evident in the fact that it rigidly and consistently divided humanity into two camps, characterised as masculine or feminine. To use Gleason's description, these two groups are the legitimate and illegitimate.[176] In such a social context and according to such rigid social and gender division, it may be appropriate and significant to ask if Paul would be perceived by his critics as belonging to the feminine and, therefore, illegitimate category.

If Paul's social standing, according to the current perception about masculinity, was indeed illegitimate, how could he possibly lead and exercise his apostolic authority in competition with the so-called super-apostles? Questions like these are relevant because Paul operated in a face-to-face society where there were constant suspicions arising about manly adequacy and judgments forming about how one performed as a man.[177]

The above observations on masculinity have a natural association with body language. For the Greeks and Romans, masculinity, just like crucifixion in antiquity, became a system of signs and symbols by which powerful and effective body language was conveyed *vis-à-vis* social interactions. It was the sort of body language that male children began to learn from their earliest moments along with proper physical development.[178]

Masculinity became of such paramount concern and preoccupation within Greco-Roman rhetorical thought that the two were often times practically synonymous. The work of Gleason is significant for drawing attention to rhetoric and masculinity: 'In a value system that prized rhetorical skill as the quintessential human excellence, and in a society so structured that this perfection could be achieved only by adult males, arbiters of rhetoric were also arbiters of masculine deportment.'[179] Moreover, an accomplished presenter of winsome masculine deportment was also regarded as a 'good man'. For Gunderson, such value judgment was closely intertwined with the development of rhetoric, so much so that he sees the practice of oration by good men as the motivation for the development of rhetorical theory.[180]

---

[175] GILMORE, *Manhood*, 223.
[176] See GUNDERSON, *Masculinity*, 9.
[177] GLEASON, *Making Men*, xxii.
[178] GLEASON, *Making Men*, 70. Cf. Soranus, *Gyn.*2.32 (101).
[179] GLEASON, *Making Men*, 104.
[180] GUNDERSON, *Masculinity*, 9.

Gleason focuses attention on the well-known professional quarrels between the sophists Favorinus and Polemo. The feud between the two also
involved their pupils, who were expected to take sides. Gleason sees here a
case which is 'an integral part of male socialization.' She elaborates that
one explanation why these rivalries became as intense as they did is because they came to be seen as two distinct and opposing views on masculinity. As such, claims to power and status were involved, which was of
moral interest not only to philosophers, but sophists as well.[181]

This feud and the analysis of it by Gleason are relevant to the Corinthian schism. This is because, to use Gleason's expression, the Corinthian
rift was also essentially a kind of 'male socialization' and the various parties in the names of Paul, Apollos and Cephas (even Christ) are 'interested
parties in the struggle', who represent competing paradigms of masculinity, as well as competing claims to power and status. Paul expresses his
deep disappointment with these competing Corinthians because as believers they apparently forgot their Christian identity, or had placed their social identity over and above that of their divine calling. You were 'called
to be saints' (κλητοῖς ἁγίοις, 1 Cor. 1.2), Paul solemnly reminds them.
However, you were 'behaving according to human inclinations' (3.3). And
then in 3.4 he asks them: 'Are you not merely human?'

Gleason even describes the fierce competition to preserve manly integrity as analogous to the role of an athlete.[182] Moreover, the competitors
must desperately seek to maintain a profile which is truly masculine and
includes the right measure of gazing, walking and gesturing in a masculine
manner. To achieve the right level of masculinity required cultivation and
ongoing effort, not least because it was not to look pretentious but natural.
One must act without appearing to be an actor.[183] One may view Paul as a
product and member of this society. It remains to be seen if the bearer of
the message of the cross felt compelled to conform to the social conventions of such masculinity.

In Greco-Roman society gender differences were often made according
to movement of the human body because it served effectively as a kind of
body language. Similarly, different social classes were also distinguished
more or less in that way through the minutiae of body language, besides
the external language of dress. Gleason also comments on what behav-
ioural psychologists observe, that 'nonverbal behaviour encodes power
well.'[184] This is one of the ways to further elucidate Paul and his critics
when they judge his bodily presence to be weak.

---

[181] GLEASON, *Making Men*, 73.
[182] GLEASON, *Making Men*, 73.
[183] GLEASON, *Making Men*, 80.
[184] GLEASON, *Making Men*, xxvi.

The great popularity and charm of self-presentation must not be perceived narrowly in terms of formal competition between social or political rivals. According to Gleason, great sophists and declaimers are only a beginning point as all aristocrats were expected to be impressive public speakers in all sorts of occasions and functions, both public and private.[185] While rhetorical practice was an exclusive game of men, not all men were equal. It was a very elitist game, reserved predominately and often exclusively for aristocrats. Yet over the centuries, as rhetoric permeated practically the entire culture, even the non-elitist had significant roles to play: the indispensable audience, observers and even self-appointed judges. In this sense, it would be reasonable to suggest that Paul's critics or judges were more than just a few leaders. The magnitude of the Corinthian conflict and crisis may be perceived as including a much larger group which played this well-established role.

Great risk was involved in self-presentation by which true masculinity was established, maintained and constantly renewed because in the cruel and often unpredictable arena of relentless competition, the participant would ultimately end up being either honoured or shamed. It was the inescapable duty of a man to be constantly on guard for the defence of personal as well as family honour.[186] This important point is relevant to Paul's conflict. While Paul as the slave or fool of Christ crucified is not at all concerned with the defence of his own personal or family honour, he evidently considers it necessary to defend the honour and integrity of his own *apostolic* identity and integrity (e.g. 1 Cor. 4.1–13; 2 Cor. 10–13). It remains to be seen if and in what way Paul's manner of defending his apostolic identity and integrity constitutes an inversion of the current social ethos.

Respectable competition, in which true manliness is at stake, could only take place between or among people who were equal or almost equal in honour and status. Hence, a challenge presented to an inferior or somebody without social honour could only bring shame and humiliation to the challenger.[187] In this cruel game, one need be mindful of the significant role the audience played which often acted as the 'arbiter of a suspenseful process.'[188] The winner of such a competitive exchange was naturally thought to have defended his honour, while the loser would have to endure great shame and damage to his status in the community.[189] Paul seems to be reminding the competing parties in Corinth of their foolishness and

---

[185] GLEASON, *Making Men*, xx–xxi.

[186] H. MOXNES, 'Honour and Shame', in R. L. ROHRBAUGH (ed.), *The Social Science and New Testament Interpretation* (Peabody: Hendrickson Publishers, 1996), 19–49, at 20.

[187] MOXNES, 'Honour', 20.

[188] GLEASON, *Making Men*, xxiii.

[189] MOXNES, 'Honour', 21.

mindlessness, for in any fight winners eventually emerge and some become losers. In Paul's view, it was senseless that such should happen as all
those who believe are already winners in Christ (1 Cor. 3.21–23) and, thus,
none need be losers.

The lack of true masculinity is also contemptuously expressed as the
appearance of 'effeminate signs'. In Clement's words, 'a noble man should
bear no sign of effeminacy upon his face or any other portion of his body.
Nor should the disgrace of unmanliness ever be found in his movements or
his posture.'[190] And again that: 'The orderly man (*ho kosmios*) reveals his
self-restraint through his deportment: he is deep-voiced and slow-stepping,
and his eyes, neither fixed nor rapidly blinking, hold a certain indefinably
courageous gleam.'[191] As such, 'the slightest sign of softness or slackening
will undo the whole effect [of a man].'[192]

On the subject of effeminate appearance and behaviour the research of
Caesar draws attention to two words. The first is *androgynos* ('effeminate'), which is used to describe the appearance of someone who is some-
where between a man and woman. The second is *cinaedus*, which refers to
sexual deviance, especially to males who prefer to play a feminine (i.e. re-
ceptive) role in intercourse with other men. Both terms are used quite in-
discriminately of men who are effeminate in appearance and behaviour.[193]

Dio Chrysostom is particularly critical of effeminate mannerisms:
'someone who is a male, and retains a male's distinctive marks
(χαρακτῆρα) and his proper speech-being incapable of eradicating also the
marks of Nature (τὰ σημεῖα τῆς φύσεως), even though he makes effort to
hide them from the world, just as the thief hides stolen goods-being smit-
ten by Furies and perverted and in every way made effeminate, is ready to
do anything at all, but nothing in accord with his own nature.'[194] The Stoics often regarded men's hair as 'symbolic language of masculinity' which
was 'established by Nature itself.'[195] Epictetus instructs his students to
'leave the care of their hair to God or Nature who made it' and avoid any
'effeminate appearance.'[196]

---

[190] Clement of Alexandria, *Paed.* 3.11.73–74.

[191] Adamantius 2.49.1.413–14F. GLEASON, *Making Men*, 61.

[192] GLEASON, *Making Men*, 62.

[193] CAESAR, *Taking it*, 64.

[194] Dio Chrysostom, *Or.* 33.60.

[195] GLEASON, *Making Men*, 69.

[196] Epictetus 3.1.26, 31: 'But for a man not to be hairy is the same thing, and if by nature he has no hair he is prodigy, but if he cuts it out and plucks it out of himself, what
shall we make of him? Where shall we exhibit him and what notice shall we post? "I will
show you," we say to the audience, "a man who wishes to be a woman rather than a
man." What a dreadful spectacle.... Whom do you wish to please? Frail womankind?
Please them as a man. "Yes, but they like smooth men." Oh, go hang (3.1.28–29, 32)!'

Without denying the gift of nature, masculine identity is not taken for granted, for the elite of Greco-Roman society masculine identity is an achieved state. It is the result of years of hard work. The feud between the two rival rhetoricians Polemo and Favorinus demonstrate the tension between 'hyper-masculine' and 'effeminate deportment' and the crucial role of self-presentation.[197] This is so much the case that Gleason asserts that 'manliness was not a birthright [but rather it] was something that had to be won.' What constituted the boundaries of competitive space had to be repeatedly redrawn in order to exclude those far less privileged in society. In this merciless world of fierce rivalry and competition, absolutely no other form of competitive masculine activity was more electrifying to both the competitors and spectators than the kind of body language called rhetoric and its delivery. [198]

Since the art of rhetorical skill – body language – was publicly and socially acknowledged for some time as a definitive test of masculine excellence, it is quite understandable that issues pertaining to rhetorical delivery often became gender issues, as these were a primary source of the metaphorical language with which power relationships are articulated, both in the present as well as the past.[199] As such, the winning or losing party in a competition between equal rivals often depended upon one's ability to expose the opponent's alleged effeminate style, mannerism or features which betrayed true masculinity.[200]

4.5 Conclusion

Within New Testaments studies there has been a rediscovery of the importance of Greco-Roman rhetoric, especially for understanding the Corinthian context and reading Paul's epistles. A number of scholars have been discussed who make significant contributions to relating rhetoric to this line of inquiry. The various views on the subject presented here demonstrate a consensus that one need possess an understanding of Greco-Roman rhetoric in order to seriously engage the Corinthian controversy from a historico-critical perspective.

An extensive survey of the historical development of Greco-Roman rhetoric from Aristotle to Quintilian and its crucial role in ancient society based on primary sources has also been offered. This is done with special emphasis on discourses on delivery which identify body language as a

---

[197] GLEASON, *Making Men*, 159.
[198] GLEASON, *Making Men*, 159.
[199] GLEASON, *Making Men*, 160.
[200] GLEASON, *Making Men*, 160.

firmly established, powerful and effective means of communication. Special reference is made to the study of Gleason as well as the works of other scholars on the subject of masculinity. This is done in close relation to the theory and practice of rhetoric and its dominant role in the social ethos of the time.

As Corinth is one of the more important social and commercial centres at the time of Paul, one should assume that what is discovered about rhetoric broadly in society is also the case at Corinth. It should not be overlooked that society was preoccupied with masculinity, which was closely related to the theory and practice of rhetoric. Not only are the Corinthian opponents' criticism of the apostle Paul a clear reflection of the social ethos of the time, but also the apostle's response is indicative of his knowledge about the issue. Were this not so, his polemics in passages such as 1 Cor. 2. 1–5 and 2 Cor. 10.10 would be quite unintelligible to readers. This is a clear and concrete example of how placing the Corinthian epistles in their social context helps one understand Paul's message.

Attention to Greco-Roman rhetoric, and especially a preoccupation with delivery, body language and masculinity, serves to set a foundation upon which a reading of 1 Cor. 2.1–5 and 2 Cor.10.10 may be built. It is to this task that we turn.

Chapter 5

Exegesis of 1 Corinthians 2.1–5 and 2 Corinthians 10.10

5.1 Introduction

The primary concern of *Part II* is rhetoric and, in relation to this, how it relates to Paul's determination not to proclaim his gospel with 'plausible words of wisdom' (1 Cor. 2.4). Paul's self-presentation as well as his manner of 'speech' (λόγος) and 'proclamation' (κήρυγμα, 2.4; i.e. his 'delivery') appear to have led to his critics' negative verdict that 'his bodily presence is weak, and his speech contemptible' (2 Cor. 10.10).

In the previous chapter, recognition is given to the rediscovery of the importance of rhetorical studies in New Testament scholarship, especially in relation to the Corinthian context. Brief reference is also made to some recent scholarly contributions significant to the rediscovery. The emphasis of the study is on the primary literature of Greco-Roman writers, from Aristotle to Quintilian, on the theory and practice of ancient rhetoric and especially on delivery as body language. Following on from this analysis special attention is given to Gleason's study on masculinity, which was a dominant issue within the social ethos of Paul's time. This study on Greco-Roman rhetoric – especially its preoccupation with delivery, body language and masculinity – helps pave the way for an exegesis of 1 Cor. 2.1–5 and 2 Cor. 10.10.

In 1 Cor. 1.18–31, Paul takes a big risk when he confronts the current social ethos with the message of the cross. He makes a sharp contrast between divine wisdom and human wisdom. The latter was largely displayed by rhetorical eloquence in delivery, a practice cherished most dearly by the Greeks and Romans, including the Corinthians. Paul has an uncompromising conviction that divine wisdom had already been revealed and powerfully demonstrated in the crucified Christ. Paul's polemic in 1.18–31 seems to be largely directed against the unbelieving Jews and Gentiles (1.22) who were perishing (1.18). However, in 1 Cor. 2.1–5 and 2 Cor. 10.10 Paul apparently has his 'Christian' critics in mind. Their criticism of Paul and disappointment with him appears to be less with his message of the cross and more with his manner of delivery and personal appearance, judging from statements such as those in 2 Cor. 10.10 and 2 Cor. 11.6. For

Paul, his message could hardly be separated from his delivery. This last point is particularly important when dealing with the Corinthian crisis, including the apparently more practical aspect of it such as presentation or delivery (body language), as Paul's overriding concern is the message of the cross (1 Cor. 1.18; 2.2). More to the point: for Paul the content of the message should determine how one presents it and not the other way around. However, the criticism of Paul's Corinthian critics as well as the apostle's response need to be understood and appreciated in the context of rhetoric and more particularly delivery as body language and society's conception of masculinity.

Paul's deliberate refusal to use 'lofty words' or 'plausible words of wisdom' in his proclamation becomes all the more significant given the fact such rhetorical skills could well have been at his disposal. Winter is prepared to go so far as to suggest that both Philo and Paul are indebted to Greek rhetoric and used their rhetorical training to overthrow the rhetorical devices of the sophists.[1] Moreover, Winter also draws attention to the public presentation of Paul's message, suggesting that he not only rejects a rhetorical style which would impress the audience with his personal countenance, but also some of the very techniques of Greek rhetoric (1 Cor. 2.1–5). Indeed, when the accounts of 2 Cor. 10.10 and 11.6 are taken together, a composite picture emerges: Paul chose not to use some grand style of Greek rhetoric when preaching precisely because of the theological reasons given in 1 Cor. 2.5.[2] Winter's reference to Paul's theological reasons is particularly relevant in the present conversation as they are the causal root behind his inversion of the present social ethos.

In 1 Cor. 2.1–5, apart from 2.2 which refers to the core content of Paul's message of the cross, the remaining four verses are mainly concerned with the apostle's manner of proclamation. This point becomes all the more important in connection with 2 Cor. 10.10 where Paul's critics are portrayed as contemptuously remarking: αἱ ἐπιστολαὶ μέν ... βαρεῖαι καὶ ἰσ χυραί, ἡ δὲ παρουσία τοῦ σώματος ἀσθενὴς καὶ ὁ λόγος ἐξουθεῖ ημένος ('His letters are weighty and strong, but his bodily presence is weak, and his speech contemptible'). In the preceding study it was seen that a respectable orator was expected to be thoroughly consistent and impressive in his delivery as well as bodily presence. For Paul, consistency in this particular Corinthian context also implied that he did not want his personal integrity to be compromised. This would distinguish him from the sophist who would not hesitate to change or modify his approach or *modus operandi* in order to realise his desired goal. Winter's examination of 1 Cor. 2.1–5 reveals a clear clustering of rhetorical terms and allusions,

---

[1] WINTER, *Philo*, 237–43.

[2] WINTER, *Philo*, 239.

which even is recognised by those who disregard the sophistic background of the Corinthian situation.[3]

One should not simply infer from Paul's statement in 2.1 that he had completely renounced rhetoric for the sake of the gospel message. A fairly safe presupposition is that the well educated apostle to both the Jews and Gentiles was familiar with rhetoric. Pogoloff goes so far as to remark that the Greco-Roman culture itself became rhetorical through the educational practices and common use of such speech in the broader society.[4] Litfin's research also helps to fill in a view of rhetorical traditions.[5] He describes how by the 1st century the tradition was at the centre of more than half a millennium of Greek cultural history. Indeed, in the days of Paul the cultural tradition of rhetoric, with *logos* and *sophia* at its core, was thriving in Greece and, in particular, Corinth. Therefore, this wide-spread and deeply imbedded tradition is a natural starting point for an investigation of references to σοφία λόγου in 1 Corinthians. When these terms occur within a broader context or in reference to public speaking, the odds increase that the rhetorical tradition stands behind them.

It may well be possible for Paul to have used certain rhetorical skills for the sake of his own *apologia* without adopting the *modus operandi* of the sophists or his critics and without compromising his own Christian integrity. In fact, Paul's letters are not only 'weighty and strong', as his critics seem to have acknowledged (2 Cor. 10.10), but also they sound very 'rhetorical' and even eloquent at times. 1 Cor. 1.18–31 is a good example.

What is the precise nature of 2.1–5? Is it just a simple testimony[6] or an autobiographical account?[7] As Timothy Lim observes, it is clearly more, and could be regarded as 'the personal manifestation of the apostle's *theologia crucis* in preaching.'[8] But Lim is also quick to recognise that the theological and the sociological were not mutually exclusive in the case of Paul.[9] Paul distinguishes himself from other messengers who moved among the early church. When investigating his use of terminology which traditionally belongs to rhetoric, both a sociological interpretation and theological exegesis are needed. Lim explains that 'it is unlikely that 1 Cor. 2.1–5 is a rhetorical strategy, whether as a tacit admission of the effectiveness of rhetoric ... or as an attempt to disarm his audience (e.g. Dio,

---

[3] WINTER, *Philo*, 155. See also WINTER, *After Paul Left Corinth: The Influence of Secular Ethics and Social Change* (Grand Rapids MI: William B. Eerdmans, 2001).

[4] POGOLOFF, *Logos*, 48.

[5] LITFIN, *Proclamation*, 189.

[6] BARRETT, *The First Epistle*, 61.

[7] WEISS, *Der Erste Korintherbrief*, 44, 47.

[8] T. H. LIM, 'Not in Persuasive Words of Wisdom, but in Demonstration of the Spirit and Power', *NovT* 29/2 (1987), 137–49, at 145.

[9] LIM, 'Wisdom', 145.

Or. 12.15; 42.2f), for the use of a device wrought by human wisdom at this point in the letter would unravel the thematic development of 1.17–25 and 1.26–31, and would contradict his theology of the cross.'[10]

However, Winter notes that Paul's repudiation of technical rhetorical devices in presenting a gospel, which includes a theology of a crucified Messiah, would place him in a position of powerlessness in relation to the status structure of Corinth.[11] Paul was well prepared to accept such a powerless position, because he knew full well that paradoxically it was precisely in such a vulnerable position that the power of Christ crucified was manifested in his own weakness. It is, therefore, not surprising when Michael Bullmore concludes that 2.1–5 not only contains the content and manner of Paul's preaching, but also is a critique of current rhetorical expectation as well as a firmly established standard by which speakers were judged.[12]

Winter makes a similar point, suggesting that while in 2.1–5 Paul is very reliant on rhetorical language and allusions (e.g. ὑπεροχή, πίστις, δύναμις, ἀπόδειξις), his approach has been shaped by his gospel message as well as his rejection of the social conventions associated with public speaking in Corinth. Winter thus believes that the apostle's language is essentially anti-sophistic.[13] 1 Cor. 2.1–5 should not be studied and understood in isolation, but in close connection with what Paul so powerfully and eloquently states in 1.18–31.[14]

---

[10] LIM, 'Wisdom', 148, n. 29.

[11] WINTER, *Philo*, 147–48.

[12] M. A. BULLMORE, *St. Paul's Theology of Rhetorical Style: An Examination of 1 Corinthians 2.1–5 in the Light of First Century Greco-Roman Rhetorical Culture* (San Francisco: International Scholars Publication, 1995), 221.

[13] WINTER, *Philo*, 147–48. Winter illustrates his point by referring to Aristotle's use of the term πίστις in connection with other important rhetorical terms with 'the combined and simultaneous application of three proofs: τὸ ἦθος τοῦ λέγοντος, τὰ πάθη, and ἀπόδειξις' (*Philo*, 153. See Aristotle, *Rhet.* 1356a 1).

[14] Fee thus thinks that 'along with 1.26–31 it demonstrates the point of 1.18–25, this time in terms of Paul's effective ministry among them despite his weaknesses and failure to rely on the kind of "powerful" speech with which they are enamoured. Thus, not only the means (the cross) and the people (the church in Corinth), but also the preacher (Paul) declare that God is in the process of overturning the world's systems.' At the same time, Fee has also rightly noted 'a strong apologetic overtone' of the passage (*The First epistle*, 89).

5.2 Exegesis of 1 Cor. 2.1–5

2.1 Κἀγὼ ἐλθὼν πρὸς ὑμᾶς, ἀδελφοί, ἦλθον οὐ καθ' ὑπεροχὴν λόγου ἢ σοφίας καταγγέλλων ὑμῖν τὸ μυστήριον τοῦ θεοῦ. *('When I came to you, brothers and sisters, I did not come proclaiming the mystery of God to you in lofty words or wisdom.')*

1 Cor. 2.1 starts out with emphasis on the first person speaker: κἀγώ ('and I,' or 'as for I,' 'but I'). Barrett translates it as 'it was in line with this principle.'[15] Winter thinks that Paul here is making a clear contrast between himself and the sophists.[16] Whatever the case may be, what Paul states in 2.1 is consistent with what he said earlier in 1.17 (i.e. that his proclamation was not with 'eloquent wisdom'; ἐν σοφίᾳ λόγου). This point appears to be of utmost importance for Paul's *apologia*, because its persuasiveness depends largely on consistency, not only of his message of the cross but also his *manner* of proclamation ('delivery'; i.e. the whole of his *modus operandi*). As such, the word ἐλθών ('came') in 2.1 could also be rendered 'first came' – 'when I *first* came to you'. Paul seems to be saying, 'From the day when I *first* came to you *until now* my *modus operandi* has been consistently the same.' The same word κἀγώ, which reappears in 2.3, likely has the same force.

The word ὑπεροχή ('lofty'; cf. NRSV) is a common term in the language of Greco-Roman rhetoric. It is cited by Aristotle to refer to the 'superiority' men often felt based on γένος, δύναμις and ἀρετή.[17] Aristotle also refers to the sense of superiority that the eloquent orator had over against the incompetent speaker.[18] For the present exegesis, the most relevant point in Aristotle's comment is his reference to oratory. However, Aristotle also indicates that the word ὑπεροχή, in this particular context, is not confined simply to its rhetorical connotation. It also had a great deal to do with superior social status according to the social ethos of Paul's time.

The comments of Pogoloff on Greco-Roman society's preoccupation with competition and rivalry for social status are helpful. This idea of rivalry is already understood in 1.17, as σοφία λόγου would, on most occasions, indicate status-relations, particularly in the context of competition

---

[15] BARRETT, *The First Epistle*, 62.

[16] WINTER, *Philo*, 155.

[17] WINTER, *Philo*, 155.

[18] In his *Rhetoric* 1379a 7, Aristotle comments on the term ὑπεροχή: 'Now men think that they have a right to be highly esteemed by those who are inferior to them in birth, power, and virtue, and generally, in whatever similar respect a man is far superior to another; for example, the rich man to the poor man in the matter of money, the eloquent to the incompetent speaker in the matter of oratory, the governor to the governed, and the man who thinks himself worthy to rule to one who is only fit to be ruled.'

and resistance to the cross. In 1.18–25 the nature of this opposition is
brought out, as 'Paul develops the paradoxical topic of the saving power of
the "foolish" and "powerless" (low-status) λόγος τοῦ σταυροῦ versus the
boasted power (high status) of σοφία λόγου.'[19] It is precisely in response
to the Corinthians' preoccupation with social status that Paul solemnly reminds the Corinthians of their humble origin (1.26–28). That being the
case, Paul's important decision not to use ὑπεροχὴν λόγου ἢ σοφίας
('lofty words or wisdom') is not only a significant departure from current
social convention in a rhetorical context, but also tantamount to renounc-
ing his own social status. The drastic nature of the apostle's inversion of
the social ethos needs also to be perceived from this perspective.

This significant term ὑπεροχή is employed by Diodorus to describe
men's competition for social status through eloquence.[20] Raymond Collins
renders this phrase ὑπεροχὴν λόγου ἢ σοφίας as 'advantage of rhetoric or
wisdom' which is a reprise of the cleverness-of-speech motif of 1.17 (οὐκ
ἐν σοφίᾳ λόγου). The phrase ὑπεροχὴν λόγου literally means 'height of
word' and is used only once by Paul. When used metaphorically it is not
only the loftiness of one's words that are meant, but also could be used to
describe the advantage one has when holding the high ground in a battle.
In other words, when Paul proclaims the gospel to the Corinthians, he does
not use oratorical skills to achieve a competitive advantage.[21]

In the opening chapters of 1 Corinthians Paul consistently uses the word
λόγος in close connection with σοφία. This is because, for Paul, it is not
just any kind of λόγος which he arbitrarily rejects, but λόγος based on
σοφία. Since σοφία is already a well defined technical term in Greco-
Roman understanding at the time of Paul, one could quite readily assume
that the Corinthians would be well acquainted with it and closely associated connotations. Not only were they familiar with it, they also greatly
cherished and valued it.[22]

With reference to the present active participle καταγγέλλων in 2.1, Litfin describes that Paul views the role of one who preaches the gospel as
sharply contrasting with that of an orator.[23] While the Greco-Roman orators fully exploited their rhetorical skills to achieve their self-seeking
goals, Paul as a faithful preacher of Christ crucified refuses to follow that
kind of style. To resort to human wisdom, especially 'eloquence' and human 'dynamic' through rhetoric, would be unworthy of a faithful preacher

[19] POGOLOFF, *Logos*, 132.
[20] Diodorus Siculus, 34/35.5.5
[21] R. F. COLLINS, *First Corinthians*, (Collegeville, Minn: Glazier/Liturgical Press,
1999), 118.
[22] SAVAGE, *Power*, 74–75.
[23] LITFIN, *Proclamation*, 247.

of the cross. Paul's proclamation of the cross – a simple, straightforward declaration – entitled a *modus operandi* which sought to avoid usurping its power.[24] Litfin repeatedly contrasts Greco-Roman rhetorical speaking with Paul's way of preaching. While the former relied on human means, Paul depends on the working power of the Spirit to produce the desired result: πίστις (faith). Caution should be taken not to perceive a contrast between reason and irrationality, but rather between two manners of attracting an audience to the gospel.[25]

There has been some textual discussion on two phrases in the Greek manuscripts: μυστήριον τοῦ θεοῦ ('mystery of God') and μαρτύριον τοῦ θεοῦ ('witness of God').[26] Bruce Metzger suggests that μαρτύριον here could recollect 1.6 while also preparing one for its reoccurrence in verse 7.[27] Collins considers that μυστήριον (cf. 2.7) makes better sense in the Corinthian context with special reference to the eschatological significance of Paul's message of the cross which is clearly expressed in 1.18.[28]

The use of the expression μυστήριον τοῦ θεοῦ evidently suggests that Paul's determination not to resort to lofty words or wisdom is based on far more than just rhetorical considerations. For Paul, it is also a profoundly theological issue. As a bearer of the message of the cross Paul was absolutely convinced that he had been commissioned not to 'deliver' an eloquent human speech, but rather to proclaim the mystery of God. In Paul's case, it was the actual content of the message which ultimately determined the manner of the speech. This clearly distinguishes Paul from Greco-Roman orators of the time for whom the manner of delivery was just as important as, and perhaps more so, than the content of speech itself.

As suggested in the previous exegesis of 1.18–31, Paul was not rejecting human wisdom simply in terms of concept or intellect. He was trying to demolish a well established system which had become an alternative to God's way of salvation or was in real danger of becoming so.

As a system it was only natural that σοφία should have been fully integrated, together with λόγος, into the whole social ethos of a city like Corinth. Pogoloff also makes this point, elaborating that when σοφία and λόγος occur together in antiquity they often imply much more than simply technical language skills. Indeed, an entire world of social status based on

---

[24] LITFIN, *Proclamation*, 247.

[25] LITFIN, *Proclamation*, 248.

[26] While μαρτύριον ('witness') is supported by ℵ[c], B, D, G, P, Ψ, 33, 81, syr[h], Vulgate, and readings in Origen, Chrysostom and Jerome, μυστήριον ('mystery') has early backing in the Beatty Papyrus, the Codex Sinaiticus, and a number of Latin fathers.

[27] B. M. METZGER, *A Textual Commentary on the Greek New Testament: A Companion Volume to the United Bible Societies' Greek New Testament* (2nd ed.; London; New York: United Bible Societies, 1994), 480.

[28] COLLINS, *First Corinthians*, 118, 115–16.

speech is implied. Within the Corinthian cultural milieu, only one who was educated and cultured would have been described as speaking ἐν σοφίᾳ λόγου. If someone did speak in words of wisdom, this would express that in their address they spoke about a subject in a style which was persuasive and presented in a convincing manner. It was the character and ethos of the orator which communicated, not simply the subject matter.[29] Thus one may conceive of a beautifully gift wrapped package and a recipient who does not necessarily distinguish the wrapping from the 'gift' which lies within.

Horsley sees in 2.1 as well as 2.4 not just Paul's familiarity with current rhetorical practice, but also a remarkably similar statement made by the apostle's near-contemporary orator Dio Chrysostom. In his discourse, Dio Chrysostom says, 'For they are clever persons, mighty sophists, wonder workers; but I am quite ordinary and prosaic in my utterance, though not ordinary in my theme (τὰ δ'ἡμέτερα φαῦλα καὶ πεζὰ ἐν τοῖς λόγοις, οὐ μέντοι περὶ φαύλων).'[30] However, Horsley qualifies Dio Chrysostom's statement explaining that Paul's self-disparagement needs to be seen in a specific Corinthian circumstance and a proclamation and movement which have their roots in Israel's traditions. While both share comments on their own eloquence, in contrast with Dio Chrysostom Paul's preaching includes 'demonstration of the Spirit and of power' (2.4).[31] The above comparison between Dio Chrysostom and Paul, given the qualifications of Horsley, clearly indicates the difficulty of assigning Paul to any ordinary category or stereotyping. He is simply unique, especially in his dealing with the most delicate and sensitive issues of σοφία and λόγος. As one begins to view the novelty of Paul, the degree to which he is seen to invert the current social ethos becomes more drastic.

2.2 οὐ γὰρ ἔκρινά τι εἰδέναι ἐν ὑμῖν εἰ μὴ Ἰησοῦν Χριστὸν καὶ τοῦτον ἐσταυρωμένον. ('For I decided to know nothing among you except Jesus Christ, and him crucified.')

Previously noted was that the *modus operandi* Paul adopts in the preaching of the gospel is ultimately based on theological considerations. 2.2 is another good example of this. Here the Greek γάρ ('for') indicates not only a causal relation between verses 1 and 2, whereby verse 2 explains the first verse, it also provides a theological reason why Paul did not come to Corinth proclaiming his message of the cross in 'lofty words or wisdom'. Ἰησοῦν Χριστὸν καὶ τοῦτον ἐσταυρωμένον ('Jesus Christ, and him crucified') is a profoundly theological statement about Paul's core mes-

---

[29] POGOLOFF, *Logos*, 54.
[30] Dio Chrysostom, *Or.* 32.39.
[31] HORSLEY, *1 Corinthians*, 53–54.

sage. The verb ἔκρινα ('decided') denotes a serious determination and firm commitment on the part of the messenger of the gospel. It was a crucial decision which was clearly and firmly resolved in Paul's mind before he came (ἐλθών) to Corinth. The short phrase 'to know nothing' (οὐ τι εἰδέναι) is used with emphasis and has the crucified Christ as Paul's only focus.

The study in chapter one on the origin and practice of crucifixion in the ancient world, together with the exegesis of 1.18–31, demonstrates that the message of Christ crucified would have been regarded as a stumbling block to Jews and foolishness to Gentiles for many reasons. When Paul purposely adopts the *modus operandi* in view here, the unbelieving Jews and Gentiles would not only find his message itself completely unacceptable, but also the manner of his proclamation would have been contemptible.

The word ἐσταυρωμένον ('crucified'), which is already used by Paul in 1.23 in the form of a perfect passive participle in the Greek, reappears here in 2.2. In both cases the Greek perfect tense is meant to describe an action or event that occurred in the past and its effect continues into the present. Thus, when Paul places the focus on 'Christ crucified' as the core message of his gospel he is in effect suggesting that the cross has not been cancelled out by all the events which subsequently followed. This includes Christ's resurrection, so that Christ crucified became the very key to unlock the 'mystery of God' (2.1).

Joseph Lightfoot takes the phrase 'to know nothing' to simply mean 'I did not trouble myself about the knowledge of anything else.'[32] It intends to emphasise Paul's single-mindedness concerning the gospel message as well as his firm commitment to its proclamation. Schrage's German rendering is simply *'nichts anderes hat Paulus wissen wollen'* (Paul did not want to know anything else).[33] Fee qualifies it by adding that 'to know nothing' does not mean that Paul rejected all other knowledge, but rather Paul had a single-minded focus on Christ crucified.[34]

Gorman translates 2.2 as: 'I decided to know nothing among you except Jesus Christ – that is, Jesus Christ *crucified*.' He prefers this translation because of its clear focus and emphasis on the crucifixion of Jesus. When placed in context, comments Gorman, the words 'to know' mean something like 'to experience and to announce in word and deed'. Gorman agrees with Hans Küng that Paul succeeds more than anyone when he expresses the ultimate distinguishing feature of Christianity: the cross-

---

[32] J. B. LIGHTFOOT, *Notes on the Epistles of St Paul from Unpublished Commentaries* (London: Macmillan, 1895), 171.

[33] SCHRAGE, *Der Erste Brief*, 1.227.

[34] FEE, *The First epistle*, 92.

centred focus.[35] Gorman also helpfully describes that 'it is not indeed as
risen, exalted, living, divine, but as crucified, that this Jesus Christ is distinguished unmistakably from the many risen, exalted, living gods and dei-
fied founders of religion, from the Caesars, geniuses, and heroes of world
history.'[36]

2.3 κἀγὼ ἐν ἀσθενείᾳ καὶ ἐν φόβῳ καὶ ἐν τρόμῳ πολλῷ ἐγενόμην
πρὸς ὑμᾶς, *('And I came to you in weakness and in fear and in much
trembling.')*

The absence of certain details in this verse has long puzzled not only the
average lay reader, but scholars as well. One is not quite certain as to why
Paul should be 'in weakness and in fear and in much trembling' when he
first came to Corinth. Attention needs to be given to illustrate the complexity of the issues involved before suggesting various possible interpretations
which may be derived from this verse.

Savage raises a number of questions regarding this perplexing statement. Paul makes a statement that recollects for his audience that when he
was in Corinth he had a humble demeanour. Savage draws attention to the
phrase φόβος καὶ τρόμος, asking what would have caused Paul to be
afraid. One possibility is that he feared failure, such as what he experienced in Athens. Perhaps this emotion stemmed from a personal inadequacy for the ministry that lay before him. Maybe, even, Paul experienced
some sort of stage-fright and was intimidated by large crowds. Another
possibility is that he anticipated persecution.[37]

The options Savage proposes could easily be multiplied. He assumes
too that Paul's mission in Athens was a failure, based upon the account
given in Acts 17. However, the same passage also states (17.34) that some
of the Athenians joined him and became believers, including Dionysius the
Areopagite, a woman named Damaris and others. The conversion of the
Areopagite alone is certainly no small matter. Indeed, even if no conversion actually took place, if one follows the book of Acts then Paul's opportunity to address such a distinguished gathering at the Areopagus and to
debate with the Epicurean and Stoic philosophers is already remarkable.
Moreover, if one follows this train of thought, the plausibility of Paul experiencing stage-fright also diminishes.

Collins suggests that 'Paul's self-depreciation is part of his rhetorical
appeal'. On the one hand, Ancient rhetors (e.g. Isocrates and Dio Chrysostom) frequently expressed a sort of mock humility in order to win their
audience's goodwill. On the other hand, even with this tendency in mind,

---

[35] GORMAN, *Cruciformity*, 1.
[36] GORMAN, *Cruciformity*, 2.
[37] SAVAGE, *Power*, 72.

when Paul describes his weakness a real situation may be in view as well as a rhetorical strategy (cf. 2 Cor. 11.16–29).[38] It is difficult to adjudicate whether Paul's statement is truly part of his rhetorical appeal or strategy. In the words of Fee: 'from this distance it is impossible to know the exact nature of Paul's being with them "in weakness."' In his opinion, Paul is likely referring to an actual physical condition, but even if this is not the case it is clear that there is a genuine correspondence between his own personal weaknesses and his gospel (cf. Col. 1.24). For Fee, the very heart of Paul's proclamation is the 'weakness of God' as it is communicated through a narrative about the crucified Christ.[39]

Thiselton comments that the expression ἐν φόβῳ καὶ ἐν τρόμῳ is best understood with special reference to Paul's 'sense of responsibility before God to fulfill God's call.'[40] This suggestion is helpful because, as far as Paul is concerned, it is indeed an awesome responsibility to proclaim the message of the cross which the preacher conceives of as ultimately determining the hearers' eternal destiny, whether to salvation or damnation (1 Cor. 1.18). Paul's responsibility would have become heavier since he already knew that his message of the cross would be offensive to an audience which would only welcome and appreciate what was powerful and glorious according to well-entrenched cultural conditioning.[41]

Welborn suggests that Paul may have portrayed himself as a well-known figure in the mime or the befuddled orator. If this is the case, then the description in 2.1–5 would have struck Hellenistic eyes and ears as a virtual caricature.[42] This suggestion appears to have support from several classical examples. Cicero is portrayed as a comic figure: 'you always come to the court trembling, as if you were going to fight as a gladiator, and after uttering a few words in a meek and half-dead voice, you take your leave.'[43] The speech of the emperor Claudius was thought to be confused mumbling and unintelligible.[44] Zeus is portrayed as a foolish orator: 'I am confused in the head and trembling and my tongue seems to be tied.'[45] Welborn elaborates that Paul, like Seneca's Claudius, is weak and impotent. That similar to Lucian's Zeus, he is frightened and confused. When Paul is compared to Herodas' stammering Battaros, he is seen to tremble before his audience.[46]

---

[38] COLLINS, *First Corinthians*, 116.
[39] FEE, *The First epistle*, 93.
[40] THISELTON, *The First Epistle*, 213.
[41] SCHRAGE, *Der Erste Brief*, 229.
[42] WELBORN, *Fool*, 98.
[43] Cassius 46.7.
[44] Seneca, *Apoc.* 5.2; 6.1–2.
[45] Lucian, *Jup. Trag.* 14.
[46] WELBORN, *Fool*, 98.

Socrates is described by Callicles as a 'fool', whose speech is more befitting to a slave (δουλοπρεπές) and appeared ridiculous (καταγέλαστον)
and unmanly (ἄνανδρον) in front of his audience.[47] The view of Welborn
is that this Socratic precedent of making oneself and way of presentation
the object of parody is what lies behind Paul.[48]

While Quintilian emphasises that an orator must have strength and confidence, he also agrees that 'there is also a certain tacit approval to be won
by proclaiming that we are weak, unprepared, and no match for the talents
of the opposing party' (4.1.8).

Welborn's suggestion deserves serious consideration; however, similar
to the other views discussed it is equally difficult to determine if this is the
best and most convincing backdrop against which to see Paul. For one,
even granted that Paul was knowledgeable about the tradition cited by
Welborn, it is quite another issue to suggest that the apostle had in fact followed such a tradition which was based on an entirely different worldview
from Paul's own.

After stating the core gospel message concisely but powerfully in 2.2, in
2.3 Paul openly reveals to his Corinthian readers how he first came to Corinth in terms of manner and feeling: 'in weakness and in fear and in much
trembling' (ἐν ἀσθενείᾳ καὶ ἐν φόβῳ καὶ ἐν τρόμῳ πολλῷ). The
statement becomes all the more meaningful and revealing when compared
and contrasted with what Paul says earlier in 2.1 which is also about when
he first came to the Corinthians. 'Lofty words or wisdom' (ὑπεροχὴν
λόγου ἢ σοφίας) are clearly what the Corinthians expected of Paul when
he first came to them, but it did not unfold in this way, much to the disappointment of those 'lofty' ones. 'Lofty words or wisdom' (2.1) and 'weakness, fear and trembling' (2.3) form an interesting contrast. Paul's Corinthian letters are full of such comparisons and contrasts.

Precisely what kind of weakness, fear and trembling Paul is speaking
about remains unclear. In the two Corinthian letters this is the first time
where Paul describes his own 'weakness' (ἀσθένεια), although he has already referred to God's or Jesus' 'weakness' previously in 1.25. The matter of weakness arises again in 4.9–13, 2 Cor. 6.4–10 and 12.7–10 with
considerable illustrations and elaborations. Yet, none of these passages
seem to indicate clearly or precisely the nature of Paul's weakness. As
such, one is tempted to suggest that this weakness could be physical,
and/or mental, and/or spiritual. Based on 1 Cor. 4.10 – 'We are fools for
the sake of Christ, but you are wise in Christ. We are weak, but you are
strong' – which is put in a rather sarcastic way in order to provoke his Co-

---

[47] Plato, *Gorg.* 485BC.

[48] WELBORN, *Fool*, 98,

[48] WELBORN, *Fool*, 98–99.

rinthian critics to think clearly and reflect humbly, one may suggest that it is in a similar way that weakness is used in 2.3. In other words, in comparison to the so-called 'strong' in Corinth, Paul, a δοῦλος of Christ, was quite prepared to consider himself as being weak for the sake of Christ.

For the sake of Christ, Paul was ready not only to be considered weak or foolish (4.10), but even to share Christ's sufferings 'by becoming like him in his death' (Phil. 3.10). One should not rule out the possibility that weakness in 2.3 could be physical in nature, the kind of weakness that he mentions, for instance, in 2 Cor. 12.9; although no one can be certain about the precise nature of such weakness. Since Paul earlier in 1.23–25 paradoxically describes 'Christ crucified' as 'God's weakness', it may well be that the so-called 'weakness' in 2.3 is used by Paul in a similar way.

While human weakness was often perceived negatively and despised, particularly in Greco-Roman society with its understanding of masculinity and rhetoric, it is something that Paul wants to boast about, especially when a divine promise is attached to it: 'He [The Lord] said to me, "My grace is sufficient for you, for power is made perfect in weakness". So, I will boast all the more gladly of my weakness, so that the power of Christ may dwell in me. Therefore I am content with weakness, insults, hardships, persecutions, and calamities for the sake of Christ; for whenever I am weak, than I am strong' (2 Cor. 12.8–10).

In connection to 2 Cor. 12.8–10, David Black makes an insightful comment about 2 Cor. 11.29: 'It is this sympathetic statement in 11.29 – τίς ἀσθενεῖ καὶ οὐκ ἀσθενῶ; – that closes the preceding catalogue of persecutions and sufferings (11.22–28) and prepares the reader for Paul's assertion that it is only in the things which reveal his weakness does he dare to glory (11.30).'[49]

The Greek words φόβος ('fear') and τρόμος ('trembling') are perhaps just as intriguing as ἀσθενεία ('weakness'). Are fear and trembling used by Paul with reference to God, to man or to both? The passage itself is not clear; however, it is perhaps most meaningful when understood in reference to both the divine and human.

Firstly, with reference to the divine, φόβος and τρόμος are often used in combination in the LXX,[50] especially with reference to the human encounter with the divine. The response to the divine is fear and trembling, with emphasis on the majesty and holiness of the LORD.[51] An example is Moses

---

[49] D. A. BLACK, *Paul, Apostle of Weakness: Astheneia and its Cognates in the Pauline Literature* (New York: Peter Lang, 1984), 144.

[50] Exod. 15.16; Judith 2.28; 15.2; Ps. 54 (55).5; Isa. 19.16; Dan. 4.19; *4 Macc.* 4.10. E. HATCH and H. A. REDPATH, *A Concordance to the Septuagint and the Other Greek Versions of the Old Testament* (Grand Rapids: Baker Academic, 1998), 1435–36, 1374.

[51] Savage thinks that the phrase φόβος καὶ τρόμος used by Paul could be referring to his own daily experience with the awe-inspiring majesty of God: 'Hence, in the mere

and the Israelites singing the following song to the triumphant LORD who revealed his power to the Egyptians: 'Terror and dread (φόβος καὶ τρόμος) will fall upon them. By the power of your arm they will be as still as a stone–until your people pass by, O LORD, until the people you bought pass by' (Exod. 15.16).

Another noteworthy example is Isaiah 19.16 (LXX): 'On that day the Egyptians will be like women, and tremble with fear (ἐν φόβῳ καὶ ἐν τρόμῳ) before the hand that the LORD of hosts raises against them.' Although one could speculate which passages from the Bible could have inspired Paul, it is a near impossibility to know whether he reflected on this verse of Isaiah when referring to φόβος and τρόμος in 1 Cor. 2.3. If fear and trembling are associated with women this would have gender connotations in the Corinthian context, especially with reference to current views on masculinity. For the Corinthians, φόβος and τρόμος could only be the behaviour and disposition of women, children and slaves.

As a specially commissioned messenger of the gospel of salvation it is both natural and understandable that the apostle Paul should have a deep sense of fear and trembling because of the solemn and awesome nature of his task. This is particularly true as Paul is conscious of his divine calling. Indeed, he identifies himself at the very beginning of the Corinthian letters as: 'Paul, called to be an apostle of Jesus Christ by the will of God' (1 Cor. 1.1).

Secondly, Paul's possible reference to the human is inseparable from the first. David (Ps. 55.5) uses the phrase to describe his struggles and appeals to God to answer his prayer: 'Fear and trembling (φόβος καὶ τρόμος) come upon me; and horror has overwhelmed me.' While the origin of the gospel as well as Paul's call to proclaim it come from God, the gospel itself is meant for humankind to hear and hopefully to receive. Returning to a point made previously, the receiving or rejecting of the message of the cross would ultimately determine each human beings eternal destiny. Paul has already (1 Cor. 1.18) referred to 'those who are perishing' because of their rejection of the gospel message. The eternal damnation of those who reject the gospel must have caused a tremendous sense of fear and trembling on the part of the bearer of the gospel message. As such, it would be reasonable to assume that it was with a deep sense of burden and responsibility that Paul first came to Corinth. There was an element of unpredictability whenever the message of the cross was publicly proclaimed.

---

outworking of his vocation, in the regular preaching of Christ crucified (2.2), he would have been confronted daily by the awe-inspiring majesty of God – an experience which in the LXX engendered great fear and trembling and which could well now be producing the same in Paul (2.3).' (*Power*, 73).

Both the content of the gospel, especially with Christ crucified at its core message, and Paul's manner of delivery (body language), also provide ample reasons for him to be fearful and tremble and the reasons behind this statement would have been clear to both him and the Corinthian audience. This view will be returned to and clarified in the conversation to follow.

From outside the social ethos of Paul's time and place, and within cultures influenced and having progressed along the lines of the transformation he helped set in motion, it is difficult in the present to perceive just how drastic Paul's actions would have been viewed by his contemporary audience. As a general rule, within Greco-Roman society only a fool or a lunatic would publicly reveal or confess his own weakness, especially when confronted with formidable opposition and challenges, as was Paul's unenviable position at the time. A man who did that would not even be worthy of a respectable challenger according to the refined and sophisticated game of Greco-Roman rhetoric.

Admitting weakness was also completely unacceptable within the Greco-Roman perception on masculinity. A respectable man was supposed to be strong and if he was not then he should at least pretend to be so. To publicly acknowledge one's weakness in the context of masculinity was tantamount to admitting unconditional defeat even before the contest actually started. In such a situation it was even meaningless to have a contest, since under normal circumstances a contest, according to the firmly established understanding and rules of rhetoric of the time, was supposed to be a contest between equals. Thus, when one party publicly acknowledged his own weakness, any sense of equality was immediately lost and the contest aborted.

Appreciating Paul's admission or acknowledgement of personal weakness in 2.3 in light of his specific social context is crucial. To move beyond the expression of social ethos, one might also say that Paul was acting in contrast to common sense. As far as the Corinthians were concerned, Paul's actions were nonsensical. Paul, who likely ranked among the city's highly educated, may be assumed to be even more aware of his actions than his audience. With this in mind, it becomes even more startling that Paul should make such a public acknowledgement in Corinth. Common sense would suggest that it was a crucial time for the deeply troubled apostle to be assertive with regard to his status and authority in order to effectively deal with the great Corinthian crisis and controversy. Yet, even if others were confused and confounded, Paul himself appears aware of what he was doing. One might speculate that the most concise explanation he might offer about his manner would be that it is all: 'For the sake of Christ' (διὰ Χριστόν, 1 Cor. 4.10).

It cannot be ruled out that ἀσθενεία in 2.3 may also be physical in nature since the word also denotes illness. Paul explicitly mentions his bodily

infirmity (δι' ἀσθένειαν τῆς σαρκός, Gal. 4.13) for which he had been
burdened when he first preached the gospel in Galatia.[52] Additionally,
Paul's reference to the 'thorn in the flesh' (σκόλοψ τῇ σαρκί) appears to
be some sort of bodily ailment (2 Cor. 12.7).[53] It may also refer to Paul's
physical disability.[54] Hock contends that Paul's weakness could be closely
related to his manual labour as a tentmaker who would have been perceived by others as slavish and would have suffered from a lack of social
standing in the status-conscious Corinthian society.[55] Along these lines,
Lim regards Paul's refusal of support as a sign of his weakness.[56]

In the Greco-Roman world where meekness was considered a clear sign
of weakness, even a person's physical limitations, whether born with it or
experiencing it at a later stage of life, would not necessarily have aroused
sympathy or compassion. Society tended to be relentlessly merciless,
fierce competition was common place and only the fittest survived. The
cultivation of masculinity reveals that the elite or aristocratic family would
employ doctors and nurses to ensure that a male child developed normally
and healthily. This included the rectification of all physical defects,
whether they were from birth or inflicted later. Ill health or defect would
not excuse a man.[57]

These attitudes towards weakness are largely true with regard to fear
and trembling. They were equally unacceptable from a rhetorical standpoint as from that on masculinity because they were signs of weakness,
cowardice and, most telling, the traits of women and children. Even if he
were genuinely shaking with fear a respectable Greco-Roman man would
be under great pressure to try to conceal it and it would have been practically anathema to reveal it publicly. Thus, Paul was clearly someone, but
who he was was not quite a man, as he had conceded defeat and would
have been deemed defeated already before the contest had even begun.

---

[52] H. D. BETZ, *Galatians: A Commentary on Paul's Letter to the Churches in Galatia*
(Philadelphia: Fortress Press, 1979), 224–26.

[53] V. P. FURNISH, *II Corinthians* (New York: Doubleday, 1984), 548.

[54] C. FORBES, 'Comparison, Self-praise and Irony: Paul's Boasting and Conventions of Hellenistic Rhetoric', *New Testament Studies* 32 (1986), 1–30, 14.

[55] HOCK, *The Social Context*, 67.

[56] LIM, 'Wisdom', 142.

[57] GLEASON, *Making Men*, 70.

2.4 καὶ ὁ λόγος μου καὶ τὸ κήρυγμά μου οὐκ ἐν πειθοῖ[ς] σοφίας [λόγοις] ἀλλ' ἐν ἀποδείξει πνεύματος καὶ δυνάμεως,('My speech and my proclamation were not with plausible words of wisdom, but with a demonstration of the Spirit and of power,') 5 ἵνα ἡ πίστις ὑμῶν μὴ ᾖ ἐν σοφίᾳ ἀνθρώπων ἀλλ' ἐν δυνάμει θεοῦ. ('so that your faith might rest not on human wisdom but on the power of God.')

Paul's refusal to use words of human wisdom (σοφία λόγου, 1.17), 'lofty words or wisdom' (ὑπεροχὴν λόγου ἢ σοφίας, 2.1) or 'plausible words of wisdom' (πειθοῖ[ς] σοφίας [λόγοις], 2.4) is given a clear reason in 2.4, 5.[58]

For Paul not to proclaim his message of the cross with plausible words of wisdom was more a deliberate choice than an actual lack of oratory skill. One can scarcely believe that a man who could write and argue with such skill and eloquence and who spoke so powerfully for the gospel – as Paul demonstrates and is depicted as doing – was not somehow capable of impressing the public unless he was really suffering from some mysterious physical impediment. The word 'decided' (ἔκρινα) in 2.2 is an active verb and suggests deliberate and rational thinking and action. As such, the following verse (2.3) may not necessarily be a literal statement. It could well be that Paul's rhetorical device intended to provoke. Perhaps it could also indicate the intensity of Paul's sense of responsibility and the burden he felt as the messenger of the gospel, the response to which forever determined a person's destiny. If it were indeed Paul's deliberate choice not to proclaim the mystery of God in lofty words or wisdom (2.2), sense would be made of this intention when understood as part of his overriding goal to act contrary to his social ethos.

At first glance, Paul appears in 2.4–5 to express a thought that does not logically flow from the previous verse on weakness, fear and trembling. However, a closer examination of the text within its social context may help to see the logic of Paul's progression. As noted earlier, the so-called 'weakness' (2.3) was perceived only from a human perspective, with regard to both the content of the message of the cross and Paul's manner of delivery, including his allegedly unimpressive physical appearance. This may be one of the primary reasons for Paul's fear and trembling: his message of salvation could be rejected resulting in the eternal condemnation of

---

[58] The phrase πειθοῖ[ς] σοφίας [λόγοις] has several variant readings. In some texts the phrase appears before ἀνθρωπίνης while others have this adjective after σοφίας (ℵ[c], A, C, P, Ψ, 81, syr[h] *al*). Metzger regards this as 'obviously secondary' as it 'has the appearance of an explanatory gloss inserted by copyists (at different places) in order to identify more exactly the nuance attaching to σοφίας'. Metzger explains that 'in order to represent the diversity of evidence, a majority of the Committee decided to print πειθοῖ[ς], and, on the strength of 𝔓[46] G 35* which lack λόγοις, to enclose this latter word within square brackets.' (METZGER, *Commentary*, 481).

the hearers (1.18). For those who are perishing in 1.18, both the content of Paul's message of the cross and his manner of proclamation (delivery or body language) are the main reasons for their rejection. Hence the logic of the apostle's statement in 2.4 about 'speech and proclamation' (ὁ λόγος καὶ τὸ κήρυγμα). In substance what is said in the remaining part of 2.4–5 is already present in 1.17–31, except for reference to the 'Spirit' (πνεύματος) at the end of 2.4.

The Spirit is given a much fuller treatment in 3.10–15. When this passage is read in connection with 1.20–31, 'power' (δύναμις) is almost synonymous with the 'Spirit' (πνεῦμα), a sort of hendiadys, as Collins has rightly noted: '"Spirit and power" is classical Pauline hendiadys (1 Thess. 1.5; cf. Acts 1.8) in which the epexegetical "and power" identifies "the spirit" as the powerful Spirit of God.'[59] The power of God which had been demonstrated in and through Christ certainly included Christ's resurrection. And such power was closely linked to the Spirit (or 'spirit') as is the case in Romans 1.3, 4.

The polemical nature of the word δύναμις ('power') in 2.4–5 requires little explanation in this particular context. Δύναμις is a key word that appears in relation to both Greco-Roman rhetoric (esp. in the body language of delivery) and masculinity. Δύναμις is also the very thing which the Corinthians, especially Paul's critics, most cherished and claimed to possess. Moreover, the power or authority of Paul was also being seriously being challenged in Corinth. However, Paul's primary concern here and elsewhere is not so much with his own personal power or authority, but rather that of God (1.17–18, 24–25; 2.4–5).

Closely connected with the concept of δύναμις is another equally important word in Greco-Roman tradition: ἀπόδειξις ('demonstration'). Plato uses ἀπόδειξις as a means of proof of an argument.[60] Aristotle is similarly concerned with proofs (πίστεις): 'proof is a sort of demonstration (ἀπόδειξις) since we are most strongly convinced when we suppose anything to have been demonstrated (ἀποδεδεῖχθαι).' [61] Epictetus uses ἀπόδειξις in a similar sense,[62] while Plutarch regards ἀπόδειξις as a means of finding truth: 'philosophy is concerned with truth, and the illumination of truth is demonstration (ἀπόδειξις).'[63]

Lim provides an insightful observation that when Paul uses ἀπόδειξις along with πνεύματος and δυνάμεως, the word functions in a way that is

---

[59] COLLINS, First Corinthians, 120.

[60] Plato, Soph. 265D; Phaed. 77C.

[61] Aristotle, Rhet. 1355a 11.

[62] Epictetus 2.25. Cf. Diogenes Laertius 7.45.

[63] Plutarch, Mor. 387A.

different from and counter to the rhetorical meaning of the term. Paul, according to Lim, insists that his word and preaching are based upon a demonstration. This expression is not according to the rhetorical practice of the time, but rather of the Spirit and power. The divine conviction of the Spirit and power replaces a demonstration which consists of arguments and broadly assumed truths (cf. 1 Cor. 4.20).[64] However, Lim is quick to qualify that Paul's determination not to follow the current rhetorical practice does not equal a total rejection of the art. Paul simply does not want his proclamation to depend on plausible words of wisdom, but rather on the Spirit and power.[65]

In the final analysis, church schisms in Corinth were essentially a power struggle. Rise to social prominence and glory depended very much on the acquisition of power as well as its maintenance and increase in Greco-Roman society. Without real 'power', rhetoric and its body language were virtually meaningless. The phrase 'a demonstration (ἀπόδειξις) of the Spirit and power' says much about the problem in Corinth as well as Paul's controversy with his critics. Eloquent human wisdom (1.17) and lofty words or wisdom were nothing, unless they could actually be demonstrated in real power.

Judging from the overall tone of the Corinthian correspondence, the impression is that Paul does not seem really to believe that his Corinthian critics actually have as much δύναμις as they purport or imagine themselves to have. Paul's view is clearly reflected, for example, in 4.18–20 where the power issue is raised in a highly polemical manner: 'But some of you, thinking that I am not coming to you, have become arrogant. But I will come to you soon, if the Lord wills, and I will find out not the talk of these arrogant people but their power. For the kingdom of God depends not on talk but on power.' There is a temptation to conclude that no actual need existed for the apostle to find out if these arrogant people really had power or not. The tone set by Paul indicates that he did not really believe that they had power.

Λόγος may be understood in the sense of 'talk' or 'speech'. Ironically, it is λόγος that Paul identifies as a particular 'gift' (χάρισμα) which the Corinthians had at the beginning of 1 Corinthians (1.7). But equally ironic is the sad fact that this particular χάρισμα caused enormous trouble in Corinth. It is little wonder that Paul has to deal with this issue head-on and in a severe manner.

Here in 2.5, just as in 1.17–31, 'human wisdom' (σοφία ἀνθρώπων) is set in stark contrast with 'the power of God' (δυνάμει θεοῦ). Paul finally explains why he does not make his proclamation about Christ crucified

---

[64] LIM, 'Wisdom', 147.
[65] LIM, 'Wisdom', 148.

'with plausible words of wisdom, but with a demonstration of the Spirit and of power' when he first came to the Corinthians. It is: 'so that your faith might rest not on human wisdom but on the power of God.'

5.3 Exegesis of 2 Cor. 10.10

2 Cor. 10.10 ὅτι αἱ ἐπιστολαὶ μέν, φησίν, βαρεῖαι καὶ ἰσχυραί, ἡ δὲ παρουσία τοῦ σώματος ἀσθενὴς καὶ ὁ λόγος ἐξουθενημένος. *('For they say, "His letters are weighty and strong, but his bodily presence is weak, and his speech of no account."')*

Introduction

2 Cor. 10.10 is discussed in close connection with 1 Cor. 2.1–5 primarily because these two Corinthian passages are dealing with virtually the same issue: Paul's self-presentation, delivery (body language) and λόγος ('speech' or word). Yet, the context of 2 Corinthians may not be assumed to be exactly the same as 1 Corinthians. Attention to time and circumstances need also to be given.

Paul's relationship with the Corinthian church was complex with a number of complications. Indeed, from Paul's correspondences with the Corinthians, only two letters survive. According to 1 Cor. 5.9, Paul apparently wrote at least one other letter which dealt with, among other issues, sexual immorality. From the time between when the surviving two epistles are written, little to no information is available. In 2 Cor. 2.1 Paul refers to 'another painful visit'. This seems to imply that after the writing of 1 Corinthians, Paul made a visit to Corinth that for one reason or another brought with it some agony. One is reminded of what Paul promises in 1 Cor. 4.19, that 'I will come to you soon, if the Lord wills, and I will find out not the talk of these arrogant people but their power'. Paul's promise here suggests that one of the main purposes of his intended visit is to deal with the arrogant individuals in the church. His tone is somewhat severe. If this promised visit is the one that took place, the statement in 2 Cor. 2.1, that it was painful, resonates with the intentions and circumstances expressed in 1 Cor. 4.19.

According to the book of Acts (18.11), Paul's first visit to Corinth lasted a year and a half. When considering the uncertain time gap between the composition of the two epistles, a reasonable assumption is that quite a few years have passed between his first visit and when 2 Cor. 10.10 was written. Ernest Best doubts if the so-called '2 Corinthian' epistle was a single letter. This second epistle, he considers, shows signs of consisting of distinct sections which could indicate the redaction of several Pauline correspondences into a single 'letter'. Someone in Corinth may have cobbled different correspondences together after Paul was dead, perhaps intended as a suitable manner to preserve his meaningful messages. Best elaborates on this theory:

> There is a very clear break both in thought and in mood at the end of chapter 9, and a very strong case can be made for regarding the whole of chapters 10–13 as coming from another letter. Many scholars identify this with the intermediate or painful letter. More probably chapters 10–13 come from a letter written after chapters 1–9. If so, they depict another stage in which relations between Paul and the Corinthians again became worse after the improvement indicated in 7.5–16. This deterioration was caused by preachers who came into Corinth from other Corinthian communities with ideas about Jesus and the gospel which were very different from those of Paul.[66]

While one may agree that chapters 10–13 should be viewed as a literary unit, it is not necessary to conclude that the letter itself is a collection of different sources assembled after Paul's death.[67]

There are considerable autobiographical notes in 2 Corinthians. It is not surprising that this is the case, especially in chapters 10–13, as this passage is devoted primarily to Paul's defence of his own *modus operandi*. He is defending his role as apostle against false or so-called 'super-apostles' (11.5). Particularly significant is that, in special reference to the super-apostles, Paul states that while he may be untrained in speech he is, however, not untrained in knowledge. The polemical context of 10–13 seems to suggest that the perception of Paul being untrained in speech is the negative opinion of his opponents. This is most likely the origin of the critical statement in 10.10 regarding Paul's bodily presence and speech.

A question arises whether Paul really was untrained in speech, as he apparently admitted and some scholars are inclined to conclude.[68] It is with some reticence that a verdict should be reached based solely on the single statement found in 11.5, which occurs in a polemical context. As suggested previously, when Paul is seen as a product and member of his culture it is highly implausible that he is straightforwardly untrained in speech! What Paul then may be seeking to communicate is that he is technically or professionally untrained as were many orators of his time. Another option presents itself, that even if Paul was technically or professionally trained as seasoned orators were, then he had decided not to practice these skills. Reasons for this are provided, such as statements made in 1 Cor. 2.4, 5.

---

[66] E. BEST, *Second Corinthians* (Atlanta: John Knox, 1987), 2.

[67] See Barclay, '2 Corinthians', in J. D.G. DUNN and J. W. ROGERSON (eds.), *Eerdmans Commentary on the Bible* (Grand Rapids, MI: W.B. Eerdmans, 2003), 1353–73; M. E. THRALL, *A Critical and Exegetical Commentary on the Second Epistle to the Corinthians* (2 vols.; International Critical Commentary; Edinburgh: T&T Clark, 1994–2000), 1.3–49; FURNISH, *II Corinthians*, 29–54.

[68] SAVAGE, *Power*, 70.

When one views Paul as intentionally bucking the social expectations of his society, consistency is found in his thought and expression. Since the statement is made polemically, Paul may be viewed as conceding for argument's sake.

Interpreting 2 Cor. 10.10 is not wholly dependent on understanding the circumstances and factors behind its composition. Even the information that can be gathered and discussed in this regard has serious limitations. Nonetheless, what has been seen to this point indicates the complex nature of Paul's relationship with the Corinthians and that a great deal transpired between the writing of the two letters. This point, although simple, may help to appreciate the difficulty of interpreting this single verse in 10.10: 'For they say, "His letters are weighty and strong, but his bodily presence is weak, and his speech contemptible."' Although so little is known on a micro level, on a macro level the statement could be made most intelligible within the context of Greco-Roman rhetoric and body language.

That 2 Cor. 10.10 is an authentic quotation of Paul who is reflecting on his Corinthian critics seems to be beyond reasonable doubt. The mention of ἐπιστολαί ('letters') here would probably include at least 1 Corinthians as well as the letter mentioned in 1 Cor. 5.9. Perhaps also the 'painful letter' referred to in 2 Cor. 2.1 could be included. In the case of 2 Cor. 10.10, Winter believes that a continuing debate among sophists is reflected, a dispute about written versus impromptu oration that began in the 4th century BC. He cites the exchange between Alcidamas and Isocrates as an instance of this.[69] It is difficult to determine if this Corinthian verse is a true reflection of the classical tradition given by Winter. What is relatively certain is the fact that Paul's critics thought that there was a clear discrepancy between his letters, which they considered weighty and strong; his bodily presence, which they regarded as weak; and his speech, which they found to be contemptible.

Βαρεῖαι καὶ ἰσχυραι ('weighty and strong') probably refer to both the content and the tone of Paul's letters. The Corinthians could well be making a statement of simple fact here. It would be reasonable to expect the letter mentioned in 1 Cor. 5.9 to be weighty and strong since Paul was dealing with the grave matter of sexual immorality, in which he instructed that the sexually immoral person should be driven out of the congregation (5.13). This was tantamount to 'excommunication'. Although not the whole of 1 Corinthians could be considered weighty and strong, most of it, whether on matters of doctrine or conduct, was clearly worthy of such a description.

The context as well as the tone of this quotation from Paul's critics in 2 Cor. 10.10 seem to suggest that the βαρεῖαι and ἰσχυραι are likely used in

---

[69] WINTER, *Philo*, 205.

a positive sense, that is as an acknowledgement. If this is indeed the case then the critics next statement – 'but his bodily presence is weak, and his speech contemptible' – becomes all the more intriguing, especially when the two diametrically opposed opinions are set in stark contrast. The Greek expression μέν and δέ is a construction of contrast. What Paul's critics say is quite serious, perhaps even grave, because the remark virtually accuses Paul of inconsistency or discrepancy between written words and his actual 'speech' and personal conduct. That is, the apostle did not actually deliver what he promised or threatened to do (cf. 1 Cor. 4.19). In other words, Paul's critics subsequently found out that he was actually not as weighty and strong as he had earlier claimed (pretended) to be. One could even view him as bluffing.

Ironically, as far as Paul's Corinthian critics were concerned, it was they themselves who found out that the same apostle who made such promises turned out to be a poor speaker and, therefore, not truly a 'man' of what they deemed to be actual power and substance. Indeed, there should be no inconsistency or discrepancy between written words and oral delivery ('bodily presence') and such an opinion about Paul would have been seriously damaging to him within the context of Greco-Roman rhetoric. A good orator was ultimately judged by his overall self-presentation which should be a great performance in itself. The Corinthians would not only be familiar with the rules of such a game but had apparently subscribed to it themselves. Consequently, Paul was judged by the same firmly established rules. As Winter observes, if the public was to be persuaded, they expected a certain quality from an orator or sophist, and Paul's presentation simply fell short. His opponents were drawn to this shortcoming as it was an 'irreparable deficiency'.[70]

Much has been said in scholarly circles about Paul's 'bodily presence' (ἡ παρουσία τοῦ σώματος), which was judged by his Corinthian critics to be 'weak' (ἀσθενής, 2 Cor. 10.10). As discussed, there are those who believe Paul was most likely hampered by ill health, which made his bodily presence unimpressive.[71] Whether this is the most plausible interpretation needs further consideration.

Victor Furnish draws attention to the contrast between 'weak' and 'strong', stating that an accusation of being weak would be to say that in person Paul 'cuts a sorry figure'.[72] But in what sense was Paul a sorry figure? Hans Betz links 1 Cor. 2.3 with 2 Cor. 10.10, and points out that weakness here refers to Paul's unattractive appearance rather than inner feelings. Betz points to the Socratic-Cynic tradition in which a public

---

[70] WINTER, *Philo*, 217.
[71] THISELTON, *The First Epistle*, 261.
[72] FURNISH, *II Corinthians*, 468.

speaker's appearance is just as important and powerful as his speech.[73] Again, Paul's allegedly unattractive appearance remains largely a matter of speculation as there is a lack of corroborating evidence.

While modern scholars' interpretation of Paul's 'bodily presence' remains largely conjecture, the Corinthians' expectation of a good orator to have impressive physical demeanour and presentation is undoubtedly an expectation of the time. Epictetus highlights the importance of the physical appearance of a true Cynic: 'Such a man needs also a certain kind of body, since if a consumptive comes forward, thin and pale, his testimony no longer carries the same weight.... That was the way of Diogenes, for he used to go about with a radiant complexion, and would attract the attention of the common people by the very appearance of his body.'[74] Arignotus, 'a man of superhuman wisdom', describes his unattractive teacher Pancrates as 'a holy man, clean shaven, in white linen, always deep in thought, speaking imperfect Greek, tall, flat-nosed, with protruding lips and thinnish legs' (Lucian, *Phil.* 34). Betz compares Paul's weakness to Lucian's Pancrates whose speech and appearance were unfit for public oratory.[75]

Lucian in his writing makes a sharp contrast between educated noble men with a 'dignified appearance' (σχῆμα εὐπρεπές) and men with a 'servile appearance' (σχῆμα δουλοπρεπές).[76] Given their Greco-Roman context, it is reasonable to assume that Paul's Corinthian critics would be rather familiar with these or similar comparisons, although there is no clear suggestion in the Corinthian correspondence that his critics had in fact made any comparison between Paul and any of the classical figures.

Larson makes the point that whereas noble birth is immutable, masculinity is a matter of perception.[77] That Paul's bodily presence is weak and his speech contemptible would have been largely a matter of perception. Larson's observation also helps to confirm that the performance of a speaker was also gender performance. Returning to the theme of masculinity and manhood, a male's deficiency in self-presentation could easily create an opening for his rivals to ridicule him as 'effeminate' (*mollior*).[78] Barton describes this further, explaining how spotting an effeminate man is a practice that appears in tragedies, comedies, Greek and Roman oratory, poetry and even graffiti. One identified such a man by his physique or

---

[73] BETZ, *Der Apostel Paulus und die sokratische Tradition: Eine exegetische Untersuchung zu seiner „Apologie" 2 Korinther 10–13* (Tübingen: Mohr, 1972), 44–57.

[74] Epictetus 3.32.86–89.

[75] BETZ, *Paulus*, 53–4.

[76] Lucian, *Somn.* 13.

[77] LARSON, 'Masculinity', 86.

[78] LARSON, 'Masculinity', 88.

physical movement. Moreover, sexual passivity was a tell tale sign of the effeminate man (κιναιδός, or *mollis*).[79]

Larson also observes that there were two basic reasons one would be considered weak. The first is if they lacked a forceful self-representation. Orators should dominate and master their audiences. The second is physical disability or small stature.[80] One is inclined to think that Paul's weak bodily presence in 2 Cor. 10.10 is more likely related to his self-presentation as a whole rather than to any actual physical weakness (e.g. physical handicap or defect). Although one cannot dismiss the possibility that Paul had a physical problem or was slight in stature, the audience's perception of him should be given priority as the reason he was perceived as he was. In the present context, the Corinthian critics' impression about Paul is perhaps more important than his actual physical body. As the study on Greco-Roman society has already indicated, the audience's opinion about the orator was part and parcel with the rhetorical game.

The controversy between Paul and his opponents has much to do with 'speech' (λόγος). Paul's speech was openly censured by his opponents as contemptible or of no account (2 Cor. 10.10). Whether λόγος in this context refers to style or content is an issue. Larson, in describing characteristics of weak rhetoric, adds to physiognomy and physical appearance the sound of one's voice. She makes the suggestion that in Paul's case, his opponents were most likely referring to both an unimpressive masculine deportment (bodily presence) and the sound of his voice (speech). When weighing the masculine performance of an orator, speech played a crucial role.[81]

Pogoloff also connects speech with social status and describes a wise speaker as one who uses language suited to the upper echelon of society. The upper class was educated, cultured, literate and persuasive in speech.[82] In Liftin's view, the reason why the Corinthians were not impressed by Paul's public speaking was because he simply did not live up to such standards. He seems to have lacked sophistication and the 'polish' of that class. Perhaps also his diction, word choice and voice were also lacking. Without the right speech, and of course physical presence and charm, a Greco-Roman audience would be near impossible to please.[83]

Whether Paul was actually deficient in masculine virtues or willingly allowed these virtues to be abrogated for the sake of the gospel needs consideration. If he freely abandoned these virtues, the reason would be to al-

---

[79] BARTON, 'Physionomics', 116.
[80] LARSON, 'Masculinity', 88.
[81] LARSON, 'Masculinity', 89.
[82] POGOLOFF, *Logos*, 119.
[83] LITFIN, *Proclamation*, 162.

low the power of God to truly manifest itself in and through his own human weakness, so that the faith of the Corinthians might rest 'not on human wisdom but on the power of God' (1 Cor. 2.5). According to the Greco-Roman concept of masculinity, a real man did not cede power or control to another, as slaves and women did. Indeed, setting aside others perception of manhood dovetails with Paul's willingness to become a δοῦλος of Christ.[84] The choice to become weak and a slave is thoroughly consistent with his overall intention to challenge social values through both his message and novel *modus operandi*.

Whether it was by choice or by actual deficiency, Paul's allegedly weak physical appearance and contemptible speech would have disqualified him from being a respectable member of the elite by the long and firmly established standards of the time. The consequence of not fitting into the category of respectable orator is that he would have become an embarrassing figure as far as his Corinthian critics were concerned.[85]

Savage thus regards Paul's unimpressive physical appearance as crucial in the Corinthian critics' judgment against him,[86] while Larson suggests that his physical appearance was a main cause for the critics' rejection of him.[87] Black comments that the Corinthian critics' charge against Paul relates to the perceived discrepancy between his letters and his conduct, so that what was supposed to be a positive opinion about his weighty and strong letters turned out to be an extremely negative issue due to his weak physical presence and contemptible speech.[88] One may summarise that Paul is accused of being duplicitous, disingenuous and even phony.

Despite how much conjecture there has been and the number of educated guesses made, there is little certainty as to just how unimpressive Paul's physical presence really was and the precise manner in which his speech was contemptible. A graphic description of Paul's physical appearance is found in the *Acts of Paul and Thekla* 3, where Paul is portrayed as 'a man small in size, bald-headed, bandy-legged ... with eyebrows meeting, rather hook-nosed.'[89] This is clearly not a complimentary portrait; however, whether one should take anything historical from this late apoc-

---

[84] LARSON, 'Masculinity', 91.

[85] LITFIN, *Proclamation*, 161.

[86] SAVAGE, *Power*, 54.

[87] LARSON, 'Masculinity', 87.

[88] BLACK, *Paul, Apostle of Weakness*, 136.

[89] J. K. ELLIOTT, *The Apocryphal New Testament: A Collection of Apocryphal Christian Literature in an English Translation* (Oxford: Clarendon, 1993), 364. See MALINA and J. H. NEYREY, *Portraits of Paul: An Archaeology of Ancient Personality* (Louisville, KY: Westminster John Knox Press, 1996). R. M. GRANT, 'The Description of Paul in the Acts of Paul and Thecla', *Vigiliae Christianae* (1982), 36.1–4. A. J. MALHERBE, 'A Physical Description of Paul', *Harvard Theological Review* (1986), 79.170–75.

ryphal source is dubious.[90] Nonetheless, Savage infers from late sources such as this that maybe Paul's humble physical presence affects his speech.[91]

Two points may be considered in light of the uncertainty surrounding what is meant by Paul's 'weak' bodily presence:

(1) The bodily presence of Paul may be unimpressive similar to the way it is described in sources such as the *Acts of Paul and Thekla* 3. If this is indeed the case, there would be every reason for Paul to be despised according to the social ethos of the time. As discussed throughout, in ancient rhetoric the speaker was expected to be a 'man', handsome, self-confident, assertive, strong and imposing. As such, he commanded respect, attention and ultimately approval and even praise. When it came to the actual delivery of speech, self-presentation was crucial, which included an attractive and symmetrical body that allowed the orator to use each body part – quite literally from head to toe – to fully and skilfully enhance the whole presentation.

It was at the point of delivery that the power and charm of body language became most evident. If the apostle's physical presence was really as portrayed in some apocryphal sources, Paul certainly had very little in terms of physiognomy to work with when presenting. If he were given a chance to deliver a formal speech, Paul's self-presentation would make him look, if one takes these late sources at face value, more like a feeble clown who was only fit for public entertainment rather than a serious and respectable orator. Moreover, even if Paul's allegedly unimpressive physical presence was something that he was born with, or was due to certain bodily defects suffered later, the sources lead one to believe that he would certainly not expect nor solicit public understanding or sympathy. Any failure or inability to monitor or correct the physical development of a male from birth would simply not be acceptable in his society.

(2) The allegedly weak bodily presence of Paul need not necessarily imply that he was actually suffering from any noticeable bodily defect. The previous study demonstrates that according to the stringent rules of Greco-Roman rhetoric and the rigid perception of masculinity that even the self-presentation and delivery of a perfectly normal, healthy person could be considered weak if the individual members of the body were not effectively orchestrated. Paul, who firmly decided to know nothing among the Corinthians except Jesus Christ crucified (1 Cor. 2.2) and was equally determined to proclaim the gospel without eloquent wisdom (1.17; cf. 2.4), was most unlikely to adhere to the strict rules and conventions of Greco-Roman rhetoric or uncritically share the current perception on masculinity.

---

[90] The document was written in the late 2nd century. MALINA, *Portraits of Paul*, 127.

[91] SAVAGE, *Power*, 71.

To do so would be equivalent to emptying the cross of Christ of power (1.17) and allow the faith of the Corinthians to rest on human wisdom rather than the power of God (2.5).

Like the weak bodily presence of Paul, his allegedly contemptible speech also becomes more intelligible and meaningful when put in the context of Greco-Roman rhetoric and masculinity. Λόγος is rather problematic in the passage, as Kennedy notes, this word for 'speech' is ambiguous and even used at times as a mystical concept which may 'refer concretely to a word, words or an entire oration, or may be used abstractly to indicate the meaning behind a word or expression or the power of thought and organization or the rational principle of the universe or the will of God.'[92]

Judging from the frequent appearance of the term λόγος in various contexts in the Corinthian letters and given the complexity of the Corinthian problems, which had a great deal to do with speech, eloquence, and wisdom, it is unlikely that λόγος in 2 Cor. 10.10 would only denote ordinary 'word' or 'words'. As Paul in the Corinthian letters was equally concerned with both the content of the message of the cross and the manner of its proclamation (i.e. delivery), it is reasonable to assume that λόγος also has to do with content and manner of delivery (i.e. the whole of self-presentation in rhetorical terms). Kennedy also describes that λόγος has a human side and denotes 'artistic creativity and the power of personality', a description that is relevant for the current discussion.[93]

If λόγος were to be regarded as the content of Paul's gospel, in what sense was it so negatively regarded as contemptible? It is safe to assume that these Corinthian critics were part of a church and, thus, it is unlikely that they would regard the core gospel message as contemptible. That is, they would have embraced something one could call a 'Christian faith'. As such, it is reasonable to suggest that if the content of Paul's gospel was in any way contemptible to the Corinthian critics, it would probably not be the gospel itself as such, but its lack of sophistication, by the standard they had accepted from the Greco-Roman social ethos.

If the core message of Paul's gospel was as simple and unsophisticated as the apostle put it, 'Jesus Christ and him crucified' (e.g. 1 Cor. 2.2) or as he writes in 15.3–5 as simply about Christ's death, burial and resurrection, the sophisticated and philosophically minded may have found it contemptible. It is less likely the case when the critics make the accusation of it being 'contemptible' (ἐξουθενημένος) that they were describing the content of Paul's λόγος. It is rather more likely that the contemptible λόγος refers to Paul's manner of presentation (body language). This would make better sense in view of what the critics said about Paul's weak bodily pres-

---

[92] KENNEDY, *Persuasion*, 8.
[93] KENNEDY, *Persuasion*, 8.

ence (ἡ παρουσία τοῦ σώματος ἀσθενής). It would also find a more than satisfactory explanation within the context of Greco-Roman rhetoric and masculinity.

One crucial and perplexing question remains: why did it take so long for the Corinthian critics to realise, or for the criticism to be echoed by Paul, that while his letters were weighty and strong, his bodily presence was weak and his speech contemptible? A number of years had passed since Paul first brought the gospel to them in Corinth. Had these observant, intelligent and critical Corinthians not noticed Paul's weaknesses, especially his unimpressive bodily presence and his contemptible speech, while he was with them (a year and a half according to Acts 18.11)? One explanation of this dilemma may be offered. Perhaps when the Corinthians initially encountered Paul they were so fascinated by the new and challenging message of the gospel that his weaknesses were overlooked. The old adage that familiarity breads contempt may be at play.

There is another factor that is less speculative: no letter seems to have been written in the course of Paul's first visit. As such, there was just no occasion at that time for the critical Corinthians to compare the apostle's letters with his bodily presence and speech. But a lot had transpired since then. At least two letters had been written before 2 Corinthians and the church situation had now turned from bad to worse, including church schisms which involved Paul himself and many others. The Corinthians, especially Paul's critics, naturally did not like some of his threatening words. In what was apparently Paul's first letter (1 Cor. 5.9), he already demands excommunication for the sexually immoral and exhorts them to drive out the wicked from among them (5.13). In 4.18–21, those who feel threatened and hurt by Paul's severe warning are far more numerous. Paul tells them that he will come soon and bring a stick with him to chastise them. For some of the Corinthians, Paul's words sounded not only threatening, but also they may well have been misconstrued as arrogant, or demeaning.

1 Corinthians is clearly weighty and strong at a number of points, although this remark of Paul's critics may be taken either as a compliment or indication of their displeasure, especially when some of its content is directed against them. Although the letter mentioned by Paul in 1 Cor. 5.9 cannot be traced, one may reasonably assume that it would have been weighty and strong as well, especially as it was dealing with serious matters such as sexual immorality.

With at least two of Paul's correspondences to hand and, presumably, also having been visited by the apostle at least twice now, the Corinthian critics were in a good position to make a comparison and sharp contrast between his letters ('weighty and strong') and his bodily presence ('weak'), as well as his speech ('contemptible'). Unlike Paul's first visit when they might have looked at all aspects of Paul, including his bodily presence and speech in a more innocent and unbiased way, at this later point they may have changed their initial attitude and impression about Paul due to a drastic change in situation. Such a big alteration in the Corinthians' attitude towards Paul may be due, at least in part, to the powerful presence and influence of the super-apostles. Otherwise, Paul would not have used such strong words to compare himself with them (2 Cor. 11.16–23). If Paul in his first visit were regarded by all as a friend, at a later stage those who were supporters of the super-apostles or other leaders would now have to treat him differently, perhaps even as an enemy.

In view of what Paul promises in 4.18–19, his critics would now be watching closely to see if he could deliver what he threatened to do. Paul's critics apparently did not like his menacing words from the time they first received them. Through critical, even hyper-critical eyes, they would understandably assess and examine Paul from a very different perspective now; and through their scrutiny, they discovered a very disturbing inconsistency between what he had written and how he actually appeared and spoke. Hence the remark: 'His letters are weighty and strong, but his bodily presence is weak, and his speech contemptible.' Paul did not live up to their high expectations of him. Indeed, when a man was charged with inconsistencies, it was nearly indistinguishable to saying that he was a fraud or fake. That discrepancy is an important issue for Paul in his dealings with the Corinthians is clearly reflected in passages such as 1.17–20, where he insists that he is thoroughly consistent and has never vacillated.

Unfortunately, the Corinthian correspondence gives no clue as to the precise way Paul's speech was contemptible. Was it about the content or structure of the apostle's speech? Was it a matter of presentation or delivery which involved voice, tone, body gestures and movements? Without reliable information, one may only conjecture in broad terms that in his critics' opinion Paul failed to meet the standard of a good orator. According to current rhetorical practice, not only should the social standing and character of the speaker be acceptable and his physical appearance impressive, but also the structure of speech must strictly follow recognizable conventions. The entire delivery must visibly and audibly demonstrate the harmonious coordination of the body members. The negative remark and impression of Paul's critics indicates that he failed to meet these expectations.

In a work that draws together physiognomy and slavery with rhetoric and manhood as they relate to criticisms of Paul in 2 Cor. 10.10, Harrill demonstrates that slave physiognomics were commonly used in the Roman time to maintain 'a somatic hierarchy between the slave and the free.'[94]

---

[94] HARRILL, 'Invective', 200.

According to Josephus, the freeman Celadus was once sent by the Emperor Augustus to find out if a certain young man was Prince Alexander. Celadus unveiled a plot simply by noting the young man's servile appearance: 'Celadus had no sooner set eyes on him than he detected the points of difference in the face, and noting that his whole person had a coarser and servile appearance (δουλοφανές), penetrated the whole plot' (*B. J.* 2.106–7).

Philo goes so far as to say that a slave actually possessed a 'naturally slavish body' (*Quod Omn.* 40). Apollonius tries to prove that a certain Arcadian boy was a free person simply because he did not look 'slave-like in appearance' but possessed 'all the good-looks' (Philostratus, *Vit. Apoll.* 8.12). Livy regards all Syrians as being 'far better fitted to be slaves, on account of their servile dispositions (*servilia ingenia*), than to be a race of warriors' (35.49.8). Harrill's research refers to a number of Greco-Roman writers who made 'a physiognomic connection between somatic inferiority – a weak, ugly bodily presence – and the condition of natural slavery.'[95]

In the political arena somatic invective was frequently used among the Greco-Roman elite against their rivals. However, as Harrill helpfully points out, such abusive rhetoric was very seldom used against slaves. Instead, it was directed at freeborn men, especially political opponents who were regarded as being slavish. As such, physiognomic distinctions between slave and freeman have very little to do with the actual description of slaves but far more to do with the rhetoric of manhood in Greco-Roman society. According to Harrill the dichotomy in the appearance between servile and free serves to mask disputes about manhood in the current culture, whether in regard to oratory, history, moral philosophy, comedy or satire.[96] In this connection, Cicero's somatic invective directed at Piso is well known: 'Do you begin to see, monster, do you begin to realize how men loathe your impudence? No one complains that some Syrian or other, some member of a crew of newly-made slaves, has become Consul. We were not deceived by your slavish complexion (*color servilis*), your hairy cheeks, and your discoloured teeth; it was your eyes, eyebrows, forehead, in a word, your whole countenance, which is a kind of silent speech of the mind, which pushed your fellow-men into delusion' (*Pis.* 1).

Harrill's work also has important implications for the study of the Corinthian controversy because in New Testament scholarship 2 Cor. 10.10 has been too commonly cited as 'evidence for Paul's actual physical appearance', which could be misleading in the context of Greco-Roman rhetoric. This is because the problem that the Corinthian critics had with Paul may have very little to do with the apostle's actual physical appearance, but with his perceived deception and inconsistency, very much in the

---

[95] HARRILL, 'Invective', 201.
[96] HARRILL, 'Invective', 201.

tradition of the caricatured Piso. Harrill thus concludes that it is appropriate to draw an analogy between Cicero's invective against Piso and the
criticism of the Corinthians against Paul. In both cases, there was the perceived inconsistency between what was once mistakenly believed to be
stern and authoritative (or to use the expression of 2 Cor. 10.10, 'weighty
and strong') and the actual physical presence ('weak' in 10.10). In both
cases, the consequence was grave, because the perceived inconsistency
would eventually rob the person under attack of all the credentials and attributes of a respectable free citizen. In other words, just like Piso in the
eyes of Cicero, the apostle Paul virtually becomes a sort of 'natural slave'.
Exegetical studies on some of the relevant Corinthian passages, such as 1
Cor. 2.1–5 and 2 Cor. 10.10, may now become more intelligible in light of
Harrill's attention to Greco-Roman rhetoric, especially his discussion on
physiognomics and manhood.

Harrill also draws attention to beliefs about deportment as a system of
signs which reflect on an individual's self-control as well as suitability to
rule over others. It is in light of such views on personal demeanour that 2
Cor. 10.10 should be read. Harrill also describes that in Greco-Roman invective, 'to accuse a person of a weak bodily presence and deficient speech
is to call that person a slavish man unfit for public office or otherwise to
dominate others.'[97] An important moral issue is involved which leads
Philip Hughes to describe the critics' accusation as damaging the very authority of Paul and not a mere ridicule of some physical disability.[98]
Glancy suggests that 'the adjective ἀσθενής refers ultimately to low social
status, a lack of honour, or simply a weak claim to apostolic authority.'[99]
The seriousness of 2 Cor. 10.10 together with its profound implications
must therefore take these points into consideration.

Despite their diversity, the many handbooks and other relevant literature
on Greco-Roman rhetoric clearly speak with one voice on the fragility of
manhood: 'weak demeanour is slavish and leads to a loss of manhood.'[100]
A great many examples are given to constantly warn against the flatterer
and his weak bodily presence.[101] Aristotle warns that 'flatterers are always
servile' (*Eth. nic.* 1125a). Seneca despises the flatterer for his servile ob-
sequiousness (*obsequium servile*).[102] Dio Chrysostom regards the flatterer
as one 'who lacked a free man's spirit (ἀνελεύθερος) and was of a servile
nature (δουλοπρεπής)' (*Or.* 15.29). Even a free man could be a slave 'in-

---

[97] HARRILL, 'Invective', 204.

[98] P. E. HUGHES, *Paul's Second Epistle to the Corinthians: The English Text with Introduction, Exposition and Notes* (Edinburgh: Marshall, Morgan & Scott, 1962), 362.

[99] GLANCY, 'Boasting', 128.

[100] HARRILL, 'Invective', 205.

[101] Curtius Rufus, *Hist. Alex.* 8.4.30; Tacitus, *Ann.* 1.7; 5.61; 12.4; *Hist.* 1.36.

[102] Seneca, *Ben.* 6.30.5.

significant in appearance, servile (δουλοπρεπής), unsleeping, never smil-
ing, ever quarrelling and fighting with someone, very much like a pan-
derer, who in garb as well as in character is shameless and niggardly,
dressed in a coloured mantle, the finery of one of his harlots' (*Or.* 15.29).
According to Epictetus, shameful actions could turn a free man into a slave
(4.1.8–18). Harrill elaborates:

> All these examples demonstrate that flattery and inconstancy were physiognomic signs of
> the slavish man whose ignoble gestures and weak bodily presence served as a rhetorical
> *topos* for the antitype of manhood in Greco-Roman moral philosophy. Such moral
> preaching assumes rhetoric of manhood similar to that in the moral *exempla* of historical
> literature and in the invective of judicial oratory aimed at typecasting an enemy as physi-
> ognomically servile.[103]

The implications of this observation for the Corinthian controversy are
clear. Instead of taking 2 Cor. 10.10 simply as evidence for Paul's actual
physical presence – a practice that fails to take Paul's social setting seriously – the expression may also be interpreted as slave physiognomics. Although Harrill may be somewhat assertive when making his point in regard
to Paul and his critics, there is little doubt that his research is very valuable.

Despite the critics' admittedly strong invective against Paul, he evidently remains committed to explore all ways and means to try and resolve
the issue in a way befitting his faith in Christ. There are good reasons to
assume that Paul is, after all, very conscious of the fact that he is dealing
with critics who already embraced his message of the cross. They were
quite certainly not those who were perishing (1 Cor. 1.18). Quite to the
contrary, there are also reasonably good grounds to suggest that as far as
Paul is concerned these critics would probably be among the saints mentioned in the opening verses of the Corinthian letters: ἡγιασμένοις in 1
Cor. 1.2 and ἁγίοις in 2 Cor. 1.1.

5.4 Conclusion

In this second and final chapter of *Part II* attention is given to rhetoric, delivery, body language and masculinity as it relates to the Greco-Roman social ethos. This is done as preparation for an exegesis of 1 Cor. 2.1–5, a
passage concerned with Paul's manner of proclamation ('delivery' in rhetorical terms) and 2 Cor. 10.10, in which Paul refers to the Corinthians' invective against him. Understanding the Corinthian critics' disparagement
of Paul is elucidated by the studies of Larson and Harrill, who both give
significant attention to Greco-Roman physiognomics and manhood.

---

[103] HARRILL, 'Invective', 204.

Throughout this study the importance of putting the Corinthian correspondences in their socio-historical contexts has been the focus. *Part II* again demonstrates how Paul's social context helps to interpret several passages which would otherwise be obscure.

In the course of the exegesis of 1 Cor. 2.1–5 and 2 Cor. 10.10 a number of crucial issues have been discussed and important questions raised. Although scholars have made great efforts to deal with these issues and questions critically and fairly, the nature of the task and material available for research makes conclusions rather tentative. This is especially true when considering the precise nature of Paul's weakness, fear and trembling when he first came to Corinth (1 Cor. 2.3). The precise way in which Paul's bodily presence was weak and his speech contemptible (2 Cor. 10.10) remains somewhat elusive. Nonetheless, this study has begun to demonstrate that there are convincing reasons to consider that Paul's intention is to invert the current social ethos and that his *modus operandi* is as an apostle of Christ and all that this entails.

In *Part III*, Paul's apostolic life will be the focus of attention. His personal tribulations will be explored with special reference to the concept of suffering in the Greco-Roman tradition in close connection with Paul's autobiographical comments related to this theme in 1 Cor. 4.8–13 and 2 Cor. 11.23–33.

Part III

Hardship (*Peristasis*) in Greco-Roman Social Ethos and Pauline Understanding

Hardship as 'Virtue' in Classical Writings, with Special Reference to Stoicism

Introduction

Part III has as its focus Paul's perception and experience with suffering and hardship. The physical aspects of his travails are conveyed largely in terms of body language. The lists of hardship in Paul's autobiographical notes may be illuminated when set within particular Greco-Roman contexts.

This final part consists of three chapters, each dealing with suffering in antiquity: Chapter 6 discusses hardship portrayed as a virtue, especially in Stoicism; Chapter 7 considers hardship as a sign of degradation and humiliation; and Chapter 8 looks at hardship as a witness to divine power in human weakness.

6.1 Stoicism: A General Introduction

Zeno of Citium (334–262 BC) is commonly regarded as the founder of Stoicism. This Greek school of philosophy derived its popular name from the στοὰ ποικίλη or 'painted porch' in Athens, the well-known location of their teaching. Zeno's thought was further developed by Cleanthes and Chrysippus. The trio could be regarded as the early representatives of Stoicism.[1] With the exception of Cleanthes' short 'Hymn to Zeus', virtually no work of the early Stoics survives intact. The leading figures of the next period of Stoicism were Panaetius (c. 185–c. 110 BC) and Posidonius (135–51 BC), who operated and developed the school largely at Rhodes. Their influence on Cicero's philosophical treatises (mid-1st c. BC) was considerable. The following phase of Stoicism, sometimes known as Roman Stoi-

---

[1] R. W. SHARPLES, 'Stoicism', in H. TED (ed.), *The Oxford Companion to Philosophy* (Oxford: OUP, 1995), 852–53, at 852. See A. A. LONG, 'Stoicism', *Hellenistic Philosophy: Stoics, Epicureans, Sceptics* (London: Duckworth, 1986), 107–209. J. M. RIST, *Stoic Philosophy* (Cambridge: Cambridge University Press, 1969).

cism,[2] left behind some of the most important Stoic writings. The Roman phase of Stoicism is represented especially by Seneca the Younger (c. 2 BC–65 AD), Epictetus (c. 55–135 AD) and the Roman emperor, Marcus Aurelius (121–80 AD).[3] The primary concern of these Stoics and their followers was on practical and personal ethics. The influence of these men and their school lives on, so that the descriptions 'stoic' and 'stoical' are well-known and common expressions to indicate acceptance of misfortune without complaint.[4] Many leading Roman political figures were Stoics.

Generally speaking, Stoicism was characterised by a philosophy of nature, an empiricist epistemology and an absolutist conception of moral duty. Writings of the founder Zeno are all lost; but his influence persists. The Stoic idea of the divine reason (λόγος) was central to their understanding of the universe as a highly unified entity, including the harmony of the universe (permeated with the λόγος) and man (endowed with the 'seed of logos', λόγος σπερματικός). Personal happiness and the well-being of human society are perceived in highly and consistently moral terms, with great emphasis on human moral obligation. Man would not be able to fulfill his moral obligation and obtain true happiness and virtue unless reason became the true master of his life, thought and action.[5]

Important to the Stoic philosophy was the belief in God and his providential work over the whole of the orderly universe in which man occupies a prominent place.[6] Man's reason enabled him to recognise the supreme plan of God and to submit himself willingly to it. This would also allow him to transcend his own personal interest and natural desire, so that even his own suffering was believed to be serving a wider purpose predetermined by the divine will.[7]

The belief that the world was completely ruled by Providence not only had a strong appeal to the ruling class, but also was a source of great comfort to those who had to deal with all sorts of misfortunes in life. For this as well as other reasons, Stoicism remained a great fountain of moral strength and social force in ancient Greco-Roman society.[8]

---

[2] See E. V. ARNOLD, *Roman Stoicism: Being Lectures on the History of the Stoic Philosophy with Special Reference to Its Development within the Roman Empire* (Cambridge: CUP, 1911).

[3] D. N. SEDLEY, 'Stoicism', in R. AUDI (ed.), *The Cambridge Dictionary of Philosophy* (Cambridge: CUP, 1995), 768–69.

[4] SHARPLES, 'Stoicism', 852.

[5] P. P. HALLIE, 'Stoicism', E. PAUL, *et al.,* (eds.), *The Encyclopedia of Philosophy* (London: Collier Macmillan Publishers, 1967), vol. 8.19–22, at 21–22. SEDLEY, 'Stoicism', 769. LONG, 'Stoicism', 147–50.

[6] LONG, *Epictetus: A Stoic and Socratic Guide to Life* (Oxford: Clarendon Press, 2002), 143.

[7] F. H. SANDBACH, *The Stoics* (London: Chatto & Windus, 1975), 35.

[8] SANDBACH, *The Stoics*, 16.

6.2 The Stoic View on Virtue, Good and Evil

The subject of virtue had a prominent place in ancient Greco-Roman philosophy and ethics. In the Platonic view, virtue was essentially an inner
state which governed and guided a person's moral behaviour and action.[9]

According to Stoic ethics, a person's inner state was not an autonomous
and independent entity. It must be in harmony with the orderliness of nature (φύσις). As such, a morally responsible person must always try to act
'according to nature' (κατὰ φύσιν). It was only in this way that a person
secured a life of ἀπάθεια or εὐθυμια, namely, spiritual peace and well-
being as well as εὐδαιμονία, the happiness for his soul (δαίμων).[10] In such
a happy and blessed state, a person could be said to be in perfect harmony
with nature and become almost god-like.[11] This was a true Stoic's ultimate
concern. The Stoics' belief in the attainment of such a content and blissful
state was based on their understanding of the λόγος as the soul of the universe as well as man's potential to participate and share in the λόγος due to
the λόγος σπερματικός that had been implanted in each person. Such was
the philosophical context in which the Stoic view on virtue, good and evil
is to be understood.

In Stoicism, 'virtue' might sometimes appear highly philosophical and
abstract. However, this important word could also be understood in more
concrete terms, so that the Stoics could more tangibly talk about certain
cardinal virtues such as intelligence, which was the ability to distinguish
the good from evil. The virtue of bravery could be discerned, to know what
it was to fear and what to not. So too justice, the notion of rendering to a
person what they really deserved. Of these and other important virtues, the
most important one for the Stoics was undoubtedly self-control, which was
the inner mental state of a person that governed all thinking and action in
life.[12]

For the Stoics, virtue was inseparable from wisdom, so that a 'virtuous'
man was also a 'wise' man or only the wise could be virtuous. Although
the Stoics had their own particular view on good and evil, it would be too
simplistic to think that things in life were either simply good or evil for the
Stoics. This was because, beside things good and evil, there were also
things which were considered 'indifferent' (ἀδιάφορα) to the virtuous and
wise man. However, the virtuous Stoics also acknowledged that certain

---

[9] M. SLOTE, 'Virtues', in *The Oxford Companion to Philosophy*, 900–01, at 900.

[10] Diogenes Laertius 7.88: 'The virtue of the happy man and the smooth current of life,
when all actions promote the harmony of the spirit dwelling in the individual man with
the will of him who orders the universe.'

[11] HALLIE, 'Stoicism', 8.21.

[12] HALLIE, 'Stoicism', 8.22. LONG, 'Stoicism', 199–200.

things they considered indifferent could also be 'advantages' (though not necessarily to be needed or essential). Health, wealth and honour, for example, were among these 'advantages'. Their opposites were 'disadvantages' to be avoided by the wise (but not at all costs) as well as those things which were totally 'indifferent' (ἀδιάφορα) to the wise.[13] For the Stoics 'advantages' were not in themselves 'good' and 'disadvantages' necessarily 'bad'. Advantages and disadvantages were thus outside the Stoic concept of good and bad in moral terms.

In his *De Officiis*, Cicero mentions four cardinal ethical virtues which are concerned 'either (1) with the full perception and intelligent development of the true; or (2) with the conservation of organized society, with rendering to every man his due, and with the faithful discharge of obligations assumed; or (3) with the greatness and strength of a noble and invincible spirit; or (4) with the orderliness and moderation of everything that is said and done, wherein consist temperance and self-control' (1.5.15). Cicero's emphasis on temperance and self-control is consistent with the general teaching of Stoicism.

The Stoics believed that the road to virtue was a well-trained reason which enabled a person to think and act correctly. In the Platonic tradition there are basically four cardinal virtues: justice, temperance (self-control), bravery and wisdom. But Zeno tries to re-define these four cardinal virtues in terms of wisdom; so that justice is primarily concerned with distribution, temperance with acquisition and bravery with endurance. All these virtues could be obtained only through wisdom. Wisdom is inseparable from knowledge which enables a person to make a distinction between what should and should not be done and between what is good, evil or neither (i.e. things that are just indifferent [ἀδιάφορα]).[14] This point about knowledge was of great importance to the Stoics, because a person could do what is right only if he always knew what 'right' was.

The word virtue (ἀρετή) in ordinary usage had a wider and more general sense, which could be rendered 'excellence', but in Stoicism it was often taken absolutely to mean moral excellence or perfection which could be obtained only by those who were truly virtuous. Only those who were truly virtuous could be regarded as truly good (ἀγαθόν) and happy. In this sense, virtue, goodness and happiness nearly became synonymous in Stoic ethics. Moreover, due to its particular emphasis and focus on the moral aspect of virtue, moral excellence and human excellence became identical in the end, and should thus be the ultimate goal of one's life. Following this simple logic, what was considered 'evil' or 'bad' in the Stoic concept was confined only to what was morally imperfect. In this context, misfortune,

---

[13] HALLIE, 'Stoicism', 8.22. LONG, 'Stoicism', 189–99.
[14] SANDBACH, *The Stoics*, 42.

suffering, sickness and even death itself, matters which were normally regarded as 'evil', belonged only to the morally indifferent and were not
'evil' *per se* in the Stoic sense.[15] However, the Stoics were also quick to
acknowledge that among things morally indifferent some 'have precedence' (προηγμένα) over others. Thus for example, good fortune, health,
wealth and beauty would generally be preferred rather than misfortune,
sickness, poverty and ugliness by a normal and sensible person if there was
a choice.[16]

For the Stoics, such preference was just natural. Generally speaking, for
Zeno and his followers, the 'preferred' things could never lead to true happiness (εὐδαιμονία). Throughout the history of Stoicism this remained a
key point in its philosophy. A man's virtue never depended on his ability
and success in obtaining anything in the external world. It only depended
on his having the right mental attitude towards those 'indifferent' things.
The Stoics' confidence in one's self-reliance were not only of immense
importance to the Stoics themselves, but also a source of great inspiration,
comfort and strength to those who had to face the harsh realities of life, including severe suffering and death.[17]

In Stoicism emotions were often interpreted in intellectual terms. Emotions such as distress, fear and the like only reflected a false judgment
about what was evil, and should thus be ignored. Such mental attitude
sometimes gives people the impression that the Stoics were a class of people with very little or no human feelings.

For the Stoics there were actually two very different categories of so-
called 'good' and 'evil': one morally vital and the other morally indifferent. The values that were attached to the two categories were very different. The vast difference between the two must always be maintained and it
required great wisdom to do that. The Stoics were most particular about
the vital distinction between the two, so much so that different vocabulary
and expressions were actually employed. Thus, things that were regarded
as morally good were 'to be won' (αἱρετόν) and the morally evil 'to be
fled from' (φευκτόν). Indifferent matters were either 'to be taken'
(λῆπτον), 'picked' (ἐκλέκτεον) or 'not to be taken' (ἀλῆπτον). The morally good were described as 'beneficial' (ὠφέλιμον) or 'useful'
(χρήσιμον) and the evil 'harmful' (βλαβερόν). Indifferent things could either be 'serviceable' (εὔχρηστα) or 'unserviceable' (δύσχρηστα).[18] These
are some of the 'serviceable' (εὔχρηστα) things according to Seneca (*Ep.*

[15] SANDBACH, *The Stoics*, 28. See T. BRENNAN, *The Stoic Life: Emotions, Duties, and Fate* (Oxford: OUP, 2005), 119–34.
[16] SANDBACH, *The Stoics*, 31.
[17] SANDBACH, *The Stoics*, 29.
[18] SANDBACH, *The Stoics*, 30.

82.11): 'I classify as "indifferent," – that is, neither good or evil, – sickness, pain, poverty, exile, death.'

Cicero in *Tusculan Disputation* 5.10.29–30 links happiness with goodness:

> Let us see who are to be described as happy: for my part I think it is those who are compassed about with good without any association of evil, and no other sense underlies the word happy, when we use it, except the fullness of combined good and complete separation of evil ... for there will come as it were a throng of evils, if we regard them as evils, poverty, obscurity, insignificance, loneliness, loss of property, severe physical pain, ruined health, infirmity, blindness, fall of one's country, exile and, to crown all, slavery – in all these distressing conditions – and more still can happen – the wise man can be involved; for chance occasions them, and chance can assail the wise man; but if these are 'evils,' who can show that the wise man will be always happy, seeing that he can be involved in all of them at one and the same time? ... And if the noble distinction of this title of 'wise,' most worthy of Pythagoras, Socrates and Plato, so delights them, let them constrain the soul to despise the things which dazzle them, strength, health, beauty, riches, distinctions, wealth, and count as nothing the things that are their opposites: then will they be able in clearest accents to claim that they are terrified neither by the assault of fortune nor the opinion of the mob nor by pain or poverty, and that they regard all things as resting with themselves, nor is there anything beyond their control which they reckon as good.

A couple of comments may be made on the above statement of Cicero: (1) the expressions, 'if we regard them as evils', and 'if these are evils' suggest that nothing is actually evil, only thinking makes it so; and (2) the belief in chance relates to what is beyond human control. In Stoic vocabulary, chance, fate, divine will and so forth, are often synonymous.[19]

In the end it is the mental attitude which separates the wise man from others, according to Cicero (*Fin.* 3.13.42): 'Again, can anything be more certain than that on the theory of the school that counts pain as an evil, the Wise Man cannot be happy when he is being tortured on the rack? Whereas the system that considers pain no evil clearly proves that the Wise Man retains his happiness amidst the worst torments. The mere fact that men endure the same pain more easily when they voluntarily undergo it for the sake of their country than when they suffer it for some lesser cause, shows that the intensity of the pain depends on the state of mind of the sufferer, not on the pain's own intrinsic nature.' For Cicero, it is 'the state of mind of the sufferer, not the pain's own intrinsic nature,' that is decisive. A similar attitude is found in Seneca (*Const.* 10.4): 'The wise man does receive some wounds, but those that he receives he binds up, arrests, and heals; these lesser things he does not even feel, nor does he employ against them his accustomed virtue of bearing hardship, but he either fails to notice them, or counts them worthy of a smile.'

---

[19] Cf. Epictetus (4.1.128–31; 4.4.6–7; 4.5.27–37) highlights when it is 'up to us' (ἐφ' ἡμῖν). LONG, *Epictetus*, 27–31; 211; 218–22.

For Seneca, things good or evil are not just matters of mental attitude and human perception, it is also God's way of thinking: 'It is God's purpose, and the wise man's as well, to show that those things which the ordinary man desires and those which he dreads are really neither good nor evils. It will appear, however, that there are goods, if these are bestowed only on good men, and that there are evils, if these are inflicted only on the evil' (*Prov*. 5.1–2). The Stoic idea that God's purpose could be in harmony with human thinking is consistent with their fundamental belief in the unity of the divine λόγος and the λόγος σπερματικός in man.

Seneca (*Ep.* 82.17), in profoundly Stoic spirit and composure, stresses that man's voluntary decision to confront hardship is a great virtue: '... nothing glorious can result from unwillingness and cowardice; virtue does nothing under compulsion (*Non est autem gloriosum, quod ab invito et tergiversante fit; nihil facit virtus, quia necesse est.*)' (cf. 66.16). For Seneca, a virtuous man 'welcomes (*amplexatur*) that which all other men regard with fear.'[20] The virtuous man is fearless when confronted with hardship: 'He reckons all these things as the bugbears of man's existence. Paint him a picture of slavery, lashes, chains, want, mutilation by disease or by torture, or anything else you may care to mention; he will count all such things as terrors caused by the derangement of the mind' (*Ep.* 85.27).

In *Ep.* 71.26–27 Seneca makes it clear it is not hardship itself that is evil but the breakdown of the human mind, and it is only in the rational part of man where 'supreme good' may be found:

What element of evil is there in torture and in the other things which we call hardships? It seems to me that there is this evil, — that the mind sags, and bends, and collapses. But none of these things can happen to the sage; he stands erect under any load.... I do not withdraw the wise man from the category of man, nor do I deny to him the sense of pain as though he were a rock that has no feelings at all. I remember that he is made up of two parts: the one part is irrational — it is this that may be bitten, burned, or hurt; the other part is rational — it is this which holds resolutely to opinions, is courageous, and unconquerable. In the latter is situated man's Supreme Good.

Seneca holds that 'the wise man is a skilled hand at taming evils. Pain, want, disgrace, imprisonment, exile – these are universally to be feared; but when they encounter the wise man, they are tamed' (*Ep.* 85.41).

According to Epictetus the virtuous man is the one 'who though sick is happy, though in danger is happy, though dying is happy, though condemned to exile is happy, though in disrepute is happy' and 'suffers no harm, even though he is soundly flogged, or imprisoned, or beheaded' (2.19.24; cf. 4.1.126). 'How, then, does it come about that he suffers no harm, even though he is soundly flogged, or imprisoned, or beheaded?' asked Epictetus. The answer is: the virtuous man bore it in 'a noble spirit'

---

[20] Seneca, *Ep.* 71.28; cf. 30.9; *Ir.* 1.5.2.

(4.1.127). Epictetus has great confidence in the human mind's freedom to choose between good and evil (1.25.1–4; cf. 2.4-7; 2.5.1, 7–8).

The Stoics were keenly aware of the fact that while a morally right attitude and action were within man's power to decide and do according to his nature-endowed reason, there were often the unforeseen circumstances which could prevent him from realising his noble goal. However, this was not their primary concern, because as long as the attitude and action were morally right, the mature Stoics could commit the end-result to God, fate or chance with peace of mind and a clear conscience (συνείδησις). Varying degrees of belief in fate or determinism seemed to be quite common among Stoics. In the end, what brought happiness to a man was not necessarily success in terms of the actual realisation of the desired goal, but the morally good intention, attitude and action. While accepting certain factors which could be beyond human control, the Stoics were generally very strong and consistent in their conviction that self-reliance, informed by knowledge and guided by wisdom and reason, was the road to happiness.

6.3 Hardship as God's Gift

The idea that human hardships have a divine origin is quite ancient. It may be found, for example, in Homer's *Iliad* (24.527–51) and *Odyssey* (4.236–37; 1.32–33). In the mythology of Homer, both good and evil come from God. However, in order to justify God's goodness and the divine purpose behind evil, Plato (*Rep.* 617E) boldly affirms that 'God is blameless (θεὸς ἀναίτιος)'. He repeats this in *Rep.* 380A: '… we must either forbid them to say that these woes are the work of God, or they must devise some such interpretation as we now require, and must declare that what God did was righteous and good, and they were benefited by their chastisement.' It is this conviction that provides the wise with the fortitude to endure suffering and misfortune, as Plato puts it in *Rep.* 387E: '"Least of all then to him is it a terrible thing to lose son or brother or his wealth or anything of the sort." "Least of all." "Then he makes the least lament and bears it most moderately when any such misfortune overtakes him."' Plato's point is clear: (1) the God/gods could not be held responsible for evil; and (2) even if hardship or any evil should befall man, it could only be for his benefit.

While the Stoics put great emphasis on self-reliance and were fully confident about human potential and ability to do the best in life, they also believed that all human lives were predetermined by some providence, whether the gods, fate or both. Yet, the human person was ultimately responsible for things good or bad. To them, providential determinism and human moral responsibility were fully compatible.

Seneca's *De Providentia* (c. AD 41–42) is a kind of theodicy, in response to Lucilius' question: if Providence is indeed in control, how does one account for the disturbing fact that many evils often seem to come upon good people. In his reply, Seneca says that the world of nature is orderly and well planned so that one could only assume that whatever happens to men is providential. But the strong and virtuous must not be shaken by what are commonly regarded as 'evils', such as misfortune, sickness and even death itself. All these should be matters of indifference to them. In real life God often puts those whom he loves and trusts to severe tests and struggles and God is usually not disappointed. Following this simple logic, the weak and the timid are not worthy of God's trial. As such, the mature and the highly motivated should really welcome sufferings and calamities as God-sent opportunities for their own good. God 'does not make a spoiled pet of a good man; he tests him, hardens him, and fits him for his own service (*Bonum virum in deliciis non habet, experitur, indurat, sibi illum parat*)', Seneca explains (*Prov.* 1.6). He elaborates on this point further:

> God, I say, is showing favour to those whom he desired to achieve the highest possible virtue whenever he gives them the means of doing a courageous and brave deed, and to this end they must encounter some difficulty in life.... Do not, I beg of you, shrink in fear from those things which the immortal gods apply like spurs, as it were, to our souls. Disaster is Virtue's opportunity (*calamitas virtutis occasio est*).... In like manner God hardens, reviews, and disciplines those whom he approves, whom he loves (*Hos itaque deus quos probat, quos amat, indurat, recognoscit, exercet*) (*Prov.* 4.5–7).

For Seneca the trial of the virtuous and his ultimate victory is also part of God's grand and mysterious design to question common conceptions concerning the nature of good and evil, conceptions which fail to distinguish the morally good and evil from the indifferent things (*Prov.* 5.2).

Seneca believes that even the gods are sometimes moved by the virtuous man's struggle with God-sent calamity: 'Do you wonder if that God, who most dearly loves the good (*deus ille bonorum amantissimus*), who wishes them to become supremely good and virtuous, allots to them a fortune that will make them struggle? For my part, I do not wonder if sometimes the gods are moved by the desire to behold great men wrestle with some calamity' (*Prov.* 2.6–7).

The pedagogical value and discipline in man's struggle is also described by Seneca: 'And so, in the case of good men the gods follow the same rule that teachers follow with their pupils; they require most effort from those of whom they have the surest hopes' (*Prov.* 4.11).

Man in his struggle must take great comfort from the fact that 'God has deemed us worthy instruments of his purpose to discover how much human nature can endure (*Digni visi sumus deo in quibus experiretur quantum humana natura posset pati*)' (*Prov.* 4.8. See *Ep.* 11.8–10; 52.2.7–8). But for Seneca, such great comfort is not enough to sustain man in his life-long struggle. Besides being a man of fortitude and courage, he must also commit himself to God or Fate, with the strong conviction that his struggle is part of the grand design of the universe determined by a sovereign will. This philosophy is well stated, for example, by Seneca in *Prov.* 5.6–8:

> I am under no compulsion, I suffer nothing against my will, and I am not God's slave but his follower.... Therefore everything should be endured with fortitude ... let us be cheerful and brave in the face of everything, reflecting that it is nothing of our own that perishes. What, then, is the part of a good man? To offer himself to Fate. It is a great consolation that it is together with the universe we are swept along; whatever it is that has ordained us so to live, so to die, by the same necessity it binds also the gods.

Seneca's last statement that not only men, but also the gods, are bound by 'the same necessity' is not only a great consolation to those who are caught in hardship, it also serves to reiterate the Stoics' fundamental belief in the unity between the virtuous man and the divine λόγος or God himself.

Sometimes Seneca goes even further with the seemingly incredible suggestion that the one who endures the most severe hardship with the strongest fortitude might even 'outstrip God', because God is 'exempt from enduring evil, while you are superior to it' (*Prov.* 6.6).

The Stoics' focus on reason and the mind together with their attitude to things indifferent often gave people the impression that they had totally disregarded the harsh reality of physical pain and were void of human feelings and emotions. Such an impression, however, is not altogether correct. Seneca, for instance, takes the reality and experience of physical pain quite seriously. In Seneca's *Ep.* 14.4–5 a vivid and graphic description of bodily pain and the extreme endurance of the sufferer are given: 'Picture to yourself under this head the prison, the cross, the rack, the hook, and the stake which they drive straight through a man until it protrudes from his throat. Think of human limbs torn apart by chariots driven in opposite directions, of the terrible shirt smeared and interwoven with inflammable materials, and of all the other contrivances devised by cruelty, in addition to those which I have mentioned!'

The Stoics' emphasis on the mastery and strength of human reason is sometimes accompanied by a humble acknowledgement of divine assistance in man's struggle, such as Seneca puts it in *Ep.* 41.2: 'Indeed, no man can be good without the help of God. Can one rise superior to fortune unless God helps him to rise?' And in *Ep.* 41.4: 'If you see a man who is unterrified in the midst of dangers, untouched by desires, happy in adversity, peaceful amid the storm, who looks down upon men from a higher plane, and views the gods on a footing of equality, will not a feeling of reverence for him steal over you? Will you not say: "This quality is too great and too lofty to be regarded as resembling this petty body in which it dwells? A divine power has descended upon that man."'

The following statement by Seneca (*Ep.* 73.16) would certainly be a great encouragement to those in the midst of trial: 'The gods are not disdainful or envious; they open to you; they lend a hand as you climb. Do you marvel that man goes to the gods? God comes to men; nay, he comes nearer, he comes into men. No mind that has not God, is good.'[21] The word 'reason' in the following statement (*Ep.*74.21) could well be taken as a kind of synonym for God: 'Love reason! The love of reason will arm you against the greatest hardships (*Ama rationem! Huius te amor contra durissima armabit*).'

Sometimes Epictetus conceives of God as someone who is 'within' man himself, so that he becomes a kind of 'God-bearer'. Such a thought naturally places great responsibility on man:

> Do you not know that you are nourishing God, exercising God? You are bearing God about with you, you poor wretch, and know it not! Do you suppose I am speaking of external God, made of silver or gold? It is within yourself that you bear Him, and do not perceive that you are defiling Him with impure thoughts and filthy actions. Yet in the presence of even an image of God you would not dare to do anything of the things you are now doing. But when God Himself is present within you, seeing and hearing everything, are you not ashamed to be thinking and doing such things as these, O insensible of your own nature, and object of God's wrath! (2.8.12–14)

Following his great predecessors, Marcus Aurelius holds firm to the belief that everything in the world is the design of the divine Reason or God, which or whom man must gladly accept and co-operate with. To do so is also to follow the dictate of Nature. 'Why should I live in a world where there are no gods and no Providence?' asked Marcus Aurelius in *Meditations* 2.11.

In certain contexts, 'reason' and 'god' are almost synonymous for Marcus Aurelius. As such, one should always 'keep the god within us safe from violation or harm, stronger than pleasures and pains, doing nothing without purpose or by mistake or in pretence, having no need that anyone else should do something or not do something and accepting what happens and what is assigned to us coming from the same source as that from which it has itself come' (*Med.* 2. 17).

Like Seneca, Marcus Aurelius is equally convinced that a man's hardship is God's assignment, as he puts it simply but clearly in 3.11: '... and what virtue it calls for from me, such as gentleness, manly courage (ἀνδρείας), truth, fidelity, guiltlessness, independence, and the rest. In each case therefore must thou say: this has come from God.' Once a man accepts what has been predetermined by 'destiny', his duty is to be obedient to God without complaint: '... there is left as the characteristic of the good man to delight in and to welcome what befalls and what is being spun

---

[21] See also Seneca, *Ep.* 31.11; 41.1; 120.14; Epictetus 2.8.9–14.

for him by destiny ... but to maintain it to the end in a gracious serenity, in orderly obedience to God, uttering no word that is not true and doing no deed that is not just.'[22] As a faithful 'follower of God', a Stoic should totally disregard others' opinion about him and be free from all cares and concerns, and just set his mind on the course that God has assigned for him: 'What others may say or think about him or do against him he does not even let enter his mind, being well satisfied with these two things – justice in all present acts and contentment with his present lot. And he gives up all engrossing cares and ambitions, and has no other wish than to achieve the straight course through the Law and, by achieving it, to be a follower of God' (*Med.* 10.11).

6.4 Suicide

The constant recurrence of the topic of suicide among the Roman Stoics, and Seneca's glorification of it as 'the path to freedom' has prompted some to remark that Seneca is 'in love with death.'[23] Whatever the case may be, it is Seneca's view that 'the best thing which eternal law ever ordained was that it allowed to us one entrance into life, but many exits.... This is the one reason why we cannot complain of life: it keeps no one against his will' (*Ep.* 70.14).

For all his apparent glorification of death and his praise of the freedom it brings, it is Seneca's view that everything in life, including death itself, has its appointed time. As such, there is no need to either hasten its arrival or to try to turn away from it: 'It is folly to die through fear of dying. The executioner is upon you; wait for him. Why anticipate him? Why assume the management of a cruel task that belongs to another? Do you grudge your executioner his privilege, or do you merely relieve him of his task?' (*Ep.* 70.8).

For the Stoics, 'appropriate action' (καθῆκον) was an important factor in regard to suicide. Reason must ultimately decide what course of action was appropriate or inappropriate in a particular set of circumstances. However, to act appropriately was not necessarily good, and to act inappropriately necessarily bad, in the strictly moral sense. In this case suicide was not a strictly moral issue.

It was quite impossible for the Stoics to talk about human suffering and hardship without having to deal with the issue of death, whether it was natural or otherwise. Here the noble death of Socrates, the philosopher *par excellence*, is undoubtedly the *locus classicus* for people to imitate. Plato,

---

[22] Marcus Aurelius, *Med.* 3.16. Cf. 2.17; 3.7; 5.27.
[23] SANDBACH, *The Stoics*, 50.

Cicero, Seneca and Epictetus each regard Socrates' death as a response to 'divine sign' (see §2.2.1.3). When a divine sign was given, the issue of death, including suicide, was beyond mere human judgment to decide whether an action was appropriate or not. This was because when a divine sign was believed to have been given to a person, some kind of moral 'ought' or imperative became a major factor in that person's ultimate decision. In this case, the Stoics, like Socrates, would think that a person could only be obedient to the divine sign, whether to willingly surrender to some outside agent or to commit suicide.

Socrates consistently holds that the body is the soul's prison and there is one way in which a man could be free from all anxiety about the fate of his soul.[24] Philosophically or religiously, the Socratic attitude toward death is evidently prompted by the Greek belief in the immortality of the soul as well as its ability to find true wisdom in the other world.[25]

Seneca thinks that once the nature of death is properly understood, a man could actually scorn death because not even death is able to strike his soul and 'the way out' (i.e. suicide) is always open to him with the divine assurance that 'of all things that I have deemed necessary for you, I have made nothing easier than dying.'[26] Seneca (*Ep.* 65.22–23) even goes so far as to suggest that 'to despise our bodies is sure freedom': 'For my body is the only part of me which can suffer injury. In this dwelling, which is exposed to peril, my soul lives free. Never shall this flesh drive me to feel fear, or to assume any pretence that is unworthy of a good man. Never shall I lie in order to honour this petty body. When it seems proper, 1 shall sever my connection with it. At present, while we are bound together, our

---

[24] Plato, *Phaed.* 65C, 66E, 67CD, 115A.

[25] Plato, *Phaed.* 67E–68B: 'the true philosophers practise dying, and death is less terrible to them than to any other men…. When human loves or wives or sons have died, many men have willingly gone to the other world led by the hope of seeing there those whom they longed for, and of being with them; and shall he who is really in love with wisdom and has a firm belief that he can find it nowhere else than in the other world grieve when he dies and not be glad to go there? We cannot think that, my friend, if he is really a philosopher; for he will confidently believe that he will find pure wisdom nowhere else than in the other world. And if this is so, would it not be very foolish, for such a man to fear death?' Cf. 82C.

[26] Seneca, *Prov.* 6.6–7: 'Above all, I [God] have taken pains that nothing should keep you here against you will. The way is open…. I have made nothing easier than dying … and you will see what a short and easy path leads to freedom.' Seneca, *Ir.* 1.112: 'In any kind of slavery the way lies open to freedom. If the soul is sick and because of its own imperfection unhappy, a man may end its sorrows and at the same time himself … in whatever direction you turn your eyes, there lies the means to end your woes. Do you see that cliff? Down there is the way to freedom. Do you see that ocean, that river, that well? There sits freedom at the bottom. Do you see that tree …? From its branches hangs freedom. Do you see that throat of yours, that stomach, that heart? They are ways of escape from slavery. Do you ask what is the path to freedom? Any vein in your body!'

alliance shall nevertheless not be one of equality; the soul shall bring all quarrels before its own tribunal. To despise our bodies is sure freedom.'

For Seneca, however, there is nothing honourable about death *per se*: 'Death is honourable when related to that which is honourable; by this I mean virtue and a soul that despises the worst hardships (*id est virtus et animus extrema contemnens*)' (*Ep.* 82.14).

Epictetus subscribes to Socrates' view that the body is an encumbrance. Yet this in itself is not a sufficient reason for a person to take suicide as an option (1.9.10–11). It would be equally wrong to commit suicide in order to escape from one's adverse circumstances. The right way to treat one's body is simply to regard it as completely unimportant (1.9.17).[27]

Epictetus is sometimes fond of using a phrase like 'the door stands open' to indicate that suicide always remains an option for people (1.25.18). However, one should always be certain about God's call before suicide is committed: 'If thou sendest me to a place where men have no means of living in accordance with nature, I shall depart this life, not in disobedience to thee, but as though thou wert sounding for me the recall.'[28] Also, no one should take his own life unless certain that he has completed his God-given assignment on earth: 'Men, wait upon God. When he shall give the signal and set you free from this service, then shall you depart to him; but for the present endure to abide in this place, where he has stationed you' (1.9.16).

6.5 Courage and Manliness

In order to make a clearer comparison and contrast between the Stoic and Pauline perceptions on the matter of hardship and suffering, it is necessary to highlight the Stoic view on courage and manliness.

Despite the distinctiveness of Stoicism as a philosophical school, its leaders and followers continued to be inspired by Plato and Xenophon's Socrates, especially in the area of moral virtues, such as fortitude and self-control over mental, physical and emotional stress.[29] The Stoics were also mindful of Socrates' famous saying: 'No harm can come to the good man in life or in death, and his circumstances are not ignored by the gods' (Plato, *Apol.* 41D).

Cicero expresses his deep conviction in a very Stoic manner that the courage and discipline of the human soul would enable a man to endure all the odds in life and eventually make life worth living: 'The soul that is al-

[27] LONG, *Epictetus*, 159.
[28] Epictetus 3.24.101–02; cf. 1.24.20.
[29] LONG, *Epictetus*, 68.

together courageous and great is marked above all by two characteristics: one of these is indifference to outward circumstances.... The second characteristic is that, when the soul is disciplined in the way above mentioned, one should do deeds not only great and in the highest degree useful, but extremely arduous and laborious and fraught with danger both to life and to many things that make life worth living' (*Off.* 1.20.66). He praises the Stoic understanding of courage, especially courage that is prompted by its response to danger and for the cause of justice: 'The Stoics, therefore, correctly define courage as "that virtue which champions the cause of right." Accordingly, no one has attained to true glory who has gained a reputation for courage by treachery and cunning; for nothing that lacks justice can be morally right' (*Off.* 1.19.62).

Cicero (*Tusc.* 2.18.43) elaborates on the definition of virtue with special emphasis on manliness:

> It is universally agreed then, not merely by the learned but by the unlearned as well, that it is characteristic of men who are brave, high-spirited, enduring, and superior to human vicissitudes to suffer pain with patience.... And yet, perhaps, though all right-minded states are called virtue, the term is not appropriate to all virtues, but all have got the name from the single virtue which was found to outshine the rest, for it is from the word for 'man' that the word virtue is derived (*appellata est enim ex viro virtus*); but man's peculiar virtue is fortitude (*viri autem propria maxime est fortitudo*), of which there are two main functions, namely scorn of death and scorn of pain. These then we must exercise if we wish to prove possessors of virtue, or rather, since the word for 'virtue' is borrowed from the word for 'man,' if we wish to be men (*Utendum est igitur his, si virtutis compotes vel potius si viri volumus esse, quoniam a viris virtus nomen est mutuata*).

Manly bravery and endurance occupied a prominent place in the social ethos of the Romans because these were highly regarded as the very qualities which enabled them to conquer places and build their empire. In this particular context, the one word they had in mind would most probably be *virtus* (a word cognate with *vir,* 'man' as seen above). *Virtus* was, therefore, a particularly manly quality in the face of extreme suffering and pain was a litmus test of masculinity. Therefore, it is quite natural that great Roman thinkers such as Cicero and Seneca repeatedly use the adjective 'womanly' (*muliebriter*) as the pejorative term to characterise a man's failure to endure pain.

Using the analogy of the athletes in fierce competition, Seneca (*Ep.* 78.17) makes special reference to virtue and manliness: 'What blows do athletes receive on their faces and all over their bodies. Nevertheless, through their desire for fame they endure every torture, and they undergo these things not only because they are fighting but in order to be able to fight. Their very training means torture. So let us also win the way to victory in all our struggles, for the reward is not a garland or a palm or a trumpeter who calls for silence at the proclamation of our names, but rather virtue, steadfastness of soul, and a peace that is won for all time, if fortune has once been utterly vanquished in any combat. You say, "I feel severe pain." What then; are you relieved from feeling it, if you endure it like a woman (*si illum muliebriter tuleris*)?'

In *Tusc.* 4.24.53 Cicero attempts a definition of bravery (ἀνδρεία, *fortitudo*): 'Bravery is, he [Chrysippus] says, the knowledge of enduring vicissitudes or a disposition of soul in suffering and enduring, obedient to the supreme law of our being without fear (*Fortitudo est, inquit, scientia rerum perperendarum vel adfectio animi in patiendo ac perferendo summae legi parens sine timore.*).' 'Supreme law' here could refer to the law of nature or of God. However, it is perhaps more likely that Cicero had in mind the 'reason' that was believed to be in man's inner being, as his next statement in *Tusc.* 2.20.47–48 seems to indicate:

When then we are directed to be master of ourselves, the meaning of the direction is that reason should be a curb upon recklessness…. It is man's duty to enable reason to have rule over that part of the soul which ought to obey. How is it to be done? You will say. Even as the master over the slave, or the general over the soldier, or the parent over the son. If the part of the soul, which I have described as yielding, conducts itself disgracefully, if it give way in womanish fashion to lamentation and weeping (*si se lamentis muliebriter lacrimisque dedet*), let it be fettered and tightly bound by the guardianship of friends and relations; for often we find men crushed by a sense of shame at being overcome without any reason. Such persons therefore we shall have almost to keep in chains and guard closely like slaves, whilst those who shall be found more steadfast, though not of the highest strength, we shall have to warn to be mindful of honour, like good soldiers recalled to duty.

For Cicero, no insult to a person's manly ego could be greater than being tauntingly described as 'womanish', an adjective used by Cicero in the previous statement as well as in the following one in *Tusc.* 2.23.55: 'But the principal precaution to be observed in the matter of pain is to do nothing in a despondent, cowardly, slothful, servile or womanish spirit (*ne quid abiecte, ne quid timide, ne quid ignave, ne quid serviliter muliebriterve faciamus*).' It is worth noting that for Cicero being womanish is closely parallel to being slavish.

For Cicero as well as the committed Stoics, true manliness and other closely related virtues or qualities were essentially mental and not physical. Their main concern was with inner strength and fortitude and not physical power. But the mind required a great deal of alertness and readiness. This meant strict discipline and constant exercise, without which courage, manliness, etc., were just empty talk. To the Stoics, ultimately it was the human mind or reason which was in tune with the law of Nature, God or the divine *Logos* that made everything possible – courage, manliness, virtue, wisdom, goodness, beauty and happiness: 'Happiness depends on what is entirely a man's own doing, the operation of his mind: if he judges correctly and holds steadfastly to truth he will be a perfect being, whom misfortune may strike but will never harm. The wise man will be more rightly called a king.... All things will rightly be called his, for he alone knows how to use them; rightly too will he be called beautiful, for the features of the mind are more beautiful than those of the body, rightly the only free man, since he obeys no master and is the servant of no greed, rightly invincible, for though his body may be bound, no fetters can be put on his mind.... If it is true that none but the wise are good and all the good are blessed, is anything more to be studied than philosophy or anything more divine than virtue?' (Cicero, *Fin.* 3.22.75–76).

6.6 The True Stoic Worthy of Imitation and Praise

In classical Greco-Roman thinking, the great value of suffering and hardship endured by the virtuous was not confined to their own personal life. Equally important was the common belief that they could be inspiring exemplars for others. Great pedagogical value was thus attached to their examples (Seneca, *Prov.* 4.8, 11).

For Cicero, it is man's display of virtue in situations of extreme danger and difficulty that deserve the greatest praise: 'the greater the difficulty, the greater the glory' (*Sed quo difficilius, hoc praeclarius*) (*Off.* 1.19.64). Cicero believes that the glory that now belongs to the one who has made it is perceived largely in terms of bravery, nobility and masculinity: 'We must realize ... that achievement is most glorious in the eyes of the world which is won with a spirit great, exalted, and to the vicissitudes of earthly life. And so, when we wish to hurl a taunt, the very first to rise to our lips is.... "For ye, young men, show a womanish soul, yon maiden a man's;" and this: "Thou son of Salmacis, win spoils that cost no sweat nor blood." When, on the other hand, we wish to pay a compliment, we somehow or other praise in more eloquent strain the brave and noble work of some great soul' (*Off.* 1.18.61).

In Cicero's *De Oratore* 2.346–47, those who manage to overcome adversity and misfortune in difficult situations with wisdom, bravery and dignity deserve 'the most welcome praise':

But the most welcome praise is that bestowed on deeds that appear to have been performed by brave men (*viris fortibus*) without profit or reward; while those that also involve toil and personal danger (*cum labore ac periculo ipsorum*) supply very fertile topics for panegyric, because they admit of being narrated in a most eloquent style and of obtaining the readiest reception from the audience; for it is virtue that is profitable to others, and either toilsome or dangerous or at all events not profitable to its possessor, that is deemed to mark a man of outstanding merit (*praestantis viri*). Also it is customarily recognized as a great and admirable distinction to have borne adversity wisely, not to have been crushed by misfortune, and not to have lost dignity (*dignitatem*) in a difficult situation.

Seneca expounds upon his idea of the 'honourable and glorious' in an eloquent manner (*Ep.* 82.10–12): 'Mere death is, in fact, not glorious; but a
brave death is glorious.... I classify as "indifferent," – that is, neither good
nor evil, – sickness, pain, poverty, exile, death. None of these things is in-
trinsically glorious; but nothing can be glorious apart from them. For it is
not poverty that we praise, it is the man whom poverty cannot humble or
bend. Nor is it exile that we praise, it is the man who withdraws into exile
in the spirit in which he would have sent another into exile. It is not pain
that we praise, it is the man whom pain has not coerced. One praises not
death, but the man whose soul death takes away before it can confound it.
All these things are in themselves neither honourable nor glorious; but any
one of them that virtue has visited and touched is made honourable and
glorious by virtue; they merely lie in between, and the decisive question is
only whether wickedness or virtue has laid hold upon them.'

The idea of God sending a good example for the learner to imitate is
also present in Epictetus (3.22.45–49): 'And how it is possible for a man
who has nothing, who is naked, without home or hearth, in squalor, without a slave, without a city, to live serenely? Behold, God has sent you the
man who will show in practice that it is possible. "Look at me," he says, "I
am without a home.... Yet what do I lack? Am I not free from pain and
fear, am I not free? ... Who, when he lays his eyes upon me, does feel that
he is seeing his king and his master?"' In Epictetus' ideal, a true philosopher becomes god-like in the end: 'Of such character will I show myself to
you – faithful, reverent, noble, unperturbed ... one who dies like a god,
who bears disease like a god. This is what I have; this is what I can do; but
all else I neither have nor can do. I will show you the sinews of a philosopher (νεῦρα φιλοσόφου)' (2.8.27–29).

6.7 A Jewish Counterpart: the Maccabean Tradition

In the Jewish tradition, a likely counterpart to Stoicism on the virtues of
courage and endurance would probably be the moving example of the
Maccabean martyrs in the face of extreme suffering. As such, it may be
helpful to make a brief reference to it before examining the case of Paul on
the matter. Brent Shaw thinks that it was the intention of the author of *4
Maccabees* to show that, by using the power of the human spirit and mind
to control the body, one could be a 'master of oneself' (αὐτοδέσποτος) under adverse circumstances.[30] This is most evident in the author's recounting, in graphic detail, the extreme suffering the Maccabean martyrs went

---

[30] B. D. SHAW, 'Body/Power/Identity: Passions of the Martyrs', *JECS* 4 (1996), 269–
312, at 277.

through. They were Eleazar, the seven young men and finally, their mother. The moral of the story is clear: the martyrs emerged victorious in their confrontation with the tyranny of their oppressor because they powerfully showed that the tortured body, under the control of the spirit and mind, was able to endure and finally overcome all the tortures inflicted upon it. The victims' victory eventually earned them a noble reputation as worthy martyrs of the nation.

The author of *4 Maccabees* sums up the virtue of endurance of the Jewish martyrs in 17.11–16: 'Truly divine was the contest in which they were engaged. On that day virtue was the umpire and the test to which they were put was a test of endurance. The prize for victory was incorruption in long-lasting life. The first to enter the contest was Eleazar, but the mother of the seven sons competed also, and the brothers as well took part. The tyrant was the adversary and the world and the life of men were the spectators. Piety won the victory and crowned her own contestants.'[31]

Like the Stoics, and perhaps more so, the Maccabeans also took God's sovereignty and divine assistance seriously. However, also similar to the Stoics, except somewhat less explicit and pronounced, the focus of the Maccabeans in their περίστασις was on the human qualities or virtues which enabled them to overcome extreme adversity and emerge as victors. For the admiring public, readers or hearers, attention was also largely on the human efforts and virtues of their sages or martyrs, so that in the end it was both 'praise be to man on earth' and 'glory be to God on high'. Whatever the case may be, one suspects that for Paul's Corinthians, the interest may well have been more in 'praise be to man on earth' rather than in 'glory be to God on high'. There is good reason to consider that this would certainly not be Paul's way of thinking. It was always divine grace and glory that the apostle sought. Moreover, Paul was ever conscious of his own identity as the δοῦλος of Christ. As such, he did not seek glory for himself.

The Greco-Roman as well as the Maccabean traditions on endurance also seem to have been reflected in the thinking of the early church fathers. In his letter, Ignatius bishop of Antioch, also associates martyrdom with the virtue of endurance.[32] Similarly, Tertullian also believes that *patientia* or endurance is important to the mind as well as the body, to the extent that it virtually becomes the lord and master of one's mind and body.[33] When this happened, a person would be well prepared for all the adversities in life, including 'whips, fire, the cross, wild beasts and ... the sword'.[34] Con-

---

[31] ANDERSON (trans.), '4 Maccabees', 2.562–63.
[32] Ignatius, *Eph.* 3.1.
[33] SHAW, 'Body', 298.
[34] Tertullian, *Pat.* 13.8.

sequently, the martyrs were regarded as 'athletes of piety' (εὐσεβείας ἀθλητῶν) and it was their 'valour, manliness and courage (ἀνδρείας)' which won them their battles.[35]

6.8 Conclusion

Special reference has been made to Stoicism in this chapter as an essential background in the lead up to an inquiry into Paul's understanding of hardship based largely on 1 Cor. 4.8–13 and 2 Cor. 11.23–33. For the purposes of this research, it is of little use and far beyond the scope of the study to look at Stoicism in the broadest and most general of terms. Attention has, therefore, been given only to several issues which are assumed to be characteristic of the Stoic school and relevant to the apostle's *peristasis* catalogues; issues such as the Stoic view on virtue, good and evil, human hardship as a divine gift, and severe suffering as a welcome opportunity to demonstrate a man's courage and endurance, which were regarded as the most obvious traits of masculinity. Last but not least is the Stoic attitude towards death and suicide. The pedagogical values which the Stoics' attached to the great examples set by the truly virtuous man are also noted.

The study on virtue, good and evil has shown that for the Stoics these concepts were only important and meaningful morally, and judgment on them depended largely, if not entirely, on the human reason or mind. Things external, including hardship and physical pain, even death itself, were matters of 'indifference' to Stoics. As such, these indifferent matters were not within the Stoics' moral concerns. Although the Stoics' attitude toward hardship was indicative of their moral character as well as being relevant to the issues of virtue and wisdom, hardship itself was not a moral issue. Therefore, the Stoics were thought to be members of a class which was able to transcend things, including hardship, pain and even death itself; things which were generally the deep concerns of other people.

It remains to be seen where Paul really belongs. It is almost unnecessary to say that the Stoics' belief in hardship as a God-sent gift to the 'worthy' as a test of their moral character lifted their burden in the face of severe hardship. While suicide was not treated lightly by the Stoics, there was the general understanding that it was largely a matter of human judgment at the dictate of a man's reason as well as being sensitive to the divine call.

Although the Stoic view of courage was essentially consistent with the general Greco-Roman position on the matter, its moral overtone needs to be especially noted. On the matter of masculinity, the Stoic emphasis was also on man's moral fortitude and mental stamina rather than on his out-

---

[35] Eusebius, *Hist. Eccl.* 5.1.1. SHAW, 'Body', 307.

ward features and physical strength. The great importance that the Stoics attached to pedagogical values of moral virtue obtained by the good and wise was essential to the core of their teaching. This concern became the more important when the virtuous was seriously regarded as a God-sent witness. It remains to be seen whether Paul's view on the matter is in any way comparable to the Stoic's.

It is particularly worth noting that, by introducing the unique idea of the 'indifferent' (ἀδιάφορα), the Stoics had more or less re-defined 'good' and 'evil' both philosophically and morally. In the conversation to follow, attention will be given to whether Paul also subscribed to such ideas in his attitude towards hardship and suffering, or if the apostle looked at those issues quite differently. Whatever the case may be, the Stoic idea was clearly out of the ordinary. As far as the common people were concerned, most of them could not and would not look at those harsh realities of life in such a detached or indifferent manner and remain stoical about them.

Generally speaking, the Stoic attitude toward hardship was positive for reasons which have been given in this study. This is, however, only one side of the coin. There is another side of the coin which has yet to be looked at. This other side will seek to reveal the significant fact that there was also a tradition in the Greco-Roman society which viewed hardship, especially its physical aspects, with contempt and suspicion, regarding it as personally and socially humiliating and degrading and thus unworthy of true manliness. It was probably from this negative perspective that Paul's Corinthian critics judged the apostle's hardship. Moreover, it was also likely from a similarly negative position that Paul presented his περίστασις in order to witness to the power of God in his degradation and humiliation in a typically paradoxical fashion. This will be the remaining task in chapter 7 before embarking on an exegesis of 1 Cor. 4.8–13 and 2 Cor. 11.23–33 in chapter 8.

Chapter 7

Suffering and Hardship as Signs of Shame and Degradation: the Other Side of the Coin

7.1 Introduction

The possible background of Paul with reference to περίστασις has been a matter of considerable interest to New Testament scholars, especially in relation to the Corinthian correspondence – Paul's autobiographical notes concerning his own suffering and hardship. A number of opinions have been expressed on what lies behind Paul's *Peristasenkataloge*, ranging from pinpointing singular traditions to widespread practices.

Two positions are thought to be representative of the most widespread scholarly opinions on the provenance of the lists. These may be represented by Bultmann, who attributes Paul's lists to the Stoic tradition, and Schrage, who regards them as Jewish apocalyptic.[1] However, Robert Hodgson argues that Paul's diverse background is not confined to Stoic philosophy or Jewish apocalyptic, but rather sees a broader literary convention in the 1st century which was taken up quite diversely, for instance by: Josephus, Pharisaic Judaism of the Mishnah and even nascent 'Gnosticism'.[2] One need not agree with the breadth of Hodgson's claims to arrive at the view that the background to Paul may well be more complex than the respective views of Bultmann and Schrage. However, Hodgson's claims are far too sweeping for the present study to engage with exhaustively. In the previous chapter considerable attention was given to the Stoic tradition since there is some consensus that it is a crucial background, if not only, on the study of *peristasis* catalogues.

Fitzgerald's thesis serves as an appropriate point of departure for the current discussion. He seeks not only to demonstrate the positive use of the *peristasis* catalogues in the Greco-Roman tradition, but also asserts that Paul in fact followed that tradition very closely. As both the Stoic tradition and Fitzgerald's thesis are only concerned with the positive use of the *peristasis* catalogues, it is necessary to look at the other side of the coin,

---

[1] R. HODGSON, 'Paul the Apostle and First Century Tribulation Lists', *ZNW* 74 (1983), 59–80, at 60.

[2] HODGSON, 'Paul the Apostle and First Century Tribulation Lists', 69, 60.

which is an attempt to show that the suffering and hardship in the lists could also be perceived negatively as signs of shame and degradation. The exegesis of Paul's biographical notes on the subject (ch. 8) seeks to demonstrate that it is the negative aspect of the *peristasis* catalogues that Paul has in mind when he lists them out in his *apologia* as the apostle of Christ. If this negative aspect is convincing then Paul's approach would be seen as consistent with his seemingly bizarre decision to know nothing except Jesus Christ and him crucified (1 Cor. 2.2) and his deliberate refusal to use eloquent wisdom (1.17) or plausible words of wisdom (2.4) in his proclamation. In all these Paul's overall intention remains consistent and clear, namely, the inversion of the current social ethos.

7.2 Review of Fitzgerald's Thesis

Fitzgerald argues that classical literature shows that the Greco-Roman sage generally used the *peristasis* catalogues positively to demonstrate the best of human virtues. The sage's ability to endure extreme hardships was so highly regarded in the Greco-Roman society that Epictetus actually views περίστασις as 'the test of the philosopher' (2.19.24; 3.10.11) and of true masculinity.

The propagandistic and pedagogical purposes of the use of the *peristasis* catalogues in the classical tradition are also well documented by Fitzgerald. What is even more important, as far as the present research is concerned, is Fitzgerald's view that it is for the same reason that Paul lists the *peristasis* catalogues in 2 Corinthians.[3] Fitzgerald further conjectures that Paul in 2 Corinthians thus frequently depicts himself in terms of the typically 'ideal philosopher' of the Greco-Roman tradition and that the *peristasis* catalogues are used by him as 'an integral part of this *Selbstdarstellung*'. In the end, the catalogues serve the same literary function for Paul. Fitzgerald is convinced that clear examples are found in 2 Cor. 4 and 6 where Paul 'enumerates nine hardships in order to magnify and prove the greatness of his endurance (cf. also 2 Cor. 1.23–28).'[4] Paul's purpose in the use of the catalogues is to show that he is not driven to despair in the face of suffering and severe hardship. Quite to the contrary, Fitzgerald explains that 'the emphasis falls on Paul's superiority to suffering and his triumph over it.'[5]

Fitzgerald identifies *Peristasenkataloge* not only in the Corinthian correspondence (1 Cor. 4.9-13; 2 Cor. 4.8-9; 6.4-10; 11.23-28; 12.10), but

---

[3] FITZGERALD, *Cracks*, 44.
[4] FITZGERALD, *Cracks*, 204.
[5] FITZGERALD, *Cracks*, 204.

also in Romans, Philippians and 2 Timothy (Rom. 8.35–39; Phil. 4.11–12; 2 Tim. 3.11). He argues for this designation based upon the widespread recognition that what is found in other ancient documents is similar to what is found in Paul's lists of circumstances.[6] Fitzgerald also discusses the influence Bultmann has on the use of '*Peristasenkataloge*' as a designation for Paul's list of difficulties – an influence that continues to the present.[7] Fitzgerald generally subscribes to Bultmann's position and stresses the similarity in the use of the catalogues by the ideal sage and the apostle Paul.[8]

Fitzgerald provides a useful survey of the term περίστασις, beginning from the 5th century BC. As the term develops, it essentially comes to mean 'a catalogue of circumstances' for good, bad or both. However, it is adverse circumstances, difficulties or hardships that the term more commonly designates, as is the case in Paul's use in the Corinthian correspondence.[9] The following insights of Fitzgerald are particularly noteworthy:

> *Peristasis* catalogues frequently serve as rhetorical and literary foils for the depiction of various aspects of the wise man's existence and character ... they serve to depict such characteristics as 1) the sage's serenity despite the direst calamities of life, 2) his virtue, especially his courage, 3) his endurance of the greatest and most demanding hardships, 4) his perseverance in doing noble deeds despite the dangers involved and his refusal, at any cost, to depart from what justice dictates, 5) his contempt for Fortune, 6) his victory over adversity, 7) his *askesis* and the role it plays in his victory, 8) his invincibility and invulnerability as a person, 9) his perfect rationality, 10) his demeanour and his response to his adversaries, 11) his consent to the hardships of his life and the volitional character of his suffering, and 12) his conformity to the will of God and the place of his suffering within the divine plan. In short, the catalogues depict and celebrate the greatness of his invincible virtue, the power and tranquillity of his philosophically informed mind.[10]

It remains to be seen if, and to what extent, Paul's use of the catalogues is similar to that of the ideal sage.

From the Greco-Roman tradition Fitzgerald singles out *Phaedo* 67E – 68B, *Respublica* 387DE and Diogenes Laertius 3.78 where the sangfroid attitude of Socrates' confrontation with death is commonly believed to be a great revelation about the true philosopher. This is also true of Aristotle's 'virtuous man' who 'endures repeated and severe misfortune with patience' (*Eth. nic.* 1.10.11) as well as Cicero's 'no one can be just who fears death or pain or exile or poverty' (*Off.* 2.11.38). Epictetus holds basically the same view in 2.19.24 and 4.1.127.[11]

---

[6] FITZGERALD, *Cracks*, 1.
[7] FITZGERALD, *Cracks*, 7.
[8] FITZGERALD, *Cracks*, 12–13.
[9] FITZGERALD, *Cracks*, 203.
[10] FITZGERALD, *Cracks*, 115.
[11] FITZGERALD, *Cracks*, 60–65.

Fitzgerald's study shows that the wise man's hardship is often attributed to two sources: Fortune and God. Whatever the case might be, the will of the wise man is decisive in his response to adverse circumstances. For ancient philosophers like Socrates, response to hardship involves not only the rational disposition of the person but also his voluntary attitude.[12] The notion of the 'death wish' of Socrates (Plato, *Phaed.* 62C; 64A) has an abiding influence in the Greco-Roman tradition. Seneca stresses that the virtuous man 'welcomes (*amplexatur*) that which all other men regard with fear' (*Ep.* 71.28). On Quintilian, Fitzgerald comments: 'his attitude toward Fortune and her hardships is thus one, not of fear, but of utter contempt. Fear is servile, but contempt is the attitude of a superior to an inferior (Quint. *Inst.* 12.8.14), and the sage's disdain for Fortune is a sign that he feels himself superior to her and what she is able to inflict.'[13]

Fitzgerald notices a significant difference in the Greco-Roman tradition between 'Fortune' and 'God' in relation to adversity or hardship. While Fortune was often thought to be working against man and was thus the author of evil, sages and moralists tended to regard or welcome adversity as a gift from God. Fitzgerald elaborates that the combination of an exalted notion of deity and an unwillingness to call difficulties 'evil' are what lead to Stoic circles regarding hardships as a blessing given to humanity out of divine love. This tradition, with a clearly Platonic foundation, portrays God as the author of adversity, but hardships are part of the greater divine plan for the sage.[14] As such, Seneca believes that the wise and virtuous should thankfully welcome hardships as a divine favour (*Prov.* 4.5, 7–8).

God's testing of the good and wise men through trials and travails was not only for their own sake, but also they were expected to be good examples for others to follow (*Prov.* 4.8, 11). Moreover, the fact that good and wise men also experienced 'evils' while evil men enjoyed 'goods' and blessings also served as part of the divine plan to question the common notion about good and evil (*Prov.* 5.2).[15]

For both Seneca and Epictetus hardship should in no way be regarded as a sign of divine hostility towards a good man or as an indication of God's neglect of him. Quite to the contrary, it should be understood as divine acknowledgment of a person's value (*Diss.* 1.29.47).[16]

Fitzgerald cites the works of Xenophon (*Agesilaus* 6.2), Pliny (*Naturalis historia* 7.28.102–04) and others to highlight the great value of hardship in classical tradition, especially in the demonstration and cultivation of ἀνδρεία: A sage or ideal philosopher has all the virtues in his posses-

---

[12] FITZGERALD, *Cracks*, 70.

[13] FITZGERALD, *Cracks*, 74.

[14] FITZGERALD, *Cracks*, 76.

[15] FITZGERALD, *Cracks*, 79.

[16] FITZGERALD, *Cracks*, 81.

sion and uses them when confronted with hardship. In a situation when confronted with adversity, ἀνδρεία comes especially to the fore. While ἀνδρεία straightforwardly means 'courage' it also has clear connotations of 'manliness'. 'Ανδρεία is the archetypal virtue and encompasses the notion of possessing courage deemed worthy of honour. This virtue gives rise to independence, confidence, pride and boasting.[17]

Fitzgerald also makes a significant reference to Plato's *De Republica* (357A–362C), where the good and wise man is portrayed not only as the righteous sufferer, but also as a fool, hence 'the foolish righteous sufferer'. For Socrates, the so-called 'foolish righteous sufferer' is actually 'the just man' who is loved by the gods and that 'all things that come from the gods work together for the best for him that is dear to the gods' (612E–613A). Socrates firmly states that in most cases the 'just man' would end his life in honour (613C).[18]

Fitzgerald also makes the case that the pedagogical purpose of the *peristasis* catalogues in the Greco-Roman tradition and in Paul's writings is similar. Moreover, both the classical sage and Paul attribute their respective hardships to God (1 Cor. 4.9; 2 Cor. 6.9). As such, they accept their hardships willingly and joyfully.[19]

Agreement may be found with Fitzgerald's reading of Paul in 2 Cor. 4: 'It is in 2 Cor. 4, however, that Paul points to the appearance of divine power in his human frailty. As a consequence, the catalogue of his hardships serves both to show the power of God at work in him and to demonstrate at the same time his own weakness (cf. also 2 Cor. 11.30; 12.10). His serenity and endurance are thus the work of God, and, for this reason his boasting of his hardships in 2 Corinthians is 'boasting of the Lord' (1 Cor. 1.31).'[20] Fitzgerald is perceptive when recognising that it is precisely in Paul's understanding of the divine power and his own human weakness that the apostle stood 'in radical contrast to those … who saw in their triumph the demonstration of their own power and thus boasted of their victory as their own achievement.'[21]

The study offered by Fitzgerald is undoubtedly significant and confirms much of what was previously discussed about *peristasis* catalogues in the Stoic tradition (ch. 6). Fitzgerald goes beyond the confines of the Stoic tradition, providing a larger picture.

Fitzgerald's comparison of the Greco-Roman sages with Paul regarding the use and function of the *peristasis* catalogues are made on an important

---

[17] FITZGERALD, *Cracks*, 87–88.

[18] FITZGERALD, *Cracks*, 100–01.

[19] FITZGERALD, *Cracks*, 204.

[20] FITZGERALD, *Cracks*, 206.

[21] FITZGERALD, *Cracks*, 206.

assumption that not only was the apostle familiar with the Greco-Roman tradition, but that he is using it in precisely the same manner as the sages. However, he also acknowledges that in his Corinthian correspondence Paul also adapts the classical traditions 'for his own purposes' and his use of them is 'highly creative'.[22] Moreover, Fitzgerald points out that Paul's creative use is also informed by traditions derived from the OT where prophets and righteous men suffer; arguing that Paul transforms these *vis-à-vis* his obsession with the cross of Christ.[23] As far as Paul's theology and perspective are concerned, what Fitzgerald states about the approach of Paul being, in his words, 'transformed by his fixation on the cross of Christ', is particularly relevant.

Paul's familiarity with the Greco-Roman tradition concerning the *peristasis* catalogues seems to be beyond reasonable doubt, given the apostle's broad background and education. However, it remains to be seen if Paul indeed uses it in the ways that have been so readily assumed by Fitzgerald. The Greco-Roman sages and Paul may not have operated on the basis of the same philosophies and they each have very different goals in mind. For the sages, the 'ultimate concern' seems to have been more the demonstration of human virtues and manliness than the enabling grace of God (the gods). In the chapter to follow, Paul's motivating concerns are the focus of attention and specific differences spelled out in greater detail.

There is little doubt that ancient sources sufficiently show that Greco-Roman philosophers and moral teachers often use the noble example of the 'suffering sage' to admonish their followers in moral teaching and character training. It is also clear that Paul recognises the moral and pedagogical values of his own experience in suffering and hardships, such as the case in 1 Cor. 4 ('be imitators of me', 4.16). Are the Greco-Roman sages and Paul really that similar on this particular point? In Greco-Roman tradition, sages are worthy of imitation largely because of the manly virtues they demonstrate in the face of adversity. In the case of Paul, with his focus on divine grace and power, this may well be significantly different. Moreover, the main reason Paul considers himself worthy of imitation is because he is himself an imitator of Christ in the first place (11.1).

Comparing the sage's suffering with Paul, Fitzgerald observes that hardship plays a role in the divine plan for both. Adversity for Paul and the

---

[22] 'Paul's use of *sophos*-imagery and *peristasis* catalogues clearly shows that he is familiar with the traditions about the sage and the means used to depict him. In his Corinthian correspondence he adopts and adapts these traditions for his own purposes and uses them in the ways that have been indicated. Such adoption and adaptation of these traditions are not unique to Paul but occur as well in other authors (cf., for example, Philo and *T. 12 Patr.*). But Paul's own use of these traditions and the catalogues associated with them is highly creative.' (FITZGERALD, *Cracks*, 207).

[23] FITZGERALD, *Cracks*, 207.

sage is intertwined with the mission they are called to.[24] *Pace* Fitzgerald, caution should be taken in drawing too close a parallel between the Greco-Roman sage and Paul. The classical texts referred to indicate that the idea of divine plan is sometimes present or assumed in the suffering of the sage; however, the focus is almost inevitably on things human or, more precisely, on those virtues which are considered particularly manly. In the end, God (the gods) remains in the background rather than forefront. Is this, however, the case with Paul?

While there is no denying that the sage had a sense of mission in enduring the odds in life, the mission or goal was largely anthropocentric. Even when his anthropocentrism goes beyond mere self-interest, so as to include service and even sacrifice for people and the nation, was its ultimate concern God's glory? Several Corinthian passages may be read as reflecting Paul's ultimate mission and goal as consistently theocentric. Despite Paul's Christ-centred mission, the apostle is also mindful of human interests and needs, so that he even confesses to the Corinthians that he is under daily pressure because of his anxiety for all the churches (2 Cor. 11.28).

Somewhat misleading is Fitzgerald's comparison of the sage with Paul in relation to power: 'For both Paul and the sage, what enables this victory over adversity is power [Phil. 4.13]. *Peristaseis* provide the occasion for displaying this power, and with this display comes the victory and the vaunting that goes with it.'[25] This does not tell the whole story, for while Greco-Roman sages do sometimes attribute their victory over adversity to divine power or assistance, the idea of manly merit or worthiness is either clearly present or implied in the context. Moreover, generally speaking, divine assistance and power are thought only to be available to the 'wise', 'good' and 'noble' because they deserve it. It is thus merited favour. Such a perception is in stark contrast to Paul's theology of the cross which only knows unmerited favour and grace. In the case of Paul, even if divine power were present in his suffering and hardships, it was demonstrated in and through human weakness – and this in a paradoxical way.

In the listing of a *peristasis* catalogue, ancient writers were not only concerned with the person's reactions to hardships, but also the resulting status implications. If the reactions were characterised by endurance and courage, the result would clearly be high status for the one who endured. Conversely, if the person simply succumbed to hardship, the result would be low status for him.[26] That such social status was of any real concern to Paul is questionable.

---

[24] FITZGERALD, *Cracks*, 204.

[25] FITZGERALD, *Cracks*, 205.

[26] S. B. ANDREWS, 'Too Weak Not To Lead: The Form and Function of 2 Cor. 11.23b–33', *NTS* 41 (1995), 263–76, at 276.

With this said, Fitzgerald recognises that in 2 Corinthians (11.30, 12.10) the list of Paul's adversities serves to demonstrate God's power and work in him as well as to show his own weakness.[27] Once this is acknowledged, one wonders how Paul's portrayal of himself can elsewhere be described in terms of a typical ideal philosopher, as Fitzgerald has.[28] Such an assertion seems to make it difficult for Fitzgerald to consistently perceive several crucial differences between the Greco-Roman sage and Paul when using a *peristasis* catalogue. In his eagerness to draw close comparisons and parallels between the two, the markedly different philosophies or theologies on which they respectively operate become rather blurred in the end. This is so despite Fitzgerald's significant observation that Paul not only 'adopts' the classical model in his use of the *peristasis* catalogues, but also 'adapts' it in his own creative way and for his own particular purposes.[29]

One more point to be considered is that it is generally not Paul's *modus operandi* to compare himself with others. As seen in 2 Corinthians 10.12: 'We do not dare to classify or compare ourselves with some of those who commend themselves. But when they measure themselves by one another, and compare themselves with one another, they do not show good sense.' That being the case, it is questionable whether Paul had any intention of comparing himself to the 'suffering sages' when presenting the catalogues in 11.23b–29 and elsewhere.

As Fitzgerald's focus is almost exclusively on the positive side of the use of *peristasis* catalogues in the case of both sages and Paul, it is equally important, especially for the purposes of the present study, to look at the other side of the coin, to show that *peristasis* catalogues could also be perceived contemptuously, so that they are indicative of human degradation and indignity rather than honour and glory. It is to this task that we now turn.

---

[27] FITZGERALD, *Cracks*, 206.

[28] 'Paul's depiction of himself in 2 Corinthians in terms typically used to describe the ideal philosopher and his extensive use, in that connection, of *peristasis* catalogues as part of his self-commendation, are grounded in the fact that he is concerned with showing the Corinthians that he is a person of integrity in whom they may have both confidence and pride. Since *peristasis* catalogues were a traditional means of demonstrating virtue, it was natural that he should choose to employ them for this purpose.' (FITZGERALD, *Cracks*, 206).

[29] Paul's *peristasis* catalogues 'represent the convergence of several traditions and reflect his own personal experiences of suffering and divine power. They take us to the centre of Paul's understanding of God and his own self-understanding, yet anchor him in the culture and conventions of his time.' (FITZGERALD, 207).

7.3 Suffering and Hardship as Signs of Shame and Degradation

The review of Fitzgerald along with the research and conversations in the previous section illustrate how Greco-Roman sages used *peristasis* catalogues to show the virtues and masculinity of those who managed to overcome great adversities and sufferings in life. While the divine design and assistance behind men's suffering are sometimes mentioned or implied in those classical texts, the emphasis is consistently on the ability and virtues of those men who succeeded. The impressive qualities or virtues displayed and vivid body language, often conveyed in very dramatic and moving manner, were unmistakably masculine in nature. The victors became great and abiding exemplars to others and the pedagogical values of their success stories were self-evident. However, all these represent just one perspective, another less gratifying one is also apparent.

Not everyone accepts the full argument of Fitzgerald. Glancy questions his suggestion that Paul's endurance of hardships testifies to his fortitude.[30] For Glancy, the realisation that there is another viewpoint on how the catalogues are perceived is also important. In regard to body language in the ancient Greco-Roman world, scars and bodily wounds could convey both positive and negative messages, depending on the context and situation. In terms of social status and public recognition, bodily scars were often visible marks and signs of the suffering sages, true philosophers and nobles, or of the courageous warriors who suffered wounds in the battlefield. However, in the case of people who belonged to the lower strata of society (e.g. beaten slaves; criminals; soldiers who have fled a battle; those who surrendered for fear of death; defeated fighters), bodily scars as body language would communicate shame and humiliation. Such negative aspects of bodily wounds have already been partly dealt with in the study on crucifixion (ch. 1). Socio-politically, body scars or wounds could well be powerful and vivid signs and symbols of a man's power, honour and glory. But the opposite was also true, because they might connote defeat, enslavement, submission and ultimately could become a person's στίγματα.

As powerful symbols and effective body language, the scarred body was often used rhetorically in a man's self-presentation in which status and honour were of paramount concern. Body wounds were also symbols of a man's virile self-control, courage and perceived superhuman endurance. A classic example of this is found in Plutarch's *Moralia* 331C where reference is made to King Philip who fought courageously in battle: 'When the thigh of his father Philip had been pierced by a spear in battle with the Triballians, and Philip, although he escaped with his life, was vexed with his lameness, Alexander said, "Be of good cheer, father, and go on your way

---

[30] GLANCY, 'Boasting', 121.

rejoicing, that at each step you may recall your valour.'" 'Are not these the words of a truly philosophic spirit which, because of its rapture for noble things, already revolts against mere physical encumbrances?' asked Plutarch rhetorically. He continues,

> How, then, think you, did he glory in his own wounds, remembering by each part of his body affected a nation overcome, a victory won, the capture of cities, the surrender of kings. He did not cover over nor hide his scars, but bore them with him openly as symbolic representations, graven on his body, of virtue and manly courage (ἀλλ᾽ ὥσπερ εἰκόνας ἐγκεχαραγμένας ἀρετῆς καὶ ἀνδραγαθίας περιφέροτα).

It is hardly necessary to elaborate further on what Plutarch says concerning the power of body language which a man of valour conveyed.

Quintilian says that the scars on a man's body speak for him more powerfully than his own declamation: 'Thus when Antonius in the course of his defence of Manius Aquilius tore open his client's robe and revealed the honorable scars which he had acquired while facing his country's foes, he relied no longer on the power of his eloquence, but applied directly to the eyes of the Roman people.'[31] Quintilian preserves a viewpoint on how, in many cases, body language which included scars conveyed honour far more powerfully and effectively than mere human words.

Josephus narrates Antipater's self-defence against accusations of disloyalty before Julius Caesar by letting his body speak (*B.J.* 1.197): 'At these words Antipater stripped off his clothes and exposed his numerous scars. His loyalty to Caesar needed, he said, no words from him; his body cried it aloud, were he to hold his peace.' Josephus preserves a similar view of Quintilian on body language. Once the defendant's body cries aloud, not a single word more is necessary. Cicero also attaches great importance to the masculine character of a warrior's body scars (*Tusc.* 2.18.43). Glancy describes that the scars of a warrior are like a 'tabloid of masculinity' shouting out to the observer.[32] Indeed, bodily scars are testimony that a man has risked his life, giving no heed to pain or death.

However, not all scars were necessarily marks of courage and honour. Thus, while scars in the front (e.g. on the face, chest, throat) were often read as marks of true courage in battle or any other combat, bodily scars on the back of a man were often regarded as visible signs of cowardice. As such, the very location of one's scars became an important issue. Thus, Servilius could boast of the glorious fact that all the 'honourable scars' he received were 'in front' (*Livy* 45.39.16): 'I have on twenty-three occasions challenged and fought an enemy; I brought back the spoils of every man with whom I duelled; I possess a body adorned with honourable scars, every one of them received in front.' The drama continues: 'He then

---

[31] Quintilian 2.15.7.
[32] GLANCY, 'Boasting', 106.

stripped, it is said, and told in which war he had received each wound.' Significantly, Paul also says (Gal. 6.17): 'I carry the marks of Jesus branded on my body.' When Paul makes this statement, a question arises whether he says this to show his manliness with all its implications. This seems unlikely, as Paul in this particular Galatian context is actually acknowledging that as a faithful δοῦλος of Christ it is his destiny and privilege to share in Christ's suffering.

In the classical texts, sages often speak about the fact that their bodies have endured various afflictions. However, not all physical afflictions suffered necessarily signified courage and endurance. Only the precise context or occasion could distinguish courage from cowardice. Glancy's study focuses on the meaning and related connotations of the 'whippable body' and discovers that 'in Roman *habitus*, whipping was the archetypal mark of dishonor'.[33] This is a mark of shame, for being beaten communicates vulnerability to another person, and as such is not a rite of passage so much as a diminishing of one's manhood.[34] Flogging was commonly used as corporal slave punishment in Roman practice.

Subjection to bodily punishment clearly signaled enslavement, humiliation and debasement. As Richard Saller notes, 'precisely because *uerbera* were fit for slaves and encouraged a servile mentality of grudging fear, such punishment was considered inappropriate and insulting for freeborn adult *filiifamilias*.'[35] Therefore, a 'whippable body' was dishonourable and disgraceful. Richard Alston also comments on this, describing beating, especially in public, as a dramatic demonstration of a person being subjugated to another, which was a sign of the victim's servility.[36] Dominic Montserrat makes the powerful analogy that being beaten is similar to being sexually penetrated, as it is both invasive and demeaning. Being beaten or penetrated enforces a distinction between slave and free.[37] A slave whose body was assaulted and injured would also find themselves in a permanent physical state of passivity and subjection.[38] Glancy's study also refers to this theme, explaining that penetration as well as bodily violation cannot be harmonised with a respectable masculine portrayal. Moreover, manhood required that one be able to protect not only his status and repu-

---

[33] GLANCY, 'Boasting', 107.

[34] GLANCY, 'Boasting', 108.

[35] SALLER, 'Corporal Punishment, Authority, Obedience', in B. RAWSON (ed.), *Marriage, Divorce, and Children in Ancient Rome* (Oxford: Clarendon, 1991), 144–65, at 165.

[36] R. ALSTON, 'Arms and the Man: Soldiers, Masculinity and Power in Republican and Imperial Rome', in *When Men Were Men*, 205–23, at 208.

[37] D. MONTSERRAT, 'Experiencing the male body in Roman Egypt', in *When Men Were Men*, 153–64, at 157.

[38] Montserrat, 'Experiencing', 157.

tation, but also the boundaries of his own body.[39] There were qualitative differences between free and slave bodies.

Based on the consistency of the use of whipping or flogging in Roman society, one could quite safely infer that it was established as an important distinguishing mark between slave and free. It is a sad fact that some Roman slaves often bore humiliating and debasing marks on their backs due to past whippings. Jesus, the suffering servant *par excellence*, also endured such physical abuse in the final hours of his life – a connection which is certainly not lost to Paul.

In Rome, it would be the greatest dishonour, shame and humiliation for a free person to be subjected to public whipping. Cicero gives a vivid and moving description of the Roman citizen Gavius' suffering at the hands of Verres, highlighting the severe flogging which was inflicted on his body as a mark of gross injustice and humiliation for a Roman citizen.[40]

Philo's account of Flaccus' campaign against the Jews of Alexandria relies heavily on a kind of body language which is closely associated with flogging and is indicative of one's social standing in Roman society. According to this account, Flaccus ordered the members of the Jewish council to be rounded up and brought to a theatre as a spectacle, highlighting in particular the awful corporal torture through whipping: 'Then as they stood with their enemies seated in front to signalize their disgrace he ordered them all to be stripped and lacerated with scourges which are commonly used for the degradation of the vilest malefactors, so that in consequence of the flogging some had to be carried out on stretchers and died at once, while others lay sick for a long time despairing of recovery' (*Flacc.* 75). Horrified by the Roman's humiliating and undignified treatment of the Jewish leaders, Philo makes the following critical remarks:

For it is surely possible when inflicting degradation on others to find some little thing to sustain their dignity.... Surely then it was the height of harshness that when commoners among the Alexandrian Jews, if they appeared to have done things worthy of stripes, were beaten with whips more suggestive of freemen and citizens, the magistrates, the Senate, whose very name implies age and honour, in this respect fared worse than their inferiors and were treated like Egyptians of the meanest rank and guilty of the greatest iniquities (*Flacc.* 79–80).

---

[39] GLANCY, 'Boasting', 111.

[40] Cicero, *Verr.* 5.158–61: 'Everyone was wondering how far he [Verres, governor of Sicily] would go and what he was meaning to do, when he suddenly ordered the man to be flung down, stripped naked and tied up in the open market-place, and rods to be got ready. The unhappy man cried out that he was a Roman citizen.... To this Verres replied that he had discovered that Gavius had been sent to Sicily as a spy by the leaders of the fugitive army, a charge which was brought by no informer, for which there was no evidence, and which nobody saw any reason to believe. He then ordered the man to be flogged severely all over his body.'

Similarly, Josephus also voices his protest (*B.J.* 2.308): 'For Florus ventured that day to do what none had ever done before, namely, to scourge before his tribunal and nail to the cross men of equestrian rank, men who, if Jews by birth, were at least invested with that Roman dignity.'

Ironically, according to the book of Acts, it is the members of the Jewish council who unjustly flog the innocent apostles: 'and when they had called in the apostles, they had them flogged (δείραντες). Then they ordered them not to speak in the name of Jesus, and let them go.' But as the apostles left the council, 'they rejoiced that they were considered worthy to suffer dishonour (ἀτιμασθῆναι) for the sake of the Name' (Acts 5.40–41). Thus, instead of complaining about injustice and being perturbed by any sense of humiliation, the apostles counted it a privilege to have gone through such an experience of great 'dishonour' (ἀτιμασθῆναι). It was a blatant inversion of Roman social ethos.

The profound meaning of Paul's body language is not only confined to the wounds and scars borne by the body, but also has important implications for his manual labour: his tentmaking profession. Although Paul is never explicitly called a tentmaker, in 1 Cor. 4.12 he mentions 'the work of our own hands'. In connection to Paul's so-called 'tentmaking' activities, Hock's study is important. Paul's profession, mentioned in Acts 18.3, and implicitly by Paul in 1 Cor. 4.12, has often been taken positively as his ability (and pride) to support himself and thus make the gospel free to others. It is also sometimes taken as a kind of 'sideline', without thinking that it was central to Paul's self-identity and lifestyle as a δοῦλος of Christ.

Hock seeks to demonstrate that Paul's manual labour was very much the trade of a slave or person of very low social status. His hunger and thirst, mentioned in the Corinthian letters, may also be an indication that this trade did not always provide sufficiently for him. In other words, Paul's tentmaking labour was also socially a considerable σκάνδαλον in this status-conscious society.

After attempting to establish that Paul was a leatherworker and maker of tents (as well as other leather goods), Hock discusses the daily experiences of a 1st century artisan.[41] Craftsmen worked for long hours in dirty, noisy and dangerous environments and were regularly stigmatised as slavish, poor and uneducated with a modest income (i.e. daily bread and not much more).[42] Hock summarises Paul's condition, that his trade had a significant impact on his social status and daily experiences. In Hock's view, Paul's daily life was found in a workshop surrounded by common tools, bent over a work bench like a slave, in the company of artisan-friends (e.g. Aquila and Barnabas). Therefore, he not only would have been perceived as slav-

---

[41] HOCK, *The Social Context*, 26–31.
[42] HOCK, *The Social Context*, 31–35.

ish and humble, but would have viewed himself this way as well: a reviled, abused, low class labourer.[43]

Savage also makes a contribution to the discussion on the social implications of Paul's manual labour. He questions several rather popular views that the Corinthian criticism of Paul was largely due to his refusal to accept help or pay for his ministry, thus setting him apart from other Hellenistic and Jewish teachers. Savage convincingly challenges that this may not be the most important issue. The main problem was probably the social implications of manual labour, such as tentmaking, and to a lesser degree inconsistency on the part of Paul, since he himself also believed that a worker deserved his pay (1 Cor. 9.6–7, cf. Jesus' teaching Matt. 10.10; Lk. 10.7).[44]

Paul may well have been keenly aware that he would need to maintain the grounds of his boasting by continuing his manual labour. If this were the case, the social implications of such servile work clearly demanded a high price. That Paul himself was aware of this is an attractive thought. He seems to be well prepared for such weakness, through which, paradoxically, God's power might be manifested, just as it was through the cross of Christ. Yet, in order to do that Paul had to deal with the misunderstanding and criticism of his Corinthian critics who, according to the broader ethos, would likely have viewed the entire circumstance negatively.

Two diametrically opposed social perceptions met. Paul's theology of the cross, his communication of it and lifestyle because of it appear to be unexpected and clashed with the cultural expectations of the day. Savage takes the view that 'the key to understanding the Corinthians' criticisms of Paul for refusing their material support would be found, not in positing hypothetical groups of rival missionaries (who did not refuse support), but in seeking to discover the prevailing first-century attitudes to matters such as pay, money, wealth, poverty and employment.'[45] Paul's labour was undoubtedly undignified and contemptible according to the current social ethos.

Cicero explicitly expresses his contempt for manual labour, saying that 'vulgar are the means of livelihood of all hired workmen whom we pay for mere manual labour, not for artistic skill; for in their case the very wage they receive is a pledge of their slavery' (*Off.* 1.150). Similarly, Lucian writes that a labourer has only his hands, he lives and toils with his body and has nothing else.[46]

Given the fact that in 1st century Roman society, where material possessions were one of the most important criteria to assess a person's social

---

[43] HOCK, *The Social Context*, 67.

[44] SAVAGE, *Power*, 81.

[45] SAVAGE, *Power*, 84.

[46] Lucian, *Somn.* 9. See also Seneca, *Ep.* 88.2; Juvenal, *Sat.* 9.140.

standing, the poverty of Paul would understandably be an important issue for which a solution must be found. Judging from Paul's strategy in the Corinthian correspondence, instead of changing or improving his working and living conditions, Paul apparently decided to deal with the issue both socially and theologically rather than evading it. Socially, Paul wants the Corinthians to adopt a new 'Christian' social ethos which is markedly different from the current one. Theologically, he confronts them with the cross, which, when rightly understood, virtually turns the old world of the Corinthians up-side-down. Humanly speaking, this was a daunting task, especially in a great commercial centre such as Corinth where one would imagine that social status and all the values involved were the main concerns of residents. As such, the conflict of diametrically opposed perceptions between that of Paul and his critics was inevitable. In light of the contents of 2 Corinthians, Paul's solution was not yet as persuasive as he likely would have hoped.

7.4 Conclusion

Περίστασις was commonly regarded as a true test of the sage's manliness, courage and endurance. According to this Greco-Roman tradition, those who overcame hardships were highly regarded as noble, praiseworthy and exemplary. In marked contrast, those who failed would be viewed in terms of unmanliness and cowardice.

The degree to which Paul would have been aware of the details of this tradition is difficult to gauge. On the basis of the apostle's breadth of learning and experience in diverse Hellenistic and Jewish contexts, one may safely assume that he was indeed aware and effected by the tradition. It has been called into question whether Paul uses the *peristasis* catalogues in the way that they were commonly used by Greco-Roman sages, as argued by Fitzgerald and others. The view taken here is that Paul most likely does not use it in the manner portrayed in the classical tradition (i.e. positively to demonstrate or prove one's own human endurance and courage so that glory and honour might be conferred). To use it in this way would work contrary to Paul's goal, in effect robbing God of His glory and honour, and this would have been the last thing that Paul, the δοῦλος of Christ, would want to do.

A more convincing interpretation of the *peristasis* catalogues in Paul's writings is that they are negatively used. This then is seen to fit with the main concern of Paul, as only through a negative self-portrayal is the apostle able to offer a paradoxical witness to the divine power that was manifested in and through his own weakness. Only in this way was he able to boast of his own weakness, an idea which would certainly be considered absurd according to the thinking of the time. For Paul, it was precisely this perceived irrationality that made his message of the cross and his own *modus operandi* such a drastic inversion of the social ethos.

In the chapter to follow two pertinent passages (1 Cor. 4.8–13 and 2 Cor. 11.23–33) will be turned to as this subject is further explored. The *peristasis* catalogues in Paul's own biographical notes may be seen and discussed as serving his overall purposes in his Corinthian polemics, namely, to challenge certain perceptions of his critics which he considered incompatible with Christian thinking and to act boldly in reaction to certain key social values of the time.

Chapter 8

Suffering and Hardship as Demonstration of Divine Power in Human Weakness: Exegesis of 1 Cor. 4.8–13 and 2 Cor. 11.23–33

8.1 Introduction

Suffering and hardship occupied a prominent place in Greco-Roman tradition. Generally speaking, adversity was welcomed as a means of proving a man's endurance and masculinity. While divine design and assistance are sometimes referred to or assumed in the Greco-Roman tradition, the focus is consistently anthropocentric with its emphasis on human virtues such as courage and fortitude, both mental and physical. Suffering and hardship, especially its physical aspects, also had negative implications in this status-conscious Greco-Roman society, which were considered humiliating and humanly degrading. It has been suggested it is this negative perspective that Paul's Corinthian critics judged his lists of adversity; and this, together with other possible factors, such as his lack of eloquence and unimpressive physical appearance, caused them to question his apostleship and authority.

The negative perception of Paul's *peristasis* may be viewed as the flip side of the positive. While bodily wounds and scars inflicted, for instance in courageous battle or for a just cause and noble act, were often considered as marks of moral virtues. They were perceived much differently and even in an opposite way if they were the result of punishment (e.g. in the case of runaway slaves and criminals). The same would be true if scars were found on the backside of an individual rather than the front, or if they were the result of manual labour (e.g. Paul's manual work as a tentmaker, a task commonly regarded as befitting slaves or lowest strata of society).

While Paul may well be familiar with the tradition of a positive use of *peristasis* catalogues, with their focus on manly virtues, the apostle himself most likely used the lists in ways that were different from his Greco-Roman counterparts. They functioned to show how divine power and grace were demonstrated in and through his human weakness. This was done in a paradoxical fashion.

1 Cor. 4.8–13 and 2 Cor.11.23–33, which should be read in the overall context of Paul's *apologia* in his dealing with the Corinthian polemics, are

probably among the best examples of Paul's human weakness. Interpreting these passages helps demonstrate that Paul's intention is to react and even challenge the social ethos of his time, indeed to invert it.

8.2 Exegesis of 1 Cor. 4.8–13

The Corinthians' problem was basically one of perception which resulted in, among other things: church divisions, false impressions about Paul and an unrealistically high regard for themselves. These serious problems were both social and theological. Socially, the Corinthians remained bound up in their inherited social context and did not yet grasp the implications of Paul's preaching. This also relates to theology, as Paul's message of the cross and the manner in which it was proclaimed were not yet appreciated or understood.

Paul's opening statement in 1 Cor. 4.1 is intended to correct the Corinthians' false perception about him and his fellow-workers who should only be regarded as 'servants of Christ and stewards of the mysteries of God' (ὑπηρέτας Χριστοῦ καὶ οἰκονόμους μυστηρίων θεοῦ). However, even in this apparently simple statement, Paul's typically subtle and paradoxical way of stating his case is not difficult to detect. This is because while the word 'servants' generally suggests humble social status and denotes humility and unworthiness, the phrase 'stewards of the mystery of God', on the other hand, indicates privilege and honour from the Christian point of view.[1] As such, the marked contrast between this present worldly and the Christian perceptions are clear right from the start in Paul's *apologia*.

Verse 4.7, expressed in the form of a mild rebuke, is unmistakably Paul's direct response to the Corinthians' state of mind: 'For who sees anything different in you? What have you that you did not receive? If then you received it, why do you boast as if it were not a gift?' The key word here is 'different', from Greek the verb διακρίνει, which simply means 'judges', 'distinguishes' or 'makes a distinction'. Therefore, it is a matter of opinion involving a value judgment and which was the very source of the Corinthian troubles (cf. 1 Cor. 2.14–15, ἀνακρίνω). In this particular case, Paul is most likely referring to the Corinthians' unwarranted high opinion of themselves as well as to things that they wrongly thought they possessed. Even if they did possess what they claimed, there was still the equally erroneous act of forgetting that everything came as an unmerited gift of God.

---

[1] Cf. D. MARTIN, *Slavery as Salvation: The Metaphor of Slavery in Pauline Christianity* (New Haven; London: Yale University Press, 1990).

4.8 ἤδη κεκορεσμένοι ἐστέ, ἤδη ἐπλουτήσατε, χωρὶς ἡμῶν ἐβασιλεύσατε· καὶ ὄφελόν γε ἐβασιλεύσατε, ἵνα καὶ ἡμεῖς ὑμῖν συμ βασιλεύσωμεν. (*'Already you have all you want! Already you have become rich! Quite apart from us you have become kings! Indeed, I wish that you had become kings, so that we might be kings with you!'*)

Verse 8 is expressed in the form of rebuke and sarcasm. The idea of fullness and richness, as well as being kings, may have come from Cynic and Stoic thinking. In Epictetus' opinion the true Cynic could say, 'Who, when he lays eyes upon me, does not feel that he is seeing his king and master (τίς με ἰδὼν οὐχὶ τὸν βασιλέα τὸν ἑαυτοῦ ὁρᾶν οἴεται καὶ δὲ σπότην)?' Moreover, within Cynic thought, the philosopher's reign was a 'sharing in the kingly rule of Zeus (ὡς μετέχων τῆς ἀρχῆς τοῦ Διός).'[2] According to the Stoics, wealth (πλοῦτος), kingship (βασιλεία), happiness (εὐδαίμων) and freedom (ἐλεύθερια) could only belong to the wise man.[3]

Weiss suggests that the slogan in the Corinthian parties reflects Stoic influence.[4] In line with Weiss, Terence Paige also conjectures that certain terms and vocabulary in Paul's letter echo Stoic thought, and 4.8 is a good example.[5] Paige concludes that it is plausible to consider that an aspect of the Corinth problem may well have been a Stoicising, or perhaps Cynic and Stoicising, influence. If this were indeed the case, argues Paige, the Stoic-like terminology may be explained along with the growth of an elite group of self-styled *sophoi* within the community who developed a highly individualistic and self-centred ethic. The result would have been self-centred spirituality which would have developed from Stoic influence. The concept of Christian freedom would have been advocated which was counter to the community. Consequently, there would have been a breakdown of the community, leading to Paul's response which was 'to display the fully dependent status of their existence in Christ.'[6] Paige is not alone in viewing the Corinthians' idea of richness and fullness, as well as being kings, as originating in Cynic and Stoic philosophies. This is a view advocated by, for instance, Hays.[7]

Paul's sarcastic and ironic statement is indicative of his disproval of the Corinthians' perception, because their view was simply inconsistent with his humble gospel. The rebuke becomes all the more obvious as Paul modestly considers himself and his fellow-workers as no more than servants of

---

[2] Epictetus 3.22.49, 95.
[3] Plutarch, *Mor.* 1060B; 1062E.
[4] WEISS, *Der Erste Korintherbrief*, 158–59.
[5] T. PAIGE, 'Stoicism, ἐλευθερία and Community at Corinth', in J. WILKINS and T. PAIGE (eds.), *Worship, Theology and Ministry in the Early Church : Essays in Honour of Ralph P. Martin* (Sheffield : JSOT, 1992), 180–93, at 184.
[6] PAIGE, 'Stoicism', 192.
[7] HAYS, *First Corinthians*, 70.

Christ at the very beginning of the chapter. Hence, the contrast is between
humble servants and exalted kings.

Hodgson describes Paul as having abandoned his *theologia crucis* in favour of a *theologia gloriae*. In so doing, the dissenters are 'reminded of the
actual conditions of Christian life between the ages by means of a list of
Paul's tribulations.'[8] Hodgson draws our attention back to Paul's lists of
adversity, which stand in contrast to the claim of being rich and kings.
Within this context, he also describes the function of Paul's lists as didactic rather than apologetic and autobiographical. However, in the broader
Corinthian context one should show caution in viewing Paul as only interested in the didactic (1 Cor. 4.6–21), as this verse also has an apologetic
and autobiographical overtone (4.1–4; 9.1–2).

Thiselton contends that verse 8 needs to be appreciated in light of two
significant factors: (1) the problem of overrealized eschatology and (2) the
effects of perceived conversion experiences within many Greco-Roman
and especially Greco-Oriental cults.[9] In general, 1 Corinthians 1–14 evidence both a realized eschatology and an enthusiastic theology of the
Spirit.[10] Thiselton's suggestion has not been accepted by all, Barclay
counters those who seek to interpret the Corinthian theology simply as an
example of realized eschatology based on 4.8. He draws awareness to how
Paul's perspective on the Corinthian community tends to determine how
one describes them.

Barclay writes that in 'Paul's view the freedom, knowledge and spiritual
ecstasy enjoyed by the Corinthians constituted a falsely claimed pre-
emption of eschatological glory.'[11] Barclay's point is convincing, and he
goes on to explain that 'the Corinthians apparently see nothing pitiable
about the present, because their non-apocalyptic perspective anticipates no
radical disjunctions in the future. Their Spirit-filled lives are not an early
experience of the future; they simply consider themselves to have reached
the heights of human potential.'[12] If one accepts Barclay's suggestion, the
word 'already' (ἤδη), which occurs twice in 4.8, simply means that the Corinthians had considered themselves, to use Barclay's expression, 'to have
reached the heights of human potential.' Whether Thiselton's 'realized eschatology' or Barclay's 'heights of human potential', Paul had to sternly

---

[8] HODGSON, 'Paul the Apostle and First Century Tribulation Lists', 65.

[9] THISELTON, *The First Epistle*, 357.

[10] THISELTON, 'Realized Eschatology at Corinth', in *Christianity*, 107–18, at 118.

[11] BARCLAY, 'Thessalonica and Corinth', 64.

[12] 'But did the *Corinthians* see their experience as related to an eschatological time-
frame like this? Did they consider that they had already entered the future, or did they
simply not operate with Paul's typical contrast between present and future?' asks Barclay
('Thessalonica and Corinth', 64).

remind the Corinthians that the whole thing was not yet.[13] The sarcasm of Paul's statement is powerful: 'would that you did reign, so that we might share the rule with you!' The simple fact is that the Corinthians were 'not yet' in a position to either reign or rule. They were simply self-conceited, which is a clear indication of their Christian immaturity and that they were still very much reacting as members of their world.

4.9 δοκῶ γάρ, ὁ θεὸς ἡμᾶς τοὺς ἀποστόλους ἐσχάτους ἀπέδειξεν ὡς ἐπιθανατίους, ὅτι θέατρον ἐγενήθημεν τῷ κόσμῳ καὶ ἀγγέλοις καὶ ἀνθρώποις. *('For I think that God has exhibited us apostles as last of all, as though sentenced to death, because we have become a spectacle to the world, to angels and mortals.')*

In the opening verse of chapter 4, Paul describes himself and his fellow-workers as 'servants' and 'stewards.' He applies the term 'apostles' in 4.9 to himself as well as others. Rengstorf explains that in the NT Paul is the classical representative of apostleship. This is largely due to the dramatic nature of his calling and the extraordinary range of his missionary and pastoral activities (15.10). The polemics and apologetics Paul is engaged in also contribute to his deep sense of apostleship and calling.[14] However, apostleship was inseparable from the authority which he was expected to exercise. Dunn sees Paul's apostolic authority as an excellent opportunity to compare Paul's theology and practice. Paul's success in founding churches demonstrates his apostolic commissioning. He is, then, an apostle at least to these churches and it is to them that he writes as their apostle.[15] Nonetheless, the Corinthian church founded by Paul clearly challenges his apostolic authority.

For Paul who decided to know nothing except Jesus Christ and him crucified (2.2), and whose gospel was the message of the cross (1.18), the words 'exhibited', 'sentenced to death' and 'spectacle' could well be intended to remind his readers of Christ's own crucifixion. As an apostle of Christ crucified, Paul was also expected to walk in the steps of his master. What Paul writes here in 4.9 not only strongly contrasts with 4.8, but also there is strong irony: while the Corinthians received the gospel from Paul, they now considered themselves kings, Paul the messenger of the gospel and his fellow apostles now appear like men sentenced to death. Yet, the humanly appalling condition of Paul should not take anyone by surprise, as

---

[13] Barrett suggests that 'the Corinthians are behaving as if the age to come were already consummated, as if the saints had already taken over the kingdom (Dan. 7.18); for them there is no "not yet" to qualify the "already" of realized eschatology' (*The First Epistle*, 109).

[14] RENGSTORF, *TDNT* 1.437.

[15] DUNN, *The Theology of Paul the Apostle* (Edinburgh: T & T Clark, 1998), 571–72.

Karl Plank observes, 'humiliation and affliction characterized his apostle-ship (4.9–13).'[16]

Plank makes the case that despite obvious sarcasm and apparent anger, which is immediately followed by a stark contrast between the Corinthians' highly exalted state and the apostles' pitiable condition, Paul's purpose is 'to reestablish his position of preeminence among them as their spiritual πατήρ (4.14–15), not to shame them.'[17]

Following on from 4.8 are even stronger words of sarcasm which are elaborated on (4.9–13). Paul does far more than just utter mere words; he actually paints a very vivid and moving picture. Paul's self-conceited Corinthian Christians probably thought that they were now occupying a commanding position in an arena or a theatre like kings, just waiting for a great procession to gradually pass in front of them. The procession was heralded by victorious generals who were just returning from a great conquest. Last in the procession were those captured soldiers who had already been sentenced to death (ἐπιθανατίους). These captured men are virtually good for nothing, except for short-term public exhibition and entertainment. It is probably in this kind of context that Paul speaks about becoming 'a spectacle (θέατρον, "theatre") to the world, to angels and to men' (4.9). Paul intentionally likens himself and his fellow-apostles to men sentenced to death. Such a vivid portrayal of himself and his fellow-apostles has a strong element of irony and is intended to provoke the self-conceited and haughty Corinthians.

Paul's portrayal may also be a show in a theatre rather than a procession. Whatever the case, he thought that instead of just allowing the Corinthians to read or hear his words in the form of a letter that they would also be able to see it explained with meaningful images, for the latter would be far more provocative. There was also effective body language in Paul's portrayal. Welborn suggests that the term θέατρον literally means 'a place for seeing', especially in dramatic performances. It was a place increasingly used for public assemblies in the early empire, corresponding to the growing significance of the theatre in public life. At the time, θέατρον meant what one sees at a theatre or a play. Welborn's opinion is that this latter sense is intended by Paul rather than the general meaning 'spectacle'.[18] He suggests too that allusions to the mime are present throughout 1 Cor. 1–4.[19] Welborn's thesis rests on a very crucial hypothesis: Paul is not only familiar with the 'comic-philosophic tradition', but also consciously

---

[16] K. A. PLANK, *Paul and the Irony of Affliction* (Atlanta: Scholars Press, 1987), 16.

[17] BLACK, *Weakness*, 104.

[18] WELBORN, *Fool*, 51.

[19] WELBORN, *Fool*, 50–54.

adopts it in the precise way that Socrates and Aesop do (i.e. for his own purposes).

That the well educated apostle would be familiar with theatrical work such as mime is very plausible. However, to suggest that he strategically adopts it, especially with the conscious assumption of the role of the 'wise fool' is quite a different matter. There is simply no solid evidence to make the case that Paul in fact followed the practice of Socrates and Aesop. If Socrates, Aesop and Paul were put on a stage in a 'theatrical' context, there would be some points of similarity. However, one suspects that in real life where a more complete picture is available; such similarities would turn out to be far less convincing. As noted previously in the comparison between Socrates' and Jesus' respective attitudes towards death, any such comparison needs qualification and should be done with caution.

That Paul regarded himself to be a kind of fool and was also being put on stage as a spectacle (4.9, 10) for the sake of the gospel should not be confused with Welborn's thesis that Paul in fact deliberately assumes the role of a mime, especially in the well-defined comic-philosophic tradition of the Greco-Roman world. Even granted that Paul assumes the role of fool and adopts the fool's speech for his own particular purposes, Welborn may unwittingly overstretch his parallels by identifying the apostle too closely with Socrates and Aesop. Perhaps those New Testament scholars who 'routinely dismiss the notion that Paul derived the role of the fool and the genre of the "fool's speech" (2 Cor 11.1–12) from the Greek and Roman mime' may well have a valid point.[20]

Thiselton uses dramatic language in explaining Paul's metaphor. He describes it as a great 'pageant', wherein criminals, prisoners and professional gladiators march off to fight. Within this metaphor, the apostles bring up the rear and are destined to fight to the death. The main verb of the sentence (ἀπέδειξεν) is used in the aorist (ἀποδείκνυμι) and means 'put on display'. Displaying here is in the sense of 'theatrical entertainments or gladiatorial shows.'[21] Whether Welborn's 'mime' or Thiselton's 'pageant', Paul's point remains sufficiently clear when he uses the word 'spectacle' (4.9).

Both problematic and questionable is the close comparison Fitzgerald draws between the Greco-Roman sage and Paul with regards to the use of περίστασις. Fitzgerald's comparison is inappropriate because of the irony in this passage: Paul is simply not concerned with the exhibition of his own manly virtues as sages were. However, Fitzgerald is perceptive about

---

[20] Welborn, *Fool*, 3.
[21] Thiselton, *The First Epistle*, 359.

Paul's skilful use of paradox in his ironical admonition, even if Fitzgerald does not view Paul as having finally accomplished his purpose.[22]

If the Corinthians' self-image was indeed correct, they truly would appear as kings, occupying the most commanding position on a grandstand or seats in a theatre, where the apostles, who now looked like 'men sentenced to death', were in full view. Thiselton notes that in the NT ἐπιθανάτιος is only used here, but that it appears in the LXX for those thrown to the lions (*Bel and the Dragon* 31). Schrage suggests that the idea of 'death' here may be suggestive of sharing with Christ in his crucifixion.[23] Paul's reference to 'the world, angels and men' (τῷ κόσμῳ καὶ ἀγγέλοις καὶ ἀνθρώποις) seems to suggest a kind of cosmic significance of the apostolic ministry, including the suffering and possible martyrdom of the apostles.

4.10 ἡμεῖς μωροὶ διὰ Χριστόν, ὑμεῖς δὲ φρόνιμοι ἐν Χριστῷ· ἡμεῖς ἀσθενεῖς, ὑμεῖς δὲ ἰσχυροί· ὑμεῖς ἔνδοξοι, ἡμεῖς δὲ ἄτιμοι. *('We are fools for the sake of Christ, but you are wise in Christ. We are weak, but you are strong. You are held in honour, but we are in disrepute.')*

The irony of Paul continues in 4.10 with three sets of sarcastic contrasts. This irony, which is enshrined in the three catchwords μωρός ('foolish'), ἀσθενής ('weak') and ἄτιμος ('dishonor'), is already present in 1.18ff., where it is stated that the message of the cross and its messenger are regarded as foolish and weak by the unbelieving world. The word ἔνδοξος ('splendid', 'glorious' or 'respected') stands in sharp contrast to ἄτιμος ('despised', 'insignificant' or 'dishonoured'). The word ἄτιμος in 4.10 clearly has social status in mind in the Corinthian context, with special reference to those who were poor and weak and were thus treated with disrespect in contemporary society. In the context of the theatrical metaphor in the Greco-Roman tradition, ἄτιμος could also be used for public entertainers such as actors and gladiators who often had no ownership of themselves, and thus had no real social status.[24]

Theissen, who seeks to provide a sociological perspective for understanding the Corinthian church situation, suggests that the social composition of the Corinthian church was diverse and seemed to be dominated by those who came from the upper class; and 4.10 refers to the three categories of high ranking people first mentioned in 1.26 – the wise, the powerful and those of noble birth. Each term has a strong sociological significance, and 'Paul contrasts his circumstances with those of the Corinthians in terms bearing indisputable sociological implication. For example, Paul

---

[22] FITZGERALD, *Cracks*, 148.

[23] SCHRAGE, as cited by THISELTON, *The First Epistle*, 360.

[24] WELBORN, *Fool*, 60–61.

works with his hands, experiences hunger, has no permanent home, and is persecuted. He is "the refuse of the world, the offscouring of all things (1 Cor. 4.11–13)."'[25]

Unlike Theissen who interprets 1 Cor. 4.10 as proof of the presence of an upper class, Meggitt argues that Paul was actually not referring to the socio-economic situation of specific groups, but rather to the spiritual pretensions of the self-conceited Corinthian: '1 Cor. 4.10 should be read in the light of the apostle's preceding words in 1 Cor. 4.8 which surely cannot describe his opponents' actual social situation.... [in] 1 Cor. 4.10 Paul is contrasting the bleak nature of his daily life as an apostle with the Corinthians' exalted, heavenly pretensions, in order to highlight the absurdity of their claims, and to bring them back to earthly reality. His words do not tell us anything at all about the Corinthians' socio-economic location.'[26] Meggitt's argument is persuasive.

Of the three sets of contrast between: (1) 'fools' (μωροί) and 'wise' (φρόνιμοι); (2) 'weak' (ἀσθενεῖς) and 'strong' (ἰσχυροί); and (3) those 'held in honour' (ἔνδοξοι) and those 'in disrepute' (ἄτιμοι) – the word fools in the first set of contrasts deserves some special treatment in view of its connotations and implications which were most probably familiar to the Corinthians and Paul. Moreover, Paul's own self-designation as a fool for Christ's sake is thoroughly consistent with his earlier description of the message of the cross, namely the Christian gospel as folly to those who refused to believe (1.18, 21, 23).

While the fool in the comic-philosophic tradition and in Paul's self-designation have their respective social contexts and circumstances, the more significant difference between them lies far deeper beneath the social surface. In the case of the comic-philosophic tradition, the social context and circumstance were based on the basic social ethos of the Greco-Roman world. Whereas in the case of Paul the concept of fool derived essentially from his whole understanding of the cross of Christ. As Welborn rightly notes, 'because of the event of the crucified Christ, Paul has come to believe that God has chosen the nothings and nobodies.'[27] As such, Paul's appropriation of the role of the 'fool' for Christ's sake is a matter of theology and of faith. Welborn also sees Paul's adoption of the role of fool as being inspired, at least in part, by Christ's own crucifixion as well as the sufferings of his first disciples.[28]

---

[25] THEISSEN, *The Social Setting*, 73, 71–72.

[26] MEGGITT, *Poverty*, 106–07.

[27] WELBORN, *Fool*, 250.

[28] WELBORN, *Fool*, 250, 'Paul's appropriation of the role of the fool is a profound, but not unexpected, maneuver, given the way in which Jesus was executed and the socially shameful experience of Jesus' early followers.'

Paul's language about his self-designation as the 'fool' is not only ironical and rhetorical, but also it subtly demolishes all wisdom that is humanly conceived. If Paul's foolishness was indeed the way or the wisdom that God had chosen in his dealings with human existence and predicament, then there would be absolutely no place for human wisdom. As such, the sarcasm of Paul's following statement – 'you are wise in Christ' – was immediately apparent to his audience.

In a typically Pauline paradox, the strong contrast set between weak and strong, as well as between honour and disrepute, is ultimately the contrast between two diametrically opposed worldviews. This is an indicator of Paul's consistent attention to portraying values which run counter to the current social ethos. Moxnes takes note that the earliest Christian church, as part of a broader honour-shame culture, would therefore have carried this culture over into their own sub-group.[29]

The term 'honour' (*dignitas*), which was based on power, life-style and wealth, was the principal criterion of legal privilege in Roman legal practice.[30] In Neyrey's words, 'honour resides in one's name, always an inherited name.... Honour resides in certain public roles, statuses, and offices.... That is, honour is expressed and measured by one's possessions which must be on display. Wealth in general denotes honour – not simply the possession of wealth, but its consumption and display: e.g., banquets, fine clothes, weapons, houses, etc.'[31]

Neyrey's comments on 'shame' are particularly relevant: 'Contempt, loss of face, defeat, and ridicule all describe shame, the loss of honour.... Shame can be ascribed or achieved. A magistrate may ascribe shame by declaring one guilty and so worthy of public flogging (2 Cor. 11.23–25).... Yet shame may be achieved by one's folly or by cowardice and failure to respond to a challenge. One may refuse to participate in the honour-gaining games characteristic of males, and thus bring contempt on oneself.'[32] In the case of Paul, shame could be said to be both ascribed and achieved. His Corinthian critics poured contempt on him, whether his shame was ascribed or achieved, and the latter was perhaps more contemptible because, to borrow the expression of Neyrey, Paul refused 'to participate in the honour-gaining games characteristic of males, and thus bring contempt on oneself.'[33]

As the first two parts of this study seek to demonstrate, both crucifixion and rhetoric essentially involve body language. The same is largely true of the *peristasis* catalogues in Paul's Corinthian correspondence. As such,

[29] MOXNES, 'Honor', 36.
[30] NEYREY, 'Shame ', 156.
[31] NEYREY, 'Shame ', 156.
[32] NEYREY, 'Shame', 158.
[33] NEYREY, 'Shame', 158.

Neyrey's statement, which closely associates honour with a man's body, is particularly significant: 'the bodily grammar for honour works also for shame. If the honourable parts of the body, the head and face, are struck, spat upon, slapped, blindfolded, or otherwise maltreated, shame ensues.... If one is publicly stripped naked, flogged, paraded before the crowds, and led through the streets, one is shamed.'[34]

In Corinth, Paul's honour was challenged more than claimed. In fact, the moment when Paul decided to know nothing among the Corinthians except Jesus Christ crucified (1 Cor. 2.2) and came to them in weakness, fear and much trembling (2.3), he virtually surrendered any claim to 'honour' as far as the Greco-Roman society was concerned. Paul consequently made himself vulnerable in this very status-conscious society. Yet, paradoxically, it is precisely in his vulnerability that the messenger of the cross sought to demonstrate God's power and wisdom in and through Christ, who himself willingly became vulnerable.

4.11 ἄχρι τῆς ἄρτι ὥρας καὶ πεινῶμεν καὶ διψῶμεν καὶ γυμνιτεύομεν καὶ κολαφιζόμεθα καὶ ἀστατοῦμεν *('To the present hour we are hungry and thirsty, we are poorly clothed and beaten and homeless,')*

In marked contrast to the Corinthians' thinking that they were now enjoying the fullness and kingly reign promised by Christ, Paul suddenly responded with a down-to-earth and fairly grim statement, beginning from 4.11, to describe their present *Sitz im Leben*: 'To the present hour we hunger and thirst, we are ill-clad and buffeted and homeless.' The phrase 'to the present hour' (ἄχρι τῆς ἄρτι ὥρας) is made with considerable emphasis. One can almost hear Paul saying, 'My dear friends in Corinth, while you may think that you have *already* reached the fullness of your Christian experience, to the present hour, we are still *not yet!*' The pitiful physical condition to which Paul refers may be regarded as largely true. To an ordinary person in the days of Paul, that the apostle of the now exalted King and Lord should be hungry, thirsty and poorly clothed is almost unimaginable. To also be beaten and homeless only takes the description farther. Paul's body language is unmistakable. Under normal circumstances, the status of an ambassador naturally would be expected to correspond with the one who sent him. However, this is clearly not the case with Paul and his fellow apostles in the eyes of others. Indeed, one may view this as another σκάνδαλον!

In Rome, food problems were certainly not unknown. There was often a lack of sufficient supply, at times contamination, a general absence of hy-

---

[34] NEYREY, 'Shame', 158.

giene, and the river was so polluted that fish even became sick.[35] According to Lucian, hunger was the common experience and complaint of artisans (*Sat.* 31). Paul's condition in this verse (πεινῶμεν καὶ διψῶμεν) may well be literally true. According to Lucian, 'labourers are barely able to supply them with just enough' (*Fug.* 12–13). He elaborates: 'you see if you get a single sandal done before the sun rises you will be much ahead earning your daily bread.... Take care, however, that you don't dream you are rich and then starve when you wake up' (*Gall.* 1). In the *Cataplus*, the cobbler Micyllus still has to face hunger even though he laboured for many long hours (*Cat.* 20). In some cases, poor families sold their daughters as prostitutes to avoid dying of starvation (Lucian, *Dial. Mer.* 6.293).

The verb γυμνιτεύω (γυμνότης, noun) in this verse communicates far more than just poor clothing, as it is also indicative of the low social-status of the person who is poorly clothed. At the time of Paul, good clothing was expensive and only the rich could afford costly garments while poor people, including manual workers, could only afford won-out, dirty clothing and sometimes even appeared half-naked. In the words of Meggitt, 'the importance given to clothing as a means of articulating socio-economic distinctions in antiquity also suggests that it necessitated significant financial outlay.'[36]

According to Lucian's story, the artisan Micyllus is so desperate for food and clothing that he eventually welcomes death: 'Unlucky man that I am, never again will I go hungry from morning to night or wander about in winter barefooted and half-naked, with my teeth clattering from cold' (*Cat.* 20). Juvenal witnessed that the poor were often being ridiculed for their dress: 'of all the woes of luckless poverty none is harder to endure than this, that it exposes men to ridicule' (*Sat.* 3.147–52).

The verb κολαφίζω also has a wide range of meanings, from violent beating to physical harm or injuries caused by intense manual labor, such as Paul's tent-making work, and the latter would imply the low social status of a slave-like artisan.[37]

---

[35] See GARNSEY and R. SELLER, *The Roman Empire: Economy, Society, and Culture* (London: Duckworth, 1987). GARNSEY, 'Food Consumption in Antiquity: Towards a Quantitative Account', in P. GARNSEY (ed.), *Food, Health and Culture in Classical Antiquity* (Cambridge: Classical Department Working Papers, 1989), 36–49. GARNSEY, 'Grain for Rome', in P. GARNSEY, K. HOPKINS and C. R. WHITTAKER (eds.), *Trade in the Ancient Economy* (London: Chatto & Windus, 1983), 118–30. V. NUTTON, 'Galen and the Traveller's Fare', in J. WILKINS, D. HARVEY and M. DOBSON (eds.), *Food in Antiquity* (Exeter: Exeter University Press, 1995), 359–69.

[36] MEGGITT, *Poverty*, 61. See G. HAMEL, *Poverty and Charity in Rome Palestine, First Three Centuries C. E.* (Berkeley: University of California Press, 1990), 57–93.

[37] THISELTON, *The First Epistle*, 362.

Consistent with his thesis, Welborn seeks to interpret 'buffeted' (κὸ λαφιζόμεθα, 'brutally treated' or 'beaten')[38] in reference to the mime: 'it is not difficult to comprehend why the beating of the fool provided amusement: the explanation lies in the complex social function of this theatrical type. For the rich in the audience, the blows that rained down upon the fool's bald head were a sign of his helplessness and humiliation, and thus welcome reminders of the power of the rich to inflict punishment, and their invulnerability to such mistreatment.'[39] Although Welborn's understanding is plausible, this particular nuance remains only one possibility among others. However, points of his argument are insightful and much may be gleaned from his overall analysis.

In his research on Greco-Roman urban housing, Ramsey MacMullen makes the memorable comment that 'no one has sought fame through the excavation of slums.'[40] Artisans normally lived and worked in small workshops (*tabernae*).[41] The poor lived in tombs, cellars and vaults, below bridges and theatre awnings, while the poorest had little choice but to sleep in the open air.[42] MacMullen paints a vivid picture, describing these lodgings in the open air as porticoes, street corners and the less trodden parts of the marketplace.[43]

Meggitt also addresses the 'appalling slums' where nearly all *plebs urbana* dwelled.[44] He elaborates that the poor, whether one speaks of their dwelling place, food or clothing, lived a subsistence or near-subsistence existence. The reward for their toils, under the best of circumstances, would not have sufficiently provided for them to improve their lot in life.[45]

In Welborn's work on the 'fool' as mime, he discusses ἀστατοῦμεν (often translated 'homeless') as possibly translated as 'unsettled', according to the context of the comic-philosophic tradition: 'Homeless was the con-

---

[38] See more on body 'beatings' in the light of § 7.3.

[39] WELBORN, *Fool*, 70–71.

[40] MACMULLEN, *Roman Social Relations 50 BC to AD 284* (New Haven: Yale University Press, 1974), 93.

[41] A. WALLACE-HADRILL, *Houses and Society in Pompeii and Herculaneum* (Princeton: Princeton University Press, 1994), 139. A. BURFORD, *Craftsmen in Ancient Greek and Roman Society* (Ithaca: Cornell University Press, 1972), 79.

[42] MEGGITT, *Poverty*, 63. B. W. FRIER, 'The Rental Market in Early Imperial Rome', *Journal of Roman Studies* 67 (1977), 27–37. A. SCOBIE, 'Slums, sanitation, and mortality in the Roman World', *Klio* 68 (1986), 399–433. A. G. MCKAY, *House, Villas and Palaces in the Roman World* (London: Thames & Hudson, 1975), 139. J. STAMBAUGH, *The Ancient Roman City* (Baltimore: Johns Hopkins University Press, 1989), 90.

[43] MACMULLEN, *Roman Social Relations*, 87.

[44] MEGGITT, *Poverty*, 66. Z. YAVETZ, 'The Living Conditions of the Urban Plebs in Republican Rome', in R. SEAGER (ed.), *The Crisis of the Roman Republic* (Cambridge: W. Heffer & Sons, 1969), 162–79.

[45] MEGGITT, *Poverty*, 66–67.

dition of many of the poor in the Roman Empire ... the term is more con-
sonant with the theatrical metaphor than one might have assumed. For the
mime's life was a vagabond life, constantly roving from town to town, in
search of audiences and suitable venues for performance.'[46] On the one
hand, accepting Welborn's view might be seen to soften the impact of a
more of common rendering 'homeless'. On the other hand, however, if
Welborn is correct, he has shed significant new light on a metaphor previously not appreciated.

4.12 καὶ κοπιῶμεν ἐργαζόμενοι ταῖς ἰδίαις χερσίν· λοιδορούμενοι
εὐλογοῦμεν, διωκόμενοι ἀνεχόμεθα, (*'and we grow weary from the work
of our own hands. When reviled, we bless; when persecuted, we endure;'*)
13 δυσφημούμενοι παρακαλοῦμεν· ὡς περικαθάρματα τοῦ κόσμου
ἐγενήθημεν, πάντων περίψημα ἕως ἄρτι. (*'when slandered, we speak
kindly. We have become like the rubbish of the world, the dregs of all
things, to this very day.'*)

Paul continues with his description of the apostles' appalling living condition in 4.12–13. His confession about growing weary from the work of
their hands once again indicates the demand and burden of manual labour.
It was not only the manual labour that was difficult for Paul and his fellow
apostles to bear. The social stigma that it brought to the labourers was
equally burdensome and humiliating, as Martin comments: 'the dative
χερσίν, with our hands (v.12), is instrumental, and calls attention to the
status of manual labour, which was in general despised in Greek culture by
those who secured an income in other ways.'[47] The so-called 'dignity of
labour' was certainly a novel idea to people of Paul's time.

Just as in many other cases in the Corinthian correspondence, the 'we'
here – 'we labour, working with our own hands' – could either literally refer to Paul with some of his fellow-apostles and co-workers or only to Paul
himself. If it were the former, one would think of Aquila, a fellow Jew
whom Paul first met in Corinth and who was of the same trade as Paul
(Acts 18.1–3). The fact that Paul was a kind of tentmaker would automati-
cally bring him down to a lower social stratum of society (cf. ch. 7).
Hock's research on the social, economic and physical conditions of Paul's
trade leads him to the compelling suggestion that Paul's hunger, thirst, nakedness as well as other social stigma and abuse he bore were closely related to his manual labour as a tentmaker.[48] Hock elaborates that based
upon a number of scattered references artisans were often reviled and
abused, being judged slavish, uneducated and even useless. When Paul's
statements are lined along with others, they match well. As such, one

---

[46] WELBORN, *Fool*, 70–71.
[47] MARTIN, *Corinthian Body*, 79–86.
[48] HOCK, *The Social Context*, 35.

would hardly deem Paul's situation enviable, as an apostle of Christ he spent a lot of time travelling. Hock believes that Paul would have most often been on the road or in the workshop, undertaking exhausting labour that could be thankless and which resulted in his lists of suffering.[49] If manual labour was a matter of Paul's own choice, and the resultant weariness was in this sense self-inflicted, revilement and persecution were certainly not. Paul's determination not to respond in like kind may be said to be part of his *imitatio Christi*. In other words, Paul might well be following Jesus' principle of non-violence here. While this might be a 'virtue' from the Christian perspective, it was unmistakably a blatant sign of weakness and cowardice according to the Greco-Roman social ethos of the time.

Superficially, words in 4.12 such as λοιδορούμενοι ('reviled') appear only like some kind of verbal abuse. Welborn's study, however, indicates that something far more serious could be implied here: 'predictably, verbal abuse devolves into physical violence – hitting, spitting, etc. – in these passages, as it does in 1 Cor. 4.12.'[50] If one follows Welborn's reading, Paul's reference to persecution immediately after being reviled would make logical sense.

Just as in 4.11 ('to the present hour'), the expression 'we have become' (ἐγενήθημεν) and 'are now' (or 'until now', ἕως ἄρτι) in 4.13, apart from being a true description of the apostles' present living condition, also provide an apt contrast to the self-elevated status of the Corinthians. As far as the struggling apostles were concerned, all the good things were still 'not yet'. Paul must have been convinced that his suffering would not be in vain. Having a clear vision of 'the revealing of our Lord Jesus Christ' (1.7), which is Paul's true eschatology, he was certain that his present anguish was a suffering in hope. Such hope was not only for Paul's own self-consolation, but for the encouragement of others as well: 'Therefore, my beloved brethren, be steadfast, immovable, always abounding in the work of the Lord, knowing that in the Lord your labour is not in vain' (15.58).

Paul's final statement in 4.13 – 'We have become like the rubbish of the world, the dregs of all things, to this very day' – appears as a continuation of the thought in 4.9, 10: 'like men sentenced to death; we have become a spectacle to the world, to angels and to men. We are fools.' Welborn sees this as 'the climax of the account,' because Paul echoes here 'the judgment of the world upon the clownish apostles.' The words περικαθάρματα ('rubbish') and περίψημα ('dregs'), according to Welborn, are powerful terms of abuse in the Greek language.[51] Indeed, Hays emphasises that Paul's statement should not be underplayed, as he is using the worst terms

---

[49] HOCK, *The Social Context*, 37.
[50] WELBORN, *Fool*, 81.
[51] WELBORN, *Fool*, 79, 80.

of abuse to describe following Christ, to follow Christ is to share his fate
of scorn and rejection by the world.[52] Judge views Paul as deriving from a
high ranking sector of society and having well-balanced social qualifications. As such, this social distinction serves as an explanation to why Paul
was so sensitive to the disgrace he endured from time to time. When Paul
(1 Cor. 4.13) describes becoming like the rubbish of the world, it does not
sound like the statement of one who is accustomed to such indignities, indeed the words resonate with feelings that he should not be subject to
them.[53]

Meggitt, who locates Paul in the social grouping of the poor, argues that
'in Roman law codes, there was almost an infinite variety of ways a person
could suffer insult.'[54] Meggitt disagrees with Judge, arguing that regardless
of one's social status it is difficult to conceive of anyone who would have
been content, as Judge implies, being treated as the world's rubbish or the
dregs of all things. If one follows Judge's reasoning, states Meggitt, ultimately the humanity of the impoverished in the 1st century is denied.[55]
While Meggitt's criticism of Judge is understandable, especially from the
perspective of modernity in which human dignity and rights are often
taken for granted, Meggitt's view may be overly idealistic and sentimental
when the broader social context is taken into account.

If Paul's social qualifications were indeed as impressive as Judge says,
the irony of Paul's statement is all the more startling. This is because the
great majority of Corinthians were likely among those who were socially
low and despised in the world (1.28). However, these chosen ones of God
now believed that they had become rich and even kings (4.8). In a reversal
of this, someone with the right social qualifications had, quite ironically,
become like rubbish and the dregs of humanity (4.13).

While reviling, persecution and slander directed against Paul and his
fellow-apostles were ill-intended, the apostles' response – blessing, endurance and words of kindness – could only be derived from their Lord who
had gone through far more than they had so far experienced.[56] Such power
was paradoxically demonstrated in the apparent weakness of the apostles.

Language, in both verbal and body forms, has already been discussed as
vital in Paul's dealing with the complex Corinthian situation. Paul's language in 4.8–13 is another good example of this. Plank summarises this
important point well: 'Paul confronts the Corinthian situation armed with
the weapons of irony. Through the careful use of ironic language he challenges the Corinthian system of value and asserts the force of his own fun-

---

[52] HAYS, *First Corinthians*, 72.

[53] JUDGE, *The Social Pattern*, 58.

[54] MEGGITT, *Poverty*, 90.

[55] MEGGITT, *Poverty*, 90.

[56] The paradox of weakness as source of power as in 1 Cor. 1.18–23.

damental convictions.'[57] Although this passage, just like others in the Corinthian correspondence, is put in the form of irony and sarcasm, Paul's intention remains positive because those words, however strong and disturbing, are ultimately meant to provoke and correct.

8.3 Exegesis of 2 Cor. 11.23–33

The polemical and apologetic nature of 2 Cor. 11.23–33 is clear from the
start of chapter 11, in which Paul speaks about his own foolishness (11.1)
and about the Corinthians being led astray by those who proclaim another
Jesus and a different gospel (11.3, 4). Further into the chapter, Paul makes
a reference to those who want to be recognised as equals (11.12). Paul describes those boasters as false apostles and deceitful workers, who are the
ministers of Satan (11.13–15). Jerry Sumney seeks to link these 'ministers'
to the 'Pneumatics' whose 'powerful demeanour includes recounting successes and visionary experiences, as well as demanding pay and obedience.'[58]

Anthony Hanson identifies the opponents of Paul as Jewish Christians
who are influenced by Greek philosophy and pneumatics.[59] Peter Marshall's interpretation is more persuasive: Paul's rivals are rhetorically
trained and attribute to themselves virtues and deeds belonging to traditional measures of one's greatness. Others at Corinth would have shared
the same values and expected 'an apostle to be a man of culture, basing
this on those qualities which they have ascribed to themselves in an open
and unashamed self-display.' Thus, they portray Paul as someone who fails
to live up to their standards, both socially and intellectually. They would
have viewed him as unrestrained in speech, his physical appearance ridiculous and his actions shameful as only befitting to a fool.[60]

Towards the middle of the chapter Paul first makes it clear to the Corinthians that he was actually no fool (11.16). However, if the Corinthians
really thought that he was a fool, he would boast a little and speak as a fool
(11.16, 17). The concluding statement in 11.18 is very important: 'since
many boast according to human standards (κατὰ σάρκα, lit. "according to
the flesh"), I will also boast.' This statement is significant because, had
Paul not been provoked by the Corinthians, he would not have spoken like

---

[57] PLANK, *Affliction*, 33.

[58] J. L. SUMNEY, *Identifying Paul's opponents: The Question of Method in 2 Corinthians* (Sheffield: JSOT Press, 1990), 189, 190.

[59] A. T. HANSON, *The Paradox of the Cross in the Thought of St Paul* (Sheffield:
JSOT Press, 1987), 87–88.

[60] P. MARSHALL, *Enmity in Corinth: Social Conventions in Paul's Relations with the
Corinthians* (Tübingen: Mohr Siebeck, 1987), 339–40.

a fool as he does in this chapter. This is especially the case in 11.23–33, which is sometimes described as 'the fool's speech' (e.g. by Barrett,[61] Sumney[62] and Jerome Murphy-O'Connor[63]). In other words, it was only for polemical and apologetic purposes that he reluctantly chooses to speak like a fool in his conflict with the Corinthian 'fools' (1.19). It would be far too low or unworthy of the apostle of Christ to come down to such a level, to boast according to human standards or according to the flesh under normal circumstances.

The sarcasm in 11.19 is evident: 'for you gladly put up with fools, being wise yourselves!' If the Corinthians were indeed as 'wise' as they claimed or pretended to be they would not have allowed those 'fools' to make slaves of them, to prey upon them and to take advantage of them (11.20). In a derisive tone and with a certain amount of anger Paul makes a rather unusual remark: 'to my shame, I must say, we were too weak for that!' (11.21). It was certainly foolish of the 'wise' Corinthians to have allowed those 'fools' to have made slaves of them, to have preyed upon them and to have taken advantage of them. Had Paul wanted to do that he would have greater advantage over those 'fools', since the Corinthians owed him the gospel. However, Paul had to confess that he was too weak for that. Paul's sarcastic remark is uttered in the heat of polemical statements. Paul would not allow himself to do so, for this would be blatantly inconsistent with his *modus operandi* as the apostle of Christ crucified. Indeed, Paul's *peristasis* catalogues in 2 Cor. 11.23–33 should be perceived and interpreted from this perspective.

Chapter 6 *peristasis* in the Greco-Roman tradition is discussed with special reference to the Stoics, who generally saw the lists positively as part of human virtues of endurance and courage. Chapter 7 examines the other side of the catalogues, as indicators that suffering could also be perceived negatively to connote cowardice, humiliation and human degradation. This study argues that it is the negative side that Paul has in mind when he provides *peristasis* catalogues in the Corinthian correspondence.

Returning to the *Peristasenkataloge*, Savage also contemplates the negative response which likely came from Paul's readers. He sees the list of personal afflictions as so horrific that 'it would have elicited feelings of extreme contempt among his readers.' When Paul boasts of such degrading

---

[61] BARRETT, *Second Epistle*, 288. See R. P. MARTIN, *2 Corinthians* (Waco: Word Books, 1986); FURNISH, *II Corinthians*, 512–13; PLUMMER, *A Critical and Exegetical Commentary on the Second Epistle of St. Paul to the Corinthians* (Edinburgh: T. & T. Clark, 1915), 311.

[62] SUMNEY, *Opponents*, 153–55.

[63] J. MURPHY-O'CONNOR, *The Theology of the Second Letter to the Corinthians* (Cambridge: CUP, 1991), 107. See M. J. HARRIS, *The Second Epistle to the Corinthians: A Commentary on the Greek Text* (Grand Rapids: Eerdmans, 2005), 789.

experiences, he would appear to almost revel in his humiliation.[64] Ralph
Martin notes the basic differences between the Greco-Roman tradition and
Paul's use of the *peristasis* catalogues: 'this section is dominated by the
use of the *peristaseis*-list, i.e., a list of trials, endured by moral philosophers and teachers.... There are obvious differences as well; not least in
that the popular moral philosopher suffered *peristaseis* as a totally human
experience, where Paul saw a divine purpose running through all his life's
hardships.'[65] Martin's observation is helpful, although it is noteworthy that
the moral philosopher sometimes refers to divine assistance or presence in
the midst of struggle, as the earlier study on Stoic περίστασις demonstrates.

11.23 διάκονοι Χριστοῦ εἰσιν; παραφρονῶν λαλῶ, ὑπὲρ ἐγώ· ἐν
κόποις περισσοτέρως, ἐν φυλακαῖς περισσοτέρως, ἐν πληγαῖς
ὑπερβαλλόντως, ἐν θανάτοις πολλάκις. *('Are they ministers of Christ? I
am talking like a madman – I am a better one: with far greater labours, far
more imprisonments, with countless floggings, and often near death.')* 24
Ὑπὸ Ἰουδαίων πεντάκις τεσσεράκοντα παρὰ μίαν ἔλαβον, *('Five
times I have received from the Jews the forty lashes minus one.')*

Boasting was usually done in Paul's time with public recognition in
mind.[66] However, here Paul is doing it in a particularly polemical context.
Under normal circumstances, it would be the very last thing he wanted to
do.

That 11.23–33 is basically about boasting is made clear from the two
immediately preceding verses: 'But whatever any one dares to boast of – I
am speaking as a fool – I also dare to boast of that. Are they Hebrews? So
am I. Are they Israelites? So am I. Are they descendants of Abraham? So
am I' (11.21, 22). Paul in 11.22 boasts about his Hebrew/Jewish identity,
and the polemic indicates that at least some of his opponents (i.e. the other
'ministers of Christ'; 11.23) are also of Jewish descent. Furnish believes
'Hebrews' in 11.22 is a title of honour and would have been understood as
referring to one's ethnicity; whereas 'Israelites' would have been used
primarily of one's ethnic descent and the term 'Israelites' had religious
connotations while still implying something about ethnicity.[67] Margaret
Thrall suggests that this emphasis on Jewishness may indicate that within
the Corinthian church the Jewish-Christian component may have been a

---

[64] SAVAGE, *Power*, 63.

[65] MARTIN, *2 Corinthians*, 368.

[66] 'Boasting was often seen as a demand for public recognition of honour. Words for
"boast" and "boasting" (καύχημα, *kauchēma*; and terms with the καυχ-, *kauch*-, stem)
are common in the NT (Rom 2:17, 23; 3:27; 4:2).' MOXNES, 'Honor', 24.

[67] FURNISH, *II Corinthians*, 514.

fairly large contingent.[68] This is an impression one gets from the book of Acts where Paul visits synagogue after synagogue.

The two expressions in following verse 11.23 – 'I am speaking as a fool' and 'I am talking like a madman' – seem to imply that Paul does not intend to boast. Rather, he finds himself in a circumstance in which he is forced to do so, much against his own wishes and Christian character. This is despite boasting being part and parcel of the lifestyle within Greco-Roman society. Ben Witherington draws attention to this side of society, describing shaming and boasting as a normal phenomenon in this honour-shame society. Within this honour-shame culture, describes Witherington, public recognition was of the utmost concern and did not necessarily relate to the actual facts of a person's character. Reputation came first and one would not want for it to be publicly tarnished.[69] Pogoloff comments on another but related aspect of this culture, that in addition to competing with others, there would have been a great deal of class and status envy.[70]

Both in the general context of the Greco-Roman world and in the particular context of the Corinthian situation, boasting was not just a matter of personal attitude and behaviour, it was an essential feature in the whole of rhetorical training and practice, especially in public oratory where the speaker was judged and praised for his eloquent communication. He was expected to be boastful, as it was inherent in the social ethos.

As previously noted, boasting and comparison, neither of which Paul wanted to do, unfortunately begin in the passage just before 11.23–33. An expression of purposeful intent, κἀγω ('and I', or 'I also'), occurs six times in 11.16–22 alone, clearly indicating the frequency and intensity of Paul's reluctant comparison with his rivals. In each case Paul establishes his parity with his rivals. What he does in 11.23 is a natural continuation of what he already started, however reluctantly. If the expression κἀγω is used to indicate the similarity or equality between Paul and his rivals, the other expression, ὑπὲρ ἐγώ in 11.23a ('I am far more' or 'I am better'), is meant to show his superiority over them. These two expressions, κἀγω and ὑπὲρ ἐγώ, although relatively simple, are indicative of Paul's rhetorical skill in the context of polemics and *apologia*.

Instead of providing an impressive list of achievements and credentials to show his superiority over rivals, Paul provides a *peristasis* catalogue, itemising his sufferings, especially physical aspects and the body language he seeks to convey. To be sure, such an exercise in itself is not surprising,

---

[68] THRALL, *A Critical and Exegetical Commentary on the Second Epistle to the Corinthians* (Edinburgh: T&T Clark, 2000), 2.730.

[69] B. WITHERINGTON, *Conflict and Community in Corinth* (Grand Rapids: Eerdmans, 1995), 8.

[70] POGOLOFF, *Logos*, 211.

as the sages and philosophers of the ancient Greco-Roman world were also quite accustomed to doing so. What is surprising is that, unlike his Greco-Roman counterparts, it is not human virtues (e.g. courage, endurance and manliness) that Paul tries to exhibit, but rather blatant human weakness and even cowardice (e.g. 11.32, 33)! While this presentation would understandably be surprising to the Greeks and Romans, including the Corinthians, both foe and friend, it is a typical Pauline presentation of paradox to deal with the Corinthian problem. For Paul it was far more than just a matter of strategy, it was also theologically motivated and prompted by his understanding of the cross.[71]

11.23a reveals the real bone of contention between Paul and his Corinthian rivals. The word 'ministers' (διάκονοι) here appears somewhat harmless, since by itself it does not really confer any particularly significant social status. However, in the context of the Corinthian controversy the word is problematic and indicative of a serious issue. Although Paul does not explain why at the beginning of his *apologia*, the whole Corinthian correspondence may be understood as dealing with the controversial issue which basically has to do with Paul's *modus operandi*. And he is a 'minister' of Christ, with a particular manner of speech, socially unacceptable life style, and even problematic physical appearance. All these clearly place him in a bad light in comparison to his rivals, especially the 'super-apostles', powerful, rich and eloquent. In the same chapter (11.12–15), Paul already uses strong words to describe and expose some of these 'boasters'.

Unlike 1 Cor. 4.8–13, for instance, where Paul identifies himself and his fellow-apostles with the first person plural 'we' in his *apologia,* in the whole passage of 2 Cor. 11.23–33 he uses the singular 'I', thereby making the issue far more personal. The *peristasis* catalogues he itemises should also be viewed in this context. The contention is essentially between him and his rivals.

The expression, 'I am a better one' (11.23a) is extraordinary, even somewhat shocking, to those who know Paul as a humble δοῦλος of Christ. Paul is apparently conscious of it when he confesses that he is speaking like a madman. Paul's self-confessed 'madness' may be seen here as communicating that it is out of character for him to boast and compare himself with others in order to show his own superiority. Not only was Paul 'mad' in the context of the Greco-Roman ethos, he also appears like the 'fool' in accordance with the study on mimes by Welborn.

---

[71] 'Appeal is made to evidence of his shame and dishonor. "What he has endured is the seal of his Apostleship."' (PLUMMER, *Commentary*, 322). See HARRIS, *The Second Epistle*, 797–98.

It needs to be asked in what manner Paul is a 'better' minister than other 'ministers of Christ' (11.23). The answer is found in the following *peristasis* catalogues Paul provides. It is in personal tribulations and sufferings that he wants to show that he is better than the rest and not in a manner likely anticipated in Greco-Roman or Jewish (i.e. Maccabean martyrs) virtue paradigms defined by courage, endurance, manliness and such. This is another sign of Paul's 'madness' for, according to societal expectations on *peristasis* which prove one's manly virtues (e.g. the great moral philosophers and teachers), he would indeed have been viewed as mad.

In 11.23 Paul refers first to his 'labours'. It is with 'far greater labours' that Paul claims to be superior to his rivals. Such an argument is hardly valid in the context of current Greco-Roman expectations for at least three reasons:

(1) If 'greater labours' here is simply meant to indicate in general terms that one was working harder than others in whatever work, such 'greater labours' would not have any particular merit in themselves nor earn any social status to the hard labourer. In fact, in a society where most hard work was performed by people of the lower strata of society, including ordinary artisans and slaves, manual labourers, instead of having grounds for boasting, were usually the very cause of social prejudice and contempt. The so-called 'dignity of labour' or 'sanctity of labour' could only be a bad joke for Paul's audience.

(2) If by 'greater labours' Paul has in mind all the hard work he does for the sake of the gospel, appreciation would only be expected from his close associates and supporters, and certainly not his rivals who were understandably jealous of his 'hard work' as well as its fruit.

(3) If by 'greater labours' Paul is referring specifically to his manual labours as a tentmaker, it would only cause society, including the Corinthian Christians who are part of it, to further despise him for reasons which have been demonstrated by scholars such as Glancy and Hock (cf. §7.3). However, it is precisely in such an apparently poor or invalid argument that the power and subtlety of Paul's irony and paradox become clearest and most provocative. This explanation would relate to an unspoken view challenging social values, the reason for which is found in an understanding of the cross of Christ.

The phrase φυλακαῖς περισσοτέρως ('far more imprisonments') is just as problematic as Paul's earlier reference to κόποις περισσοτέρως ('far greater labours'). The reason for this is: (1) 'imprisonments' as a general term could only negatively connote crimes and other illegal or anti-social activities and would thus work against the apostle; and (2) from Paul's biographical notes alone or from the witness of the book of Acts, one could reasonably infer that the apostle's imprisonments were not only realities, but perhaps far more frequent than what is recorded. Since they are apparently not the result of any noble and heroic acts, but closely or exclusively due to the preaching of the message of the cross, such an argument would draw sympathy neither from those who were perishing nor from Paul's jealous rivals. Forbes comments that imprisonment and beatings do not exactly inspire confidence that someone is respectable.[72] This was as true then as it is now. Marshall comments on how Paul would have been perceived: as a 'man of shame'.[73]

Perhaps far more serious and with greater implications is Paul's reference to the physical assaults that he painfully experienced, beginning from 11.23b to 11.24: 'with countless floggings, and often near death. Five times I have received at the hands of the Jews the forty lashes less one.'[74] Paul's reference to thirty-nine lashes is interesting because this is the number of official punishment given by the synagogue. In Matt. 10.17 Jesus warns his disciples about the possibility of being delivered up to Jewish councils (συνέδρια) and being flogged in their synagogues (ἐν ταῖς σὺ ναγωγαῖς αὐτῶν). The origin of such corporal punishment is found in Deut. 25.2–3.

Under normal circumstances the number of lashes was determined by the nature of the offence, but in no case should it to exceed forty. This was to prevent the offender from having to suffer gross public humiliation.[75] The Deuteronomic origin of the practice found its later development in *m. Makkoth* 3.10 and is also attested, for instance, in Josephus (*Ant.* 4.238, 248). Although there is some uncertainty as to how often and under what conditions the 40 lashes, or fewer, would have been given, Paul's statement here appears to be substantiated by external sources. Therefore, it is certainly plausible that Paul would have endured a known practice of punishment from the 1st century. Synagogue floggings were administered for various offences, which are itemized in *m. Makkoth* 3.1–9.[76] However, how the Mishnaic description relates to actual practice is debated.

History is full of ironies. Paul, who was once notorious for persecuting the first Christians, is portrayed in the book of Acts as being responsible for flogging early followers of Jesus (Acts 22.19). The persecutor himself now became the victim. According to *m. Makkoth* 3.14, the possibility of a person's dying during or after the thirty-nine strokes was real; no wonder

---

[72] FORBES, 'Comparison', 19.

[73] MARSHALL, *Enmity*, 361.

[74] Since Paul's own accounts as well as those in Acts cannot literally verify the precise locations or the exact number of times regarding the physical assaults mentioned by Paul in the above verses, their historicity seems to be beyond reasonable doubt. The fact that Paul was actually stoned 'near death' was witnessed at least once in Acts 14.19, and this occurred in Lystra.

[75] HARRIS, *The Second Epistle*, 801

[76] BARRETT, *Second Epistle*, 296.

Josephus describes this frightening punishment as 'most ignominious' (αἰσχίστη) for a free man (*Ant.* 4.238).[77] In view of the severity of the punishment, it is remarkable that Paul managed to survive after enduring such floggings five times.

Thrall highlights the fact that Paul as a Jew suffered heavily at the hands of his own people.[78] This point is worth noting because of Paul's earlier pride in his own identity (11.22). The social stigma associated with such corporal punishment is not difficult to imagine. And especially because he was a Roman citizen, a 'free' man, his humiliation would have been intensified. This was very different from the kind of manliness and other virtues which the Greco-Roman sages or philosophers were committed to exhibit in their use of the *peristasis* catalogues.

How one interprets perceptions of corporal beatings in the 1st century has tremendous importance for understanding Paul's rhetorical strategy. When commenting on 11.23b–33, Glancy points out that while there are those who regard Paul's listing of adversities here as an ironic inversion of 1st century values, there appears to be a greater consensus that he is simply acting according to Greco-Roman rhetorical practice.[79] Sustained attention to this rhetorical tradition (cf. ch. 7), as it relates to Paul's preaching, poses a serious challenge to the perceived consensus.

In their commentaries, Best and Martin understand Paul's endurance of hardship as a sign of courage and manliness.[80] Fitzgerald proposes that 'Paul's scars attest to a praiseworthy endurance of hardship'[81] while Martyn argues that Paul's suffering testifies to the virtue of his fortitude and loyalty to Jesus.[82] Glancy, however, contends that in their emphasis on the 'manliness of confronting manifold physical challenges', the wounds inflicted on Paul are counted by contemporary scholars as emblems of martial valour while ignoring power relations (e.g. legal status, domination and submission, honour and shame) brought about in corporal beatings.[83] This last point is significant. Just as Glancy criticises Fitzgerald for being one-sided in associating bodily suffering (including whipping or flogging) only as signs of honour or manliness, without recognising its negative aspects, she does so now to other scholars such as Best and Martin. One cannot ignore the negative side – the dishonouring aspect – that Paul has in mind in 11.23–25 when he refers to 'floggings' and so forth. To highlight the honourable and glorious side of being flogged, according to the social ethos of

---

[77] HARRIS, *The Second Epistle*, 802–03.
[78] THRALL, *II Corinthians*, 736.
[79] GLANCY, 'Boasting', 119.
[80] BEST, *Second Corinthians*, 114; MARTIN, *2 Corinthians*, 376.
[81] FITZGERALD, *Cracks*, 43.
[82] MARTYN, *Galatians*, 568, n.73.
[83] GLANCY, 'Boasting', 121.

the time, would have weakened Paul's argument in the Corinthian controversy.

It would appear rather unlikely that in 11.23–25 Paul intends to defend his honour in the manner of the Greco-Roman sages. Thus, when he seeks to compare himself with the 'super-apostles' with the listing of his suffering and hardship, the real purpose is to show how much more than them he had endured (if they had indeed ever really been afflicted!). Suffering too is not just in physical terms, but also is related to other types of social humiliation and degradation. Paul's statement in 11.23 – 'with far greater labors, far more imprisonments, with countless floggings, and often near death' – should be understood in this context. Paul's concluding remark in the list also suggests that he is referring to humiliation and weakness and not glory and strength: 'Who is weak, and I am not weak?' (11.29). Moreover, his reference to escape in Damascus (11.32, 33) is also intended for the same purposes.

Unlike Fitzgerald, who regards *peristasis* catalogues only as signs of virtues based on the views of Seneca and Epictetus, Glancy convincingly argues that 'we cannot rely on Seneca (or, later, Epictetus) to reconstruct the *habitus* that shaped the Corinthian response to Paul's whippable body.'[84] Neither from the immediate context of 2 Cor. 11 nor within the overall purview of the two Corinthian letters (esp. in relation to polemical passages) could the Corinthians, especially Paul's fierce critics, simply regard Paul's 'whippable body' as a sign of virtue. Indeed, Paul himself does not view it this way. To regard the *peristasis* catalogues according to the social ethos of the Greco-Roman tradition (i.e. to list them in order to show the greatness of human endurance and true masculinity) goes against Paul's express purpose to boast of his weakness and God's enabling grace in and through his weakness.

If Paul really has any intention in the heat of his polemics against his critics to show his superiority over them, it is certainly not in the matter of human endurance and courage. The fact that he is let down in a basket through a window in the wall of Damascus and escapes from King Aretas' hands (11.32, 33; cf. Acts 9.23–25) is a sure sign of cowardice according to the common Greco-Roman understanding of courage and masculinity. If Paul has any sense of superiority over his Corinthians critics or the 'super-apostles', it would be in the area of suffering and hardship: 'with far greater labors, far more imprisonment, with countless floggings, and often near death' (11.23). This is really the main point of Paul's argument and the listing of the περίστασις in chapter 11 and elsewhere. Yet, paradoxically again, what was considered shameful according to the Greco-Roman

---

[84] GLANCY, 'Boasting', 124.

ethos turns out to be honour for Paul. He counts it a great tribute to suffer
for Christ, even being beaten.

At this particular point about honour, even John Chrysostom appears to
have been somewhat unwittingly misled by centuries of Christian tradition
concerning suffering and martyrdom, which tends to regard and even welcome Christian hardship positively as a glorious path to share in Christ's
suffering. John Chrysostom thus reads what Paul writes in Gal. 6.17 – 'I
carried the marks of Jesus branded on my body' – as a sign of 'manly virtue' (ἀνδραγαθία), in the way that it was often regarded in Greco-Roman
period, although Chrysostom himself is not entirely unaware that the apostle's bodily scars could also signify something disgraceful (ὄνειδος, *Hom,
Gal.* 6.4).[85] Not only does Paul openly acknowledge that he carries 'the
marks of Jesus' branded on his body, he goes even further to confess that
he always carries in the body the death of Jesus (2 Cor. 4.10). Such was
the extent of Paul's *imitatio Christi*.

There is a strong case to be made that according to the social ethos of
Paul's time, the apostle's testimony concerning his own weakness and the
abuse of his body were likely perceived by his opponents as marks of servile submission and insignia of humiliation which were unworthy of a man
of any social standing, dignity and honour. For Paul's critics, αἰσχρός
(dishonourable, degraded, and ultimately, morally suspect) and ταπεινός
connoted shame, humiliation and degradation.[86] Shaw points out that 'it is
the Christian writings of the New Testament that revolutionize these values
wholly by their total inversion. Paul boasts of his self-abasement and humility, and draws attention to the effort one must make to strive towards
the final virtue that should be claimed by the Christian, that of being *tapei-
nos*. Indeed, he actually creates a new virtue – *tapeinophrosunê*
(ταπεινοφροσύνη) – the voluntary abasement of the self and one's
body.'[87] Paul's mindset is thoroughly consistent with his deep desire to be
an imitator of Christ, especially Christ's self-emptying (κένωσις in Phil.
2.5–8).

One can scarce ignore the basic conflict between the Greco-Roman
ethos and Paul's theology of the cross. Glancy endorses Harrill's view that
'social status was somatically expressed', and since Paul's bodily appearance was weak, even by his own confession (1 Cor. 2.3; 2 Cor. 11.30), his
critics questioned his manhood and right to authority. Glancy too is aware
of the importance of body language, stating that 'because NT scholars have

---

[85] Cited in Glancy, 'Boasting', 126, n.103.
[86] Larson thinks that 'Paul's open admission that he had been flogged by both Jewish
and Roman authorities (2 Cor. 11.23–25) was certainly the boasting of a "madman" because of the shame and humiliation incurred by the recipients of such punishments' (94).
[87] SHAW, 'Body', 303–04.

not acknowledged that relationships of power were embodied, they have not appreciated the centrality of Paul's body to the super-apostles' campaign against him.'[88] Glancy also argues that Paul's boasting of beatings is for strategic reasons (i.e. as marks of identification with the sufferings of the crucified Christ), although the Corinthians failed to appreciate the 'manly valour in Paul's storytelling body'.[89]

Larson goes even further, suggesting that Paul is in fact using a dangerous strategy (i.e. by strongly identifying with Christ in his weakness) since weakness in a man denotes humiliation and degradation in this power-conscious society. Paul is reproached by his opponents for reasons which may be divided into two primary categories: (1) lack of physical appearance and skills as a public speaker, which lead to a miserable failure in terms of rhetorical performance; and (2) personal character, seen in his impoverished lifestyle, manual labor and so on. However, 'taking Christ as his model, Paul argues that weakness, humility, and suffering in the cause are badges of honour in God's eyes (2 Cor. 12.5–10).'[90] There seems to be little doubt that Paul's conformity to Christ crucified ('cruciformity') is a deliberate choice and a life-long commitment (1 Cor. 2.2; cf. Gal. 6.14).

Paul refers to his countless floggings (2 Cor. 11.23) in connection with his self-confessed weakness (11.29, 30) and not with any intention to boast of his own endurance, although he also apparently possessed such manly quality, even by Greco-Roman standards. Paul is not ashamed to confess his own weakness because such a confession is thoroughly consistent with his theology of the cross and his strong commitment to *imitatio Christi*. In this connection, what Paul says in 13.4 is important: for Christ was crucified in weakness. However, this is not the end of the story; otherwise there would not have been any good news for Paul to proclaim. Thus, what immediately follows is equally important: but Christ now lives by the power of God, so that as one who has been fully identified with Christ, Paul is able to remind the Corinthians with confidence that although he and his fellow apostles are 'weak in him [or with him]', they also live with Christ by the power of God.

It is the human weakness of Paul that the Corinthians, especially his critics, saw and perceived according to the current social ethos, rather than by the power of God which could only be perceived from the divine perspective and in paradoxical terms. Noteworthy is that part of Christ's weakness in the eyes of the Greco-Roman world would surely have been the floggings which Pilate inflicted on him (Jn. 19.1; cf. Mk. 15.15, par. Matt. 27.26). One is tempted to consider that when the apostles rejoiced,

---

[88] GLANCY, 'Boasting', 127–28.
[89] GLANCY, 'Boasting', 135.
[90] LARSON, 'Masculinity', 95.

that they were considered worthy to suffer the dishonour of floggings for the sake of the name of Jesus (Acts 5.40, 41), that they may well have had Christ's own sufferings in mind. As such, the profound sense of solidarity with Christ, who was also afflicted, would be quite unmistakable.

11.25 τρὶς ἐρραβδίσθην, ἅπαξ ἐλιθάσθην, τρὶς ἐναυάγησα, νυχθήμερον ἐν τῷ βυθῷ πεποίηκα· *('Three times I was beaten with rods. Once I received stoning. Three times I was shipwrecked; for a night and a day I was adrift at sea;')*

In 11.25 the verb ἐρραβδίσθην (from ῥαβδίζω, Latin *virgis caedere,* 'beating with rods') refers to a specific Roman punishment.[91] Martin elaborates that there is a technical side to the sentence of being beaten with rods: it refers to a penalty inflicted by Roman magistrates. Here in 11.25, Paul says that he has suffered this sentence three times. Martin describes this as 'a fact which is sad evidence that Roman governors were not always meticulous in upholding the law (Livy 10.9), and a miscarriage Paul comments on' as having been treated outrageously at Philippi (1 Thess. 2.2). When Paul was beaten, Martin writes, it was in public and either served as a warning or was the treatment of a social pest.[92]

In the case of Paul, the actual legality of these cases of beatings from which he suffered is not as significant as the social implications and symbols that are attached to it. This is just the negative side of the *peristasis* catalogues. In Greco-Roman society it would be the greatest dishonour, shame and humiliation for a free person to be subjected to whippings publicly (see §7.3).[93]

Philo's account of Flaccus' campaign against the Jews of Alexandria relies heavily on a kind of body language which is closely associated with whipping or flogging and which is indicative of one's social class and standing in the Roman society. According to the account, Flaccus orders the members of the Jewish council to be rounded up and brought to the theater as a spectacle, highlighting in particular the awful corporal torture through flogging (*Flacc.* 75).

The beating of Paul by the Roman authorities is tantamount to the denial of his Roman citizenship and the implications and consequences are evidently very serious because one of the main differences between the condition of a slave and a free man in Roman society was the vulnerability of the former to repeated corporal punishments. Saller notes that whipping

---

[91] HARRIS, *The Second Epistle,* 803.

[92] MARTIN, *2 Corinthians,* 377. Cf. FURNISH, *II Corinthians,* 516.

[93] Cicero gives a very vivid and moving description of a Roman citizen Gavius's suffering at the hands of Verres, highlighting the severe flogging that was inflicted on his body, as a mark of gross injustice and humiliation for a Roman citizen (*Verr.* 5.158–61, cf. 5.139–40; 4. 24, 26; 1.9, 13). A severe flogging could lead to death (*Verr.* 5.142).

or beating in Roman society 'symbolically put a free man in the servile category and so degraded him.' Thus, 'the act of being whipped affected a Roman's status by detracting from his honour through public humiliation and association with the lowest human form in the Roman world, the slave.'[94]

The debate about Paul's social origins and status continues. A considerable number of NT scholars take the position that Paul enjoyed his privilege as a Roman citizen (Acts 16.37)[95] before his Christian conversion. Judge proposes that Paul, who came from a distinguished Jewish circle, belonged to 'the privileged group of Hellenistic families' and possessed 'an unusually well balanced set of social qualifications.'[96] Hengel suggests that Paul came from a 'petty-bourgeois' middle-class family while Nils Dahl believes that Paul was born to a well-to-do family.[97] Ed Parish Sanders thinks that Paul had a middle class upbringing.[98] Both William Ramsay and Theissen believe that Paul belonged to the higher strata of society and possessed citizenship of both Tarsus and Rome and thus enjoyed 'an unusual, privileged status.'[99] Marshall also insists that Paul's social status and education were equal to his rivals.[100] Thrall concludes that 'Paul's own mention of the three Roman floggings he endured does not cast serious doubt on the claim in Acts that he was a Roman citizen. A mixture of various external circumstances and inward motives would be sufficient to account in each case for his silence concerning his possession of the citizenship.'[101]

Because Paul was Jewish and most likely a Roman citizen as well, it would be reasonable to assume that he would be knowledgeable about the sanctity of the human body, especially that of a man, in both Jewish and Roman traditions. Moreover, now as a follower of Christ crucified, he goes even further theologically to assert that the body of the believer is in fact

---

[94] SALLER, 'Punishment', 154.

[95] See BARRETT, *A Critical and Exegetical Commentary on the Acts of the Apostles* (Edinburgh: T. &T. Clark, 1998), 2.801–02; DUNN, *The Acts of the Apostles* (Peterborough: Epworth Press, 1996), 223; BRUCE, *The Acts of the Apostles* (London: Tyndale Press, 1965), 340–41.

[96] JUDGE, *The Social Pattern*, 57–58.

[97] HENGEL, *The Pre-Christian Paul* (London: SCM Press, 1991), 17. DAHL, *Studies in Paul: Theology for the Early Christian Mission* (Minneapolis: Augsburg, 1977), 35.

[98] E. P. SANDERS, *Paul* (Oxford: OUP, 1991), 10.

[99] W. M. RAMSAY, *St. Paul the Traveller and the Roman Citizen* (London: Hodder and Stoughton, 1895), 30–31; THEISSEN, *The Social Setting*, 36.

[100] MARSHALL, *Enmity*, 400.

[101] THRALL, *II Corinthians*, 742. However, Meggitt takes an opposite view that 'just as the early Church Fathers recognised him [Paul] as a "common man" (ἀγοραῖος), and his contemporaries saw him as one of poor (πτωχός) so we should also place him in this economic context' (*Poverty*, 96).

'a temple of the Holy Spirit' (ναὸς τοῦ ἁγίου πνεύματος, 1 Cor. 6.19) by
which to glorify God (6.20). In 4.11–13 Paul openly speaks about his body
being hungry, thirsty, poorly clothed and beaten as well as growing weary
from the work of manual labour. In 2 Cor. 4.8–10 he tells of being afflicted
in every way, crushed, persecuted, struck down and always carrying in the
body the death of Jesus. In 6.5–9, he continues his account of being beaten,
imprisoned and punished. When compared with others, Paul feels very personally and deeply that he experienced far greater labours, far more imprisonments, countless floggings and was often near death (11.23). He is
not ashamed to confess his physical sufferings openly (11.24–25), although humanly speaking, as a servant of God as well as a Roman man, he
should have felt ashamed. The suffering apostle is not speaking in parables
but rather rich, vivid and solid body language which could only be fully
understood according to the social ethos of the Greco-Roman world.

Earlier in this study reference is made to Antipater who exposed his
numerous bodily scars to prove his loyalty to Caesar (§7.3).[102] Martyn
draws a close comparison between Antipater and Paul: 'as Antipater was
said to bear on almost every part of his person the marks of wounds showing his loyalty to Caesar, so Paul points to his body as it testifies to his belonging to the crucified Jesus.'[103] He also makes reference to 2 Cor. 11.24–
26 where Paul lists the many ordeals he suffered, including stoning and
whippings, describing the scars received by Paul as reflecting the 'wounds
of a soldier sent into the front trenches of God's redemptive and liberating
war.'[104] Martyn's comments appear to place a positive spin on the matter,
and are perhaps an appreciative contemporary perspective. However, *pace*
Martyn, for those who were perishing, even for the worldly Corinthian
Christians and especially Paul's critics, Paul's physical sufferings and
scars would have been viewed contemptuously.

Martyn's comparison between Antipater and Paul, while interesting and
valid to a certain extent, requires some important qualification. To begin
with, it is the praise of Caesar and perhaps other possible motives that are
the concern of Josephus' account. However in the case of Paul, human
praise and other ambitions had long since been 'crucified', and the loyalty
he now pledges for Christ was in obedience to the divine calling he received from his Lord and his whole life is testimony to this fact. As such,
even in the heat of the Corinthian controversy, his loyalty to Christ was
never challenged by his rivals and critics.

Martyn makes several important insights, including a recognition that
the miserable afflictions Paul endured when preaching are comparable to

---

[102] Josephus, *B.J.* 1.193, 197.
[103] MARTYN, *Galatians*, 568, n.73.
[104] MARTYN, *Galatians*, 568.

Jesus. The same powers that crucified Jesus are those that are inflicted on Paul (1 Cor. 2.8, Gal. 4.19). As such, the scars that he bore 'are nothing other than the present epiphany of the crucifixion of Jesus' and his 'physical body is thus a place in which one finds a sign of the present activity of the redeemer in the world (2 Cor. 4.7–10).'[105]

It may be elaborated that it is Paul's identification with his Lord (or *imitatio Christi*) that in Gal. 6.17 he says he carries 'the marks of Jesus branded on his body'. In 2 Cor. 4.10 a similar reference is found, this time in a paradoxical statement about life and death; that he is 'always carrying in the body the death of Jesus, so that the life of Jesus may also be made visible in our bodies.' Bruce explains how slaves were tattooed and branded to show who owned them, in a similar way Paul's marks, which Bruce calls the 'marks of Jesus', function to show ownership.[106] John Pobee points out that the scars Paul carried are 'the sign of apostleship.'[107] Taking Gal. 6.11–17 as a whole, 'the paradox of the cross is central to this passage, and so is the representation of Jesus' sufferings by his disciple.'[108]

In Phil. 3.10 Paul in fact goes beyond carrying 'the marks of Jesus', and writes about his full identification with Christ: 'I want to know Christ and the power of his resurrection and the sharing of his sufferings by becoming like him in his death.' Such is perhaps the uppermost limit of *imitatio Christi*. The statement that immediately follows suggests that such a profound desire to want to be fully identified with the crucified Christ is also deeply inspired by the eschatological hope of resurrection: 'if somehow I may attain the resurrection from the dead' (3.11). Here, Paul's statement is rather unassuming when he qualifies his hope with the words 'if somehow'. Indeed, Paul's paradoxical statements about death and life in 2 Cor. 4.10 in this regard are both revealing and powerful.

Based upon Paul's corporal suffering, including 'rod-beatings' as well as floggings by the Jews, it would be quite reasonable to suggest that being a δοῦλος and imitator of Christ crucified, Paul is very conscious of the fact that he is actually identifying himself with his Lord as well as with Christ's body and the Church in all that he had gone through.

Although there is no other NT record about Paul having been shipwrecked and being adrift at sea except the later part of his missionary journeys (Acts 27), the historicity of his reference is plausible. While shipwrecks are a common feature of ancient historiographies, the inclusion of three such incidents here should be aligned not so much with adventure

---

[105] MARTYN, *Galatians*, 569.

[106] BRUCE, *The Epistle of Paul to the Galatians: A Commentary on the Greek Text* (Exeter: The Paternoster Press, 1982), 275.

[107] J. S. POBEE, *Persecution and Martyrdom in the Theology of St. Paul* (Sheffield: Sheffield Academic Press, 1985), 95.

[108] HANSON, *Paradox*, 86.

and daring, but rather adversity and affliction. As discussed throughout, Paul is not seeking to use this list, including the ship-wrecks, to demonstrate or boast about his manhood.

11.26 ὁδοιπορίαις πολλάκις, κινδύνοις ποταμῶν, κινδύνοις λῃστῶν, κινδύνοις ἐκ γένους, κινδύνοις ἐξ ἐθνῶν, κινδύνοις ἐν πόλει, κινδύνοις ἐν ἐρημίᾳ, κινδύνοις ἐν θαλάσσῃ, κινδύνοις ἐν ψευδαδέλφοις, *('on frequent journeys, in danger from rivers, danger from bandits, danger from my own people, danger from Gentiles, danger in the city, danger in the wilderness, danger at sea, danger from false brothers and sisters;')*

Eight types of 'dangers' (κινδύνοις) are singled out in 11.26. Some are closely associated with Paul's constant travels, such as danger from rivers, robbers and the perils of the wilderness. All these were only to be expected when travelling in the ancient world, despite the *Pax Romana* which people generally enjoyed. Other dangers came from people who were hostile to Paul as a messenger of the gospel, whether Jews ('my own people') or Gentiles. The danger from false brothers and sisters is mentioned separately from the dangers from both (presumably unbelieving) Jews and Gentiles. This is particularly significant because unlike the unbelieving Jews and Gentiles, these false brothers and sisters would most likely be people who claimed or pretended to be fellow Christians of Paul. As such, it would be reasonable to suggest that Paul may have entrusted himself to them or confided in them, a rather dangerous action in a society where hostilities against the emerging Christian movement were present.

The particular danger from false brothers and sisters would, arguably, be harder than most others for Paul to bear because it involved betrayal against him. Paul must have taken this quite personally. It may also be conjectured that false brothers and sisters would also have been present in the Corinthian congregation and worked against him just as his other rivals and critics did. Harris observes that '"dangers among false brothers" stands alone at the end of Paul's list, probably because he viewed it as the most hurtful and insidious peril of all. External dangers that threatened his own life were one thing; treacherous opposition that undermined his work was quite another thing. He could cope with life-threatening hazards from without more easily than with work-undermining perils from within.'[109]

---

[109] HARRIS, *The Second Epistle*, 808.

11.27 κόπῳ καὶ μόχθῳ, ἐν ἀγρυπνίαις πολλάκις, ἐν λιμῷ καὶ δίψει, ἐν νηστείαις πολλάκις, ἐν ψύχει καὶ γυμνότητι· (*'in toil and hardship, through many a sleepless night, hungry and thirsty, often without food, cold and naked.'*)

Much of what Paul mentions in 11.27 has already occurred in the other *peristasis* catalogues (e.g. 1 Cor. 4.11, 12). Although the words 'many a sleepless night' and 'cold and naked' are additions here, they add no significant substance to what Paul says. One would expect that such common difficulties would normally accompany the harsh lifestyle the apostle describes, one which in his words included his own equation with the world's rubbish and dregs of society (4.13) – all for the sake of Christ and the gospel.

Paul's abusive treatment and unpleasant adventures, including at times extreme material poverty, form a stark contrast to the fullness and richness (4.8; cf. 11.21) of the self-conceited and boastful Corinthians, who seem to enjoy material abundance. This is, of course, only one side of the story. The other side is that Paul's material poverty is, at least in part, due to his refusal of support by the Corinthians, which significantly contributed to their estranged relationship. Yet, the 'fool' of Christ could always draw, paradoxically, great comfort and self-consolation from his *imitatio Christi*: 'as sorrowful, yet always rejoicing; as poor, yet making many rich; as having nothing, and yet possessing everything' (2 Cor. 6.10).

The problem between Paul and his critics in Corinth apparently had to do with his refusal of material support from them, especially since he appears to accept support from other churches.[110] It is evident from the Corinthian correspondence that certain influential and powerful patrons in the church were already exerting a great deal of influence on members of the congregation. Sensible and perceptive Paul would not have wanted to come under the influence of these patrons as he would have felt indebted to them by accepting their favour.

Paul's behaviour in not accepting support may well have been perceived as 'a violation of the convention of friendship or patronage',[111] as Chow states. Marshall focuses on the conflict between Paul and his Corinthian critics in light of Greco-Roman social conventions. He suggests that the Greco-Roman conventions of friendship were based on the pattern of giving, receiving and returning. Failure to adhere to these obligations of friendship could bring about enmity.[112] Paul, who is probably familiar with such social conventions, is prepared to take the risk and thus pays the price

---

[110] E.g., Phil. 4.15, 16; 2 Cor. 11.8.

[111] CHOW, *Patronage*, 188.

[112] MARSHALL, *Enmity*, 1–21.

by constantly facing hunger and thirst in order to be free from obligation and indebtedness to his would-be 'patrons'.

11.28 χωρὶς τῶν παρεκτὸς ἡ ἐπίστασίς μοι ἡ καθ' ἡμέραν, ἡ μέριμνα πασῶν τῶν ἐκκλησιῶν. ('And, besides other things, I am under daily pressure because of my anxiety for all the churches.')

Those sufferings and dangers which Paul mention until this point in the *peristasis* catalogues (11.23–27) largely involve the material and physical aspects of life. However, 'the daily pressure' upon him resulting from his 'anxiety for all the churches' (ἡ μέριμνα πασῶν τῶν ἐκκλησιῶν) may be explained as fundamentally mental and spiritual. Such was the pastoral side of the servant of Christ, which was sometimes hidden, especially in the midst of heated debate and controversy. The reference to 'all the churches' indicates the extent and magnitude of Paul's pastoral anxiety.

Based on the study of the term παρεκτός in 11.28, Harris suggests that 'as we move from vv.23b–27 to vv.28–29 we are not merely progressing from external to internal hardships but from various intermittent physical hardships that lay in the past to a single constant spiritual burden of the present.'[113] Best also provides a helpful comment that 'Paul's final point about his service to Christ relates to the inward wear and tear on his mind and soul, something even more difficult to bear than his physical sufferings. There were sleepless nights arising from his anxiety about one or another of his churches.'[114] The burdened apostle seems to wish that he could quickly resolve the Corinthian problem in order to lighten this weight and release his anxiety. The picture of Paul is of someone who wants to be rid of this time and energy waste so that he could attend to the more pressing needs of some of the struggling churches. Unfortunately for him, no promising solution seems to have been forthcoming at the time he wrote.

11.29 τίς ἀσθενεῖ καὶ οὐκ ἀσθενῶ; τίς σκανδαλίζεται καὶ οὐκ ἐγὼ πυροῦμαι; ('Who is weak, and I am not weak? Who is made to stumble, and I am not indignant?')

From the surrounding context of 11.23–33, it is difficult to know precisely what Paul is trying to say when he asks this question. Interpreting this verse may depend largely on the broader context of the Corinthian correspondence. One thing seems to be certain as far as the composition of the Corinthian congregation is concerned. In terms of social strata, only some were rich and powerful and stood in marked contrast to the majority who were poor and weak (1 Cor. 1.26). It may be assumed that the rich and powerful were often boastful and self-conceited. As such, the poor and

---

[113] HARRIS, *The Second Epistle*, 811.
[114] BEST, *Second Corinthians*, 113.

weak may quite easily have become the prey of those who were in the upper strata of society and they were apparently socially disregarded by those above them.[115] Moreover, the social and moral behaviour of those in the upper strata seems to have often caused the weak and poor to stumble and fall. It is probably for this reason that the apostle, who is not ashamed to identify himself with the weak and poor, became indignant whenever he saw them fall.

The rhetorical question 'who is weak, and I am not weak?' may indicate that Paul is not unaware of human frailty and the weaker members of his flock in Corinth. It may also be intended as encouragement to the weak with whom he fully identifies. As one who is keenly aware of his own weakness in many ways, Paul was in the best position to protect the interest of the weak and to champion their cause.

Furnish provides a summarisation of three basic scholarly views on this aspect of Paul's weakness, it is due to: (1) some kind of personal anxiety or spiritual torment; (2) some form of physical or mental illness or (3) persecution which Paul often experienced.[116] Martin notes that the verb ἀσθενεῖν ('to be weak') in 11.29 is a key word in the 'Fool's Speech' (11.21a, 30; 12.5, 9, 10). He explains that the word has a wide range of meanings: bodily weakness or sickness, the religious connotation of a sensitive conscience (Rom. 14.1, 2; 15.1; 1 Cor. 8.11, 12) or a trait of inability to lead within the congregation (1 Cor. 8.9–11; 10.15, 31).[117] Barrett also points out the paradoxical nature of Paul's statement in his comment on 11.29: 'Paul declares that he is weak, and that it is in his weakness – his humble and humiliated behaviour, his poverty, his unimpressive appearance – that the power of Christ is made known.'[118]

Forbes suggests while popular exegesis tends to perceive that Paul's self-confessed weakness is the apostle's awareness of his own inadequacy before God, in common Hellenistic usage as well as in Pauline writings the term ἀσθένεια carries strong social undertones. On the one hand, 'weakness' refers to the state of those without power or status. On the other, 'weakness' denotes humiliation in other's eyes, rather than inadequacy in one's own.[119] Forbes' observation is certainly helpful, although in the complexity of Paul's thinking and experience, the word ἀσθένεια probably has a wider range of meanings for Paul than just the social aspect.

Paul may perhaps think that his entire apostleship is characterised by 'weakness'. Therefore, Andrews is quite right in describing Paul's apostle-

---

[115] Paul could have the rich and powerful in mind when he makes the remark in 2 Cor. 11.18–20.

[116] FURNISH, *II Corinthians*, 548–49. See §5.2.

[117] MARTIN, *2 Corinthians*, 382.

[118] BARRETT, *Second Epistle,* 302

[119] FORBES, 'Comparison', 19.

ship as an 'apostleship of weakness'.[120] Black also points out that for Paul 'weakness is a sign of apostleship', for Christ himself was 'crucified in weakness, but lives by the power of God' (13.4). There is no contradiction with the gospel, for Paul's suffering and weakness are entirely consistent with it – the passion of Christ comprises the very heart of the gospel message.[121] Black also weighs in on the subject, breaking the weakness motif into three sub-themes: (1) the anthropological; (2) the Christological and (3) the ethical. Black sees these three as inseparable and interrelated aspects of Paul's gospel.[122]

Harris links Paul's anxiety with his deep sense of solidarity with all the churches. In 11.29 Paul's emphasis is on his 'empathetic identification' with others who are weak, whatever this means here (physical, spiritual or social). This verse is preceded by statements about pressure and anxiety related to pastoral care, and there too empathetic identification may be found (11.28). Overall, these verses reflect an intense and zealous concern for the spiritual welfare of fellow believers.[123]

For Paul, unlike the worldly Corinthians who viewed human strength and weakness largely from the perspective of the current social ethos, there was another dimension to weakness from the perspective of his understanding of the cross. 2 Cor. 13.4 describes Christ being crucified in weakness. It is with and by the same power that Paul deals with the Corinthians in 13.4, however difficult and complex the problem might be. This perspective seems to be the basis of Paul's boasting in 11.30.

11.30 Εἰ καυχᾶσθαι δεῖ, τὰ τῆς ἀσθενείας μου καυχήσομαι. *('If I must boast, I will boast of the things that show my weakness.')*

If the power of God is indeed demonstrated in the weakness of Christ's crucifixion, which is symbolic of human suffering in its extremity, it is thoroughly logical for Paul. He now shares the suffering of the crucified Christ. With this bold and paradoxical statement, which appears almost like a sort of theological manifesto, Paul's *apologia* may now be said to have reached its intended climax. Not only is Paul's statement here a pinnacle of his argument, but also some of the statements he subsequently makes show that there is consistency in what he says about his boasting in weakness.[124]

Paul's boasting of weakness provides a marked contrast to the Greco-Roman sages in their respective use of *peristasis* catalogues. While the latter uses it to exhibit their own human virtues (e.g. courage, endurance and

---

[120] ANDREWS, 'Too Weak', 263.
[121] BLACK, *Weakness*, 139.
[122] BLACK, *Weakness*, 228.
[123] HARRIS, *The Second Epistle*, 814–15.
[124] E.g., 12.3, 5, 9–10.

manliness), Paul applies it to his own situation, unashamedly highlighting his own human weakness so that in the end, if there were any power to speak about, it is entirely divine power which is manifested in human weakness. While his Greco-Roman counterparts may sometimes attribute their success to divine assistance, it is often put in the background rather than up front. Moreover, in some cases, even when divine assistance is clearly or explicitly acknowledged, the idea of merited favour (i.e. God/gods only chose the wise and virtuous for exhibition) is present. With reference to Paul's catalogue of suffering in chapter 11, Anthony Harvey remarks that had the catalogue come from a philosopher or a sage, such great ordeals successfully overcome would be a very powerful testimony to the strength of human endurance. However, it is in the midst of heated polemics against his opponents and critics that Paul refers to those ordeals from which he suffered physically and mentally.

As one whose thinking has consistently been a drastic inversion of the current social ethos, Paul again surprises his critics by using the catalogue to boast of his weakness, rather than his own strength.[125] Similarly, it is also in a polemical context that Paul, in his concluding remark in Gal. 6.17 refers to the carrying of the 'marks of Jesus' that are branded on his body. It is not for human praise and admiration that Paul uses this vivid body language. Such body language needed to be conveyed so that no one would make trouble for him (Gal. 6.17a). One imagines that at the back of Paul's mind, just like in 2 Cor. 11 where his many ordeals are itemised, is the theology of the cross: 'May I never boast of anything except the cross of our Lord Jesus Christ, by which the world has been crucified to me, and I to the world' (Gal. 6.14).

11.31 ὁ θεὸς καὶ πατὴρ τοῦ κυρίου Ἰησοῦ οἶδεν, ὁ ὢν εὐλογητὸς εἰς τοὺς αἰῶνας, ὅτι οὐ ψεύδομαι. (*'The God and Father of the Lord Jesus, (blessed be he forever!) knows that I do not lie.'*) *32* ἐν Δαμασκῷ ὁ ἐθνάρχης Ἀρέτα τοῦ βασιλέως ἐφρούρει τὴν πόλιν Δαμασκηνῶν πιάσαι με, (*'In Damascus, The governor under King Aretas guarded the city of Damascus in order to seize me,'*) *33* καὶ διὰ θυρίδος ἐν σαργάνῃ ἐχαλάσθην διὰ τοῦ τείχους καὶ ἐξέφυγον τὰς χεῖρας αὐτοῦ. (*'but I was let down in a basket through a window in the wall, and escaped from his hands.'*)

Realizing the serious nature of his testimony in 11.23–30, Paul believes it proper to appeal to God the Father as witness to the truth, he states: The God and Father of the Lord Jesus knows that I do not lie (11.31). The incident Paul recalls (11.32, 33) shows that he is indeed not lying, for no liar would publicly recall such an embarrassing story and certainly not in such

---

[125] A. E. HARVEY, *Renewal through Suffering: A Study of 2 Corinthians* (Edinburgh: T. & T. Clark, 1996), 102.

a polemical context as part of a personal *apologia*. On Paul's rather dramatic escape from Damascus, Martin remarks that 'whatever the precise reason for this recall of the Damascus interlude, it is a powerful ironical and playful story, tinged with humor and exactly in place; and it is biographical as well as rhetorical as a parody in form.'[126] Although there is consensus among scholars that the incident in 11.32–33 is not an interpolation, there are, nonetheless, a number of different suggestions to try to explain the recounting of the story here.[127] Furnish makes a persuasive point, which stands out among the many comments made, that this is 'a story about Paul's humiliation, not about his heroism.'[128] The story is intended to give a concrete example of Paul's weakness, since his plan to escape as well as the means used are clear signs of cowardice.[129]

There is nothing heroic about such an escape, especially in comparison to the sages in the Socratic and Stoic traditions. The Socratic or Stoic idea of bravery, with its emphasis on manliness, never seems to have crossed Paul's mind. This point also serves as a warning to any attempt to try to compare the Greco-Roman sages or philosophers with Paul, the 'fool' and δοῦλος of Christ. The weak apostle hardly fits into Cicero's ideal of the brave and wise: '… when the Wise Man is suffering torments of pain, he will say "How pleasant this is! How little I mind"' (*Fin.* 5.27.80)![130]

Paul is also not keen to be an 'Olympic victor', which is Epictetus' concern with regards to training and discipline, as he puts it in *Diss.* 1.24.1–2: 'It is difficulties that show what men are. Consequently, when a difficulty befalls, remember that God, like a physical trainer, has matched you with a rugged young man. What for? Someone says, so that you may become an Olympic victor; but that cannot be done without sweat.'

It is necessary to bear in mind that in some ways Paul actually was brave as well as disciplined, even by Stoic standards (e.g. when facing violent mobs, rulers of various importance and type, catastrophes, etc.). Moreover, as one who is 'always carrying in the body the death of Jesus' (2 Cor. 4.10) or 'the marks of Jesus' (Gal. 6.17), Paul may well be said to be as equally prepared as the Stoics for the expected as well as unexpected; indeed, even death itself. Paul is equally well prepared because he is absolutely convinced that neither death, life, angels, rulers, things present,

---

[126] MARTIN, *2 Corinthians*, 371, 372.

[127] THRALL, *II Corinthians*, 763.

[128] FURNISH, *II Corinthians*, 542.

[129] THRALL, *II Corinthians*, 764.

[130] Cicero, *Pis.* 42: '… the wise man, even were he to be shut up in the bull of Phalaris and roasted above a fire, would assert that he was happy and felt perfect calm of mind. What they meant was that the power of virtue is so great that the good man can never be otherwise than happy.' *Off.* 2.11.38: '… for no one can be just who fears death or pain or exile or poverty, or who values their opposites above equity.'

things to come, powers, height, depth or anything else in creation is able to separate the believer from the love of God in Christ Jesus our Lord (Rom. 8.38–39).

There is yet another fundamental point, one noted previously, which is to caution when making a positive comparison between Greco-Roman sages (e.g. Socrates) and Paul. This is especially the case of efforts which tend to extol and glorify the philosopher's great courage and composure as an analogue or explanation of Paul's apparent weakness. In stark contrast to Socrates' dualism, which regards the physical body as essentially evil and death as the liberation of the soul from the burdensome body, Paul takes the human body as a divine gift, even as a temple of the holy spirit (1 Cor. 6.19). As such, the suffering and mutilation of the body became all the more painful for Paul both physically and spiritually. This point needs to be seriously considered when discussing suffering and hardship in which the human body and body language are deeply involved.

Although Paul manages to bear bodily pains by the enabling power and grace of his Lord, at no point does the suffering apostle indicate that these pains are not real. He does not indicate that they are easy to bear or that he does not mind them. Perhaps one may be justified in inferring that Paul is not as detached as his Greco-Roman counterparts in matters of corporal sufferings. Even if Paul's physical endurance could be compared to those of his Greco-Roman counterparts, his real concern is not 'endurance' (ὑπομονή) as such, nor is it other virtues, but rather divine power and glory revealed in his weakness. It is not some kind of moral ideal, however noble, that occupied the troubled mind of the apostle (troubled because he never claims to have the kind of steel mind expected of Stoics like Seneca), but the kind of daily pressure and the anxiety for all the churches (e.g. in 2 Cor. 11.28). Conceptually, no moral ideal or sophisticated philosophy of the present world order provided the kind of mental and spiritual resources and inspiration that would enable the apostle to sustain his *modus operandi*, except his understanding of the cross.

8.4 Conclusion

In the ancient Greco-Roman world, a man had to be assertive if he wanted to establish himself in this competitive society. This is demonstrated in the study of Greco-Roman rhetoric, especially with reference to the crucial matter of self-presentation which involved both oral and bodily delivery (body language). Therefore, when Paul deliberately and unashamedly states that if he were to boast at all it would be in his weakness, it should be perceived as another inversion of the current social ethos: 'if I must boast, I will boast of the things that show my weakness' (2 Cor. 11.30). In this particular case, the things that show his weakness would undoubtedly include his escape from Damascus (11.32, 33) as well as the catalogue of ordeals he supplies earlier in 11.23–28, and which concludes with a personal confession: 'Who is weak, and I am not weak?' (11.29). Paul's confession appears to mean that he is just an ordinary man of flesh and blood, and most certainly not the kind of superman that the Greco-Roman sages and wise philosophers were often thought to be or claimed to be. As such, any talk about true masculinity would be nothing more than a bad joke in the case of the apostle.

Paul's escape from the hands of King Aretas in Damascus would have been regarded as an embarrassing act of cowardice. No true 'Socrates' would ever have done that. As to the catalogue of hardship in 11.23–28, the wise and virtuous sages would only use it to establish themselves in the status-hungry Greco-Roman society, and no sane man would ever use it as a confession of one's own weakness. As such, only the 'fool' in the ancient mime would perhaps do so. However, for the sake of Christ as well as for the message of the cross, Paul willingly became the 'fool' of Christ. No inversion of the social ethos is more drastic than this.

As far as Paul is concerned, the confession of his own personal weakness is not only meant to be, paradoxically, a powerful testimony to divine grace in his own life, but also an authentication of his apostleship which was in serious dispute due particularly to the strong challenge of the 'super-apostles' (11.5). This point is made clearly in the strong and unambiguous statement Paul makes just prior to the listing of his many ordeals. 'Are they servants of Christ,' he asks. Then he states that he is talking like a madman before declaring he is a better servant with far greater labours and having endured countless floggings (11.23).

Important to note at this point is that if it were not for the provocation and challenge of his opponents, Paul would most probably not have referred to his suffering and ordeals in such a manner. The expressions, 'I am speaking as a fool' (11.21) and 'I am talking like a madman' (11.23) suggest the provocative and polemical nature of his catalogue of ordeals. Moreover, while the suffering of Christ is not explicitly mentioned in chapter 11, it is reasonable to assume that it would probably have been in the mind of Paul whenever his own suffering was mentioned or hinted at. As one who so fully identifies himself with Christ crucified, to have such a mind would be natural. It is also in close connection to this assumption that a brief cross-reference has been made to the relevant verses in Galatians and Philippians in the above exegesis. Just as Christ's sacrificial suffering is the authentic mark of his messiahship, so Paul's affliction could also be regarded as the sure sign of his apostleship.

One suspects that Paul's opponents, amongst them the 'super-apostles', most likely could not have produced a more impressive list of afflictions than what Paul has. Paul's statement, 'with far more imprisonment, with countless floggings' (11.23) implies that such was likely the case. Even if Paul's opponents were able to list something equal or even more impressive, they would probably have employed it in accordance to the Greco-Roman tradition. It is most unlikely that they would have used it in the way that Paul does. There is a temptation to suggest that Paul in fact uses his *peristasis* catalogues here in 11.23–33 and in other places (cf. 1 Cor. 4.9–13; 2 Cor. 6.4–5) out of careful strategic consideration. Even if this were the case, the perceptive apostle would have been keenly aware of the risk he was taking when he boasts of his weakness, rather than strength.

Unless the Corinthians perceived the paradox that it is precisely in Paul's human weakness that divine power is made manifest and effective, then there was no way that they would acknowledge and accept his apostolic authority. According to this way of thinking, it was impossible for mere humans to ever conceive that any leader could have real authority and exercise it in weakness.

Judging from the overall background of the Corinthians, who had yet to be set free from the social ethos of the time, the likelihood of them being able to understand and appreciate what Paul said did not appear promising. In the final analysis, the whole issue is profoundly theological, although the background behind the Corinthian polemics is also deeply social. As such, it would really have required a considerable grasp of Paul's theology, especially the theology of the cross, to discern the real crux of his message to them. However, such discernment would understandably be hard to expect from the average Corinthian at that point of time.

Conclusion

Powerful and effective means to use body language have been viewed in relation to three areas: (1) crucifixion and the idea of noble death in antiquity; (2) Greco-Roman rhetoric, especially its preoccupation with delivery and masculinity; and (3) the Greco-Roman concept of περίστασις. Socio-historical studies of these three subjects have provided the necessary contexts to exegete the relevant passages in Paul's Corinthian polemics. Together with the interpretation of pertinent Corinthian passages it has been demonstrated that there is indeed a conscious attempt on the part of Paul to invert the current social ethos in his polemics and that body language is one vital link between these three dimensions of his theology and social practice.

Throughout this study there has been an attempt to maintain a balance between the socio-historical and the exegetical-theological. This desired balance is reflected in both the contents and proportions of the work. Connecting the three parts is body language in the three areas of study.

The focus of *Part I* is the socio-historical studies on crucifixion in antiquity based on primary literature. In order to demonstrate socio-historically many of the more horrible and disturbing aspects of human degradation in crucifixion, a number of examples have been discussed based upon these ancient sources together with modern scholarly views on them. Special weight is given to the crucifixion of people from the lower strata of society, including slaves and sometimes Jews, because this detestable form of capital punishment was commonly applied to them, including Jesus. The humiliation that the crucified victims endured in some of the cases cited is straightforward and needs very little elucidation.

The public nature of crucifixion, the kind of body language conveyed by the crucified victims and the entire scene of execution made this form of capital punishment the most horrific and cruellest manner of human death known from antiquity. Thus, the cross became not only a powerful visual symbol, but also a very striking form of body language. Cases of crucifixion and the commentaries on them are not made in a vacuum, but rather in the concrete and harsh reality of their socio-historical contexts which moulded and shaped the social ethos of Paul's time. In this study on crucifixion, the question is addressed why Paul's 'message of the cross' was such obvious 'folly' and great offence within the Greco-Roman world.

Following on from the study of crucifixion is an analysis of the idea of noble death in both Greco-Roman and Maccabean traditions. In these contextual studies, an important background is provided for the exegesis of 1 Cor. 1.18–31. Since it is assumed that Paul was knowledgeable about the

practice of crucifixion and current public perception of it, his acknowledgement that the message of the cross was foolishness (1.18) and his decision to know nothing except Jesus Christ and him crucified (2.2) could
reasonably be interpreted as a clear intention to present values that stood in
contrast to those of the Corinthian society at large.

The classic example of noble death in the Greco-Roman tradition,
which is given significant attention is most likely the death of Socrates, the
philosopher *par excellence*. For Jews, the classic example known is the
martyrdom of the Maccabees. In marked contrast, the crucifixion of Christ
was the most ignoble death in the eyes of the Greco-Roman world, and
may be viewed as a terrible 'curse' according to the Hebrew Scriptures
(Deut. 21.23). Paradoxically, it is this negative side of the comparison, especially between Socrates and Christ, which is the most significant, revealing and challenging from a Christian perspective. This is because it brings
out sharply the uniqueness of Christ crucified, making Paul's message of
the cross such utter μωρία and σκάνδαλον to the world, turning its ethos
completely upside down. Moreover, according to the main categories of
the crucified victims, which are identified as the crucifixion of rebels,
lower class people, slaves and Jews, Jesus could be said to have died the
death of each category. This point is seen to have profound significance in
relation to the description of the foolishness of the message of the cross.

When it comes to the message of the cross being perceived as foolishness (1.18–31), Paul needed to deal with some of the most crucial and
complex issues arising in his Corinthian correspondence. These issues included dealing with the wisdom, power and status which would have been
the most sought-after in Greco-Roman society. Methodologically, Paul
skilfully uses antithetical and paradoxical ways of speaking. He first de-
thrones the 'wisdom of the wise' with the perceived 'foolishness' of 'the
message of the cross' and puts in its place the power and wisdom of God,
which is revealed in and demonstrated through the crucified Christ. However, both the power and wisdom of God are not conceived by the apostle
in abstraction, but in and through the crucified body of Christ which, as a
medium, communicated *vis-à-vis* powerful body language, and which demanded a response from those who heard about it to either accept it for
their own salvation or reject it for their own damnation (1.18).

The main problem with the self-conceited Corinthians is that of boastfulness, which was most likely the main contributing factor to their divisions. Paul's paradoxical approach left them no grounds for human boasting, because even by worldly standards, or within their cherished social
ethos, not many of them were actually wise, powerful and of noble birth
(1.26). Here lies the great divine paradox: God chose what was foolish to
shame the wise, the 'weak' to shame the 'strong'; God chose things that
'were not' to reduce to nothing things that 'were' (1.27, 28). In the end,

what is presented by Paul in 1.18–31 is a revolution of immense proportions. Perhaps no inversion of the current social ethos could be more radical.

Having dethroned the wisdom of the world and reaffirmed God's wisdom and power in His calling of those who were being saved, Paul concludes his polemics by simply, but most significantly, reminding the Corinthians that Christ alone had now become for them wisdom from God,
righteousness, sanctification and redemption. The Corinthians should now
fully understand their calling and identity on this basis alone. If anyone
dared to boast, they were to boast in (or of) the Lord, but boasting could
only be justified on this basis (1.31).

Part II focuses primarily on aspects of delivery and masculinity as they
relate to Greco-Roman rhetoric. Because much of the Corinthian polemics
have to do with human eloquence and one's self-presentation in society it
is necessary to address how this relates to the social context. Indeed, not
only is there a need to deal with this setting, but also to navigate the ever
growing number of scholarly views on the subject. It was in rhetoric, especially the orator's delivery, that body language was most obvious and
powerful in displaying some of the most important traits of masculinity.
With this background in mind, the exegesis of 1 Cor. 2.1–5 and 2 Cor.
10.10 endeavours to explain why Paul deliberately chose not to use lofty
words or wisdom in Corinth, and why his bodily presence was so adversely
perceived by his Corinthian critics. Paul's decision to refrain from following the current social conventions in his proclamation of the gospel, especially as this included self-presentation, is understood as a clear indication
that he intended to act in a manner distinctly contrary to what society expected of an orator.

The view is taken that what has been said about rhetoric in the Greco-
Roman tradition also pertains to Corinth. Not only is the Corinthian opponents' criticism of Paul a clear reflection of the social ethos of the time, the
apostle's response is also indicative of his knowledge about the whole issue, otherwise his polemics in passages such as 1 Cor. 2.1–5 and 2 Cor.
10.10 would be quite unintelligible to his readers. While Paul, on the one
hand, decides not to resort to current rhetorical practice in his proclamation
of the gospel, his determination to know nothing among the Corinthians
except Jesus Christ and him crucified (1 Cor. 2.2) is, in itself, a most ironical and paradoxical manner of affirming the power and effect of body language. Given the socio-historical background of crucifixion and its implications in Paul's time, it would have been virtually impossible for the
apostle's contemporaries not to think about the kind of body language
which the crucifixion of Christ conveyed. Although in 1 Cor. 2.1–5 and 2
Cor. 10.10 Paul may seem less concerned with his message of the cross
and more concerned with his manner of delivery as well as his personal

appearance, it needs to be pointed out again that for Paul his message could hardly be separated from his delivery.

Part III concentrates on the study of περίστασις with special reference to Stoicism which uses it positively. This is followed by a close look at the flipside of περίστασις. The humiliating and humanly degrading aspects of the lists are highlighted and studied in close relation to Paul's personal tribulations mentioned in the Corinthian correspondence. Similar to crucifixion, noble death, rhetoric and delivery, the kind of body language which Paul's personal tribulations conveyed is equally clear and thus more relevant. It should be noted that the pain, sufferings and punishments were actually inflicted on Paul's physical body according to his *peristasis* catalogues (1 Cor. 4.8–13; 2 Cor. 11.23–33).

Generally speaking, the Stoic attitude towards hardship was basically positive and the reasons for this have been provided. This, however, is only one side of the coin. There is also the other side of the coin, which is a tradition in Greco-Roman society that viewed hardship, especially its physical aspects, with contempt and suspicion. Hardship was regarded as personally and socially degrading, and thus unworthy of true manliness. It is contended that this negative perspective is in view when Paul's Corinthian critics judge the apostle's hardship. Moreover, it is likely from a similarly negative position that Paul presents his περίστασις, in order to witness to the power of God in his degradation and humiliation. This use of the lists also demonstrates how Paul's preaching functions paradoxically when set within his social context.

In the opening investigation on *peristasis* catalogues, extensive references to classical Greek and Roman authors are provided. These lists are seen to represent a view that adversity was commonly regarded as a true test of the sage's manliness, courage and endurance. For lack of substantial evidence in the writings of Paul, it is difficult to be certain if he was aware of the tradition. However, on the basis of the apostle's vast knowledge and learning about Jewish practice and tradition as well as Hellenistic ones, it may be assumed that he was indeed aware. Nonetheless, the view taken is that Paul most likely did not use *peristasis* catalogues according to the classical tradition (i.e. positively to demonstrate or prove his own human endurance and courage so that glory and honour might be conferred upon him). To do so would be to rob God of His glory and honour, and this would be the last thing that the δοῦλος of Christ wanted to do.

It is rather the negative or derogatory use of the *peristasis* catalogues which is the main concern of Paul because only in this way was he able to witness the divine power manifested in and through his own weakness. Only in this manner is he able to boast of his own weakness, an idea which would certainly be considered absurd according to the thinking of the time. For Paul, it is precisely this perceived absurdity that makes his message of the cross such a drastic inversion of the social ethos. When 1 Cor. 4.8–13 and 2 Cor. 11.23–33 are interpreted, the results indicate that this view of the *peristasis* catalogues is consistent with Paul's own *modus operandi* as well as his intention to challenge the values of the Corinthian community. The current social ethos held manly virtues such as courage, endurance, power and strength in the highest regard – Paul came to proclaim humility in suffering which could overcome the world.

In the ancient Greco-Roman world, a man had to be assertive if he wanted to establish himself in this competitive society. It must, therefore, be perceived as another inversion of the current social ethos when Paul deliberately and unashamedly states that if he were to boast at all, it would be in the area of his weakness (2 Cor. 11.30). As such, perhaps only the fool in the ancient mime would do so. However, for the sake of Christ as well as for the message of the cross, Paul willingly becomes the fool of Christ. No inversion could be more drastic than this.

As far as Paul is concerned, the confession of his own personal weakness is not only meant to be, paradoxically, a powerful testimony to divine grace in his own life, but also an authentication of his apostleship which was seriously disputed due particularly to the strong challenge of the so-called 'super-apostles' (2 Cor. 11.5) and the like. This point is made clearly in the strong and unambiguous statement Paul makes just prior to the listing of his many ordeals (11.23). At this juncture, it is also noteworthy that, if not for the provocation and challenge of his opponents, Paul would most likely not have referred to his own suffering and ordeals in such a manner. The expressions 'I am speaking as a fool' (11.21) and 'I am talking like a madman' (11.23) suggest the provocative and polemical nature of his catalogue of ordeals.

This study has been built upon the broad shoulders of many scholars. As such, it is recognised that much of the discussion about crucifixion, noble death, Greco-Roman rhetoric and περίστασις is indebted to studies on these subjects. One contribution made to these subjects is the presentation of primary classical sources. Moreover, sustained attention to the ancient literature together with a number of ongoing dialogues has helped demonstrate the validity of the overall hypothesis presented throughout.

The idea of body language is certainly not novel in New Testament studies generally or Pauline studies more specifically. What may be considered new or original, in relative terms, is the attempt to identify them consistently in each of the three parts: (1) crucifixion and noble death; (2) rhetoric, especially in its emphasis on self-presentation and delivery; and (3) περίστασις, with special reference to Paul's own bodily suffering and pain and the body language it conveyed socially and symbolically.

The emphasis throughout the study has been that of inversion. The appropriateness of this term is justified in the presentation and argument of the three areas of study. Paul is seen to have had a clear intention to invert the current social ethos when responding to the Corinthian crisis. Admittedly, 'inversion' is a strong term which needs some justification. Indeed, the value and originality of this study hinges on the appropriateness of the use of the word. In a way, the argument on this important point is rather straightforward. Unlike the Corinthians, including his Corinthian critics who followed the current Greco-Roman ethos, Paul was operating within a worldview which was diametrically opposed to it.

Opposition may be viewed on a number of important occasions. Paul places divine and human wisdom in diametrically opposing positions. The socio-historical study on crucifixion shows, almost beyond a shadow of doubt, that the cross was symbolic of some of the most detestable and abhorrent aspects in Greco-Roman society. It is in this context that Paul is keenly aware that the message of the cross is foolishness to those who are perishing (1 Cor. 1.18). Yet, despite the apostle's full knowledge of it, he overtly declares that he has decided to know nothing among the Corinthians except Jesus Christ and him crucified (2.2). Similarly, knowing full well the importance of rhetoric, especially its emphasis on self-presentation, eloquence and wisdom, Paul again openly announces that his speech and proclamation are not with plausible words of wisdom (2.4). Moreover, while the sage in Greco-Roman society would refer to περίστασις to show his manly virtues, Paul deliberately uses them to boast of his own weakness (2 Cor. 11.30).

On a number of occasions a clear intention on the part of Paul is identified to invert the current social ethos. This determination seems clear from the start of the Corinthian correspondence, where Paul tries to deconstruct the firmly established values and perspectives concerning wisdom, eloquence and social status (1 Cor. 1.18–31).

In conclusion, this study attempts, in each of its three parts (crucifixion in antiquity, Greco-Roman rhetoric and *peristasis*), to locate Paul's theology of the cross within its socio-historical context. The body language employed by the apostle Paul provides a vital link between these three. It also demonstrates that Paul intends to invert the current Greco-Roman social ethos in language that is both paradoxical and provocative. The placing of Paul's message in its socio-historical setting intends to restore how the message would have been heard in its original context.

The concern of this work is not only with understanding the apostle's theology from a historical point of view. As an integral part of Christian Scripture, the Corinthian correspondence is also meaningful for the present and future. Therefore, the task of those who take Paul's message of the cross seriously is to consider and reflect on it within their own respective contexts. Although the task here has not been relating the original context of Paul's message of the cross to the many settings in which his words

resonate today, there can be little doubt that relating the two brings significant depth and meaning to the message. Indeed, Paul's message of the
cross, when listened to within its social context, is not made remote, but
rather more relevant, meaningful and challenging for communities today.

Bibliography

1. Primary Texts

Apostolic Fathers, vol. I, eds. G. P. Goold, *et al.*, trans. Kirsopp Lake (Loeb Classical Library; Cambridge, Harvard University Press, 1985).

Aristotle, *The 'Art' of Rhetoric*, vol. XXII, eds. G. P. Goold, *et al.*, trans. John Henry Freese (Loeb Classical Library; London: William Heinemann Ltd, 1926).

_____, *Ethica Nicomachea*, vol. XIX, eds. G. P. Goold, *et al.*, trans. H. Rackham (Loeb Classical Library; Cambridge, Harvard University Press, 1934).

_____, *Poetics*, eds. G. P. Goold, *et al.*, trans. S. Halliwell; Longinus, *On the Sublime*, trans. W.H. Fyfe; Demetrius, *On style*, trans. W.R. Roberts (Loeb Classical Library; London: William Heinemann Ltd, 1932).

_____, *Poetics* and Demetrius, *On style,* ed. Rev. T. A. Moxon (London: J. M. Dent, 1949)

_____, *Politics*, eds. T. E. Page, *et al.*, trans. H. Rackham (Loeb Classical Library; London: William Heinemann Ltd, 1932).

Artemidorus, *Oneirocritica*, trans. Robert J. White (Torrance, Calif: Original Books, 1990).

Augustine, *De civitate Dei*, vol. I–VII, eds. T. E. Page, *et al.*, trans. G. E. MaCrachen, *et al.* (Loeb Classical Library; London: William Heinemann Ltd, 1957–72).

Cassius, Dio Cocceianus, *Roman History*, vol. I–IX, eds. T. E. Page, *et al.*, trans. E. Cary (Loeb Classical Library; London: William Heinemann Ltd, 1914–27).

Cicero, Marcus Tullius, *Brutus and Orator*, eds. T. E. Page, *et al.*, trans. G. L. Hendrickson and H. M. Hubbell (Loeb Classical Library; London: William Heinemann Ltd, 1939).

_____, *De Finibus Bonorum Et Malorum*, eds. T. E. Page, *et al.*, trans. H. Rackham (Loeb Classical Library; London: William Heinemann Ltd, 1961).

_____, *De Inventione, De Optimo Genere Oratorum, Topica*, eds. T. E. Page, *et al.*, trans. H.M. Hubbell (Loeb Classical Library; London: William Heinemann Ltd, 1949).

_____, *De Natura Deorum, Academica*, eds. T.E. Page, *et al.*, trans. H. Rackham (Loeb Classical Library; London: William Heinemann Ltd, 1930).

_____, *De Officiis*, eds. T. E. Page, *et al.*, trans. W. Miller (Loeb Classical Library; London: William Heinemann Ltd, 1961).

_____, *De Oratore*, vol. II, eds. T. E. Page, *et al.*, Trans. H. Rackham (Loeb Classical Library; London: William Heinemann Ltd, 1942).

_____, *De Partitione Oratoria*, vol. IV, eds. E. H. Warmington, *et al.*, trans. H. Rackham (Loeb Classical Library; London: William Heinemann Ltd, 1968).

_____, *De Re Publica, De Legibus*, eds. T. E. Page, *et al.*, trans. Clinton Walker Keyes (Loeb Classical Library; London: William Heinemann Ltd, 1929).

_____, *Letters to Atticus*, vol. II, eds. G. P. Goold, *et al.*, trans. E. O. Winsted (Loeb Classical Library; Cambridge, Harvard University Press, 1984).

_____, *Philippics*, eds. T. E. Page, *et al.*, trans. Walter C. A. Ker (Loeb Classical Library; London: William Heinemann Ltd, 1951).

_____, *Pro Milone, In Pisonem, Pro Scauro, Pro Fonteio, Pro Rabirio Postumo, Pro Marcello, Pro Ligario, Pro Rege Deiottaro*, vol. XIV, eds. Jeffrey Henderson and G. P. Goold, trans. N. H. Watts (Loeb Classical Library; Cambridge, Harvard University Press, 2000).

_____, *The Speeches: Pro lege Manilia, Pro Caecina, Pro Cluentio,Pro Rabirio Perduellionis*, eds. T.E. Page, *et al.*, trans. H. Grose Hodge (Loeb Classical Library; London: William Heinemann Ltd, 1927).

_____, *The Verrine Orations*, vol. I–II, eds. T. E. Page, *et al.*, trans. L. H. G. Greenwood (Loeb Classical Library; London: William Heinemann Ltd, 1928–35).

_____, *Tusculan Disputations*, vol. XVIII, eds. Jeffrey Henderson and G. P. Goold, trans. J. E. King (Loeb Classical Library; Cambridge, Harvard University Press, 2001).

[Cicero], *Rhetorica ad Herennium*, eds. G. P. Goold, *et al.*, trans. Harry Caplan (Loeb Classical Library; Cambridge, Harvard University Press, 1981).

Curtius Rufus, Quintus, *Historia Alexandri Magni*, vol. I–II, eds. T. E. Page, *et al.*, trans. J. C. Rolfe (Loeb Classical Library; London: Heinemann, 1946).

Dio Chrysostom, *Works,* vol. I–V, eds. T. E. Page, *et al.*, trans. J. W. Cohoon (Loeb Classical Library; London: William Heinemann Ltd, 1932–51).

Diodorus Siculus, *Bibliotheca Historica,* vol. 1–V (Lipsiae: In aedibus B. G. Teubneri, 1888–1906).

Diogenes Laertius, *Lives of Eminent Philosophers*, vol. I–II, eds. T. E. Page, *et al.*, trans. R. D. Hicks (Loeb Classical Library; London: William Heinemann Ltd, 1925).

Dionysius of Halicarnassus, *The Critical Essays*, vol. I–II, eds. E. H. Warmington, *et al.*, trans. Stephen Usher (Loeb Classical Library; Cambridge, Harvard University Press, 1974–85).

Ennius, Quintus, *Annales*, ed. Otto Skutsch (Oxford: Clarendon Press; New York: Oxford University Press, 1985).

Epictetus, eds. E. Capps, *et al.*, trans. W. A. Oldfather (Loeb Classical Library; London: William Heinemann Ltd, 1927).

Eusebius, Bishop of Caesarea, *Historia Ecclesiastica*, vol. I–II, eds. T. E. Page, *et al.*, trans. K. Lake (Loeb Classical Library; London: William Heinemann Ltd, 1926–32).

Gaius, Institutes, vol. I–II, trans. Francis de Zulueta (Oxford: Clarendon Press, 1946–53)

Gellius, Aulus, *The Attic Nights,* vol. I–III, eds. E. Capps, *et al.*, trans. J. C. Rolfe (Loeb Classical Library; London: William Heinemann Ltd, 1927–28).

Gorgias, of Leontini, *Encomium of Helen,* trans. D. M. MacDowell (Bristol: Bristol Classical Press, 1982).

Herodotus, vol. II, eds. T. E. Page, *et al.*, trans. A. D. Godley (Loeb Classical Library; London: William Heinemann Ltd, 1928).

Horace, *Satires, Epistles, and Ars Poetica*, eds. T. E. Page, *et al.*, trans. H. Rushton Fairclough (Loeb Classical Library; London: William Heinemann Ltd, 1929).

Ignatius, Bishop of Antioch, *Epistolae*, trans. J. H. Srawley (London: SPCK, 1900).

Isocrates, *Antidosis*, vol. II, eds. T. E. Page, *et al.*, trans. George Norlin (Loeb Classical Library; London: William Heinemann Ltd, 1930).

_____, *Oration to Philip*, vol. I, eds. T. E. Page, *et al.*, trans. George Norlin (Loeb Classical Library; London: William Heinemann Ltd, 1930).

_____, *Panegyricus*, vol. I, eds. T. E. Page, *et al.*, trans. George Norlin (Loeb Classical Library; London: William Heinemann Ltd, 1930).

John Chrysostom, *The Homilies of S. John Chrysostom, Archbishop of Constantinople: on the first Epistle of St. Paul the Apostle to the Corinthians* (Oxford; London: Parker: Rivington, 1839), Part 1, Homilies 1–24.

Josephus, Flavius, *Jewish Antiquities*, vol. I–IX, eds. T. E. Page, *et al.*, trans. Ralph Marcus (Loeb Classical Library; London: William Heinemann Ltd, 1937–62).

_____, *The Jewish War*, vol. I–IX, eds. T. E. Page, *et al.*, trans. H. St. J. Thackeray (Loeb Classical Library; London: William Heinemann Ltd, 1930–61).

Justin Martyr, Saint, Dialogue with Trypho (Berlin; New York: Walter de Gruyter, 1997).

_____, *Apologies*, trans. Leslie William Barnard (New York: Paulist Press, 1997).

Juvenal, *Juvenal and Persius*, eds. G. P. Goold, *et al.*, trans. G. G. Ramsay (Loeb Classical Library; London: William Heinemann Ltd, 1940).

Livy, *Works,* vol. I–VIII, eds. T. E. Page, *et al.*, trans. Frank Gardner Moore, *et al.* (Loeb Classical Library; Cambridge, Mass.: Harvard University Press; London: William Heinemann Ltd, 1919–59).

Lucian, *De morte Peregrini*, vol. V, eds. T. E. Page, *et al.*, trans. A. M. Harmon (Loeb Classical Library; London: William Heinemann Ltd, 1961).

_____, *Iudicium vocalium*, vol. I, eds. T. E. Page, *et al.*, trans. A. M. Harmon (Loeb Classical Library; London: William Heinemann Ltd, 1961).

_____, *Works*, vol. I–VIII, eds. T. E. Page, *et al.*, trans. A. M. Harmon (Loeb Classical Library; Cambridge, Mass.: Harvard University Press; London: William Heinemann Ltd, 1913–67).

Marcus Aurelius, *Meditations,* ed. C. R. Haines, trans. C. R. Haines (Loeb Classical Library; London: William Heinemann Ltd, 1930).

Minucius Felix, eds.T. E. Page, *et al.*, trans. W. C. A. Kerr (Loeb Classical Library; London: William Heinemann Ltd, 1934).

Origen, *Contra Celsum* (Augustae Vindelicorum: [Imprimebat David Franck], 1605).

_____, *Contra Celsum* (Cambridge: University Press, 1953)

Petronius Arbiter, *Satyricon*, trans. P. G. Walsh (Oxford world's classics; Oxford: Oxford University Press, 1999).

Philo, vol. I–X, eds. T. E. Page, *et al.*, trans. F. H. Colson and G. H. Whitaker (Loeb Classical Library; London: William Heinemann Ltd, 1930–62).

Philodemus, *De Rhetorica,* ed. Siegfried Sudhaus (Amsterdam: Hakkert, 1964).

Philostratus, *The Life of Apollonius of Tyana, the Epistles of Apollonius, and the Treatise of Eusebius,* vol. I–II, eds. G. P. Goold, *et al.*, trans. F. C. Conybeare (Loeb Classical Library; London: William Heinemann Ltd, 1912).

Plato, *Euthyphro, Apology, Crito, Phaedo, Phaedrus*, eds. E. H. Warmington, *et al.*, trans. Harold North Fowler (Loeb Classical Library; London: William Heinemann Ltd, 1971).

_____, *Laches, Protagoras, Meno, Euthydemus* eds. T. E. Page, *et al.*, trans. W. R. M. Lamb (Loeb Classical Library; London: William Heinemann Ltd, 1962).

_____, *Lysis, Symposium, Gorgias,* vol. III, eds. G. P. Goold, *et al.*, trans. W. R. M. Lamb (Loeb Classical Library; Cambridge, Harvard University Press, 1975).

_____, *Laws*, vol. II, eds. E. Capps, *et al.*, trans. R. G. Bury (Loeb Classical Library; London: William Heinemann Ltd, 1931).

_____, *Republic*, vol. I, eds. T. E. Page, *et al.*, trans. Paul Shorey (Loeb Classical Library; London: William Heinemann Ltd, 1953).

_____, *Theaetetus, Sophist*, vol. II, eds. E. Capps, *et al.*, trans. H. N. Fowler (Loeb Classical Library; London: William Heinemann Ltd, 1921).

Plautus, Titus Maccius, *Works*, vol. I–V, eds. T. E. Page, *et al.*, trans. Paul Nixon (Loeb Classical Library; London: William Heinemann Ltd, 1916–38).

Pliny, *Letters*, vol. I–II, eds. E. Capps, *et al.*, trans. W. Melmoth (Loeb Classical Library; London: William Heinemann Ltd, 1923–24).

Plutarch, *Lives*, vol. I–XI, eds. E. Capps, *et al.*, trans. Bernadotte Perrin (Loeb Classical Library; London: William Heinemann Ltd, 1914–26).

_____, *Moralia*, vol. III, eds. T. E. Page, *et al.*, trans. Frank Cole Babbitt (Loeb Classical Library; London: William Heinemann Ltd, 1931).

_____, *Moralia*, vol. IX, eds. T. E. Page, *et al.*, trans. Edwin L. Minar (Loeb Classical Library; London: William Heinemann Ltd, 1961).

_____, *Moralia*, vol. XIII, eds. G. P. Goold, *et al.*, trans. Harold Cherniss (Loeb Classical Library; Cambridge, Harvard University Press, 1976).

Propertius, eds. E. Capps, *et al.*, trans. H. E. Butler (Loeb Classical Library; London: William Heinemann Ltd, 1912).

Quintilian, *Instititio Oratoria*, vol. I–III, eds. Jeffrey Henderson and G. P. Goold, trans. Donald A. Russell (Loeb Classical Library; Cambridge, Harvard University Press, 2001).

_____, *Instititio Oratoria*, vol. IV–V, eds. E. Capps, *et al.*, trans. H. E. Butler (Loeb Classical Library; London: William Heinemann Ltd, 1926).

Seneca, Lucius Annaeus, *Apocolocyntosis*, ed. P. T. Eden (Loeb Classical Library; Cambridge: Cambridge University Press, 1984).

_____, Lucius Annaeus, *Epistulae Morales*, vol. I–III, eds. T. E. Page, *et al.*, trans. John W. Basore (Loeb Classical Library; London: William Heinemann Ltd, 1928–35).

Suetonius, vol. I–II, eds. T. E. Page, *et al.*, trans. J. C. Rolfe (Loeb Classical Library; London: William Heinemann Ltd, 1920).

Tacitus, *Annals*, vol. V, eds. E. H. Warmington, *et al.*, trans. John Jackson (Loeb Classical Library; Cambridge, Harvard University Press, 1937).

_____, *Histories*, vol. II, eds.T. E. Page, *et al.*, trans. John Jackson (Loeb Classical Library; London: William Heinemann Ltd, 1962).

Tertullian, *Apologeticus*, eds.T. E. Page, *et al.*, trans. T. R. Glover (Loeb Classical Library; London: William Heinemann Ltd, 1934).

Valerius Maximus, vol. I, eds. Jeffrey Henderson and G. P. Goold, trans. D. R. Shackleton Bailey (Loeb Classical Library; Cambridge, Harvard University Press, 2000).

Virgil, vol. I–II, eds. G. P. Goold, *et al.*, trans, H. Rushton Fairclough (Loeb Classical Library; Cambridge, Mass.: Harvard University Press; London: William Heinemann Ltd, 1986).

Xenophon, *Agesilaus,* ed. R.W. Taylor (London: Rivingtons, 1880).

_____, *Cyropaedia*, vol. I–II, eds. E. Capps, *et al.*, trans. W. Miller (Loeb Classical Library; London: William Heinemann Ltd, 1914–25).

_____, *Memorabilia*, trans. J. S. Watson, in A. D. Lindsay (ed.), *Socrates Discourses by Plato and Xenophon* (London: J. M. Dent & Sons, Ltd., 1918).

_____, *Memorabilia* and *Oeconomicus*, eds.T. E. Page, *et al.*, trans. E. C. Marchant (London: William Heinemann Ltd, 1923).

2. Commentaries on New Testament Texts

Barrett, C. K., *The First Epistle to the Corinthians* (Black's New Testament Commentaries; London: Adam & Charles Black, 1968).

_____, *The Second Epistle to the Corinthians* (Black's New Testament Commentaries; London: Adam & Charles Black, 1973).

_____, *A Critical and Exegetical Commentary on the Acts of the Apostles* (2 vols.; International Critical Commentary; Edinburgh: T&T Clark, 1998).

Balz, Horst and Gerhard Schneider, *Exegetical Dictionary of the New Testament* (Grand Rapids MI: William B. Eerdmans, 1990).

Best, Ernest, *Second Corinthians* (Interpretation; Atlanta: John Knox, 1987).

Betz, H. D., *Galatians: A Commentary on Paul's Letter to the Churches in Galatia* (Philadelphia: Fortress Press, 1979).

Bruce, F. F., *The Acts of the Apostles* (London: Tyndale Press, 1965).

_____, *The Epistle of Paul to the Galatians: A Commentary on the Greek Text* (New International Greek Testament Commentary; Exeter: The Paternoster Press, 1982).

Collins, R. F., *First Corinthians* (Sacra Pagina Series 7; Collegeville, Minn: Glazier/Liturgical Press, 1999).

Conzelmann, H., *1 Corinthians: A Commentary on the First Epistle to the Corinthians* (*Hermeneia*; Philadelphia: Fortress Press, 1975).

Dunn, J. D. G., *1 Corinthians* (Sheffield: Sheffield Academic Press, 1995)

_____, *The Acts of the Apostles* (Epworth Commentaries; Peterborough: Epworth Press, 1996).

Ellingworth, P. and H. A. Hatton, *Paul's First Letter to the Corinthians* (United Bible Societies Handbook; New York: United Bible Societies, 1994).

Fee, G. D., *The First Epistle to the Corinthians* (New International Commentary on the New Testament; Grand Rapids MI: William B. Eerdmans, 1987).

Furnish, V. P., *II Corinthians* (Anchor Bible 32A; New York: Doubleday, 1984).

Garland, David E., *1 Corinthians* (Baker Exegetical Commentary on the New Testament; Grand Rapids: Baker Academic, 2003).

Harris, Murray J., *The Second Epistle to the Corinthians: A Commentary on the Greek Text* (New International Greek Testament Commentary; Grand Rapids MI: William B. Eerdmans, 2005).

Hays, R. B., *First Corinthians* (Interpretation: A Bible Commentary for Teaching and Preaching; Louisville KY: Wesminster John Knox Press, 1997).

Horsley, R. A., *1 Corinthians* (Abingdon New Testament Commentaries; Nashville: Abingdon Press, 1998).

Hughes, Philip Edgcumbe, *Paul's Second Epistle to the Corinthians: The English Text with Introduction, Exposition and Notes* (New International Commentary on the New Testament; Edinburgh: Marshall, Morgan & Scott, 1962).

Lightfoot, J. B., *Notes on the Epistles of St Paul from Unpublished Commentaries* (London: Macmillan, 1895).

Martyn, J. Louis, *Galatians: A New Translation with Introduction and Commentary* (Anchor Bible 33A; New York; London: Doubleday, 1997).

Martin, Ralph P., *2 Corinthians* (Word Biblical Commentary 40; Waco: Word Books, 1986).

Metzger, Bruce M., *A Textual Commentary on the Greek New Testament: A Companion Volume to the United Bible Societies' Greek New Testament* (4th rev. ed.; Stuttgart; New York: United Bible Societies, 1994).

Plummer, A., *A Critical and Exegetical Commentary on the Second Epistle of St. Paul to the Corinthians* (International Critical Commentary; Edinburgh: T. & T. Clark, 1915).

Robertson, Archibald and Alfred Plummer, *A Critical and Exegetical Commentary: First Epistle of St Paul to the Corinthians* (International Critical Commentary; Edinburgh: T. & T. Clark, 1967).

Schrage, Wolfgang, *Der Erste Brief an die Korinther* (Evangelisch-katholischer Kommentar zum Neuen Testament 7; Zürich: Benziger Verlag, vol. 1, 1991).

Thiselton, A. C., *The First Epistle to the Corinthians: A Commentary on the Greek Text* (New International Greek Testament Commentary; Carlisle: Paternoster Press, 2000).

Thrall, Margaret E., *A Critical and Exegetical Commentary on the Second Epistle to the Corinthians* (2 vols.; International Critical Commentary; Edinburgh: T&T Clark, 1994–2000).

Weiss, J., *Der Erste Korintherbrief* (Kritisch-exegetischer Kommentar über das Neue Testament 5; Göttingen: Vandenhoeck & Ruprecht, 1910).

3. General/Other Works Cited

Adams, E., *Constructing the World: A Study in Paul's Cosmological Language* (Edinburgh: T & T Clark, 2000).

Adams, E. and D. G. Horrell (eds.), *Christianity at Corinth: The Quest for the Pauline Church* (Westminster John Knox Press: Louisville, 2004).

Allegro, J. M., 'Further Light on the History of the Qumran Sect', *Journal of Biblical Literature* 75 (1956), 89–95.

Alston, R., 'Arms and the Man: Soldiers, Masculinity and Power in Republican and Imperial Rome', in L. F. and J. Salmon (eds.), *When Men Were Men: Masculinity, Power, and Identity in Classical Antiquity* (London: Routledge, 1998), 205–23.

Anderson, R. D., *Ancient Rhetorical Theory and Paul* (Kampen: Kok, 1996).

Anderson H. (trans.), '4 Maccabees', in J. H. Charlesworth (ed.), *The Old Testament Pseudepigrapha* (New York: Doubleday & Company, 1985), vol. 2.562–63.

Andrews, S. B., 'Too Weak Not To Lead: The Form and Function of 2 Cor 11.23b–33', *New Testament Studies* 41 (1995), 263–76.

Arnold, E. V., *Roman Stoicism: Being Lectures on the History of the Stoic Philosophy with Special Reference to Its Development within the Roman Empire* (Cambridge: Cambridge University Press, 1911).

Aspegren, K., *The Male Woman: A Feminine Ideal in the Early Church* (Stockholm: Almqvist & Wilksell, 1990).

Balch, D. L., 'Paul's portrait of Christ Crucified (Gal. 3.1) in Light of Paintings and Sculptures of Suffering and Death in Pompeiian and Roman Houses', in D. L. Balch and C. Osiek (eds.), *Early Christian Families in Context: An Interdisciplinary Dialogue* (Grand Rapids: William B. Eerdmans, 2003), 84–108.

Barclay, J. M. G., 'Thessalonica and Corinth: Social Contrasts in Pauline Christianity', *Journal for the Study of the New Testament* 47 (1992), 49–74.

_____, *Jews in the Mediterranean Diaspora* (Edinburgh: T & T Clark, 1996).

_____, '2 Corinthians', in J. D.G. Dunn and J. W. Rogerson (eds.), *Eerdmans Commentary on the Bible* (Grand Rapids, MI: W.B. Eerdmans, 2003), 1353–73.

Barnett, P. W., 'Opposition in Corinth', *Journal for the Study of the New Testament* (1984), 3–17.

Barrett, C. K., 'Christianity at Corinth', *Bulletin of the John Rylands University Library of Manchester* 46 (1964), 269–97.

_____, 'Cephas and Corinth', in *Essays on Paul* (London: SPCK, 1982).

Barton, C. A., *The Sorrows of the Ancient Romans* (Princeton, N. J.: Princeton University Press, 1993).

_____, *Roman Honour* (California: University of California Press, 2001).

Barton, S. C., 'Paul and the Cross: A Sociological Approach', *Theology* 85 (1982), 13–19.

_____, '1 Corinthians', in J. D.G. Dunn and J. W. Rogerson (eds.), *Eerdmans Commentary on the Bible* (Grand Rapids, MI: W.B. Eerdmans, 2003), 1314–52.

Barton, T. S., 'Physionomics: *Voir, Savoir, Pouvoir*', in *Power and Knowledge: Astrology, Physiognomics, and Medicine under the Roman Empire* (Ann Arbor: *University of Michigan Press*, 1994), 95–131.

Bauer, W., *Das Leben Jesu im Zeitalter der neutestamentlichen Apokryphen* (Tübingen: Mohr-Siebeck, 1909; reprinted, 1967).

Bauer, W., F. W. Danker, W. F. Arndt, and F. W. Gingrich, *A Greek-English Lexicon of the New Testament and Other Early Christian Literature* (3rd ed., Chicago: University of Chicago Press, 2000).

Baumgarten, J. M., 'Does TLH in the Temple Scroll Refer to Crucifixion"? *Journal of Biblical Literature* 91 (1972), 472–81.

Baur, F. C., *Paul, The Apostle of Jesus Christ, His Life and Work, His Epistles and His Doctrine* (2 vols.; Edinburgh/London: Williams & Norgate, 1875–76).

Betz, H. D., *Der Apostel Paulus und die sokratische Tradition: Eine exegetische Untersuchung zu seiner „Apologie" 2 Korinther 10–13* (Tübingen: Mohr, 1972).

Betz, H. D. and M. M. Mitchell, 'Corinthians, First Epistle to the', in D. N. Freedman (ed.), *Anchor Bible Dictionary* (6 vols.; New York: Doubleday, 1992), vol. 1.1139–48.

Black, D. A., *Paul, Apostle of Weakness: Astheneia and Its Cognates in the Pauline Literature* (New York: Peter Lang, 1984).

Bonner, S. F., *Education in Ancient Rome* (London: Methuen, 1977).

Bowersock, G. W., *The Second Sophistic: A Cultural Phenomenon in the Roman Empire* (London: Routledge, 1993).

Bradley, K. R., *Slaves and Masters in the Roman Empire: A Study in Social Control* (Oxford: Oxford University Press, 1987).

Brennan, T., *The Stoic Life: Emotions, Duties, and Fate* (Oxford: Oxford University Press, 2005).

Brown, A. R., *The Cross and Human Transformation: Paul's Apocalyptic Word in 1 Corinthians* (Minneapolis: Fortress Press, 1995).

Brown, F., S. R. Driver, and C. A. Briggs (eds.), *A Hebrew and English Lexicon of the Old Testament* (Oxford: Clarendon, 1907).

Buckland, W. W., *The Roman Law of Slavery* (London: Cambridge University Press, 1970).

Bullmore, M. A., *St. Paul's Theology of Rhetorical Style: An Examination of 1 Corinthians 2.1–5 in the Light of First Century Greco-Roman Rhetorical Culture* (San Francisco: International Scholars Publication, 1995).

Burford, A., *Craftsmen in Ancient Greek and Roman Society* (Ithaca: Cornell University Press, 1972).

Caesar, A., *Taking it Like a Man: Suffering, Sexuality and the War Poets: Brooke, Sassoon, Owen, Graves* (Manchester; Manchester University Press, 1993).

Cairns D. L. (ed.), *Body Language in the Greek and Roman World* (Swansea: Classical Press of Wales, 2005)

Carson, D. A., *The Cross and the Christian Ministry: An Exposition of Passages from 1 Corinthians* (Grand Rapids: Baker, 1993).

Chester, S. J., *Conversion at Corinth: Perspectives on Conversion in Paul's Theology and the Corinthian Church* (London: T & T Clark, 2003).

Chow, J. K., *Patronage and Power: A Study of Social Networks in Corinth* (Journal for the Study of the New Testament Supplement Series 75; Sheffield: JSOT, 1992).

Clarke, A. D., *Secular and Christian Leadership in Corinth: A Socio-Historical and Exegetical Study of 1 Corinthians 1–6* (Leiden: Brill, 1993).

Clark, D. L., *Rhetoric in Greco-Roman Education* (New York: Columbia University, 1957).

Clines, D. J. A., 'Paul, the Invisible Man', in S. D. Moore and J. C. Anderson (eds.), *New Testament Masculinities* (Society of Biblical Literature Semeia Studies 45; Atlanta: Society of Biblical Literature, 2003), 181–92.

Coleman, K. M., 'Fatal Charades: Roman Executions Staged as Mythological Enactments', *Journal of Roman Studies* 80 (1990), 44–73.

Collins, A. Y. and M. M. Mitchell (eds.), *Antiquity and Humanity: Essay on Ancient Religion and Philosophy Presented to Hans Dieter Betz on His 70th Birthday* (Tübingen: Mohr-Siebeck, 2001).

Cornwall, A. and N. Lindisfarne (eds.), *Dislocating Masculinity: Comparative Ethnographies* (London: Routledge, 1994).

Cousar, C. B., *A Theology of the Cross: The Death of Jesus in the Pauline Letters* (Minneapolis: Fortress, 1990).

Cross, F. L. and E. A. Livingstone (eds.), *The Oxford Dictionary of the Christian Church* (3rd ed.; Oxford: Oxford University Press, 1997), 560, 1469–70.

Dahl, N. A., *Studies in Paul: Theology for the Early Christian Mission* (Minneapolis: Augsburg, 1977).

_____, 'Paul and the Church at Corinth', in E. Adams and D. G. Horrell (eds.), *Christianity at Corinth: The Quest for the Pauline Church* (Westminster John Knox Press: Louisville, 2004), 85–95.

Davis, J. A., *Wisdom and Spirit: An Investigation of 1 Corinthians 1. 18–3.20 against the Background of Jewish Sapiential Traditions in the Greco-Roman Period* (Lanham, MD: University Press of America, 1984).

Deissmann, A., *Paul, A Study in Social and Religious History* (London: Hodder & Stoughton, 1926).

deSilva, D. A., 'The Noble Contest: Honour, Shame, and the Rhetorical Strategy of 4 Maccabees', *Journal for the Study of the Pseudepigrapha* 13 (1995), 31–57.

_____, *4 Maccabees* (Sheffield: Sheffield Academic Press, 1998).

_____, *The Hope of Glory: Honor Discourse and New Testament Interpretation* (Collegeville: The Liturgical Press, 1999).

Dewey, A. J., 'A Matter of Honour: A Social-Historical Analysis of 2 Corinthians 10', *Harvard Theological Review* 78 (1985), 209–17.

Droge, A. J. and J. D. Tabor, *A Noble Death: Suicide and Martyrdom Among Christians and Jews in Antiquity* (San Francisco: HarperSanFrancisco, 1992).

Dunn, J. D. G., *The Theology of Paul the Apostle* (Edinburgh: T & T Clark, 1998).

_____, 'Reconstructions of Corinthian Christianity and the Interpretation of 1 Corinthians', in E. Adams and D. G. Horrell (eds.), *Christianity at Corinth: The Quest for the Pauline Church* (Westminster John Knox Press: Louisville, 2004), 295–310.

Edwards, C., 'The Suffering Body: Philosophy and Pain', in J. I. Porter (ed.), *Construc-tions of the Classical Body* (Ann Arbor: University of Michigan Press, 1999), 252–68.

Elliott, J. K., *The Apocryphal New Testament: A Collection of Apocryphal Christian Lit-erature in an English Translation* (Oxford: Clarendon, 1993).

Ericksson, A., *Traditions as Rhetorical Proof: Pauline Argumentation in 1 Corinthians* (Stockholm: Almqvist & Wiksell, 1998).

Finley, M. I., *Ancient Slavery and Modern Ideology* (London: Chatto & Windus, 1980).

Fiorenza, E. S., *In Memory of Her: A Feminist Theological Reconstruction of Christian Origins* (New York: Crossroad, 1983).

_____, *Searching the Scriptures. Vol 2: A Feminist Commentary* (London: SCM, 1995).

Fitzmyer, J. A., 'Crucifixion in Palestine, Qumran, and the New Testament', in *To Ad-vance the Gospel: New Testament Studies* (Grand Rapids: William B. Eerdmans, 1981), 125–46.

Fitzgerald, J. T., *Cracks in an Earthen Vessel: An Examination of the Catalogues of Hardships in the Corinthian Correspondence* (Atlanta: Scholars Press, 1988).

Forbes, C., 'Comparison, Self-praise and Irony: Paul's Boasting and Conventions of Hel-lenistic Rhetoric', *New Testament Studies* 32 (1986), 1–30.

Foxhall, L. and J. Salmon (eds.), *When Men Were Men: Masculinity, Power, and Identity in Classical Antiquity* (London: Routledge, 1998).

Frier, B. W., 'The Rental Market in Early Imperial Rome', *Journal of Roman Studies* 67 (1977), 27–37.

Friesen, S. J., 'Poverty in Pauline Studies: Beyond the So-Called New Consensus', *Journal for the Study of the New Testament* 26/3 (2004), 323–61.

Funk, R. W., *Language, Hermeneutic, and Word of God: the Problem of Languag in the New Testament and Contemporary Theology* (New York: Harper & Row, 1966).

Gardner, J. F., 'Sexing a Roman: imperfect men in Roman law', in L. Foxhall and J. Salmon (eds.), *When Men Were Men: Masculinity, Power, and Identity in Classical Antiquity* (London: Routledge, 1998), 136–52.

Garnsey, P., *Social Status and Legal Privilege in the Roman Empire* (Oxford: MacMullen, Ramsey, Oxford University Press, 1970).

_____, 'Grain for Rome', in P. Garnsey, K. Hopkins and C. R. Whittaker (eds.), *Trade in the Ancient Economy* (London: Chatto & Windus, 1983), 118–30.

_____, 'Food Consumption in Antiquity: Towards a Quantitative Account', in P. Garnsey (ed.), *Food, Health and Culture in Classical Antiquity* (Cambridge: Classical Depart-ment Working Papers, 1989), 36–49.

Garnsey, P. and R. Seller, *The Roman Empire: Economy, Society, and Culture* (London: Duckworth, 1987).

Garnsey, P. and Greg Woolf, 'Patronage of the Rural Poor in the Roman world', in A. Wallace-Hadrill (ed.), *Patronage in Ancient Society* (Routledge: London, 1990).

Geertz, C., 'Religion as a Culture System', in M. Banton (ed.), *Anthropological Ap-proaches to the Study of Religion* (London: Tavistock Publications, 1966), 1–46

_____, *The Interpretation of Cultures: Selected Essays* (London: Fontana, 1993).

Georgi, D., *The Opponents of Paul in Second Corinthians* (Edinburgh: T. & T. Clark, 1987).

_____, *Remembering the Poor: The History of Paul's Collection for Jerusalem* (Nash-ville: Abingdon Press, 1992).

Gilmore, D. D., *Manhood in the Making: Cultural Concepts of Masculinity* (New Haven: Yale University Press, 1990).

Glancy, J. A., 'Boasting of Beatings (2 Cor. 11:23–25)', *Journal of Biblical Literature* 123/1 (2004) 99–135.

Gleason, M. W., *Making Men: Sophists and Self-Presentation in Ancient Rome* (Princeton: Princeton University Press, 1995).

_____, 'Mutilated Messengers: 'Body Language in Josephus', in S. Goldhill (ed.), *Being Greek under Rome: Cultural Identity, the Second Sophistic and the Development of Empire* (Cambridge: Cambridge University Press, 2001), 50–85.

Goldstein, J. A., *II Maccabees* (Garden: Doubleday & Company, 1983).

Gooch, P. W., *Reflections on Jesus and Socrates: Word and Silence* (New Haven and London: Yale University Press, 1996).

Gorman, M. J., *Cruciformity: Paul's Narrative Spirituality of the Cross* (Grand Rapids: William B. Eerdmans, 2001).

_____, *Apostle of the Crucified Lord: A Theological Introduction to Paul and His Letters* (Grand Rapids: William B. Eerdmans, 2004).

Goulder, M., 'Σοφία in 1 Corinthians', *New Testament Studies* 37 (1991), 516–34.

Grant, R. M., 'The Description of Paul in the Acts of Paul and Thecla', *Vigiliae Christianae* (1982).

_____, *Paul in the Roman World: The Conflict at Corinth* (Louisville KY: Westminster John Knox, 2001).

Gunderson, E., 'Discovering the Body in Roman Oratory', in M. Wyke (ed.), *Parchments of Gender: Deciphering the Bodies of Antiquity* (Oxford: Clarendon, 1998), 169–89.

_____, *Staging Masculinity: The Rhetoric of Performance in the Roman World* (Ann Arbor: University of Michigan Press, 2000).

Hallie, P. P., 'Stoicism', in Paul Edwards, *et al.,* (eds.), *The Encyclopedia of Philosophy* (8 vols.; London: Collier Macmillan Publishers, 1967), vol. 8.19–22.

Hamel, G. H., *Poverty and Charity in Rome Palestine, First Three Centuries C. E.* (Berkeley: University of California Press, 1990).

Hanson, A. T., *The Paradox of the Cross in the Thought of St Paul* (Journal for the Study of the New Testament Supplement Series 17; Sheffield: JSOT Press, 1987).

Harding, C. and R. W. Ireland, *Punishment: Rhetoric, Rule, and Practice* (London: Rouledge, 1989).

Harrill J. A., 'Invective against Paul (2 Cor. 10.10), the Physiognomics of the Ancient Slave Body, and the Greco-Roman Rhetoric of Manhood', in A. Y. Collins and M. M. Mitchell (eds.), *Antiquity and Humanity: Essays on Ancient Religion and Philosophy Presented to Hans Dieter Betz on His 70th Birthday* (Tübingen: Mohr-Siebeck, 2001), 189–213.

Harvey, A. E., *Renewal through Suffering: A Study of 2 Corinthians* (Edinburgh: T. & T. Clark, 1996).

Hawley, R., 'The Male Body as Spectacle in Attic Drama', in L. Foxhall and J. Salmon (eds.), *Thinking Men: Masculinity and Its Self-Representation in the Classical Tradition* (London: Routledge, 1998), 83–99.

Hengel, M., *Crucifixion in the Ancient World and the Folly of the Message of the Cross* (Philadelphia PA: Fortress Press, 1977).

_____, *The Cross of the Son of God* (London: SCM Press, 1986).

_____, *The Pre-Christian Paul* (London: SCM Press, 1991).

Hezser, C., *Jewish Literacy in Roman Palestine* (TSAJ 81; Tübeingen: Mohr Siebeck, 2001).

Hock, R. F., *The Social Context of Paul's Ministry: Tentmaking and Apostleship* (Philadelphia: Fortress, 1980).

Hodgson, R., 'Paul the Apostle and First Century Tribulation Lists', *Zeitschrift für die neutestamentliche Wissenschaft und die Kunde der älteren Kirche* 74 (1983), 59–80.

Holmberg, B., *Paul and Power: The Structure of Authority in the Primitive Church as Reflected in the Pauline Epistles* (Lund: Liberlaromede/Gleerup, 1978).

_____, *Sociology and the New Testament* (Minneapolis: Fortress, 1990).

Horrell, D. G., *The Social Ethos of the Corinthian Correspondence: Interests and Ideology from 1 Corinthians to 1 Clement* (Edinburgh: T. & T. Clark, 1996).

_____, *Social-Scientific Approaches to New Testament Interpretation* (Edinburgh, T & T Clark, 1999).

_____, *Solidarity and Difference: A Contemporary Reading of Paul's Ethics* (London: T. & T. Clark International, 2005).

Horsley, R. A., 'Pneumatikos vs. Psychikos: Distinctions of Spiritual Status among the Corinthians', *Harvard Theological Review* 69 (1976), 269–88.

_____, 'Wisdom of Word and Words of Wisdom in Corinth', *Catholic Biblical Quarterly* 39 (1977), 224–39.

_____, 'Gnosis in Corinth: I Corinthians 8.1–6', *New Testament Studies* 27 (1981), 32–52.

_____, (ed.), *Paul and Empire: Religion and Power in Roman Imperial Society* (Harrisburg: Trinity, 1997).

Hubbell, H. M., 'The Rhetorica of Philodemus', *The Connecticut Academy of Arts and Sciences* 23 (1920), 243–382.

Ijsselling, S., *Rhetoric and Philosophy in Conflict: An Historical Survey*, trans. Paul Dunphy (The Hague: Martinus Nijhoff, 1976).

Jones, M., *St Paul as Orator: A Critical, Historical and Explanatory Commentary on the Speeches of St Paul* (London: Hodder and Stoughton, 1910).

Judge, E. A., *The Social Pattern of Christian Groups in the First Century* (London: The Tyndale Press, 1960).

_____, 'The Early Christians as a Scholastic Community', *Journal of Religious History* (1960–61), 4–15, 125–37.

_____, 'Paul's Boasting in relation to Contemporary Professional Practice', *Australian Biblical Review* 16 (1968), 37–50.

_____, 'The Social Identity of the First Christians, A Question of Method in Religious History', *Journal of Religious History* 11 (1980), 201–17.

_____, *Rank and Status in the World of the Caesars and St Paul* (Christchurch, N. Z.: University of Canterbury Publications, 1982).

_____, 'The Reaction against Classical Education in the New Testament', *Journal of Christian Education* 77 (1983), 7–14.

_____, 'Cultural Conformity and Innovation in Paul: Some Clues from Contemporary Documents', *Tyndale Bulletin* 35 (1984), 3–24.

Kennedy, G. A., *The Art of Persuasion in Greece* (Princeton: Princeton University Press, 1963).

_____, *The Art of Rhetoric in the Roman World* (Princeton: Princeton University Press, 1972).

_____, *Classical Rhetoric and Its Christian and Secular Tradition from Ancient to Modern Times* (London: Croom Helm, 1980).

Kittel, G. and G. Friedrich (eds.), *Theological Dictionary of the New Testament*, trans. G.W. Bromiley (10 vols.; Grand Rapids, Mich.: Eerdmans, 1964–76).

Kraut, R., 'Socrates', in Robert Audi (ed.), *The Cambridge Dictionary of Philosophy* (Cambridge: Cambridge University Press, 1995), 749–50.

Kuhn, H.–W., 'Die Kreuzesstrafe während der frühen Kaiserzeit. Ihre Wirklichkeit und Wertung in der Umwelt des Urchristentums', in Hildegard Temporini and Wolfgang Haase (eds.), *Aufstieg und Niedergang der römischen Welt: Geschichte und Kultur*

Roms im Spiegel der neueren Forschung (Berlin: Walter De Gruyter, 1982), vol. 25.648–793.

Kunkel, W., *An Introduction to Roman Legal and Constitutional History* (Oxford: Clarendon Press, 1973).

Kurtz, D. C. and J. Boardman, *Greek Burial Customs* (London and Southampton: Thames and Hudson, 1971).

Lampe, P., 'Theological Wisdom and the "Word about the Cross": The Rhetorical Scheme in 1 Corinthians 1–4', *Interpretation* 44/2 (1990), 117–31.

Larson, J., 'Paul's Masculinity', *Journal of Biblical Literature* 123/1 (2004), 85–97.

Leigh, M., 'Wounding and Popular Rhetoric at Rome', *Bulletin of the Institute of Classical Studies* 40 (1995), 195–215.

Levine, A.-J., *A Feminist Companion to Paul* (London and New York: T & T Clark, 2004).

Liddell, H. G. and R. Scott, *A Greek-English Lexicon* (2 vols.; Oxford: Clarendon, 1996).

Lim, T. H., 'Not in Persuasive Words of Wisdom, but in Demonstration of the Spirit and Power', *Novum Testamentum* 29/2 (1987), 137–49.

Lindsay, A. D., *Socrates Discourses by Plato and Xenophon* (London: J. M. Dent & Sons, Ltd., 1918).

Litfin, D., *St Paul's Theology of Proclamation: 1 Cor 1–4 and Greco-Roman Rhetoric* (Cambridge: Cambridge University Press, 1994).

Long, A. A., *Hellenistic Philosophy: Stoics, Epicureans, Sceptics* (London: Duckworth, 1986).

_____, *Epictetus: A Stoic and Socratic Guide to Life* (Oxford: Clarendon Press, 2002).

MacDonald, M. Y., 'The Shifting Centre: Ideology and the Interpretation of 1 Corinthians', in E. Adams and D. G. Horrell (eds.), *Christianity at Corinth: The Quest for the Pauline Church* (Westminster John Knox Press: Louisville, 2004), 273–94.

MacMullen, R., *Enemies of the Roman Order: Treason, Unrest, and Alienation in the Empire* (Cambridge: Harvard University Press, 1966).

_____, *Roman Social Relations 50 BC to AD 284* (New Haven: Yale University Press, 1974).

Malherbe, A. J., 'A Physical Description of Paul', *Harvard Theological Review* (1986), 79.170–75.

_____, *Paul and Popular Philosophers* (Minneapolis: Fortress Press, 1989).

Malina, B. J., *The New Testament World: Insights from Cultural Anthropology* (Louisville: Westminster/ John Knox Press, 1993).

Malina, B. J. and J. H. Neyrey, *Portraits of Paul: An Archaeology of Ancient Personality* (Louisville, KY: Westminster John Knox Press, 1996).

Marcus, J., 'Crucifixion as Parodic Exaltation', *Journal of Biblical Literature* 125 (2006), 73–87.

Marrou, H., *A History of Education in Antiquity*, trans. George Lamb (New York: Sheed & Ward, 1956).

_____, 'Education and Rhetoric', in M. I. Finley (ed.), *The Legacy of Greece* (Oxford: Clarendon Press, 1981), 185–201.

Marshall, P., *Enmity in Corinth: Social Conventions in Paul's Relations with the Corinthians* (Tübingen: Mohr-Siebeck, 1987).

Martin, D. B., *Slavery as Salvation: The Metaphor of Slavery in Pauline Christianity* (New Haven; London: Yale University Press, 1990).

_____, *The Corinthian Body* (New Haven: Yale University press, 1995).

_____, *The Social World of the Apostle Paul* (New Haven: Yale University Press, 1983).

Martyn, J. Louis, *Theological Issues in the Letters of Paul* (Edinburgh: T. & T. Clark, 1997).

McCane, B. R., *Jews, Christians, and Burial in Roman Palestine* (Ann Arbor: UMI Dissertation Services, 2005).

McGrath, A. E., 'Cross, Theology of the', in G. F. Hawthorne, R. P. Martin, and D. G. Reid (eds.), *Dictionary of Paul and His Letters* (Downers Grove, Ill.; Leicester: InterVarsity Press, 1993), 805–12.

Mckay, A. G., *House, Villas and Palaces in the Roman World* (London: Thames & Hudson, 1975).

Meeks, W. A., *The First Urban Christians: The Social World of the Apostle Paul* (New Haven: Yale University, 1983).

Meggitt, J. J., *Paul, Poverty and Survival* (Edinburgh: T&T Clark, 1998).

Millar, F., 'Condemnation to hard labour in the Roman Empire, from the Julio-Claudians to Constantine', *Papers of the British School at Rome* 52 (1984), 124–47.

Mitchell, A. C., 'Rich and Poor in the Courts of Corinth', *New Testament Studies* 39 (1993), 562–86.

Mitchell, M. M., *Paul and the Rhetoric of Reconciliation: An exegetical Investigation of the Language and Composition of 1 Corinthians* (Tübingen: Mohr-Siebeck, 1991).

_____, 'Rhetorical Shorthand in Paul's Argumentation: The Functions of "the Gospel" in the Corinthian Correspondence', in L. A. Jervis and P. Richardson (eds.), *Gospel in Paul: Studies on Corinthians, Galatians and Romans for Richard N. Longenecker* (Sheffield: Sheffield Academic Press, 1994), 63–88.

Montserrat, D., 'Experiencing the male body in Roman Egypt', in L. Foxhall and J. Salmon (eds.), *When Men Were Men: Masculinity, Power, and Identity in Classical Antiquity* (London: Routledge, 1998), 153–64.

Moore, S. D. and J. C. Anderson, 'Taking It like a Man', *Journal of Biblical Literature* (1998), 249–73.

Moore, S. D., '"O Man, Who Art Thou…?": Masculinity Studies And New Testament Studies', in S. D. Moore and J. C. Anderson (eds.), *New Testament Masculinities* (Society of Biblical Literature Semeia Studies 45; Atlanta: Society of Biblical Literature, 2003), 1–22.

Morris, L., *The Cross in the New Testament* (Exeter: Paternoster/Grand Rapids: William B. Eerdmans, 1965).

Moxnes, H., 'Honor and Shame', in R. L. Rohrbaugh (ed.), *The Social Science and New Testament Interpretation* (Peabody: Hendrickson Publishers, 1996), 19–49.

Munck, J., 'The Church without Factions: Studies in 1 Corinthians 1–4', in *Paul and the Salvation of Mankind* (London: SCM Press, 1959), 135–67.

Murphy-O'Connor, J., *St. Paul's Corinth: Texts and Archaeology* (Wilmington, Del: Glazier, 1983).

_____, *The Theology of the Second Letter to the Corinthians* (Cambridge: Cambridge University Press, 1991).

Nadeau, R., 'Delivery in Ancient Times: Homer to Quintilian', *Quarterly Journal of Speech* 50 (1964), 53–60.

Neyrey, J. H., '"Despising the Shame of the Cross": Honor and Shame in the Johannine Passion Narrative', in D. G. Horrell (ed.), *Social-Scientific Approaches to New Testament Interpretation* (Edinburgh, T & T Clark, 1999), 151–76.

Nutton, V., 'Galen and the Traveller's Fare', in J. Wilkins, D. Harvey, and M. D. Dobson (eds.), *Food in Antiquity* (Exeter: Exeter University Press, 1995), 359–69.

Økland, J., *Women in Their Place: Paul and the Corinthian Discourse of Gender and Sanctuary Space* (London: T & T Clark, 2004).

Olbricht, T. H., 'Delivery and Memory', in S. E. Porter (ed.), *Handbook of Classical Rhetoric in the Hellenistic Period* (330 B.C.–A. D. 400) (Leiden: Brill, 1997), 159–67.

Paige, T., 'Stoicism, ἐλευθερία and Community at Corinth', in J. Wilkins and T. Paige (eds.), *Worship, Theology and Ministry in the Early Church: Essays in Honour of Ralph P. Martin* (Sheffield : JSOT, 1992), 180–93.

Pearsall, J., *The Oxford Encyclopedic English Dictionary* (Oxford; New York: Oxford University Press, 1995).

Pearson, B. A., *The Pneumatikos-Psychikos Terminology in 1 Corinthians: A Study in the Theology of the Corinthian Opponents of Paul and its Relation to Gnosticism* (Society of Biblical Literature Dissertation Series 12; Missoula, MT: Society of Biblical Literature, 1973), 27–43.

Perkins, J., *The Suffering Self: Pain and Narrative Representation in the Early Christian Era* (London: Routledge, 1995).

Pickett, R., *The Cross in Corinth: The Social Significance of the Death of Jesus* (Sheffield: Sheffield Academic Press, 1997).

Plank, K. A., *Paul and the Irony of Affliction* (Atlanta: Scholars Press, 1987).

Pobee, J. S., *Persecution and Martyrdom in the Theology of St. Paul* (Sheffield: Sheffield Academic Press, 1985).

Pogoloff, S. M., *Logos and Sophia: The Rhetorical Situation of 1 Corinthians* (Atlanta: Scholars Press, 1992).

Porter, S. E. (ed.), *Handbook of Classical Rhetoric in the Hellenistic Period* (330 B.C.–A.D. 400) (Leiden: Brill, 1997).

Ramsay, W. M., *St. Paul the Traveller and the Roman Citizen* (London: Hodder and Stoughton, 1895).

Reardon, B. P., *Collected Ancient Greek Novels* (Berkeley: University of California Press, 1989).

Rist, J. M., *Stoic Philosophy* (Cambridge: Cambridge University Press, 1969).

Russell, D. A., Greek Declamation (Cambridge: Cambridge University Press, 1983).

Saller, R. P., 'Corporal Punishment, Authority, Obedience', in B. Rawson (ed.), *Marriage, Divorce, and Children in Ancient Rome* (Oxford: Clarendon, 1991), 144–65.

_____, *Personal Patronage under the Early Empire* (Cambridge: Cambridge University Press, 1982).

Sandbach, F. H., *The Stoics* (London: Chatto & Windus, 1975).

Sanders, E. P., *Paul and Palestinian Judaism: A Comparison of Patterns of Religion* (London: SCM Press, 1977).

_____, *Paul* (Oxford: Oxford University Press, 1991).

Satlow, M. L., 'Jewish Constructions of Nakedness in Late Antiquity', *Journal of Biblical Literature* 116/3 (1997), 429–54.

Savage, T. B., *Power through Weakness: A Historical and Exegetical Examination of Paul's Understanding of the Christian Ministry in 2 Corinthians* (Cambridge: Cambridge University Press, 1996).

Schmithals, W., *Gnosticism in Corinth* (Nashville: Abingdon, 1971).

Schottroff, L., '"Not Many Powerful": Approaches to a Sociology of Early Christianity', in D. G. Horrell (ed.), *Social-Scientific Approaches to New Testament Interpretation* (Edinburgh, T & T Clark, 1999), 275–87.

Schütz, J. H., *Paul and the Anatomy of Apostolic Authority* (London: Cambridge University Press, 1975)

Scobie, A., 'Slums, sanitation, and mortality in the Roman World', *Klio* 68 (1986), 399–433.

Sedley, D. N., 'Stoicism', in R. Audi (ed.), *The Cambridge Dictionary of Philosophy* (Cambridge: Cambridge University Press, 1995), 768–69.

Seeley, D., *The Noble Death: Graeco-Roman Martyrology and Paul's Concept of Salvation* (Sheffield: JSOT Press, 1990).

Sharples, R. W., 'Stoicism', in H. Ted (ed.), *The Oxford Companion to Philosophy* (Oxford: Oxford University Press, 1995), 852–53.

Shaw, B. D., 'Body/Power/Identity: Passions of the Martyrs', *Journal of Early Christian Studies* 4 (1996), 269–312.

Slote, M., 'Virtues', in H. Ted (ed.), *The Oxford Companion to Philosophy* (Oxford: Oxford University Press, 1995), 900–901.

Sonkowsky, R. P., 'An Aspect of Delivery in Ancient Rhetoric Theory', *Transactions of the American Philological Association*, XC (1959), 257–74.

Stambaugh, J., *The Ancient Roman City* (Baltimore: Johns Hopkins University Press, 1989).

Stegemann, E. W. and W. Stegemann, *The Jesus Movement: A Social History of Its First Century* (Minneapolis: Fortress, 1999).

Stendahl, K., *Paul among Jews and Gentiles* (Philadelphia: Fortress Press, 1976).

Sumney, J. L., *Identifying Paul's opponents: The Question of Method in 2 Corinthians* (Sheffield: JSOT Press, 1990).

Taylor, C. C. W., 'Socrates', in H. Ted (ed.), *The Oxford Companion to Philosophy* (Oxford: Oxford University Press, 1995), 836–37.

Theissen, G., *The Social Setting of Pauline Christianity* (Philadelphia: T. & T. Clark, 1982).

_____, 'Review Essay: Justin J. Meggitt, *Paul, Poverty and Survival*', *Journal for the Study of the New Testament* 84 (2001), 51–64.

_____, 'Social conflicts in the Corinthian community: Further Remarks on J. J. Meggitt, Paul, Poverty and survival', *Journal for the Study of the New Testament* 25.3 (2003), 371–91.

Thiselton, A. C., 'Realized Eschatology at Corinth', in E. Adams and D. G. Horrell (eds.), *Christianity at Corinth: The Quest for the Pauline Church* (Westminster John Knox Press: Louisville, 2004), 107–18.

Toynbee, J. M. C., *Death and Burial in the Roman World* (London and Southampton: Thames and Hudson, 1971).

Usher, S., 'Oratory', in J. Higginbotham (ed.), *Greek and Latin Literature: A Comparative Study* (London: Methuen, 1969), 342–89.

van Henten, J. W., *The Maccabean Martyrs as Saviours of the Jewish People: A Study of 2 and 4 Maccabees* (Leid: Brill, 1997).

van Henten, J. W. and F. Avemarie, *Martyrdom and Noble Death: Selected texts from Graeco-Roman, Jewish and Christian Antiquity* (London: Routledge, 2002).

Wallace-Hadrill, A., *Houses and Society in Pompeii and Herculaneum* (Princeton: Princeton University Press, 1994).

Ward, R., 'Pauline Voice and Presence as Strategic Communication', *Society of Biblical Literature Seminar Papers* (1990), 283–92.

Watson, A., *Roman Slave Law* (Baltimore: John Hopkins University Press, 1987).

Watson, D. F., 'The New Testament and Greco-Roman Rhetoric: a Bibliography', *Journal of the Evangelical Theological Society* 31/4 (1988), 465–72.

_____, 'Paul's Boasting in 2 Corinthians 10–13 as Defense of His Honour: A Socio-rhetorical Analysis', in A. Erickkson, *et al.* (eds.), *Rhetorical Argumentation in Biblical Texts: Essays from the Lund 2000 Conference* (Harrisburg, PA: Trinity Press International, 2002), 260–75.

Weinandy, T. G., *Does God Suffer?* (Edinburgh: T & T Clark, 2000).

Welborn, L. L., 'On the Discord in Corinth: 1 Corinthians 1–4 and Ancient Politics', *Journal of Biblical Literature* 106 (1987), 85–111.

_____, *Paul, the Fool of Christ: A Study of 1 Corinthians 1–4 in the Comic-Philosophic Tradition* (London: T & T International, 2005).

Wilckens, U., '*Sophia*', in G. Kittel and G. Friedrich, (eds.), trans. G. W. Bromiley, *Theological Dictionary of the New Testament* (10 vols.; Grand Rapids, Mich.: Eerdmans, 1964–76), vol. 7.519–22.

Wilcox, Max, '"Upon the Tree" – Deut 21:22–23 in the New Testament', *Journal of Biblical Literature* 96 (1977), 85–99.

Williams, C. A., *Roman Homosexuality: Ideologies of Masculinity in Classical Antiquity* (New York: Oxford University Press, 1999).

Wilson, R. McL., 'How Gnostic Were the Corinthians?' *New Testament Studies* 19 (1972-73), 65–74.

Winter, B. W., *Philo and Paul among the Sophists* (Cambridge: Cambridge University Press, 1997).

_____, *After Paul Left Corinth: The Influence of Secular Ethics and Social Change* (Grand Rapids MI: William B. Eerdmans, 2001).

Wire, A. C., *Corinthian Women Prophets: A Reconstruction through Paul's Rhetoric* (Minneapolis: Fortress, 1990).

Wisse, J., *Ethos and Pathos from Aristotle to Cicero* (Amsterdam: Hakkert, 1989).

Witherington, B., *Conflict and Community in Corinth* (Grand Rapids MI: William B. Eerdmans, 1995).

Wold, B. G., *Women, Men and Angels: The Qumran Wisdom Document Musar leMevin and its Allusions to Genesis Creation Traditions* (WUNT II/201; Tübingen: Mohr Siebeck, 2005).

Wuellner, W. H., 'Haggadic homily Genre in 1 Corinthian 1–3', *Journal of Biblical Literature* 89 (1970), 199–204.

Wuellner, W. H., 'The Sociological Implications of 1 Corinthians 1:26–28 Reconsidered', in E. A. Livingstone (ed.), *Studia Evangelica IV* (Berlin: Akademie, 1973), 666–672.

Yadin, Y., 'Pesher Nahum (4Q pNahum) Reconsidered', *Israel Exploration Journal* 21 (1971), 1–12.

Yavetz, Z., 'The Living Conditions of the Urban Plebs in Republican Rome', in R. Seager (ed.), *The Crisis of the Roman Republic* (Cambridge: W. Heffer & Sons, 1969), 162–79.

Index of References

Old Testament

Genesis		54 (55).5	165
15.6	77	55.5	166
22	78		
		Isaiah	
Exodus		19.12	94, 96
15	106	19.16	165, 166
15.16	165, 166	29	92
		29.13	92
Deuteronomy		29.14	90–93
21	76, 78	44.25	96
21.22	77	53.7–8	74
21.22–23	75–78	53.9	74
21.23	23, 32, 37, 74,	53.10–12	74
	76–79, 99, 268		
25.2–3	247,	*Jeremiah*	
27.26	77, 78	9.23	109
		9.23–24	109
Joshua		9.24	109
8.23–29	76		
		Daniel	
Judges		4.19	165
5	106	7.18	229
1 Samuel		*Hosea*	
2.1–10	106	5.13–15	75
Psalms		*Nahum*	
32.10	91	2.12–14	75

New Testament

Matthew		15.34	48
10.10	222		
10.17	247	*Luke*	
27.26	251	1.46–55	106
		10.7	222
Mark			
8.11	98		
15.15	251	*John*	
15.29–31	48	18.33	36

New Testament Apocrypha

The Acts of Paul and Thekla
3   178, 179

Qumran Writings

4Q169 (Nahum Pesher)
3–4 i 7–8   75, 76

11QT 64 (Temple Scroll)
6–13   75
12   76

1QS (Serekh haYahad)
ii 12   99
ii 17   99

1QH^a (Hodayot)
iv 15   99
viii 35   99
ix 21   99
ix 27   99
x 17   99
xvi 15   99

4Q415 (Musar leMevin)
11 7   99

Mishnah Literature

m. Makkoth
3.1–9   247
3.10   247
3.14   247

m. Semahot
12.10   50

Greek, Latin Authors and Others

Aristophanes

Clouds   54

Aristotle

Ethica nicomachea
1102a   105
1169a   61
1094ab   128
1125a   184

Rhetorica
1048a 10   130
1354a 5   130
1354a 12   130
1354a 14   129
1354b 21   129

1355a 11   170
1355b 2   121
1356a 1   156
1356a 2   123
1356a 3   128
1356a 7   128
1358a 38   123
1360b 3–5   105
1360b–62a   107
1362b 14   123
1366ab   107
1378a 2   129
1378a 2–3   129
1378a 5–7   128
1378a 8   129
1379a7   157
1403b 1   131

Euthydemus	
271–72B	124
288BC	121
Euthyphro	
58	
Gorgias	
453A	121
473BC	22
473C	26, 45
485BC	164
525B	26
De Legibus	
1.626DE	70
958D–60B	49
Meno	
91B	124
Phaedo	
30A	55
30B–31A	56
42A	56
58E	57, 60
61B	58
62C	58, 212
64A	56, 60, 212
64E	56
65C	200
66B	56
66E	59, 200
67CD	59, 200
67E–68B	60, 200, 211
77C	170
82C	60, 200
115A	60, 200
117BC	61
118	61
Phaedrus	
267A	122
271D	122
Protagogas	
315A	121
319B–323A	122
De Republica	
357A–62C	213
361E–62A	43

380A	195
387E	195
430E–31A	70
495E–96A	124
612E–13A	213
613C	213
617E	195
Respublica	
387DE	211
De Sophista	
265D	170
Plautus	
Asinaria	
940	31
Aulularia	
522	21, 31
Bacchides	
584	21, 31
902	31
Capitivi	
598	50
Casina	
93	31
416	31
641	31
977	31
Curculio	
611	31
Epidicus	
359–64	30
Miles gloriosus	
372–73	30
539–40	29, 30
610–14	30
Mostellaria	
359–64	29, 31
499–500	50
1133	29, 31

Index of Authors

1. Greco-Roman Authors

2. Modern Authors

Index of Subjects and Key Terms

Wissenschaftliche Untersuchungen zum Neuen Testament

Alphabetical Index of the First and Second Series

Betz, Otto: Jesus, der Messias Israels. 1987. *Vol. 42.*
– Jesus, der Herr der Kirche. 1990. *Vol. 52.*
Beyschlag, Karlmann: Simon Magus und die christliche Gnosis. 1974. *Vol. 16.*
Bieringer, Reimund: see *Koester, Craig.*
Bittner, Wolfgang J.: Jesu Zeichen im Johannesevangelium. 1987. *Vol. II/26.*
Bjerkelund, Carl J.: Tauta Egeneto. 1987. *Vol. 40.*
Blackburn, Barry Lee: Theios Aner and the Markan Miracle Traditions. 1991. *Vol. II/40.*
Blanton IV, Thomas R.: Constructing a New Covenant. 2007. *Vol. II/233.*
Bock, Darrell L.: Blasphemy and Exaltation in Judaism and the Final Examination of Jesus. 1998. *Vol. II/106.*
Bockmuehl, Markus N.A.: Revelation and Mystery in Ancient Judaism and Pauline Christianity. 1990. *Vol. II/36.*
Bøe, Sverre: Gog and Magog. 2001. *Vol. II/135.*
Böhlig, Alexander: Gnosis und Synkretismus. Vol. 1 1989. *Vol. 47* – Vol. 2 1989. *Vol. 48.*
Böhm, Martina: Samarien und die Samaritai bei Lukas. 1999. *Vol. II/111.*
Böttrich, Christfried: Weltweisheit – Menschheitsethik – Urkult. 1992. *Vol. II/50.*
– and *Herzer, Jens* (Ed.): Josephus und das Neue Testament. 2007. *Vol. 209.*
Bolyki, János: Jesu Tischgemeinschaften. 1997. *Vol. II/96.*
Bosman, Philip: Conscience in Philo and Paul. 2003. *Vol. II/166.*
Bovon, François: Studies in Early Christianity. 2003. *Vol. 161.*
Brändl, Martin: Der Agon bei Paulus. 2006. *Vol. II/222.*
Breytenbach, Cilliers: see *Frey, Jörg.*
Brocke, Christoph vom: Thessaloniki – Stadt des Kassander und Gemeinde des Paulus. 2001. *Vol. II/125.*
Brunson, Andrew: Psalm 118 in the Gospel of John. 2003. *Vol. II/158.*
Büchli, Jörg: Der Poimandres – ein paganisiertes Evangelium. 1987. *Vol. II/27.*
Bühner, Jan A.: Der Gesandte und sein Weg im 4. Evangelium. 1977. *Vol. II/2.*
Burchard, Christoph: Untersuchungen zu Joseph und Aseneth. 1965. *Vol. 8.*
– Studien zur Theologie, Sprache und Umwelt des Neuen Testaments. Ed. by D. Sänger. 1998. *Vol. 107.*
Burnett, Richard: Karl Barth's Theological Exegesis. 2001. *Vol. II/145.*
Byron, John: Slavery Metaphors in Early Judaism and Pauline Christianity. 2003. *Vol. II/162.*

Byrskog, Samuel: Story as History – History as Story. 2000. *Vol. 123.*
Cancik, Hubert (Ed.): Markus-Philologie. 1984. *Vol. 33.*
Capes, David B.: Old Testament Yaweh Texts in Paul's Christology. 1992. *Vol. II/47.*
Caragounis, Chrys C.: The Development of Greek and the New Testament. 2004. *Vol. 167.*
– The Son of Man. 1986. *Vol. 38.*
– see *Fridrichsen, Anton.*
Carleton Paget, James: The Epistle of Barnabas. 1994. *Vol. II/64.*
Carson, D.A., O'Brien, Peter T. and *Mark Seifrid* (Ed.): Justification and Variegated Nomism.
Vol. 1: The Complexities of Second Temple Judaism. 2001. *Vol. II/140.*
Vol. 2: The Paradoxes of Paul. 2004. *Vol. II/181.*
Chae, Young Sam: Jesus as the Eschatological Davidic Shepherd. 2006. *Vol. II/216.*
Chapman, David W.: Ancient Jewish and Christian Perceptions of Crucifixion. 2008. *Vol. II/244.*
Chester, Andrew: Messiah and Exaltation. 2007. *Vol. 207.*
Chibici-Revneanu, Nicole: Die Herrlichkeit des Verherrlichten. 2007. *Vol. II/231.*
Ciampa, Roy E.: The Presence and Function of Scripture in Galatians 1 and 2. 1998. *Vol. II/102.*
Classen, Carl Joachim: Rhetorical Criticsm of the New Testament. 2000. *Vol. 128.*
Colpe, Carsten: Iranier – Aramäer – Hebräer – Hellenen. 2003. *Vol. 154.*
Crump, David: Jesus the Intercessor. 1992. *Vol. II/49.*
Dahl, Nils Alstrup: Studies in Ephesians. 2000. *Vol. 131.*
Daise, Michael A.: Feasts in John. 2007. *Vol. II/229.*
Deines, Roland: Die Gerechtigkeit der Tora im Reich des Messias. 2004. *Vol. 177.*
– Jüdische Steingefäße und pharisäische Frömmigkeit. 1993. *Vol. II/52.*
– Die Pharisäer. 1997. *Vol. 101.*
Deines, Roland and *Karl-Wilhelm Niebuhr* (Ed.): Philo und das Neue Testament. 2004. *Vol. 172.*
Dennis, John A.: Jesus' Death and the Gathering of True Israel. 2006. *Vol. 217.*
Dettwiler, Andreas and *Jean Zumstein* (Ed.): Kreuzestheologie im Neuen Testament. 2002. *Vol. 151.*
Dickson, John P.: Mission-Commitment in Ancient Judaism and in the Pauline Communities. 2003. *Vol. II/159.*

Dietzfelbinger, Christian: Der Abschied des Kommenden. 1997. *Vol. 95.*

Dimitrov, Ivan Z., James D.G. Dunn, Ulrich Luz and *Karl-Wilhelm Niebuhr* (Ed.): Das Alte Testament als christliche Bibel in orthodoxer und westlicher Sicht. 2004. *Vol. 174.*

Dobbeler, Axel von: Glaube als Teilhabe. 1987. *Vol. II/22.*

Downs, David J.: The Offering of the Gentiles. 2008. *Vol. II/248.*

Dryden, J. de Waal: Theology and Ethics in 1 Peter. 2006. *Vol. II/209.*

Dübbers, Michael: Christologie und Existenz im Kolosserbrief. 2005. *Vol. II/191.*

Dunn, James D.G.: The New Perspective on Paul. 2005. *Vol. 185.*

Dunn, James D.G. (Ed.): Jews and Christians. 1992. *Vol. 66.*

– Paul and the Mosaic Law. 1996. *Vol. 89.*

– see *Dimitrov, Ivan Z.*

–, *Hans Klein, Ulrich Luz,* and *Vasile Mihoc* (Ed.): Auslegung der Bibel in orthodoxer und westlicher Perspektive. 2000. *Vol. 130.*

Ebel, Eva: Die Attraktivität früher christlicher Gemeinden. 2004. *Vol. II/178.*

Ebertz, Michael N.: Das Charisma des Gekreuzigten. 1987. *Vol. 45.*

Eckstein, Hans-Joachim: Der Begriff Syneidesis bei Paulus. 1983. *Vol. II/10.*

– Verheißung und Gesetz. 1996. *Vol. 86.*

Ego, Beate: Im Himmel wie auf Erden. 1989. *Vol. II/34.*

Ego, Beate, Armin Lange and *Peter Pilhofer* (Ed.): Gemeinde ohne Tempel – Community without Temple. 1999. *Vol. 118.*

– and *Helmut Merkel* (Ed.): Religiöses Lernen in der biblischen, frühjüdischen und frühchristlichen Überlieferung. 2005. *Vol. 180.*

Eisen, Ute E.: see *Paulsen, Henning.*

Elledge, C.D.: Life after Death in Early Judaism. 2006. *Vol. II/208.*

Ellis, E. Earle: Prophecy and Hermeneutic in Early Christianity. 1978. *Vol. 18.*

– The Old Testament in Early Christianity. 1991. *Vol. 54.*

Endo, Masanobu: Creation and Christology. 2002. *Vol. 149.*

Ennulat, Andreas: Die 'Minor Agreements'. 1994. *Vol. II/62.*

Ensor, Peter W.: Jesus and His 'Works'. 1996. *Vol. II/85.*

Eskola, Timo: Messiah and the Throne. 2001. *Vol. II/142.*

– Theodicy and Predestination in Pauline Soteriology. 1998. *Vol. II/100.*

Fatehi, Mehrdad: The Spirit's Relation to the Risen Lord in Paul. 2000. *Vol. II/128.*

Feldmeier, Reinhard: Die Krisis des Gottessohnes. 1987. *Vol. II/21.*

– Die Christen als Fremde. 1992. *Vol. 64.*

Feldmeier, Reinhard and *Ulrich Heckel* (Ed.): Die Heiden. 1994. *Vol. 70.*

Fletcher-Louis, Crispin H.T.: Luke-Acts: Angels, Christology and Soteriology. 1997. *Vol. II/94.*

Förster, Niclas: Marcus Magus. 1999. *Vol. 114.*

Forbes, Christopher Brian: Prophecy and Inspired Speech in Early Christianity and its Hellenistic Environment. 1995. *Vol. II/75.*

Fornberg, Tord: see *Fridrichsen, Anton.*

Fossum, Jarl E.: The Name of God and the Angel of the Lord. 1985. *Vol. 36.*

Foster, Paul: Community, Law and Mission in Matthew's Gospel. *Vol. II/177.*

Fotopoulos, John: Food Offered to Idols in Roman Corinth. 2003. *Vol. II/151.*

Frenschkowski, Marco: Offenbarung und Epiphanie. Vol. 1 1995. *Vol. II/79* – Vol. 2 1997. *Vol. II/80.*

Frey, Jörg: Eugen Drewermann und die biblische Exegese. 1995. *Vol. II/71.*

– Die johanneische Eschatologie. Vol. I. 1997. *Vol. 96.* – Vol. II. 1998. *Vol. 110.* – Vol. III. 2000. *Vol. 117.*

Frey, Jörg and *Cilliers Breytenbach* (Ed.): Aufgabe und Durchführung einer Theologie des Neuen Testaments. 2007. *Vol. 205.*

– and *Udo Schnelle* (Ed.): Kontexte des Johannesevangeliums. 2004. *Vol. 175.*

– and *Jens Schröter* (Ed.): Deutungen des Todes Jesu im Neuen Testament. 2005. *Vol. 181.*

–, *Jan G. van der Watt,* and *Ruben Zimmermann* (Ed.): Imagery in the Gospel of John. 2006. *Vol. 200.*

Freyne, Sean: Galilee and Gospel. 2000. *Vol. 125.*

Fridrichsen, Anton: Exegetical Writings. Edited by C.C. Caragounis and T. Fornberg. 1994. *Vol. 76.*

Gäbel, Georg: Die Kulttheologie des Hebräerbriefes. 2006. *Vol. II/212.*

Gäckle, Volker: Die Starken und die Schwachen in Korinth und in Rom. 2005. *Vol. 200.*

Garlington, Don B.: 'The Obedience of Faith'. 1991. *Vol. II/38.*

– Faith, Obedience, and Perseverance. 1994. *Vol. 79.*

Garnet, Paul: Salvation and Atonement in the Qumran Scrolls. 1977. *Vol. II/3.*

Gemünden, Petra von (Ed.): see *Weissenrieder, Annette.*

Gese, Michael: Das Vermächtnis des Apostels. 1997. *Vol. II/99.*

Gheorghita, Radu: The Role of the Septuagint in Hebrews. 2003. *Vol. II/160.*

Gordley, Matthew E.: The Colossian Hymn in Context. 2007. *Vol. II/228.*

Gräbe, Petrus J.: The Power of God in Paul's Letters. 2000, ²2008. *Vol. II/123.*

Gräßer, Erich: Der Alte Bund im Neuen. 1985. *Vol. 35.*

– Forschungen zur Apostelgeschichte. 2001. *Vol. 137.*

Grappe, Christian (Ed.): Le Repas de Dieu / Das Mahl Gottes. 2004. *Vol. 169.*

Gray, Timothy C.: The Temple in the Gospel of Mark. 2008. *Vol. II/242.*

Green, Joel B.: The Death of Jesus. 1988. *Vol. II/33.*

Gregg, Brian Han: The Historical Jesus and the Final Judgment Sayings in Q. 2005. *Vol. II/207.*

Gregory, Andrew: The Reception of Luke and Acts in the Period before Irenaeus. 2003. *Vol. II/169.*

Grindheim, Sigurd: The Crux of Election. 2005. *Vol. II/202.*

Gundry, Robert H.: The Old is Better. 2005. *Vol. 178.*

Gundry Volf, Judith M.: Paul and Perseverance. 1990. *Vol. II/37.*

Häußer, Detlef: Christusbekenntnis und Jesus-überlieferung bei Paulus. 2006. *Vol. 210.*

Hafemann, Scott J.: Suffering and the Spirit. 1986. *Vol. II/19.*

– Paul, Moses, and the History of Israel. 1995. *Vol. 81.*

Hahn, Ferdinand: Studien zum Neuen Testament.
Vol. I: Grundsatzfragen, Jesusforschung, Evangelien. 2006. *Vol. 191.*
Vol. II: Bekenntnisbildung und Theologie in urchristlicher Zeit. 2006. *Vol. 192.*

Hahn, Johannes (Ed.): Zerstörungen des Jerusalemer Tempels. 2002. *Vol. 147.*

Hamid-Khani, Saeed: Relevation and Concealment of Christ. 2000. *Vol. II/120.*

Hannah, Darrel D.: Michael and Christ. 1999. *Vol. II/109.*

Hardin, Justin K.: Galatians and the Imperial Cult? 2007. *Vol. II/237.*

Harrison; James R.: Paul's Language of Grace in Its Graeco-Roman Context. 2003. *Vol. II/172.*

Hartman, Lars: Text-Centered New Testament Studies. Ed. von D. Hellholm. 1997. *Vol. 102.*

Hartog, Paul: Polycarp and the New Testament. 2001. *Vol. II/134.*

Heckel, Theo K.: Der Innere Mensch. 1993. *Vol. II/53.*

– Vom Evangelium des Markus zum viergestaltigen Evangelium. 1999. *Vol. 120.*

Heckel, Ulrich: Kraft in Schwachheit. 1993. *Vol. II/56.*

– Der Segen im Neuen Testament. 2002. *Vol. 150.*

– see *Feldmeier, Reinhard.*

– see *Hengel, Martin.*

Heiligenthal, Roman: Werke als Zeichen. 1983. *Vol. II/9.*

Heliso, Desta: Pistis and the Righteous One. 2007. *Vol. II/235.*

Hellholm, D.: see *Hartman, Lars.*

Hemer, Colin J.: The Book of Acts in the Setting of Hellenistic History. 1989. *Vol. 49.*

Hengel, Martin: Jesus und die Evangelien. Kleine Schriften V. 2007. *Vol. 211.*

– Die johanneische Frage. 1993. *Vol. 67.*

– Judaica et Hellenistica. Kleine Schriften I. 1996. *Vol. 90.*

– Judaica, Hellenistica et Christiana. Kleine Schriften II. 1999. *Vol. 109.*

– Judentum und Hellenismus. 1969, ³1988. *Vol. 10.*

– Paulus und Jakobus. Kleine Schriften III. 2002. *Vol. 141.*

– Studien zur Christologie. Kleine Schriften IV. 2006. *Vol. 201.*

– Studien zum Urchristentum. Kleine Schriften VI. 2008. *Vol. 234.*

– and *Anna Maria Schwemer:* Paulus zwischen Damaskus und Antiochien. 1998. *Vol. 108.*

– Der messianische Anspruch Jesu und die Anfänge der Christologie. 2001. *Vol. 138.*

– Die vier Evangelien und das eine Evangelium von Jesus Christus. 2008. *Vol. 224.*

Hengel, Martin and *Ulrich Heckel* (Ed.): Paulus und das antike Judentum. 1991. *Vol. 58.*

– and *Hermut Löhr* (Ed.): Schriftauslegung im antiken Judentum und im Urchristentum. 1994. *Vol. 73.*

– and *Anna Maria Schwemer* (Ed.): Königsherrschaft Gottes und himmlischer Kult. 1991. *Vol. 55.*

– Die Septuaginta. 1994. *Vol. 72.*

–, *Siegfried Mittmann* and *Anna Maria Schwemer* (Ed.): La Cité de Dieu / Die Stadt Gottes. 2000. *Vol. 129.*

Hentschel, Anni: Diakonia im Neuen Testament. 2007. *Vol. 226.*

Hernández Jr., Juan: Scribal Habits and Theological Influence in the Apocalypse. 2006. *Vol. II/218.*

Herrenbrück, Fritz: Jesus und die Zöllner. 1990. *Vol. II/41.*

Herzer, Jens: Paulus oder Petrus? 1998. *Vol. 103.*

– see *Böttrich, Christfried.*
Hill, Charles E.: From the Lost Teaching of Polycarp. 2005. *Vol. 186.*
Hoegen-Rohls, Christina: Der nachösterliche Johannes. 1996. *Vol. II/84.*
Hoffmann, Matthias Reinhard: The Destroyer and the Lamb. 2005. *Vol. II/203.*
Hofius, Otfried: Katapausis. 1970. *Vol. 11.*
– Der Vorhang vor dem Thron Gottes. 1972. *Vol. 14.*
– Der Christushymnus Philipper 2,6–11. 1976, ²1991. *Vol. 17.*
– Paulusstudien. 1989, ²1994. *Vol. 51.*
– Neutestamentliche Studien. 2000. *Vol. 132.*
– Paulusstudien II. 2002. *Vol. 143.*
– Exegetische Studien. 2008. *Vol. 223.*
– and *Hans-Christian Kammler:* Johannesstudien. 1996. *Vol. 88.*
Holmberg, Bengt (Ed.): Exploring Early Christian Identity. 2008. *Vol. 226.*
– and *Mikael Winninge* (Ed.): Identity Formation in the New Testament. 2008. *Vol. 227.*
Holtz, Traugott: Geschichte und Theologie des Urchristentums. 1991. *Vol. 57.*
Hommel, Hildebrecht: Sebasmata.
Vol. 1 1983. *Vol. 31.*
Vol. 2 1984. *Vol. 32.*
Horbury, William: Herodian Judaism and New Testament Study. 2006. *Vol. 193.*
Horst, Pieter W. van der: Jews and Christians in Their Graeco-Roman Context. 2006. *Vol. 196.*
Hvalvik, Reidar: The Struggle for Scripture and Covenant. 1996. *Vol. II/82.*
Jauhiainen, Marko: The Use of Zechariah in Revelation. 2005. *Vol. II/199.*
Jensen, Morten H.: Herod Antipas in Galilee. 2006. *Vol. II/215.*
Johns, Loren L.: The Lamb Christology of the Apocalypse of John. 2003. *Vol. II/167.*
Jossa, Giorgio: Jews or Christians? 2006. *Vol. 202.*
Joubert, Stephan: Paul as Benefactor. 2000. *Vol. II/124.*
Judge, E. A.: The First Christians in the Roman World. 2008. *Vol. 229.*
Jungbauer, Harry: „Ehre Vater und Mutter“. 2002. *Vol. II/146.*
Kähler, Christoph: Jesu Gleichnisse als Poesie und Therapie. 1995. *Vol. 78.*
Kamlah, Ehrhard: Die Form der katalogischen Paränese im Neuen Testament. 1964. *Vol. 7.*
Kammler, Hans-Christian: Christologie und Eschatologie. 2000. *Vol. 126.*
– Kreuz und Weisheit. 2003. *Vol. 159.*
– see *Hofius, Otfried.*
Karakolis, Christos: see *Alexeev, Anatoly A.*

Karrer, Martin und *Wolfgang Kraus* (Ed.): Die Septuaginta – Texte, Kontexte, Lebenswelten. 2008. *Vol. 219.*
Kelhoffer, James A.: The Diet of John the Baptist. 2005. *Vol. 176.*
– Miracle and Mission. 1999. *Vol. II/112.*
Kelley, Nicole: Knowledge and Religious Authority in the Pseudo-Clementines. 2006. *Vol. II/213.*
Kieffer, René and *Jan Bergman* (Ed.): La Main de Dieu / Die Hand Gottes. 1997. *Vol. 94.*
Kierspel, Lars: The Jews and the World in the Fourth Gospel. 2006. *Vol. 220.*
Kim, Seyoon: The Origin of Paul's Gospel. 1981, ²1984. *Vol. II/4.*
– Paul and the New Perspective. 2002. *Vol. 140.*
– "The 'Son of Man'" as the Son of God. 1983. *Vol. 30.*
Klauck, Hans-Josef: Religion und Gesellschaft im frühen Christentum. 2003. *Vol. 152.*
Klein, Hans: see *Dunn, James D.G.*
Kleinknecht, Karl Th.: Der leidende Gerechtfertigte. 1984, ²1988. *Vol. II/13.*
Klinghardt, Matthias: Gesetz und Volk Gottes. 1988. *Vol. II/32.*
Kloppenborg, John S.: The Tenants in the Vineyard. 2006. *Vol. 195.*
Koch, Michael: Drachenkampf und Sonnenfrau. 2004. *Vol. II/184.*
Koch, Stefan: Rechtliche Regelung von Konflikten im frühen Christentum. 2004. *Vol. II/174.*
Köhler, Wolf-Dietrich: Rezeption des Matthäusevangeliums in der Zeit vor Irenäus. 1987. *Vol. II/24.*
Köhn, Andreas: Der Neutestamentler Ernst Lohmeyer. 2004. *Vol. II/180.*
Koester, Craig and *Reimund Bieringer* (Ed.): The Resurrection of Jesus in the Gospel of John. 2008. *Vol. 222.*
Konradt, Matthias: Israel, Kirche und die Völker im Matthäusevangelium. 2007. *Vol. 215.*
Kooten, George H. van: Cosmic Christology in Paul and the Pauline School. 2003. *Vol. II/171.*
– Paul's Anthropology in Context. 2008. *Vol. 232.*
Korn, Manfred: Die Geschichte Jesu in veränderter Zeit. 1993. *Vol. II/51.*
Koskenniemi, Erkki: Apollonios von Tyana in der neutestamentlichen Exegese. 1994. *Vol. II/61.*
– The Old Testament Miracle-Workers in Early Judaism. 2005. *Vol. II/206.*
Kraus, Thomas J.: Sprache, Stil und historischer Ort des zweiten Petrusbriefes. 2001. *Vol. II/136.*

Kraus, Wolfgang: Das Volk Gottes. 1996. *Vol. 85.*
– see *Karrer, Martin.*
– see *Walter, Nikolaus.*
– and *Karl-Wilhelm Niebuhr* (Ed.): Früh-judentum und Neues Testament im Horizont Biblischer Theologie. 2003. *Vol. 162.*
Kreplin, Matthias: Das Selbstverständnis Jesu. 2001. *Vol. II/141.*
Kuhn, Karl G.: Achtzehngebet und Vaterunser und der Reim. 1950. *Vol. 1.*
Kvalbein, Hans: see *Ådna, Jostein.*
Kwon, Yon-Gyong: Eschatology in Galatians. 2004. *Vol. II/183.*
Laansma, Jon: I Will Give You Rest. 1997. *Vol. II/98.*
Labahn, Michael: Offenbarung in Zeichen und Wort. 2000. *Vol. II/117.*
Lambers-Petry, Doris: see *Tomson, Peter J.*
Lange, Armin: see *Ego, Beate.*
Lampe, Peter: Die stadtrömischen Christen in den ersten beiden Jahrhunderten. 1987, ²1989. *Vol. II/18.*
Landmesser, Christof: Wahrheit als Grundbe-griff neutestamentlicher Wissenschaft. 1999. *Vol. 113.*
– Jüngerberufung und Zuwendung zu Gott. 2000. *Vol. 133.*
Lau, Andrew: Manifest in Flesh. 1996. *Vol. II/86.*
Lawrence, Louise: An Ethnography of the Gos-pel of Matthew. 2003. *Vol. II/165.*
Lee, Aquila H.I.: From Messiah to Preexistent Son. 2005. *Vol. II/192.*
Lee, Pilchan: The New Jerusalem in the Book of Relevation. 2000. *Vol. II/129.*
Lichtenberger, Hermann: Das Ich Adams und das Ich der Menschheit. 2004. *Vol. 164.*
– see *Avemarie, Friedrich.*
Lierman, John: The New Testament Moses. 2004. *Vol. II/173.*
– (Ed.): Challenging Perspectives on the Gos-pel of John. 2006. *Vol. II/219.*
Lieu, Samuel N.C.: Manichaeism in the Later Roman Empire and Medieval China. ²1992. *Vol. 63.*
Lindgård, Fredrik: Paul's Line of Thought in 2 Corinthians 4:16–5:10. 2004. *Vol. II/189.*
Loader, William R.G.: Jesus' Attitude Towards the Law. 1997. *Vol. II/97.*
Löhr, Gebhard: Verherrlichung Gottes durch Philosophie. 1997. *Vol. 97.*
Löhr, Hermut: Studien zum frühchristlichen und frühjüdischen Gebet. 2003. *Vol. 160.*
– see *Hengel, Martin.*
Löhr, Winrich Alfried: Basilides und seine Schu-le. 1995. *Vol. 83.*

Lorenzen, Stefanie: Das paulinische Eikon-Konzept. 2008. *Vol. II/250.*
Luomanen, Petri: Entering the Kingdom of Heaven. 1998. *Vol. II/101.*
Luz, Ulrich: see *Alexeev, Anatoly A.*
– see *Dunn, James D.G.*
Mackay, Ian D.: John's Raltionship with Mark. 2004. *Vol. II/182.*
Mackie, Scott D.: Eschatology and Exhortation in the Epistle to the Hebrews. 2006. *Vol. II/223.*
Maier, Gerhard: Mensch und freier Wille. 1971. *Vol. 12.*
– Die Johannesoffenbarung und die Kirche. 1981. *Vol. 25.*
Markschies, Christoph: Valentinus Gnosticus? 1992. *Vol. 65.*
Marshall, Peter: Enmity in Corinth: Social Con-ventions in Paul's Relations with the Corin-thians. 1987. *Vol. II/23.*
Martin, Dale B.: see *Zangenberg, Jürgen.*
Mayer, Annemarie: Sprache der Einheit im Epheserbrief und in der Ökumene. 2002. *Vol. II/150.*
Mayordomo, Moisés: Argumentiert Paulus lo-gisch? 2005. *Vol. 188.*
McDonough, Sean M.: YHWH at Patmos: Rev. 1:4 in its Hellenistic and Early Jewish Set-ting. 1999. *Vol. II/107.*
McDowell, Markus: Prayers of Jewish Women. 2006. *Vol. II/211.*
McGlynn, Moyna: Divine Judgement and Di-vine Benevolence in the Book of Wisdom. 2001. *Vol. II/139.*
Meade, David G.: Pseudonymity and Canon. 1986. *Vol. 39.*
Meadors, Edward P.: Jesus the Messianic He-rald of Salvation. 1995. *Vol. II/72.*
Meißner, Stefan: Die Heimholung des Ketzers. 1996. *Vol. II/87.*
Mell, Ulrich: Die „anderen" Winzer. 1994. *Vol. 77.*
– see *Sänger, Dieter.*
Mengel, Berthold: Studien zum Philipperbrief. 1982. *Vol. II/8.*
Merkel, Helmut: Die Widersprüche zwischen den Evangelien. 1971. *Vol. 13.*
– see *Ego, Beate.*
Merklein, Helmut: Studien zu Jesus und Paulus. Vol. 1 1987. *Vol. 43.* – Vol. 2 1998. *Vol. 105.*
Metzdorf, Christina: Die Tempelaktion Jesu. 2003. *Vol. II/168.*
Metzler, Karin: Der griechische Begriff des Ver-zeihens. 1991. *Vol. II/44.*
Metzner, Rainer: Die Rezeption des Matthä-usevangeliums im 1. Petrusbrief. 1995. *Vol. II/74.*

– Das Verständnis der Sünde im Johannesevangelium. 2000. *Vol. 122.*

Mihoc, Vasile: see *Dunn, James D.G..*

Mineshige, Kiyoshi: Besitzverzicht und Almosen bei Lukas. 2003. *Vol. II/163.*

Mittmann, Siegfried: see *Hengel, Martin.*

Mittmann-Richert, Ulrike: Magnifikat und Benediktus. 1996. *Vol. II/90.*

Miura, Yuzuru: David in Luke-Acts. 2007. *Vol. II/232.*

Mournet, Terence C.: Oral Tradition and Literary Dependency. 2005. *Vol. II/195.*

Mußner, Franz: Jesus von Nazareth im Umfeld Israels und der Urkirche. Ed. von M. Theobald. 1998. *Vol. 111.*

Mutschler, Bernhard: Das Corpus Johanneum bei Irenäus von Lyon. 2005. *Vol. 189.*

Nguyen, V. Henry T.: Christian Identity in Corinth. 2008. *Vol. II/243.*

Niebuhr, Karl-Wilhelm: Gesetz und Paränese. 1987. *Vol. II/28.*

– Heidenapostel aus Israel. 1992. *Vol. 62.*

– see *Deines, Roland*

– see *Dimitrov, Ivan Z.*

– see *Kraus, Wolfgang*

Nielsen, Anders E.: "Until it is Fullfilled". 2000. *Vol. II/126.*

Nissen, Andreas: Gott und der Nächste im antiken Judentum. 1974. *Vol. 15.*

Noack, Christian: Gottesbewußtsein. 2000. *Vol. II/116.*

Noormann, Rolf: Irenäus als Paulusinterpret. 1994. *Vol. II/66.*

Novakovic, Lidija: Messiah, the Healer of the Sick. 2003. *Vol. II/170.*

Obermann, Andreas: Die christologische Erfüllung der Schrift im Johannesevangelium. 1996. *Vol. II/83.*

Öhler, Markus: Barnabas. 2003. *Vol. 156.*

– see *Becker, Michael.*

Okure, Teresa: The Johannine Approach to Mission. 1988. *Vol. II/31.*

Onuki, Takashi: Heil und Erlösung. 2004. *Vol. 165.*

Oropeza, B. J.: Paul and Apostasy. 2000. *Vol. II/115.*

Ostmeyer, Karl-Heinrich: Kommunikation mit Gott und Christus. 2006. *Vol. 197.*

– Taufe und Typos. 2000. *Vol. II/118.*

Paulsen, Henning: Studien zur Literatur und Geschichte des frühen Christentums. Ed. von Ute E. Eisen. 1997. *Vol. 99.*

Pao, David W.: Acts and the Isaianic New Exodus. 2000. *Vol. II/130.*

Park, Eung Chun: The Mission Discourse in Matthew's Interpretation. 1995. *Vol. II/81.*

Park, Joseph S.: Conceptions of Afterlife in Jewish Insriptions. 2000. *Vol. II/121.*

Pate, C. Marvin: The Reverse of the Curse. 2000. *Vol. II/114.*

Pearce, Sarah J.K.: The Land of the Body. 2007. *Vol. 208.*

Peres, Imre: Griechische Grabinschriften und neutestamentliche Eschatologie. 2003. *Vol. 157.*

Philip, Finny: The Origins of Pauline Pneumatology. 2005. *Vol. II/194.*

Philonenko, Marc (Ed.): Le Trône de Dieu. 1993. *Vol. 69.*

Pilhofer, Peter: Presbyteron Kreitton. 1990. *Vol. II/39.*

– Philippi. Vol. 1 1995. *Vol. 87.* – Vol. 2 2000. *Vol. 119.*

– Die frühen Christen und ihre Welt. 2002. *Vol. 145.*

– see *Becker, Eve-Marie.*

– see *Ego, Beate.*

Pitre, Brant: Jesus, the Tribulation, and the End of the Exile. 2005. *Vol. II/204.*

Plümacher, Eckhard: Geschichte und Geschichten. 2004. *Vol. 170.*

Pöhlmann, Wolfgang: Der Verlorene Sohn und das Haus. 1993. *Vol. 68.*

Pokorný, Petr and Josef B. Souček: Bibelauslegung als Theologie. 1997. *Vol. 100.*

– and Jan Roskovec (Ed.): Philosophical Hermeneutics and Biblical Exegesis. 2002. *Vol. 153.*

Popkes, Enno Edzard: Das Menschenbild des Thomasevangeliums. 2007. *Vol. 206.*

– Die Theologie der Liebe Gottes in den johanneischen Schriften. 2005. *Vol. II/197.*

Porter, Stanley E.: The Paul of Acts. 1999. *Vol. 115.*

Prieur, Alexander: Die Verkündigung der Gottesherrschaft. 1996. *Vol. II/89.*

Probst, Hermann: Paulus und der Brief. 1991. *Vol. II/45.*

Räisänen, Heikki: Paul and the Law. 1983, ²1987. *Vol. 29.*

Rehkopf, Friedrich: Die lukanische Sonderquelle. 1959. *Vol. 5.*

Rein, Matthias: Die Heilung des Blindgeborenen (Joh 9). 1995. *Vol. II/73.*

Reinmuth, Eckart: Pseudo-Philo und Lukas. 1994. *Vol. 74.*

Reiser, Marius: Bibelkritik und Auslegung der Heiligen Schrift. 2007. *Vol. 217.*

– Syntax und Stil des Markusevangeliums. 1984. *Vol. II/11.*

Reynolds, Benjamin E.: The Apocalyptic Son of Man in the Gospel of John. 2008. *Vol. II/249.*

Rhodes, James N.: The Epistle of Barnabas and the Deuteronomic Tradition. 2004. *Vol. II/188.*

Richards, E. Randolph: The Secretary in the Letters of Paul. 1991. *Vol. II/42.*

Riesner, Rainer: Jesus als Lehrer. 1981, ³1988. *Vol. II/7.*

– Die Frühzeit des Apostels Paulus. 1994. *Vol. 71.*

Rissi, Mathias: Die Theologie des Hebräerbriefs. 1987. *Vol. 41.*

Roskovec, Jan: see *Pokorný, Petr.*

Röhser, Günter: Metaphorik und Personifikation der Sünde. 1987. *Vol. II/25.*

Rose, Christian: Theologie als Erzählung im Markusevangelium. 2007. *Vol. II/236.*

– Die Wolke der Zeugen. 1994. *Vol. II/60.*

Rothschild, Clare K.: Baptist Traditions and Q. 2005. *Vol. 190.*

– Luke Acts and the Rhetoric of History. 2004. *Vol. II/175.*

Rüegger, Hans-Ulrich: Verstehen, was Markus erzählt. 2002. *Vol. II/155.*

Rüger, Hans Peter: Die Weisheitsschrift aus der Kairoer Geniza. 1991. *Vol. 53.*

Sänger, Dieter: Antikes Judentum und die Mysterien. 1980. *Vol. II/5.*

– Die Verkündigung des Gekreuzigten und Israel. 1994. *Vol. 75.*

– see *Burchard, Christoph*

– and *Ulrich Mell* (Ed.): Paulus und Johannes. 2006. *Vol. 198.*

Salier, Willis Hedley: The Rhetorical Impact of the Semeia in the Gospel of John. 2004. *Vol. II/186.*

Salzmann, Jorg Christian: Lehren und Ermahnen. 1994. *Vol. II/59.*

Sandnes, Karl Olav: Paul – One of the Prophets? 1991. *Vol. II/43.*

Sato, Migaku: Q und Prophetie. 1988. *Vol. II/29.*

Schäfer, Ruth: Paulus bis zum Apostelkonzil. 2004. *Vol. II/179.*

Schaper, Joachim: Eschatology in the Greek Psalter. 1995. *Vol. II/76.*

Schimanowski, Gottfried: Die himmlische Liturgie in der Apokalypse des Johannes. 2002. *Vol. II/154.*

– Weisheit und Messias. 1985. *Vol. II/17.*

Schlichting, Günter: Ein jüdisches Leben Jesu. 1982. *Vol. 24.*

Schließer, Benjamin: Abraham's Faith in Romans 4. 2007. *Vol. II/224.*

Schnabel, Eckhard J.: Law and Wisdom from Ben Sira to Paul. 1985. *Vol. II/16.*

Schnelle, Udo: see *Frey, Jörg.*

Schröter, Jens: Von Jesus zum Neuen Testament. 2007. *Vol. 204.*

– see *Frey, Jörg.*

Schutter, William L.: Hermeneutic and Composition in I Peter. 1989. *Vol. II/30.*

Schwartz, Daniel R.: Studies in the Jewish Background of Christianity. 1992. *Vol. 60.*

Schwemer, Anna Maria: see *Hengel, Martin*

Scott, Ian W.: Implicit Epistemology in the Letters of Paul. 2005. *Vol. II/205.*

Scott, James M.: Adoption as Sons of God. 1992. *Vol. II/48.*

– Paul and the Nations. 1995. *Vol. 84.*

Shi, Wenhua: Paul's Message of the Cross as Body Language. 2008. *Vol. II/254.*

Shum, Shiu-Lun: Paul's Use of Isaiah in Romans. 2002. *Vol. II/156.*

Siegert, Folker: Drei hellenistisch-jüdische Predigten. Teil I 1980. *Vol. 20* – Teil II 1992. *Vol. 61.*

– Nag-Hammadi-Register. 1982. *Vol. 26.*

– Argumentation bei Paulus. 1985. *Vol. 34.*

– Philon von Alexandrien. 1988. *Vol. 46.*

Simon, Marcel: Le christianisme antique et son contexte religieux I/II. 1981. *Vol. 23.*

Smit, Peter-Ben: Fellowship and Food in the Kingdom. 2008. *Vol. II/234.*

Snodgrass, Klyne: The Parable of the Wicked Tenants. 1983. *Vol. 27.*

Söding, Thomas: Das Wort vom Kreuz. 1997. *Vol. 93.*

– see *Thüsing, Wilhelm.*

Sommer, Urs: Die Passionsgeschichte des Markusevangeliums. 1993. *Vol. II/58.*

Sorensen, Eric: Possession and Exorcism in the New Testament and Early Christianity. 2002. *Vol. II/157.*

Souček, Josef B.: see *Pokorný, Petr.*

Southall, David J.: Rediscovering Righteousness in Romans. 2008. *Vol. 240.*

Spangenberg, Volker: Herrlichkeit des Neuen Bundes. 1993. *Vol. II/55.*

Spanje, T.E. van: Inconsistency in Paul? 1999. *Vol. II/110.*

Speyer, Wolfgang: Frühes Christentum im antiken Strahlungsfeld. Vol. I: 1989. *Vol. 50.*

– Vol. II: 1999. *Vol. 116.*

– Vol. III: 2007. *Vol. 213.*

Spittler, Janet E.: Animals in the Apocryphal Acts of the Apostles. 2008. *Vol. II/247.*

Sprinkle, Preston: Law and Life. 2008. *Vol. II/241.*

Stadelmann, Helge: Ben Sira als Schriftgelehrter. 1980. *Vol. II/6.*

Stenschke, Christoph W.: Luke's Portrait of Gentiles Prior to Their Coming to Faith. *Vol. II/108.*

Sterck-Degueldre, Jean-Pierre: Eine Frau namens Lydia. 2004. *Vol. II/176.*

Stettler, Christian: Der Kolosserhymnus. 2000. *Vol. II/131.*

Stettler, Hanna: Die Christologie der Pastoralbriefe. 1998. *Vol. II/105.*

Stökl Ben Ezra, Daniel: The Impact of Yom Kippur on Early Christianity. 2003. *Vol. 163.*

Strobel, August: Die Stunde der Wahrheit. 1980. *Vol. 21.*

Stroumsa, Guy G.: Barbarian Philosophy. 1999. *Vol. 112.*

Stuckenbruck, Loren T.: Angel Veneration and Christology. 1995. *Vol. II/70.*

–, *Stephen C. Barton* and *Benjamin G. Wold* (Ed.): Memory in the Bible and Antiquity. 2007. *Vol. 212.*

Stuhlmacher, Peter (Ed.): Das Evangelium und die Evangelien. 1983. *Vol. 28.*

– Biblische Theologie und Evangelium. 2002. *Vol. 146.*

Sung, Chong-Hyon: Vergebung der Sünden. 1993. *Vol. II/57.*

Tajra, Harry W.: The Trial of St. Paul. 1989. *Vol. II/35.*

– The Martyrdom of St.Paul. 1994. *Vol. II/67.*

Theißen, Gerd: Studien zur Soziologie des Urchristentums. 1979, ³1989. *Vol. 19.*

Theobald, Michael: Studien zum Römerbrief. 2001. *Vol. 136.*

Theobald, Michael: see *Mußner, Franz.*

Thornton, Claus-Jürgen: Der Zeuge des Zeugen. 1991. *Vol. 56.*

Thüsing, Wilhelm: Studien zur neutestamentlichen Theologie. Ed. von Thomas Söding. 1995. *Vol. 82.*

Thurén, Lauri: Derhethorizing Paul. 2000. *Vol. 124.*

Thyen, Hartwig: Studien zum Corpus Iohanneum. 2007. *Vol. 214.*

Tibbs, Clint: Religious Experience of the Pneuma. 2007. *Vol. II/230.*

Toit, David S. du: Theios Anthropos. 1997. *Vol. II/91.*

Tolmie, D. Francois: Persuading the Galatians. 2005. *Vol. II/190.*

Tomson, Peter J. and *Doris Lambers-Petry* (Ed.): The Image of the Judaeo-Christians in Ancient Jewish and Christian Literature. 2003. *Vol. 158.*

Toney, Carl N.: Paul's Inclusive Ethic. 2008. *Vol. II/252.*

Trebilco, Paul: The Early Christians in Ephesus from Paul to Ignatius. 2004. *Vol. 166.*

Treloar, Geoffrey R.: Lightfoot the Historian. 1998. *Vol. II/103.*

Tsuji, Manabu: Glaube zwischen Vollkommenheit und Verweltlichung. 1997. *Vol. II/93.*

Twelftree, Graham H.: Jesus the Exorcist. 1993. *Vol. II/54.*

Ulrichs, Karl Friedrich: Christusglaube. 2007. *Vol. II/227.*

Urban, Christina: Das Menschenbild nach dem Johannesevangelium. 2001. *Vol. II/137.*

Vahrenhorst, Martin: Kultische Sprache in den Paulusbriefen. 2008. *Vol. 230.*

Vegge, Ivar: 2 Corinthians – a Letter about Reconciliation. 2008. *Vol. II/239.*

Visotzky, Burton L.: Fathers of the World. 1995. *Vol. 80.*

Vollenweider, Samuel: Horizonte neutestamentlicher Christologie. 2002. *Vol. 144.*

Vos, Johan S.: Die Kunst der Argumentation bei Paulus. 2002. *Vol. 149.*

Waaler, Erik: The *Shema* and The First Commandment in First Corinthians. 2008. *Vol. II/253.*

Wagener, Ulrike: Die Ordnung des „Hauses Gottes". 1994. *Vol. II/65.*

Wahlen, Clinton: Jesus and the Impurity of Spirits in the Synoptic Gospels. 2004. *Vol. II/185.*

Walker, Donald D.: Paul's Offer of Leniency (2 Cor 10:1). 2002. *Vol. II/152.*

Walter, Nikolaus: Praeparatio Evangelica. Ed. von Wolfgang Kraus und Florian Wilk. 1997. *Vol. 98.*

Wander, Bernd: Gottesfürchtige und Sympathisanten. 1998. *Vol. 104.*

Waters, Guy: The End of Deuteronomy in the Epistles of Paul. 2006. *Vol. 221.*

Watt, Jan G. van der: see *Frey, Jörg*

Watts, Rikki: Isaiah's New Exodus and Mark. 1997. *Vol. II/88.*

Wedderburn, A.J.M.: Baptism and Resurrection. 1987. *Vol. 44.*

Wegner, Uwe: Der Hauptmann von Kafarnaum. 1985. *Vol. II/14.*

Weiß, Hans-Friedrich: Frühes Christentum und Gnosis. 2008. *Vol. 225.*

Weissenrieder, Annette: Images of Illness in the Gospel of Luke. 2003. *Vol. II/164.*

–, *Friederike Wendt* and *Petra von Gemünden* (Ed.): Picturing the New Testament. 2005. *Vol. II/193.*

Welck, Christian: Erzählte ‚Zeichen'. 1994. *Vol. II/69.*

Wendt, Friederike (Ed.): see *Weissenrieder, Annette.*

Wiarda, Timothy: Peter in the Gospels. 2000. *Vol. II/127.*

Wifstrand, Albert: Epochs and Styles. 2005. *Vol. 179.*

Wilk, Florian: see *Walter, Nikolaus.*

Williams, Catrin H.: I am He. 2000. *Vol. II/113.*

Wilson, Todd A.: The Curse of the Law and the Crisis in Galatia. 2007. *Vol. II/225.*

Wilson, Walter T.: Love without Pretense. 1991. *Vol. II/46.*

Winn, Adam: The Purpose of Mark's Gospel. 2008. *Vol. II/245.*

Winninge, Mikael: see *Holmberg, Bengt.*

Wischmeyer, Oda: Von Ben Sira zu Paulus. 2004. *Vol. 173.*

Wisdom, Jeffrey: Blessing for the Nations and the Curse of the Law. 2001. *Vol. II/133.*

Witmer, Stephen E.: Divine Instruction in Early Christianity. 2008. *Vol. II/246.*

Wold, Benjamin G.: Women, Men, and Angels. 2005. *Vol. II/2001.*

– see *Stuckenbruck, Loren T.*

Wright, Archie T.: The Origin of Evil Spirits. 2005. *Vol. II/198.*

Wucherpfennig, Ansgar: Heracleon Philologus. 2002. *Vol. 142.*

Yates, John W.: The Spirit and Creation in Paul. 2008. *Vol. II/251.*

Yeung, Maureen: Faith in Jesus and Paul. 2002. *Vol. II/147.*

Zangenberg, Jürgen, Harold W. Attridge and *Dale B. Martin* (Ed.): Religion, Ethnicity and Identity in Ancient Galilee. 2007. *Vol. 210.*

Zimmermann, Alfred E.: Die urchristlichen Lehrer. 1984, ²1988. *Vol. II/12.*

Zimmermann, Johannes: Messianische Texte aus Qumran. 1998. *Vol. II/104.*

Zimmermann, Ruben: Christologie der Bilder im Johannesevangelium. 2004. *Vol. 171.*

– Geschlechtermetaphorik und Gottesverhältnis. 2001. *Vol. II/122.*

– (Ed.): Hermeneutik der Gleichnisse Jesu. 2008. *Vol. 231.*

– see *Frey, Jörg*

Zumstein, Jean: see *Dettwiler, Andreas*

Zwiep, Arie W.: Judas and the Choice of Matthias. 2004. *Vol. II/187.*

For a complete catalogue please write to the publisher
Mohr Siebeck • P.O. Box 2030 • D–72010 Tübingen/Germany
Up-to-date information on the internet at www.mohr.de